KU-578-410

Pelican Books
*Political Leaders of the Twentieth Century*

Sukarno

J. D. Legge is Professor of History at Monash University,
Victoria, Australia. Born in Victoria, he was educated
at Geelong College, Melbourne University and Oxford.
Between 1946 and 1948 and 1951 and 1960, Professor
Legge was successively Lecturer, Senior Lecturer and
Reader in History at the University of Western
Australia. In 1960 he was appointed to his present post.
He has travelled widely in South-East Asia, concentrating
especially on Indonesia. From 1969 to 1970 he acted as
Director of the Institute of Southeast Asian Studies in
Singapore.

Professor Legge's books include *Australian Colonial
Policy* (1956), *Britain in Fiji, 1858–80* (1958), *Central
Authority and Regional Autonomy in Indonesia* (1961)
and *Indonesia* (1964).

J. D. Legge

# Sukarno

*A Political Biography*

Penguin Books

Penguin Books Ltd, Harmondsworth,
Middlesex, England
Penguin Books Inc., 7110 Ambassador Road,
Baltimore, Maryland 21207, U.S.A.
Penguin Books Australia Ltd, Ringwood,
Victoria, Australia

First published by Allen Lane The Penguin Press 1972
Published in Pelican Books 1973

Made and printed in Great Britain by
Richard Clay (The Chaucer Press), Ltd,
Bungay, Suffolk
Set in Monotype Times

# Contents

# Preface

It is too early for a definitive biography of Sukarno. His overwhelming dominance of the Indonesian scene during the years of Guided Democracy and the subsequent reaction against him make it difficult for any observer to give a detached assessment of his place in the history of Indonesian nationalism. Certainly no single view of him is likely to win more than limited acceptance. The following pages are simply one attempt at an assessment of his political career while it is still fresh in popular memory. While it may bring some details of Sukarno's life into the record for the first time it is not conceived as a work of basic research but is concerned, rather, to offer an interpretation of comparatively well-known material. There will, before long, be a need for a closer examination of many aspects of Sukarno's career such as that provided by Bernhard Dahm's thorough and fascinating study of the development of his thought up to the end of the Japanese occupation.[1]

Any biography must come to terms with Sukarno's own account of his life as he has given it in *An Autobiography as told to Cindy Adams* (Indianapolis, 1965). Despite its element of ghosting this is clearly Sukarno's own book, just as *My Friend the Dictator* (Indianapolis, 1967), in which Mrs Adams gives an account of her experience in writing the autobiography, is clearly her own. The *Autobiography* catches Sukarno's flamboyance, his charm and vitality, and also his egotism, and it gives his own view of himself and his role. In spite of Mrs Adams's diligence in researching the background of the story for herself, the book cannot of course claim to be an accurate record. It is rather an account of what Sukarno remembered, or mis-remembered, or of what he, at that particular time, wished to be believed about his

1. Bernhard Dahm, *Sukarnos Kampf um Indonesiens Unabhängigkeit*, Hamburg, 1966, published in revised and updated edition as *Sukarno and the Struggle for Indonesian Independence*, trans. Mary F. Somers Heidhues, Ithaca, 1969.

past. In all of this it is pure Sukarno. His memories were often highly coloured distortions. Mrs Adams, in her second book, tells of Sukarno's bland admission of the fact when she caught him out in a particularly flagrant fabrication (pp. 254–5). But, in some ways, though it tells the story in heroic terms, Sukarno's account does not really do himself justice. There is a certain thinness of interpretation about it as compared, for example, with Nkrumah's autobiography. It is the simple story of a nationalist leader confronting obstacles from within as well as from outside his nationalist movement, showing far-sighted boldness, overcoming difficulties gradually and emerging as the supreme figure. It does not show the complexity of the environment in which he worked and, by overplaying his sense of destiny and his prescience, it really gives little sense of his great political resourcefulness or of his intuitive skill in assessing and resolving a difficult situation. A less one-sided account may increase rather than diminish his stature.

Many people have helped me by making available the fruits of their own research and by reading successive drafts of the manuscript. It quickly became apparent that there are as many Sukarnos as there are students of him. I am grateful in particular to my colleagues Herbert Feith and Jamie Mackie and to George McT. Kahin, Rex Mortimer and Ann Ruth Willner for reading and commenting on all or part of the work. It would be difficult to name all of those in Indonesia who gave generously of their time and information, but I am particularly grateful to Molly Bondan, Soebadio Sastrosatomo and Mohammad Said who read and commented on an early draft of the manuscript. Alan Smith was an ideal research assistant who brought his own ideas to the patient research and checking that he did for me and who persuaded me in many cases that his judgement was better than mine. The Myer Foundation and the Australian Research Grants Committee gave financial support to a period of research in Indonesia. I am grateful to Mrs Cindy Adams for permission to quote a number of passages from Sukarno's *Autobiography as told to Cindy Adams*.

Finally I am indebted to many people at Monash University and at the Singapore Institute of Southeast Asian Studies for their tolerance of my preoccupation, to Miss Mollie Lam Chwee

Sing who typed much of the draft and to Betty Bradly who has seen the manuscript through from its hesitant beginnings to its final stages.

Monash University                                          (J. D. L.)

*Note on the spelling of Indonesian names:*
When the Republic changed the Dutch 'oe' to 'u' in official Indonesian usage, some Indonesians accepted the new convention in the spelling of their own names while others stuck to that with which they were familiar. Sukarno, to the end of his life, signed himself Soekarno. However, even while doing so he insisted that Sukarno was the correct official spelling and his officially published works follow that usage. In consequence it has been decided to use Sukarno rather than Soekarno in this book.

# Prologue

Over the years 17 August, the anniversary of the proclamation of Indonesia's independence in 1945, had become a festival of national renewal, and the crowds who had made their way to Djakarta's Medan Merdeka (Freedom Square) on 17 August 1959 to listen to the President's annual oration were conscious of taking part in an occasion. Sukarno, as he stepped to the podium, had no difficulty in capturing their attention:

> 'Brothers and Sisters all!
> Today is the Seventeenth of August!
> 17 August 1959.
> 17 August – precisely fourteen years since
> we made the Proclamation . . .'

As usual he began quietly as he established contact with the audience, but he quickly made his way into his central theme:

> '1959 occupies an especial place in the history of our Revolution. A place which is *unique*! There has been a year which I named "a Year of Decision". There has been a year which I called "a Year of Challenge". But for the year 1959 I shall give another title . . . 1959 is the year to be called the year of "Rediscovery of our Revolution".
>
> 'It is for this reason that the year 1959 occupies an especial place in the history of our National Struggle, a place which is *unique*!'

Each pointed emphasis evoked the attentive response of his listeners. The style was familiar: the effective pause, the repetition in slightly different words, the habit of injecting phrases and words from other languages into the flow of Indonesian – a Javanese proverb, an English expression, a phrase in German, French, Italian or Dutch. At times he would drop from the level of high rhetoric and raise a laugh through a piece of self-mockery. If the speech was a ritual act for his audience, for Sukarno too it was a ritual – a re-affirmation of his *rapport* with his people. In another speech a few years later he was to describe these occasions as a continuing dialogue:

'A dialogue with the People. A two-way conversation between myself and the People, between my Ego and my Alter Ego. A two-way conversation between Sukarno-the-man and Sukarno-the-People. . . . That is why, every time I prepare a 17 August address . . . I become like a person possessed. Everything that is non-material in my body overflows! Thoughts overflow, feelings overflow, nerves overflow, emotions overflow. Everything belonging to the spirit that is in my body is as though quivering and blazing and raging, and then for me it is as though fire isn't hot enough, as though the ocean is not deep enough, as though the stars in the heavens are not high enough!'

But 17 August 1959 was not quite the same as the Independence Days which preceded it or those which followed. A few weeks earlier, on 5 July, Sukarno had by Presidential Decree suspended the provisional constitution of 1950, dissolved the Constituent Assembly which had been trying to agree upon a new constitution, and reintroduced the old 'revolutionary' constitution of 1945. This sharp and decisive action formed the climax to three years of political upheaval and a groping for new solutions. Within the framework of the provisional constitution of 1950 Indonesia had experimented, unsatisfactorily it seemed, with the forms of parliamentary democracy. This constitution had given formal authority to parliament – or to governments which could command its confidence – and had assigned to the president an essentially figurehead role. A series of weak cabinets formed by coalitions of parties had failed to provide either political stability or a sense of forward motion, and by the mid fifties broad popular disillusionment with the fruits of independence was reinforced by growing regional hostility to Djakarta and by stirrings of military dissatisfaction with what was regarded as the selfishness and corruption of civilian politicians. Movements of regional separatism had led, in 1958, to open rebellion in parts of Sumatra and Sulawesi.

These cracks in the fabric of the nation gave President Sukarno an opportunity he was quick to grasp. Irked by his comparative impotence as constitutional head of state and disturbed by the loss of purpose in the country as a whole, he gladly stepped forward as the man whose leadership could overcome the nation's political rivalries. Calling on his immense prestige as the father of Indonesian independence he argued that liberal democracy was a Western import, unsuited to Indonesia's needs – a mere fifty-per-cent-plus-one democracy. Indonesia's traditional procedures by contrast were based on deliberation and the search for a consensus. What was needed was not liberal democracy but guided democracy. And he himself was the obvious guide. To provide a suitable basis for the exercise of his authority he urged the Constituent Assembly, elected in 1955, to bring its deliberations to an end by adopting the constitution of 1945, the constitution hastily drafted towards the end of the Japanese occupation and under which the infant Republic had carried on its struggle against the Dutch. This constitution provided for deliberative bodies, a popularly elected congress which could determine the main lines of national policy and a parliament to legislate, but its essential character lay in its provision for a strong president – a man who would be chief executive as well as ceremonial head of state.

The Constituent Assembly was reluctant to be persuaded and Sukarno at last moved, on 5 July 1959, to his decisive intervention dissolving the Assembly and reintroducing the 1945 constitution by his own *fiat*.

The decree of 5 July 1959 was of dubious constitutional propriety. Many argued that Sukarno's powers under the provisional constitution did not extend to usurping the functions of the Constituent Assembly. However, the nation was not disposed to question his action; rather it accepted his resolution of conflict and his assumption of authority with a sigh of relief and, in some sections, with real enthusiasm. When he came to meet his people on 17 August therefore, he was concerned not to justify his Presidential Decree but confidently to explain it. The rediscovered revolution of which he spoke was the revolution against imperialism. He surveyed its stages: the splendour of the stage of physical revolution, the stage of survival which followed, and then the period of preparation for social and economic revolution. He referred to the compromise which had followed the physical revolution – 'Compromise in the sense of sacrificing the Spirit of the Revolution' – and to the sense of a loss of the revolutionary *élan*.

'Where is that Spirit of the Revolution today? The Spirit of the Revolution has been almost extinguished, has already become cold and without fire. Where are the Principles of the Revolution today? Today nobody knows where those Principles of the Revolution are, because each and every party lays down its own principles. . . . Where is the objective of the Revolution today? The objective of the Revolution – that is, a just and prosperous society – is now, for persons who are not sons of the Revolution, replaced by liberal politics and liberal economy. Replaced by liberal *politics*, in which the votes of the majority of the people are exploited, blackmarketed, corrupted by various groups. Replaced by liberal *economy* wherein various groups wantonly grab riches through sacrificing the interests of the People.'

Sukarno saw himself now as recalling the nation to a true sense of itself and its direction: 'Let us slam the steering wheel around and go back to the right road.'

'I feel like Dante in his *Divina Commedia*. I feel that our Revolution has suffered all kinds of tortures, from all kinds of devils, all the kinds of suffering of the Inferno, and now, with our return to the 1945 constitution, we experience purification so that later we can enter Heaven. . . . The devil of liberalism, the devil of feudalism, the devil of individualism, the devil of suku-ism, the devil of groupism, the devil of deviation, the devil of adventurism, the devil of four kinds of dualisms, the devil of corruption, the devil of scraping up wealth at one blow, the devil of the multi-party system, the devil of rebellion – all kinds of devils have jumped on us in the realm of the Inferno, and now we are undergoing purgatory in all fields.'

And so, explaining, exhorting, attacking enemies, domestic and foreign ('Let the imperialists abroad be in an uproar') ticking off the four kinds of diseases besetting the country, the six advantageous features of the situation, the three points of the new Cabinet's programme, the three tasks to be performed, the three difficulties to be overcome, Sukarno moved towards his peroration:

'Therefore increase your National Spirit! Raise the stimulus of your National Will! Raise the stimulus of your National Actions! And you, oh Nation of Indonesia, will really become a tempered nation!'

The era of guided democracy was thus fairly launched. The political achievement, summarized in this Independence Day speech, was very much Sukarno's own. He had sketched his view of guided democracy early in 1957, and thereafter he had worked steadily to attain it with patience and political skill. His July Decree brought him at last to the height of his political power. It also, however, saddled him with responsibility. Power he had already enjoyed, but it had been power divorced from responsibility. Over the past three years he had manipulated prime ministers and ministers, he had balanced army against parliament and had intervened more and more in the country's political processes. But till now the responsibility for the state of the nation had not been his. In taking it now into his own hands he was putting himself in a more exposed position in which blame as well as praise could be his. It remained to be seen how his new authority would be used. Could he be as successfully constructive as a head of government as he had been as a national leader? The rhetoric of 17 August 1959 did not include any precise outline of programmes and policies. What Sukarno wanted was to be revealed only in practice, and even then perhaps imperfectly.

Seven years later Indonesia gave its own answer to the question by rejecting Sukarno and his policies. But was the national judgement of 1966 as one-sided as that which accepted his initiative in 1959?

Judgement upon the sum of Sukarno's achievements will always be a matter of controversy. In some ways he can be regarded as a representative figure of his age – one of the charismatic leaders of Asian and African nationalism. In the twenties and thirties, like nationalist leaders elsewhere, he helped to create in his people an awareness of the injustices and humiliations of colonial rule, and he became the embodiment of their aspirations. He also gave them a perception of an Indonesian nation over and above their sense of themselves as Javanese or Ambonese, Minangkabau or Atjehnese. But if he was a representative leader, thrown up by the tides of twentieth-century history, he was also a highly individual leader with his own distinctive and mercurial style. His vanity, his charm, his political resourcefulness and his unpredictability were a source both of admiration and exasperation to observers. Among his countrymen he inspired devotion or hostility, but

never indifference. Even his most consistent critics were fascinated by him in spite of themselves. To some he was a dedicated
leader – the real maker of Indonesia and the sustainer and pre-
server of the nation after independence. To others he was a
disaster, the waster of the nation's resources in policies of domestic extravagance and foreign adventure, a man seduced by power
and by the material pleasures of the presidency, the corrupter of
his people and himself. He was 'the kinetic and the catalytic
agent' in Indonesia's nationalist development after 1927, says one
critic, but he was also the personification of a tragic betrayal of a
nationalist revolution into opportunistic hands–'the dramatically
delinquent father of an overgrown, underdeveloped, adolescent
nation'.[2]

Sukarno's most noticeable skills were those of exhortation and
persuasion. As an orator he could hold an audience in the hollow
of his hand. By his words he sought to bridge differences, to bring
together diverse elements within the nation and to give them a
sense of common identity. He was also a brilliant player of the
game of politics, accomplished in manipulating people and in
holding contending forces in balance. He was sensitive to subtle
changes in the political climate and was uniquely able to catch
and formulate the frustration of the masses. But these technical
skills were the very ones which tended to contribute to his image
as a demagogue with no sense of the real problems facing his
country, and there were some grounds for such a view of him. He
appeared in his later years of power to be obsessed with the
external signs of national greatness as expressed in wasteful
monuments and empty slogans. His intoxicating sense of a world
in movement and his philosophy of continuing revolution diverted
attention from the immediate tasks of governing. He seemed to
have no grasp of economic problems and he was certainly less
concerned with the content of policies than with the techniques of
politics. He was not effective as a practical administrator. He did
much, indeed, to earn his reputation as an obstacle to ordered
development rather than as a creative national leader.

Any fair assessment of Sukarno must nevertheless take account

2. Willard A. Hanna, *Eight Nation Makers: Southeast Asia's Charismatic
Statesmen*, New York, 1964, pp. 1 and 92.

of the exceptional difficulties facing a nation-builder in Indonesia. Ethnically distinct societies, scattered in a chain of islands across 3,000 miles of ocean, were not the natural raw material for the creation of a sense of common purpose. Major cultural divisions existed even within particular ethnic communities. Sukarno's great contribution in this setting was his emphasis on unity, and his search for a synthesis of Indonesian and Western currents of thought to sustain it. In 1926, in an influential article, he stressed the essential community of interest between nationalism, Marxism and Islam, and this message, expounded consistently over the next forty years, went far to justify Sukarno's own view of himself as the spokesman for the nationalist movement as a whole. It is true that there were other leaders with major contributions to make. Sukarno was not the banyan tree beneath which nothing else could grow. Nonetheless, his vision of unity was overwhelmingly important in forging the nation and developing within it a sense of identity and self-respect Because of the power of his message he became almost a personification of the idea of 'Indonesia' and symbol of the national challenge to the mystique of colonial authority. After the attainment of independence the same qualities led him to claim leadership on a wider stage. His struggle against Dutch rule was followed by his attempt to personify the conflict against imperialism in its less tangible forms, and at Bandung in 1955 he staked his claim to be one of the major spokesmen for the whole Afro-Asian world.

Sukarno was a complex person and any assessment of him must consider several closely related clusters of disputed questions. One of these concerns his image as a revolutionary figure. As a nationalist leader in the 1920s Sukarno rejected the legitimacy of established institutions and chose the path of non-cooperation with the Dutch. His method was rather to oppose the enemy directly on the basis of the mobilized power of the masses, and for this he was ready to suffer imprisonment and exile. When independence was ultimately attained he insisted that it did not mean the end of the revolution. He spoke constantly of the revolution of mankind or of the revolution of humanity, and he stressed the need to think in a revolutionary way, to shake established institutions, to make and re-make, to build the world anew. His 1959 call to return to the rails of the revolution was followed by his concept of 'Continuing Revolution'. 'The activities of the Revolution go on. . . . For a fighting nation there is no journey's end,' he said in 1961. In domestic affairs the concept of revolutionary action became a legitimizing concept underpinning his direct personal interference with the 'normal' conventions of government. In foreign affairs he claimed to pursue a revolutionary diplomacy. 'The world of today is a tinder box of Revolution,' he said, and, in dealing with it, he showed that bold, unexpected and unconventional behaviour could sometimes achieve goals which could not be secured through the less spectacular channels of conventional diplomacy. But were there limits to Sukarno's revolutionary character? In 1945 he saw independence as essentially a transfer of authority to the nationalist establishment of which he was the acknowledged head. He was suspicious of many of the younger revolutionaries of the time, seeking new channels of power through which their own aspirations could be fulfilled. To them Sukarno appeared as a conservative figure. Others have argued that his idea of revolution represented merely a temper of mind, a rhetorical device, rather than a programmed approach to the achievement of definite goals through revolution.

It is not an easy question to resolve. The revolutionary posture which he maintained while President did not seem to be anchored in a clear conception of a changed society to which revolutionary action would lead. It might even be held that the whole weight of his policy under Guided Democracy, whether it was intended to be so or not, was likely to have the effect of preserving the kind of society he knew and the kind of élite with which he was familiar. Yet he could call, on occasion, for drastic innovation in political forms and social order, and there were undoubtedly radical elements in his thought and action which enabled him to change the world about him. Has the very concept of being a revolutionary perhaps acquired new meanings in the mid twentieth century? In the past men fought against class privilege or foreign domination, and their enemies were concrete and definite. In the mid twentieth century it has become possible for a man to be a revolutionary *per se*, his role being defined less by what he is seeking to achieve than by how he seeks to achieve it. It is the style which matters rather than the goals of his political action, which are likely to be vaguely defined. Yet for all their vagueness these goals may still represent a vision which can command the support of the inarticulate and poverty-bound masses. Is this the sense in which Sukarno was a revolutionary?

Secondly his role as the great unifier and synthesizer, important though it was in the making of Indonesia, needs to be examined critically and perhaps it, too, should not be taken entirely at its face value. Sukarno felt himself to belong simultaneously to a variety of traditions and he drew effectively on many sources – on Marxism, on Western democratic and radical thought, on elements of a Javanese world-view. He believed that he could express the aspirations of Islamic and secular leaders, of Javanese and Sumatran. He told one American journalist that he was simultaneously a Christian, a Muslim and a Hindu.[3] Certainly his eclecticism gave him special skill in adapting his ideas to different audiences, and it provided some foundation for his claim that he was peculiarly fitted to unite what might otherwise be opposing forces. A search for a common denominator can only be made by one who is not subject to the imperious demands of a single world-view, but Indonesian society comprised not one culture but many, and Sukarno's attempt to unite the diverse currents of nationalism was only in part successful. He was never as effective, for example, in his appeal to non-Javanese as he was to Javanese. Nor could his synthesis ever finally satisfy any but the more quiescent and Javanized representatives of Islam. Synthesis, almost by definition, implied for the devout Muslim a secular outlook, and Sukarno's attempt to embrace a variety of traditions made him, paradoxically but inevitably, a representative of one principal stream of nationalist thought rather than the uniter of all. Indeed towards the end of his political career he seemed almost less concerned to unite opposing forces than to balance them, and in this way to preserve his own independence. Yet even then he worked by conciliation, determined to seek common ground and continuing to assert his claim to be the spokesman for all.

3. Louis Fischer, *The Story of Indonesia*, New York, 1959, p. 299 .

A third group of questions concerns the importance in Sukarno's make-up of elements of traditional thought and action. Was he essentially a modernizing statesman, the architect of a twentieth-century nation, with views fashioned by Western education and by experience of the struggle against colonial capitalism and against the Indonesian aristocrats who worked with it? Or can he be understood only in terms of the Javanese culture from which he sprang?

These questions are more of a puzzle than appears on the surface. Java's syncretism – her ability to absorb cultural elements deriving from many sources and to re-shape them in her own way – has been proverbial, and Sukarno's talent for synthesis in the formulation of his political ideas may itself reflect a typically Javanese tolerance. His ability to bring together diverse currents of thought and to see them as part of a totality was very much in that tradition, with its perception of polarity and conflict but also of unity and harmony. His desire to seek a consensus before moving to a decision was certainly also a Javanese trait, but his Javanism went still deeper.

His *rapport* with his people, his gift of personal magnetism and his power of oratory have led observers to place him among the great charismatic leaders of the twentieth century. The term 'charismatic' is not precise. To Max Weber charisma was not just a matter of the special qualities appearing in a leader, it was also a matter of his followers seeing those qualities.[4] In Sukarno's case his people did see him as set apart and as possessing exceptional authority. That they did so was due only in part to the sheer force of his personality and to his positive political skills of rhetoric and persuasion. More important was the fact that he fulfilled their expectations of what a leader should be, and in this sense the roots of his power lay deep within the soil of the Javanese tradition, a tradition which he was able to tap at various levels.[5] His

4. Weber, Max, *The Theory of Social and Economic Organization*, trans. A. M. Henderson and Talcott Parsons, Glencoe, Ill., 1947, p. 359.

5. See Ann Ruth and Dorothy Willner, 'The Role of Charismatic Leaders' in *Annals of the American Academy of Political and Social Sciences*, March 1965, for a discussion of the way in which charisma might depend on a leader's ability to manipulate traditional symbols. See also Ann Ruth Willner, 'The Neotraditional Accommodation to Political Independence:

Javanese subjects saw him as possessing *kesaktian*, the super-naturally derived power inherent in a leader. Again he could draw on the messianic traditions of peasant society, appearing as the *Ratu Adil* (the Just Ruler) whose task was to bring order, to restore harmony and to re-unite the kingdom after a time of tur-moil, to re-assert the parallelism between the harmony of the terrestrial order and that of the cosmos. Social upheaval and the erosion of custom by colonial rule and capitalist penetration had created the conditions in which a Sukarno could appear as an ordained saviour within a traditional world view.[6] At a different level his presidency carried some echoes of the court tradition of Java; his style of leadership made him, in many respects, a modern version of a Hindu–Javanese ruler, manipulating tradi-tional symbols, possessing an aura of divine power, and sur-rounded by a royal entourage engaged in the intrigues of court politics. The attention given to his sexual prowess belonged to the same tradition.[7]

But if his subjects saw him in these terms, how did he see him-self? How far did he share their traditional world-view? One of his characteristics as a public speaker was his ability to convey a point to an audience by an illustration taken from the *wayang*, the Javanese shadow play whose themes were drawn largely from the Indian epics, the *Ramayana* and the *Mahabharata*. He could

The Case of Indonesia' in Lucien W. Pye (ed.), *Cases in Comparative Politics: Asia*, Boston, 1970.

6. Bernhard Dahm, *Soekarno and the Struggle for Indonesian Independence* (revised and updated edition of *Sukarnos Kampf um Indonesiens Unabhän-gigkeit*), trans. Mary F. Somers Heidhues, Ithaca, 1969, has emphasized Sukarno's Javanism and in particular his ability to project himself in terms of traditional messianic expectations.

7. In Weber's account (op. cit., pp. 328ff.) charismatic leadership was to be distinguished on the one hand from rational authority depending on the institutionalization of power and the acceptance of rules defining it, and on the other from traditional authority. But if Sukarno's charisma was in part due to his ability to play a traditional role the Weberian distinction between charismatic and traditional authority becomes blurred. His role as a tradi-tional leader was important, but so were his disruptive tendencies and his determination to break free from institutional restraints, and it was these latter characteristics which made him truly charismatic.

rely on his Javanese and Sundanese audiences to know the *wayang* stories intimately and to be able to grasp the nuances of his argument without hesitation. Was this simply a matter of rhetorical skill? Was he simply concerned to clothe his ideas in an acceptable and dramatic form? Or did he himself move in the thought world of the *wayang*? There are many signs that he did tend to think of the events of the day as illustrating *wayang* themes, with himself in a *ksatria* (warrior) role, and to see the nationalist struggle in terms of the *Bharata Yudha* story of the conflict between the Pendawas and the Kaurawas.[8] Such a frame of reference gave an heroic character to his struggle, but it may also explain his occasional miscalculations of the power realities of a situation and his tendency almost to expect miraculous solutions.

Sukarno belonged in fact to a culture which sees no firmly set barrier between the natural world and the supernatural, and which assumes the possibility of drawing power from the supernatural order to manipulate events in the terrestrial sphere. Hence his use of *dukuns* (traditional soothsayers), his possession of magically endowed *pusakas* (sacred heirlooms or other objects able to give power to their possessors) and his reverence for holy places. More fundamentally his whole cast of mind and his perception of political forces and processes where shaped in considerable measure by the basic characteristics of a Javanese cosmology in which man is seen as not responsible for controlling his environment nor indeed as capable of it. His apparent hesitation while faced with difficult choices may perhaps be explained in this way. It is a Javanese characteristic to avoid formulating a long term plan of action to control the future and to provide a criterion for the making of immediate choices. Rather a Javanese will allow the forces about him to work themselves out – to reveal themselves and enable an immediate course of action to be determined. He will tend not to look too far ahead but to leave the next phase of development to reveal itself in due course. At the political level actions will tend to be in terms of the forces which are deployed at a particular moment. Sukarno frequently seemed to reflect that disposition in his own political behaviour, yet he

8. Dahm, op. cit., casts much of his account of Sukarno's thinking in the twenties in these terms.

was also well read in the political philosophy of the West and he certainly saw himself as leading his people into the twentieth century. He had a shrewd perception of the trend of events in the world about him and was concerned to make Indonesia a modern state, drawing on the resources of modern technology and able to take a leading place in the counsels of the nations. Once again it is not easy to make a just assessment of him.

Finally there are questions which relate more deeply to his individual personality. The striking characteristic of Sukarno, at least in outward appearance, was his tremendous self-assurance. Always at the centre of events, uniformed and neat in appearance, brisk in his movements, sparkling in his assumption of his central role, he seemed to dominate every situation. He kept his followers in orbit about the focal point of his own personality. He was vain, but also willing in conversation to turn a point against himself and he was able to exert a magnetic charm even over his opponents. So compelling was this image of self-assurance that we take it perhaps too much for granted that this is what he was. There are at least some signs that his confidence was slow in developing, and that, at least for a great part of his life, his self-assurance was merely an outer shell, hiding an inner anxiety and uncertainty. As a boy Sukarno seems to have been somewhat withdrawn, uneasy in his relationships with other students at school and finding refuge in books. He read widely, identifying himself with revolutionary leaders of the past and displaying a strongly romantic element in his sense of history. He built up for himself something of a fantasy world in which he could dominate the stage, and his early steps in political life have something of the air of an attempt to act out in the real world the role he had cast for himself in his imagination. It was in the field of oratory particularly that his imaginings were able to take real shape, but even when he had discovered the intoxication of having power over large audiences he remained, in his youth, shy and withdrawn in smaller groups.

Was Sukarno the extrovert really over-compensating for his lack of assurance? Even his vanity was perhaps the obverse of a lack of confidence. His sexual athleticism, which gained him so much admiration as well as notoriety, may have sprung from the same kind of source. As a child he found security in the bed of

Sarinah, the family servant, and he spent the rest of his life, perhaps, attempting to recover it in the beds of others. In his twenties it was his wife Inggit, eleven years his senior, who supported him and gave him confidence. After the revolution his marriage to Hartini prefaced the opening of a new and more assured phase in his political life. Thereafter his interest in sex became more and more obsessive. This has sometimes been interpreted as an attempt to prove his political potency but it may equally have been that his declining powers and his fear of death revived his feelings of insecurity.

As a political thinker Sukarno was not as confident of his views as he often seemed to be.[9] In the thirties his self-esteem was easily punctured by other leaders who were critical of his expressive approach to politics, and the rest of his career was, at least in part, an attempt to prove the validity of his ideas. At the level of action he did at times show clarity of vision and an awareness of the steps he felt he should take, as when he arrested the plotter Sudarsono in 1946, rallied the Republic against communist insurrection in 1948, foiled a half-hearted attempt at a military coup in 1952, appointed himself *formateur* of a new cabinet in 1957, or dissolved a recalcitrant parliament in 1960. But he was not always decisive and in command of events. Often he seemed to drift with circumstances, to wait upon events rather than to shape them, allowing decisions to make themselves. He did this in the critical days after the Japanese surrender in 1945; he temporized in December 1948 when the Dutch launched a surprise attack on the Republic's capital, Jogjakarta; in 1959 he left the Republic in a time of crisis and allowed events to sort themselves out. It might, of course, be argued that on each of these occasions his hesitation and delay represented ripe political wisdom, and it must also be recognized that, at other times, he did direct and shape the world about him – from the mid fifties he showed remarkable zest and resourcefulness. There are paradoxes of leadership here which make him a particularly complex character for the purposes of analysis and judgement.

It will be part of the argument of the following pages that there

9. Dahm, (op. cit., p. 65) speaks of him as regarding himself as infallible. In fact the reverse was true.

were three periods in his career when his political creativity showed itself most clearly. During the late twenties he, more than any other, was responsible for the creation of the Indonesian Nationalist Party, for the shaping of its ideology and for determining its course of action. During the Japanese occupation he was a skilful mediator standing between his people and their Japanese overlords, and he used his position to prepare the way for Indonesia's bid for independence after the Japanese defeat. During the revolution itself he was, perhaps, less important than others in directing events and after the transfer of sovereignty he was for a number of years merely a figurehead president. In the mid fifties, however, he stepped once again to the centre of the political stage and played the dominating role in shaping the institutions and developing the ideas of Guided Democracy. After 1959 his dominance continued but it is questionable how far he was still the maker of history and how far he was caught up in the momentum of events over which he came to have little control.

# 1
# Boyhood

Sukarno was born on 6 June 1901.[10]

His father, Raden Sukemi Sosrodihardjo, one of the eight children of Raden Hardjodikromo, was, as the title 'Raden' indicates, a member of Java's aristocratic *priyayi* class. Born in 1869 Sukemi received elements of a Dutch education at a Junior Teachers Training School in the regency town of Probolinggo in East Java. It was not an advanced education. The 'Kweekschool', of which there were only a very few in Java at the time, was designed to give a couple of years of secondary schooling as training for primary school teachers, and, on graduation, Sukemi found himself employed in a newly opened native primary school in Singaradja, Bali. In addition to his teaching duties he eked out his income by serving as research assistant to Professor van der Tuuk, an expert on Indonesian languages, who was engaged at the time in a study of Balinese language and custom.[11]

It was at Singaradja that Sukemi met his future wife, Idayu Njoman Rai, the daughter, he claims, of a Balinese family of the Brahmana (priestly) class. Their marriage was not accomplished without difficulty. Sukemi was Javanese and nominally a Muslim, and though Bali's Hinduism did not involve an elaborate Indian-type caste system, a marriage of this kind was clearly a breach of

10. This is the generally accepted date, the one given in the official biographies, and claimed by Sukarno himself in his *An Autobiography as Told to Cindy Adams* (New York, 1965). Some scholars have cast doubt upon it. B.R.O'G. Anderson, for example, states that Sukarno was forty-five years old in April 1945 (*Some Aspects of Indonesian Politics Under the Japanese Occupation*, Ithaca, 1961, p. 20), thus making the year of his birth 1899, if the 6 June date is retained, or possibly 1900 if it is not. Sukarno entered a Dutch Higher Elementary School in 1914 (see Note at the end of this chapter). If he was born in 1900 or 1899 this would mean that he would be fourteen or fifteen at the time, and that would presuppose a primary schooling of eight or nine years. It is unlikely that the primary schooling of a schoolmaster's son would have taken so long to complete. The 1901 date would thus appear to be the more likely.

11. M. Y. Nasution, *Penghidupan dan Perdjuangan Ir. Sukarno* [The Life and Struggle of Engineer Sukarno], Djakarta, 1951, p. 10.

Balinese marriage rules;[12] her parents therefore rejected Sukemi's request for the hand of their daughter. The young couple, ignoring that refusal, eloped in customary Balinese fashion and were then married in a Muslim ceremony. The bride's family was thus faced by a *fait accompli*. This at least is Sukarno's story and it must be confessed that it contains a number of improbabilities. Would a Balinese Brahmana have married a Javanese at this stage of Indonesia's history? Was her family really that of the rajahs of Singaradja? Other stories suggest that Sukarno's mother may have been of lower caste origin and perhaps of mixed descent. One story is that Sukemi's wife was the daughter of a Balinese woman who had married a Madurese trader in Singaradja. In the absence of firm evidence one cannot be sure.

After their marriage Sukemi and his wife stayed on in Singaradja until after the birth of their eldest child, a daughter named Sukarmini. Within two years of her birth Sukemi applied for, and secured, a transfer to Surabaja and it was there that Sukarno was born. He was named Kusno Sosro Sukarno, but the first two names were dropped in his childhood and he remained thereafter, in the common Javanese fashion, simply Sukarno.[13]

The birth of a hero calls for signs and portents. In humorous vein Sukarno in his autobiography supplies at least one. The eruption of Mount Kelud, a volcano near Kediri in East Java, could serve the purpose, he suggests. But he wonders whether it was a welcome to him or a sign of anger.[14] He was perhaps a little more serious in stressing the year and the date – the dawn of a new century and an auspicious day.

12. In Bali, emphasis is placed on the importance of the four orders (*varnas*) rather than upon caste differences within those orders. Marriage is allowed across status lines, but only according to certain rules. In particular, women may not marry into a lower class. See Hildred Geertz, 'Indonesian Cultures and Communities', in R. McVey (ed.) *Indonesia*, New Haven, 1963.

13. Nasution, op. cit., p. 11, has him named Kusno Sosro Sukarno from the beginning. In Sukarno's account he was at first named Kusno, but, after early illnesses, his father changed the name to Sukarno, after Karna, one of the warriors in the *Mahabharata*, so that he might start afresh (*Autobiography*, p. 26).

14. *Autobiography*, p. 18.

'My birthday is double six. June six. It is my supreme good fortune to have been born under Gemini, the sign of twins. And that is me exactly. Two extremes. I can be gentle or exacting; hard as steel, or poetic. My personality is a mixture of reason and emotion. I am forgiving and I am unyielding. I put enemies of the state behind bars, yet I cannot keep a bird in a cage.'[15]

Portents aside, Sukarno's childhood was in fact ordinary enough. At some stage in the first few years of his life his father's parents, possibly in order to give financial relief to Sukemi, offered to take the boy into their own home at Tulungagung, in the south of East Java. He probably had his initial education in the village school there, but if so it was only for a brief period. When he was about six his family moved from Surabaja first to the nearby town of Sidoardjo, and then, very soon after, to Modjokerto where Sukemi found himself promoted to the position of *mantri-guru* (chief teacher) in the Second Class Native School. After this move Sukarno rejoined his family and entered his father's school to continue his primary education.[16]

His childhood memories of both Tulungagung and Modjokerto were of early instruction from his father, his mother's labour in polishing the unhusked rice which was all the family could afford, and his relationship with the family servant, Sarinah, whose bed he shared as a young child, and whom he was later to idealize as a symbol of Indonesian womanhood and the representative in particular of the 'little people' who made up the mass of the country's population. Many years later, during the days of Guided Democracy, she was to have her monument in 'Sarinah', a multi-storey department store to be built in Djakarta's Djalan Thamrin as a prestige building – an example of Indonesia's ability to create a modern emporium offering a profusion of consumer goods for ordinary people. Sukarno claimed that she was the greatest single influence in his life. 'It was from

15. ibid., p. 17.
16. There is some disagreement among his biographers about the exact sequence and dates of these movements. Sukarno speaks of his family's move to Modjokerto when he was six. He refers subsequently to his life with his grandparents. The above account follows broadly that of Nasution, op. cit.

her I learned to love the common people. She was of the common people herself but of uncommon wisdom.'[17]

He looked back with assertive pride to the dominance he quickly established over the friends with whom he played as a boy. He enjoyed the reputation of being a young fighting cock,[18] bolder than others, a leader in their games, organizing their activities and making himself the centre of a small gang. He claimed that he allowed no one to challenge his ascendancy and boasted that when beaten in a spinning-top competition he settled the question of his superiority by throwing his rival's top in the river.[19] (Whether this happened or not his pride in telling the story at least throws some light on the later Sukarno.)

He made much of his poverty. In his autobiography he exaggerated the extremity of his family's hardship: 'We were so poor we could barely eat rice once a day.'[20] The salary of a schoolmaster was indeed low and, whether at Modjokerto with his parents or at Tulungagung with his grandparents, he did know what poverty was. 'A man's life is unpredictable indeed,' he said in a speech when, as President, he visited the United States in 1956. 'I am the poor son of poor parents. My father was a small teacher who earned twenty-five guilders a month. This is ten dollars. I am the child of common people.'[21] There was a certain amount of romanticism here. Sukarno's poverty was that of the Javanese people as a whole. In comparative terms he was not poor. As a *mantri-guru* in Modjokerto, and later as an inspector of schools in Blitar, Sukemi was not too badly off. Sukarno was therefore not of the common people in a genuine sense, and from his birth there were many circumstances that made him different from others.

The inter-ethnic marriage from which he sprang was itself

17. Sukarno, *Sarinah*, Tebingtinggi, 1948, Foreword. *Sarinah* was subsequently republished in successive editions with an expanded text and with the subtitle *The Responsibility of Women in the Struggle of the Indonesian Republic*.

18. *Djago*, a cock, but also used in the sense of 'leader', 'cock of the walk'.

19. *Autobiography*, p. 28.

20. ibid., p. 23.

21. *Post and Times Herald*, Washington, 17 May 1956.

unusual in the late nineteenth century. The Indies were – and are – a mosaic of distinct communities, divided by language, by religion sometimes, by social organization and by distinctness of separate cultural traditions. In the one island of Java the Javanese of the eastern two-thirds of the island are a different people from the Sundanese of the western third. Outside Java a series of ethnic groups – Atjehnese, Batak, Minangkabau, Balinese, Makassarese, Buginese and others – have a continuing pride in their own distinctness. Urbanization was, in due course, to blur some of the edges of ethnic separateness and pave the way for a perception of an Indonesian nation; self-conscious nationalism was to formulate and develop this perception. But organized nationalism was still some years in the future at the time of Sukemi's courtship, and inter-ethnic marriages which were also inter-religious marriages must have been rare indeed. It is not without significance that Sukarno, who was to glory in the fact that he was deeply rooted in the traditional culture of Java and was at the same time to proclaim the doctrine of Indonesian unity in diversity should himself have been the product of such a union. From his mother he may have derived a sense of a more vigorous artistic life than was to be found in Java, where the concern is to preserve and refine a highly sophisticated cultural tradition rather than to innovate and experiment.[22] From his father he would have acquired a feeling for Java's mystical tradition and a sense of the need for order in a disordered universe.

Again it is important that, for all his talk of his poverty and of his belonging to the common people, he was not a commoner but a member of the *priyayi* class. In Javanese society the term *priyayi* strictly denotes descent from a regent and in Jogjakarta today it still refers to officials in the service of the Sultan. More generally in Java the term applies to persons of gentle birth and it derives from the administrative hierarchy of the old kingdoms of Java which grew up under Indian cultural influence in the latter half of the first millennium A D. Mataram in Central Java, Kediri and Singhasari in East Java and, in the fourteenth century, the great kingdom of Madjapahit were all elaborate states, centred on the capital of the ruler, dependent on tribute from the irrigated rice

22. Hildred Geertz in McVey, op. cit., p. 50.

lands under their control and governed through a territorial bureaucratic hierarchy. As in other Indianized states of Southeast Asia, the ruler himself was seen as a god-king, an incarnation perhaps of Vishnu or Shiva, radiating sacredness and possessed of magical power (*sakti*) to rule. His court was a centre of civilization, whose society was based on a refined and elaborate etiquette. Below the nobility the *priyayi* were the officials and the élite of this court-centred society, sharing in its world-view of the kingdom as an analogue of the cosmos, accepting its values of equilibrium and harmony and its belief in mystical contemplation as a means of penetrating the inner nature of reality.

The Dutch East India Company, in extending its sway in Java in the seventeenth and eighteenth centuries at the expense of the central Javanese kingdom of Mataram had preserved the outlines of the Javanese social order and retained also its territorial administrative system. In effect the Company cut off as it were the apex of the kingdom; in the parts of Java ceded to it, it substituted itself as sovereign in place of the Sultan's court, but below that level it did not greatly disturb existing patterns of government. It continued to rule through the existing hierarchy of territorial officials. In the nineteenth century, after the Crown had replaced the Company, closer control and intensification of government gradually curbed the privileges of this bureaucratic aristocracy and transformed it into a salaried civil service, but even in the twentieth century *priyayi* status carried with it an aura of authority drawn from an ancient cultural tradition. It remained a matter of Dutch policy to support this class and to exercise authority through it. The lower ranks of the *pangreh pradja*, the territorial civil service, were staffed from its members, who served as regents (the highest rank regularly open to Indonesians), district officers and sub-district officers.

Sukemi's *priyayi* origins had not opened a career for him in the *pangreh pradja*. His schoolteaching was a less honorific form of government service, but his rank gave his son on the one hand the opportunity of securing the all-important advantage of a Dutch education and, on the other, the advantage of an established place in traditional Javanese society.

As a child Sukarno entered that traditional culture through the world of the *wayang* – the shadow puppet plays which formed, simultaneously, a part of the high culture of the Javanese court tradition and of the folk tradition of the Javanese village. It has been said that the *wayang* themes, drawn from the Indian epics, the *Ramayana* and the *Mahabharata*, but Javanized in the process, contain the essence of the tradition of Java, that in them 'lies hidden the secret Javanese knowledge concerning the deepest significance of life'.[23] The stories of warriors and giants, of gods, kings, princes, princesses and clowns are not merely a source of entertainment but a repository of values and a subtle exploration of man's relation to the universe. They embody the idea of the parallelism of the terrestrial order and the supernatural and their themes illustrate the importance both of conflict, and of harmony and equilibrium precariously maintained through that conflict. In this view of the precarious balance of the universe can be found a perception of polarity in the natural and supernatural orders alike, an interaction of complementary opposites – male and female, light and darkness, life and death, heaven and earth, mountain and sea and so on – but these polarities do not include a simple opposition between good and evil. On moral questions there is no such simple dichotomy, but rather an inherent ambiguity which leads to a moral pluralism. As one scholar has argued, if the *wayang* offers models for human behaviour they are models where alternative actions are subtly balanced and where a profound cultural tolerance rather than an absolute morality is the ultimate prescription.[24] The *dalang*, or puppet master, in his manipulation of the puppets before the screen symbolizes the magical power of the performance to affect reality as well as to describe it; the mechanism of the performance – shadows on one side of the screen and the leather puppets on the other – also reflects the symbolic relationship of shadow and substance.

Sukarno absorbed this aspect of Javanese philosophy from his

23. K. G. P. A. A. Mangkunegara VII of Surakarta, 'On the Wayang Kulit (Purwa) and its Symbolic and Mystical Elements', (originally published in *Djawa*, Vol. XIII, 1933), translated from the Dutch by Claire Holt, Ithaca, 1957, p. 1.

24. B. R. O'G. Anderson, *Mythology and the Tolerance of the Javanese*, Ithaca, 1965.

grandparents at Tulungagung, from his father at Modjokerto and, so the official stories run, from Wagiman, a poor farmer living nearby in Modjokerto. After school Sukarno would often go to sit in Wagiman's hut and listen to his stories of *wayang* heroes – of Kumbakarna, Ardjuna, Gatutkatja, Kresna, the comical but powerful Semar, Hanuman the monkey leader and hosts of others, each with his own well-known virtues and subtleties of character. At other times he was one of those wide-eyed children sitting in front of their elders, watching the night-long performances and listening to the narration of the *dalang* with its pre-scribed turning points – at midnight the entry of the hero and at 3 a.m. the beginning of the resolution of the plot. He absorbed its moral pluralism and its ideas of a just ruler and a harmonious and ordered society. One feature of the *wayang* however did not capture him. He did not learn to follow its models of polished, refined, exquisite (*halus*) behaviour. On the contrary in later life he seemed deliberately to have rejected the refinement of the *wayang* tradition and to have projected an image rather of vigour, coarseness and earthiness in his social behaviour. It is interesting that in his student days in Surabaja and Bandung it was the figure of Bima with which he sometimes chose to identify himself. Bima was one of the five warrior brothers who were the heroes of the *Mahabharata*. His qualities were those of boldness, courage and truthfulness, but certainly not of refinement. He was blunt, uncompromising, rough, contemptuous of established authority and prepared to rebuke even the gods.[25]

The important thing, however, is that Sukarno from an early age was steeped in the *wayang* tradition. In his later speeches he could call upon *wayang* stories and characters to make a complex point to a Javanese audience. Nor was this simply a matter of oratorical gimmickry for he himself lived and moved to a high degree within the thought world of the *wayang*, seeing contemporary conflicts in its terms and even, perhaps seeing himself as the *dalang*, shaping the events of his world and expounding their inner meaning.

25. See Dahm, *Sukarno and the Struggle for Indonesian Independence*, Ithaca, 1969, pp. 26–7, for a discussion of the significance of Bima for Sukarno.

Finally, of importance in the moulding of the young Sukarno was his father's profession as a teacher and his concern as an intellectual. As a teacher Sukemi was a stern overseer of his son's schooling, but after school hours he gave him extra coaching to prepare him for the Dutch secondary education which could open wider horizons for the boy. Beyond this formal instruction Sukemi's other intellectual interests had their influence on his son. Beside his formal adherence to Islam and his accompanying adherence to an older Hindu–Javanese tradition, Sukemi had theosophical leanings.[26] (It is, perhaps, an oddity of the rise of nationalism in some colonial societies, that theosophy should have played a significant part. Despite its concern to probe the mysticism of Eastern religions theosophy was essentially a Western-based body of thought, an eclectic product of the frustrations experienced by individuals in England and America who were dissatisfied with conventional religion and morality. The oddity lies in the fact that the ideas of Colonel Alcott, Madame Blavatsky, W. Q. Judge and Annie Besant should have appealed to societies with their own elaborate and highly sophisticated mystical tradition; there is something patronizing in the earnestness with which Western enthusiasts urged Eastern wisdom upon India. The fact remains however that they did find Indian allies in their search for hidden truths and that Annie Besant did become President of the Indian National Congress. Theosophy's impact in Indonesia awaits its historian – certainly it was slighter than in India.) Through his father, then, Sukarno tapped not only Western learning but also this rather odd, rather artificial, current of Western spiritualism seeking an Eastern dress, and it is significant that the Western influence which was present in his early youth was not that of science, discipline and the Enlightenment but that of a more mystical and off-beat strain.

It is worth dwelling a moment or two more on Sukarno's relations with his parents. His father died towards the end of the Japanese Occupation. His mother lived to see her son President and in the last few years of her life he showed a proper filial piety, visiting her often in her home in Blitar when duties of state permitted. This affection for his mother was used, after his fall from

26. *Autobiography*, p. 39.

power, to support scurrilous stories that he was not Sukemi's son. In his autobiography Sukarno refers to a story that he was, in fact, the illegitimate son of a Dutch coffee planter, farmed out to Sukemi and his wife, and that his hatred of Dutch colonial rule sprang from the fact that his real father had not acknowledged him. There are many versions of the illegitimacy story in circulation. Another suggests that he was the son, not of a Dutch coffee planter, but of a Eurasian plantation overseer. Another, which had currency in sections of the Indonesian Press after his fall from power, was the romantic story that he was really the son of Sunan Pakubuwono X of Surakarta, spirited away at birth to save him from hostility within the *kraton* (palace) from half-brothers who thought that a new male child might steal the succession from them.[27]

It is, of course, not impossible that Sukarno was illegitimate, and that Sukemi and his wife were foster-parents, but no story of this kind can be verified. There is no more than initial plausibility in the argument that Sukemi could not have paid for Sukarno's education and that he must therefore have been supported by a patron, the coffee planter, the Sunan or somebody else. And the argument that Sukarno rarely mentioned his father and reserved his filial piety for his mother is not borne out by his own account of his life. It is true that he tended, when speaking of his parents together, to speak of his mother first and then of his father; but he spoke of the latter at length nonetheless, and with respect and affection. He recalled the strictness of his paternal discipline, his punishment when he came home late from a fishing expedition, his rebuke when his father found him rifling a bird's nest and destroying God's living creatures. He recalled also his father's extraordinary devotion in sleeping under his bed when he contracted typhus at the age of eleven, in order that he might be saved by his father's magical force flowing up to the sick boy. He mentioned Sukemi's concern at his imprisonment and his resigned acceptance of Sukarno's political career. The tributes were continuous and unforced.

Surrounded by these varied influences Sukarno made his way

27. See *Sketsmasa*, No. 53, 1967, for an article entitled: '*Sukarno Anak Siapa?*' ['Whose Son is Sukarno?'] by Oemar Bey.

effectively though not brilliantly through the grades of his father's primary school at Modjokerto. In 1914 he reached the fifth grade,[28] and the time came for him to move on to the next stage of the education which Sukemi had planned for him – a year or two in the Dutch-language elementary school (Europeesche Lagere School) at Modjokerto, which would give him a basis for entry into Dutch secondary education.

This was more easily obtained than would have been the case even a few years earlier. In the early years of the twentieth century the Netherlands Indies Government had sought to expand educational facilities for Indonesians. Opportunities available in the nineteenth century were meagre. A very limited amount of vernacular education was given in village schools and opportunities for further primary and secondary education for children of *priyayi* families were available either in what were called Chiefs' Schools or later, in the nineties, either in training schools for native administrators (OSVIA) or in the newly established First Class Schools. These facilities were greatly extended after 1901 when the Netherlands Government committed itself to what became known as the Ethical Policy. In the late nineteenth century there had been mounting criticism in Christian and Social Democrat circles in Holland of the oppressive aspects of colonial policy. The new humanitarianism received one of its most notable expressions in the argument of C. T. van Deventer, a Dutch lawyer who had practised in the Indies and who later became a liberal-democrat member of the States General. Van Deventer argued that Holland had drawn wealth from the Indies and owed them, in consequence, a 'debt of honour' which should be repaid in the form of a welfare policy designed to improve the lot of her Indonesian subjects. In 1901 the replacement of the liberal government by a Christian–Social-Democrat coalition injected a new sense of idealism and mission into colonial policy, one of the practical consequences of which was an expansion of educational facilities, both at the vernacular level and at the level of secondary and even tertiary education for an Indonesian élite. In addition to schools founded specifically for Indonesians a few were able to

28. Grade 6, according to Nasution, op. cit., but Native Schools did not go beyond the fifth grade.

enter Dutch schools at both primary and secondary level. Dutch schools had been open, at least in theory, to Indonesians since 1864, though unlike Eurasian pupils Indonesians were charged fees for the privilege of attending. With the establishment of First Class Native Schools in 1893 efforts were made to discourage the entry of Indonesians into Dutch Schools, but after 1901 there was some relaxation of this policy and a few were able to enjoy the opportunity.

The educational aspects of the Ethical Policy contained elements both of expediency and of a *mission civilisatrice*. It was hoped that expanded education would meet the need for clerks in the lower levels of government service and in business, and also that it would check the growth of anti-Dutch feeling by offering selected persons an entry into the heritage of Western civilization. One important aspect of the educational policy of the Indies Government was the determination to maintain standards and curricula in Dutch schools in the Indies at a level equivalent to those in Holland itself. This was the *concordantie* principle. The schools were created in the first place, of course, for Dutch and Eurasian children and it was considered of vital importance, since many of these children would spend part of their school years in Holland during their parents' leave, that an exact equivalence be preserved. This determination was both a virtue and a defect. It meant that for the select few Indonesians who could gain entry to Dutch-language schools there would be equality of instruction with Dutch children. It meant also, however, that for reasons of cost the opportunity could be available only to a tiny number. Such schools, which gave a five-year course, could not be founded in sufficient numbers to meet the Indonesian demand, and in the first twenty-eight years of this century only 279 Indonesians, drawn almost entirely from the children of civil servants and *priyayi*, graduated from them. For Sukemi it was important that his son should be one of them.

In enrolling his son at Modjokerto ELS Sukemi was faced immediately by the question of Sukarno's proficiency in Dutch – the magical key to advancement. His own school taught in the vernacular (Javanese) for the first three grades and then in Malay, the long-time lingua franca of trade in the archipelago and now the language of lower administration. Dutch was taught as a subject but was not the medium of instruction. After an interview with the headmaster of the ELS Sukarno was accepted as a student, but his Dutch was declared to be below the standard for the sixth grade in a Dutch school and it was decided he would have to start a grade behind. Sukarno protested that he would be humiliated by being placed below his age group, but Sukemi's ingenuity solved the problem. He suggested taking a year off Sukarno's age and registering him as twelve instead of thirteen.[29] And so he was admitted.

During the next two years Sukarno mastered Dutch and had his first romantic attachment, almost as part of the same operation. He fell in love with a Dutch girl and feared his father's anger when he was discovered by him in her company. Sukemi merely commented that it would be good for his Dutch. It was part of a rather ambiguous beginning to Sukarno's relations with the Dutch. He had already suffered humiliation in playing soccer with Dutch boys who had paraded their feelings of superiority towards him. Later, at school in Surabaja, he was to suffer more pinpricks of this kind. On the other hand his small affair with Rika in Modjokerto was followed by his pursuit of other Dutch girls in Surabaja. Were these merely boyish love affairs? Or did they serve to demonstrate to himself his own superiority, and to assuage the feelings of wounded pride which were born of other contacts with Dutch people? Perhaps it was a little of each.[30]

In 1916, having completed his two years of Dutch primary education in the ELS at Modjokerto Sukarno was qualified for entry into a Dutch secondary school. His father, through the good

29. This incident is one of the elements in the puzzle about Sukarno's age. In his own account he states that he was fourteen at the time and that Sukemi put his age back to thirteen (*Autobiography*, p. 29). The account as given above follows my own conclusion that 1914 was the year of his entry to the ELS and that 1901 was in fact the year of his birth. I have accepted Sukarno's account that the change of age was due to his desire to avoid shame, but it is possible that the reason was that there were upper age limits for entry into secondary schools, and he needed to falsify his age to qualify, two years later, for the Surabaja Hogere Burger School (HBS).

30. For these affairs as remembered by Sukarno see *Autobiography*, chapters 3 and 4.

offices of a Surabaja friend, Umar Sayed Tjokroaminoto, had arranged to enrol him in the Hogere Burger School (HBS) in Surabaja and had also arranged accommodation for him in Tjokroaminoto's house. This move was to be of crucial importance for the future, for Tjokroaminoto, chairman of the mass nationalist organization Sarekat Islam, was the central figure in Indonesian nationalism at the time, and Surabaja was the crucible of nationalist thought and action. In his patron's house Sukarno was to have his first experience of the ferment which was beginning to disturb Indonesian society and of the political energies of those who were preparing organized resistance to colonial rule.

Note on the main dates in Sukarno's early life:

There is some difficulty in determining the precise chronology of Sukarno's passage through the successive stages of his education. Did he enter the ELS in Modjokerto in 1913, 1914, or 1915? Was he twelve, thirteen, or fourteen at the time? Did he spend one year or two at the ELS? Did he go to the HBS in Surabaja in 1915, 1916 or 1917 and was he fourteen, fifteen or sixteen at the time? Did he spend four, five or six years there? Sukarno's account of his school career given in his *Autobiography* is not internally consistent and there are further inconsistencies between it and other standard accounts.

1. In the *Autobiography* (p. 29) Sukarno states that he entered the ELS at the age of fourteen (and put his age back to thirteen). If 1901 was the year of his birth this would have occurred in 1915. Since he was admitted to the fifth grade, according to that account, he would have presumably had to complete two further years before entering the HBS in Surabaja. Unless he was able to complete two years' work in one he would thus have entered the HBS in 1917 aged sixteen. But the *Autobiography* states that he was fifteen when he went to Surabaja (p. 31). If he did go to the HBS in 1917 he would have had only four years there instead of the normal five years of secondary schooling.

2. Nasution, op. cit., has Sukarno graduating from his father's school at the age of twelve in 1913, from the ELS at fourteen in 1915, and from the HBS at the age of nineteen in 1920, after five years of secondary schooling.

3. Dahm, op. cit., also has Sukarno entering the ELS at the age of twelve in 1913 and the HBS at fourteen in 1915 (p. 28), but he has him graduating from the HBS in 1921. This would mean that his secondary schooling lasted for six years instead of five.

All of these accounts thus need some correction. Nasution is certainly wrong in stating that Sukarno graduated from the HBS in 1920. The graduation is recorded in *Oetoesan Hindia*, 11 June 1921 (See also Dahm, op. cit., p. 43). Graduation from Surabaja in 1921 then may be taken as the one clearly established date in the whole story. If one works back from that date,

Sukarno's entry into the HBS would have occurred five years earlier – in 1916 – which is consistent with his account of his age at that time as fourteen and with his entry to the ELS in Modjokerto in 1914. It is inconsistent, however, with his own memory that he was fourteen when he entered the ELS.

This problem of chronology is further confused by the slight doubt about Sukarno's age. If he was born in 1900 he would indeed have been fourteen at the time of his entry to the ELS in 1914 (though he would have been sixteen when he went to Surabaja). However, as argued in footnote 1 of this chapter, this would imply an improbably long primary schooling.

In the view of the present writer the most likely version is that Sukarno was born in 1901, entered the ELS at the age of thirteen in 1914, entered the HBS in 1916 and graduated from there in 1921.

# 2

# Origins of Nationalism

The Java into which Sukarno was born was a society in the process of profound social change. Over the preceding quarter of a century the Indies, in common with other parts of Asia and Africa, had begun to feel the full impact of industrial Europe's expansive energies and indeed it can reasonably be argued that the colony of Netherlands India was effectively created during this period. One of the myths of Indonesian nationalism has been that the archipelago was subjected to 350 years of Dutch rule–from the beginning of the seventeenth century, when the Dutch East India Company began its operations, up to the Second World War. In fact it was only towards the end of the nineteenth century that Dutch rule was extended over the archipelago as a whole. Even in Java, where the Dutch had established a firm base of operations by the end of the seventeenth century, it was not until the early nineteenth that they developed a deeply penetrating administration. Dutch activities over the previous 200 years had merely laid the foundations.

The society encountered by the Dutch was diverse. Early patterns of migration and settlement had produced a patchwork of ethnically distinct peoples, stemming perhaps from a common Malay stock but possessing their own special characteristics – their own languages, their own cultural traditions, their own patterns of social organization. They were distinct communities which only much later would come to accept a common Indonesian nationality. Over the centuries they were subjected to a variety of external pressures. From about the fifth century Java and parts of Sumatra received independent cultural influences from India which aided the evolution of elaborate hierarchical kingdoms based on wet rice cultivation and possessing a refined, court-centred, aristocratic tradition. Hindu and Buddhist conceptions of state and kingship were superimposed on the animistic and magical world of village society. Later still Islam followed the trade routes, finding footholds first in Sumatra from about the thirteenth century but spreading more widely in the course of the fifteenth from the great trading centre of Malacca. The new religion found more ready acceptance in the commercial centres of the archipelago, but penetrated only with difficulty into the land-based, inward-looking kingdoms of Java. If one wished to classify in simple terms the complex amalgam of traditions, both indigenous and imported, to be observed in the islands, one could stress the broad difference between Java, where Hinduism has left its deepest mark and where society is hierarchical and aristocratic in character, and the outer islands, in particular Sumatra to the west and Celebes and the spice islands to the east, where trade and Islam went hand in hand.

In the sixteenth century this diverse society had its first contact with new influences from Europe, first the Portuguese and then the Dutch. In the early seventeenth century the Dutch East India Company (Vereenigde Oostindische Compagnie – VOC) secured a foothold in Jacatra in West Java and made it into its head-quarters of Batavia. From this base it established factories in the eastern islands of the group from which it could command the source of the spice trade. From Makassar and Ambon, from Banda and Tidore, it collected its cargoes of mace, nutmeg and clove. It shouldered aside the indigenous traders of the region and gathered more and more of the export trade of the islands into its own hands.

The VOC was at first concerned with commerce rather than with the establishment of a costly territorial empire, but in its search for monopoly it emerged as the paramount power in the Indies, greater than other princes and able to impose its will on others. Even so it was only gradually that Dutch power came to control, first the island of Java, and then other parts of the archipelago. The VOC was wound up at the end of the eighteenth century and its holdings in the Indies passed to the Dutch crown. Over the course of the nineteenth century Dutch economic interests expanded and the administrative machinery of the Indies' government developed in consequence to carry new responsibilities. In Java, for example, the culture system, whereby a proportion of the land of each village was to be set aside for the production of export crops to be delivered to the government in lieu of tax, required a new thoroughness of administration. Outside Java the process was slower, but by the mid nineteenth century a considerable part of Sumatra had come under Dutch authority. However it was really after 1870 that a quickening of the tempo began to expose the Indies to forces of a new kind. In fact it was less a quickening of tempo than the beginning of a new and distinctive period of Dutch expansion.

In 1870 a new agrarian law enabled private Dutch interests to acquire land under long-term leasehold and to share in this way in the exploitation of the Indies. This encouragement of private enterprise marked the beginning of what was called the 'Liberal Policy', and within the framework of the new legislation Dutch investment began to flow at a rate which was to transform the Indies' export economy within a comparatively brief period. The volume of exports increased more than tenfold between 1870 and 1930, and their character changed. While exports of coffee, sugar, tea and tobacco continued to expand, the export figures came to be dominated by industrial raw materials – rubber, copra, tin and oil. The direct production of these goods through the application of Dutch capital and through enterprises under Dutch management and employing Indonesian labour contrasted sharply with the former indirect method of acquiring export crops grown by Indonesian cultivators on their own land; for some crops such as rubber, copra, sugar, tea and tobacco, the plantation – a form of large-scale corporative enterprise – represented a new mode of economic exploitation. To support the expanding economy a new network of communications – railways and roads in Java and Sumatra and shipping between Java and the outer islands – bound the archipelago in a new unity.

This enormous expansion of the Indies' export economy resulting from direct Dutch investment was accompanied by a rapid extension of territorial control. After 1870 deliberate steps were taken to round out Dutch control of the archipelago. Between 1873 and 1908 the long drawn out and hard fought Atjeh war completed the subjugation of Sumatra. In Borneo, Celebes and the Moluccas, areas which had already been subject to a general Dutch suzerainty were riveted more firmly to Batavia and new areas were taken – south and central Celebes by 1906, Ceram and

Buru in 1907, Ternate in 1909. And so the march continued. West New Guinea was also brought, though to a more limited degree, within the framework of Dutch administration. By 1910 the process was practically complete. This sudden and explosive expansion of territory must be seen as part of the competitive surge of western European imperialism by which, in the later nineteenth century, most of the 'underdeveloped' areas of the globe which had not previously come under colonial domination were divided between Britain, France, Germany, Holland and Belgium. Though the Dutch had been in the Indies for three centuries they had moved after 1870 to the creation of what was, in effect, a new empire.

There were various ways in which the Indonesian élite could react to these developments. Some managed to accommodate themselves to Dutch rule; they occupied satisfying positions within the colonial framework and had no desire for change. Others hoped to secure autonomy for the Indies in the future, to be achieved by co-operation with the régime and by concessions gradually won from the Netherlands. Others looked to the evolution of an Indonesian partnership with the Dutch. But for others again the indignity of colonial subjection was the overwhelming fact. For them the only course was uncompromising and possibly violent struggle for complete independence. Sukarno was to belong to this latter category. From his youth he acquired a burning sense of resentment at the discriminations of colonial rule. Some of them were the major discriminations of a colonial economy or the suppression of native political activity. Perhaps more important were the apparently petty humiliations suffered at the hands of Dutchmen who, from the moment they stepped ashore at Tandjung Priok, were the masters in what was essentially a caste society. Social exclusion, the Dutch sense of superiority, and their easy assumption of authority left deep psychological marks on those who were on the receiving end of the colonial equation. For Sukarno the sense of insult and humiliation was deeply felt, and the determination to assert his own pride and to recover self-respect for himself and his people became the driving force of his actions.

The nationalist movement was not simply the sum total of individual resentments however, and if Sukarno's contribution to it is to be understood it is necessary to examine more closely the setting within which he moved.

Indonesian nationalism was essentially a new phenomenon to be distinguished from earlier movements of protest against Dutch rule. The Java War of 1825–30, for example, in which Prince Diponegoro resisted Dutch power in Central Java for five years, was a local movement reflecting local discontent, and was very different in character from the new currents of resistance to be seen in the early twentieth century. The new nationalism was the product of the new imperialism. It should be seen as part of a greater movement affecting many parts of the new empires created by Europe in Asia and Africa at the end of the nineteenth century and it was concerned not merely with opposition to colonial rule but with the development of new and self-conscious perceptions of national identity. The two aspects went together, of course: the sense of nationhood was forged in the common experience of resistance to colonial subjection; nevertheless, the ideas of nationality and of the creation, in time, of a new political order – a modern state – through which it could be expressed were essentially new concepts, going beyond the negative aspects of a struggle for independence and involving the construction of new channels of authority in traditional societies and the definition of new expectations. All of this had its parallels elsewhere – in India, in other parts of Southeast Asia and in Africa – and it was very different from the 'pre-nationalist' movements of agrarian protest which were common in Indonesian society, or from revolts under traditional leadership directed against particular grievances.

In Indonesia Sukarno helped to shape the new self-consciousness but he did not create it. Its basic causes lay in the processes of social change set in motion by the latter-day expansion of Dutch political and economic power in the Indies. In the eighteenth century the representatives of the Company collected the produce of the Indies but made only a limited impact upon the political and social orders they found there, and they managed even to accord a degree of respect to indigenous authority; but at the end of the nineteenth century Dutch government and Dutch capital were transforming Indonesia. The release of new economic energies had disturbed the balance of traditional agrarian societies. It had stimulated the emergence of new classes, eroded the position of traditional élites and loosened many of the communal ties which had provided the established environment for the great mass of the population. It had also given political unity for the first time to the archipelago and had thus created a situation in which it was possible for Indonesians to see beyond ethnic divisions to the possibility of national unity. These changes helped to create not only a growing *malaise* among the population as a whole but also, more positively, a new awareness of a changing world, and a new political leadership through which that awareness could be expressed.

The rapid urban growth of the period was at once a reflection of change and a stimulus to it. Batavia, Surabaja, Semarang and Medan became large commercial cities, the headquarters not only of central and regional government but also of the financial and commercial services of the new economy – banks, business firms, export houses and port facilities. The Dutch population of the Indies increased as an army of civil servants and business employees came to staff these services. For Indonesians too the cities offered opportunities: for the literate as clerks in the lower ranks of business or government administration; for skilled and semi-skilled workers in railway workshops, small printing works and other forms of industrial employment and for the unskilled as labourers and domestic servants. However, though the cities provided an environment for the growth of a new urban culture, for most of the Indonesians who were drawn into them it was a destructive rather than a creative environment. Most of them came to live in overcrowded *kampongs* composed of flimsy bamboo houses which rapidly degenerated into congested and unserviced slums. These settlements attempted in some measure to recreate the communal patterns of village life for many of those who lived in them, but they were increasingly the home of the unaccommodated and demoralized elements of Indonesian society, displaced from their rural background.

While economic development stimulated change in some directions, in others its effect was, paradoxically, to make existing social patterns more rigid. This was particularly so in rural Java which was faced by rising population without any parallel change in the character and organization of agrarian society. Java's population increased from about six million to almost thirty million over the course of the nineteenth century and to over forty million by 1920. This in itself was an indication of the tempo of the forces released by the new imperialism. The rapid increase, however, was accommodated in large measure by the extension of the traditional *sawah* (wet rice) method of cultivation into hitherto unoccupied areas without any significant change in technology or social order. Insofar as there was change it was in the direction of intensifying existing methods of cultivation, not of revolutionizing them. Land was fragmented into smaller and smaller holdings. Efforts were made to make two grains of rice grow where one grew before, to produce two crops in the time formerly allowed to produce one. The land itself was thus driven harder and harder and subjected to the work of more and more human hands. This process of 'involution'[31] and reinforcement of the traditional economy and society in Java confirmed the wide gap between traditional agriculture on the one hand and the new economy of the estates, oil wells and business houses created by Dutch capital on the other.

But in other ways rural society did feel the solvent effects of the growth of the Western sector of the economy. The village as a whole was brought within the orbit of a money economy which had its impact on traditional economic relationships. Plantation development placed labour demands upon rural society, and those who left the village for estate-employment inevitably slipped from their niche in an established social order into an environment in which their customary notions of value and behaviour were largely irrelevant. Many of them, on the expiry of their contracts, could no longer return to the village environment and came to swell the unskilled and unaccommodated population of the urban *kampongs*. Population pressure also drove many from countryside to city. It is not easy, from available statistics, to draw

31. For the application of this term and an analysis of the process see C. Geertz, *Agricultural Involution*, Berkeley, 1963.

firm conclusions about general living standards in different sectors of the community but the consensus of authorities is that, apart from a few years before the First World War, *per capita* income fell slowly but steadily from the 1890s onwards.[32]

Poverty and social dislocation may appear sufficient in themselves to explain the increasing unrest in Indonesian society in the early years of the twentieth century. There was, in addition, a growing awareness of the mere fact of alien rule as government penetrated more deeply into rural society, whether as tax-gatherer or as benevolent protector and well-intentioned provider of welfare services. There were also more specific aspects of colonialism's inevitable discrimination apparent to village and élite alike, whether in the protection of Dutch enterprise built into the very nature of colonial rule or in the reservation of certain levels of employment for Dutchmen or again in the thoughtless social discrimination which could be much more galling to the educated Indonesian. The Dutch were in many ways more liberal in their attitude to race and colour than were the members of some other European powers, but once they had created their own dominant society in the Indies its self-contained character inhibited social intercourse with Indonesians.

However nationalism was not a simple consequence of the oppressive, disruptive or discriminatory features of colonial rule. Indeed it is significant that an organized movement of resistance to colonial authority began to emerge just as the Dutch were becoming concerned with charting a new and more benevolent course in the administration of their empire. At the beginning of the twentieth century as we have noticed a new idealistic strain made itself apparent: the Ethical Policy was intended to repay Holland's debt of honour to the Indies. This meant different things to different people. Some saw it as making possible an

32. See Kahin, *Nationalism and Revolution in Indonesia*, Ithaca, 1952, pp. 23 ff. for a discussion of the views of authorities on this question. See also J. S. Furnivall, *Netherlands India*, Cambridge, 1939, pp. 214–16 and D. H. Burger, *Structuurveranderingen in de Javaanse Samenleving* ['Structural Changes in Javanese Society'], published in *Indonesië* in seven parts during 1949–50. Parts 1 and 3, 'The Village Sphere' and 'The Supra-village Sphere', were published in translation by the Cornell Modern Indonesia Project, 1956 and 1957.

expansion of Indonesian economic development so that the gap between the two sides of the dual economy could be closed. Others saw it rather in cultural terms. They wanted colonial rule to enable an Indonesian élite to share in the heritage of Western civilization. Others again recognized a measure of cultural arrogance in such an approach and wished the provision of aspects of Western civilization to be accompanied by the respectful protection of valuable aspects of Indonesian civilization. 'Cultural synthesis' rather than assimilation was their aim, with the ultimate goal of a new 'East Indian society', a multi-racial society, blending characteristics of East and West and able to stand on its own feet, self-governing but in some continuing relationship with the Netherlands. Whatever the precise content given to the idea of a welfare policy its exponents showed a genuine sense of mission. They felt that Holland was on the verge of a noble experiment in colonial rule which could serve the interests of colonial power and colonial subjects alike, and such an expectation inspired a new breed of paternal and devoted civil servants whose task it was to implement the new policy.

So much for the vision. In practical terms the policy meant the introduction of a series of welfare programmes. Agricultural services provided technical advice to village agriculturalists and assisted in the improvement of irrigation works; health services were improved; there were programmes for the resettlement of people from overcrowded areas and educational facilities were extended. The latter development was partly the result of the advocacy of the government's adviser on Islamic matters, Christiaan Snouck Hurgronje. Snouck had argued that a Western education could offer the best counter to the possible danger of a militant pan-Islamic movement in Indonesia, but there was a good deal more in his proposals than a mere defensive expediency. There was also an element of what might be called 'cultural imperialism' – he saw in education the means of making available the riches of Western civilization to the Indonesian élite. At the political level the creation in 1918 of the Volksraad (People's Council), representing Indonesians and 'Foreign Asiatics' as well as Dutch, can be taken as a later extension of the same general policy. It was an earnest of the government's promise to consult local opinion and to prepare for the increasing autonomy of the Indies within the Dutch empire.

The elements of idealism which lay behind the adoption of the Ethical Policy were genuine. Nonetheless the results of the Policy in the long run proved to be meagre. It did not check the declining living standards of the Indonesian population. It did not stimulate technological changes in agriculture, nor set in motion any economic revolution. Nor could it really be expected to do so. The aims set out in its founders' speeches were certainly high, implying as they did a gigantic experiment in controlled social change and economic development; but the policies justified in the name of these aims were far more modest. Colonial Minister Idenburg summarized the methods by which the experiment was to be conducted in his slogan: 'Education, irrigation, emigration'. Education was vigorously developed, though with consequences for the élite which we have still to examine, but considered against the magnitude of the problem of mass illiteracy the educational programme of the ethical period succeeded only in scratching the surface. A literacy rate of a little over six per cent by 1930 was hardly a massive achievement.[33] For the rest, irrigation and emigration may have contributed to ameliorating rural conditions but they involved no attempt to change the existing labour-intensive techniques of wet rice cultivation. The visionaries of 1900 were, of course, the prisoners of the thinking of their day. Their plans were conceived within the framework of Holland's liberal view that economic development resulting from European investment must inevitably benefit the local population as well as the Dutch investors in the long run. It was not, in any case, to be expected that the framework of existing economic policy would suddenly be set aside. The plans for welfare must be seen, then, as an appendage to the *laissez-faire* liberal policy which preceded it and not as a departure from it.

33. This figure was calculated on the basis of total population including children. A different calculation, excluding children under ten, would give a literacy rate of about 30%. See S. L. van der Wal, *Some Information on Education in Indonesia up to 1942*, The Hague, 1960, for a discussion of the question. However it is clear that by any calculation Dutch mass-education policies were not spectacularly successful.

In some ways, however, though falling far short of its goals, the Ethical Policy did contribute, perhaps unexpectedly, to the ferment of social change in Indonesia. Far from earning the responsive gratitude of a dependent people it positively accentuated the growth of Indonesian awareness of alien rule and of hostility towards it. The implementation of schemes for village improvement through the application of 'gentle pressure' on the Indonesian ranks of the administrative service and on village authorities aroused a growing resentment. It brought village society more sharply than ever before into contact with government as such, and it added to the currents of discontent and frustration which had been stimulated by the preceding quarter of a century of Dutch economic expansion.

Mass discontent required leadership and here the effects of the Ethical Policy were even more significant. Provision of a Western education for members of the élite had not been accompanied by any clear programme for using the products, even though they were comparatively few in number. The policy of allowing entry to Dutch primary and secondary schools for some Indonesians did not open the floodgates, for such education was beyond the means even of most of the *priyayi*. Even so the demand for places was greater than the supply, and there was insufficient employment even for the few hundred Indonesians who emerged annually from these schools. For a few there were jobs and status in the lower ranks of government service or in Dutch business houses, though Indonesian applicants often found themselves the victims of discriminatory policies which preferred Dutch or Eurasian employees to Indonesians. In many fields there were different rates of pay for Indonesian and Dutch employees; for many graduates there was no employment available. Two points stand out: the Western-educated élite formed but a tiny proportion of the population; despite this fact it was an under-employed and frustrated élite, resentful of its lack of opportunity, and quick to resent the slights and humiliations arising from its inferior status and from Dutch attitudes of careless superiority. From these elements emerged Indonesia's 'political élite',[34] able

34. The term is suggested by R. van Niel in his *The Emergence of the Modern Indonesian Elite* (The Hague, 1960), to distinguish the members of

to diagnose its own unhappy condition and ready to engage in political activity and to mobilize the discontent of the rural and urban masses.

If one were to try in a few words to record a brief judgement of Dutch imperialism from its hesitant beginnings in the seventeenth century to its full thrust in the late nineteenth and early twentieth centuries, the verdict would be that it was harsh and oppressive in some respects, paternal and benevolent in others, particularly after 1900, but that it was heavy-handed even in its benevolence. Such pros and cons, however, are only marginally significant for an explanation of the rise of nationalism. They were of minor importance when set against the overwhelming facts of Dutch rule and of the social changes produced by Dutch economic penetration: by urbanization, by the growth of Dutch plantations and mines, by the expansion of exports and the penetration of a money economy to the village level. The causes of twentieth-century nationalism are to be found in the disturbance to the balance of traditional societies which followed this full impact of modern industrial Europe. With the emergence of a new intelligentsia mass discontent could be channelled and organized into movements of political power challenging the colonial régime, looking forward positively to the building of an independent state based on new perceptions of national identity and transforming the patterns of a traditional order.

Even this is not the whole story. Nationalism is not merely the product of a simple equation – mass discontent plus frustrated leadership. For leaders and followers alike the crisis in which they were caught up was in some respects psychological, a crisis of individual and collective identity as an established order was subjected to new pressures and established values were eroded. It was in a sense a problem of knowing who one was and what one's group was. Custom had provided answers to those ques-

---

the older *priyayi* who staffed the older territorial administrative service, and others who had secured satisfying employment and whose concern, whatever their basic views on political questions, was primarily to keep the wheels of government turning, from those who, as an unemployed intelligentsia, turned to nationalist action. Hence the distinction between the 'functional' and a 'political' élite.

tions, but social change and shifting status systems reopened them. Western education had alienated some intellectuals from their own society and its preconceptions, making them sons of the European Enlightenment, but without making them Europeans. Sutan Sjahrir in his letters from exile expressed the intellectual's dilemma. He found himself much closer in outlook to Europe and America than to his own society until his exile enabled him, as it were, to return home spiritually.[35] For some nationalism offered a resolution of this tension. The idea of the nation was a new idea – a new collectivity able to command an individual's loyalty and to offer him a reason for his existence.

There were many variations on this theme. Some sought an answer to their alienation in a rejuvenated Islam. Western education had not only produced secular nationalists, it had its effects also within the world of Islam, reinforcing new currents of thought flowing from Cairo. The modernist movement in Islam, developing especially under the teaching of Mohammad Abduh of Cairo at the end of the nineteenth century, sought a purification of Islamic doctrine – a sweeping away of the scholastic accretions and the local superstitions which had come to obscure the faith. It also believed that Islam must accommodate itself to the modern world. The modernists regarded their faith as essentially based on reason and believed that the renewal of a purer orthodoxy, freed from obscurantism, could be reconciled with Western science and progress. The new ferment in Islam was one part of the story of Indonesia's re-awakening.

The impact of Islamic modernism was felt largely within urban society. At the same time unreformed Islam, too, had a subtly changed role to play in rural society. Javanese society is proverbially tolerant and it has accommodated over the centuries a variety of traditions. Islam has been one of them. It has been accepted and blended with a complex of older beliefs – with the animism and the communalism of village society, with Hindu thought and with the mysticism, the refinement and the sophisticated worldview of the royal courts. This is not to say, however, that is has nowhere struck deep roots. Javanese syncretism is a real trait but

35. Sjahrir, *Out of Exile*, New York, 1949, p. 33.

it did not lead to an even and universally accepted blend of diverse traditions. In some places and for some people Islam was but one element in a subtle blend. For others it was a single compelling faith making absolute demands and refusing to compromise with other beliefs. There was thus accommodation between Islam and custom and also opposition and tension between them, reflected in the continuing division in Javanese society between *santri* and *abangan* – between the devout Muslim on the one hand and, on the other, the non-Muslim or only nominal Muslim whose religion was compounded of elements of animism, magic and mysticism as well as of Islam.[36] Outside Java too a similar gulf was set in many areas between Islam and *adat* or customary law.

These divisions were of importance in Indonesia's emerging nationalism and were to continue to be important in shaping the political conflicts of the independent Republic. The point to be made here, however, is that for rural society in the early twentieth century, both for *santri* and *abangan*, Islam acquired a new appeal. As the communal ties of the village were loosened it served as an integrating factor, offering a new collective vision which could give meaning and purpose to existence and binding Muslims together against infidel rule. Traditional Islam helped to provide a sense of collective identity for the peasant as reformist Islam did for the Muslim intellectual and as secular nationalist thought did for the Western-educated élite.

These various currents contributed to the emergence of nationalism as an organized force. The ferment of social change provided a mass base for political protest and an educated élite was at hand to lead it. It is customary in surveys of Indonesian nationalism to pay tribute to the first stirrings in the late nineteenth century of a genuine nationalist consciousness, but to see the foundation of Boedi Oetomo in 1908 as the beginning of nationalism as an organized movement. Boedi Oetomo was a society founded by a retired Javanese doctor, Wahidin Soediraoesada. In its original conception its goals were essentially cultural;

36. The term *abangan* is derived from *abang*, meaning 'red'. The *abangan*, or 'red ones', are contrasted with the *santri* religious community sometimes referred to as 'the white ones'.

it sought ways of reconciling Javanese values with the demands of the modern world. Its membership was mainly aristocratic and it found its early support in medical student circles, but it also attracted members from the ranks of the civil service and from the *priyayi* in general. Though it remained for many years a not insignificant part of the wider nationalist movement, it was soon outstripped in both membership and significance by more politically motivated organizations – in particular by the mass society Sarekat Islam.

Sarekat Islam had its origins as a protection society formed by Javanese traders who were concerned at Chinese penetration into such fields as *batik* making which was considered to be a peculiarly Javanese preserve. The original Islamic Trading Association (Sarekat Dagang Islam) changed its name and its character in 1912 and, as Sarekat Islam, embarked on a spectacular expansion under the chairmanship of the charismatic Umar Sayed Tjokroaminoto, who brought passionate devotion to the task of developing a modern political role for Islam through the new organization. Its membership grew rapidly from a few thousand to several hundred thousand in the space of four years. By 1919 it claimed membership of two and a half million, but this was an inflated figure – a more accurate count would be about 400,000.[37] Nevertheless, the society clearly had an established mass base, and a wide appeal. For the peasantry it was a unifying force in a disturbed society, for urban workers in Surabaja and Semarang and other cities it appeared as a potential protector and organizer. It also offered Western-educated intellectuals, whether Muslim or not, an opportunity for positive political action. One of its remarkable features was its ability to embrace both *santri* and *abangan*. It was in effect able to anchor itself in elements of both traditions. Its Islamic content had obvious appeal for the *santri*. For non-*santri* it provided a point of collective resistance to the Dutch but it touched also the mystical and messianic strands in the *abangan* tradition – in particular the idea of the coming of a just ruler who would set a disordered world to rights again. In general it could be said to represent an interaction between the traditional foci of authority and the new urban-based leadership

37. See Dahm, op. cit., pp. 13–14 for a discussion of this question.

which, in organization and ideology, was to create the familiar outlines of modern nationalism.

While Sarekat Islam dominated organized nationalism for the decade after its foundation it was not the only expression of it. Eurasians had their own organizations, based on the view that residence in, and commitment to the Indies, rather than race, should be the basis of nationalism. A quite different approach was represented by the Indies Social Democratic Association (ISDV), founded in 1914 by a Dutch Marxist named Hendrik Sneevliet. Originally dominated by Dutch members, ISDV gradually acquired Indonesian members who prepared the way for the transformation of the association into the Indies Communist Party (PKI) in 1920.

A variety of attitudes was thus able to find organized expression after 1912. There was, however, little precise definition of ultimate goals. Sarekat Islam's original approach was set within the framework of loyalty to the colonial government. Its economic and social programme, couched at first in the most general terms, spoke of developing commerce among Indonesians and promoting their material well-being. This programme was to be implemented, presumably, by pressure exerted within the framework of Dutch government. Within a few years the organization had become much more radical, envisaging non-cooperation with the Dutch and opposition to foreign capital. During the first years of its existence precision of programme was less important than nationalist fervour. Indeed there was no occasion for it, or for other societies, to define their course clearly and only the Marxists, drawing on a ready-made general theory, were able to formulate any coherent and systematic view of the colonial condition and the remedy for it. Not until after 1926 can one discern a clearly identifiable strain of 'secular' nationalism emphasizing the primary importance of Indonesian independence and leaving a consideration of the precise nature of social objectives until after independence had been achieved.

In these circumstances the early manifestations of organized nationalism appeared to display a fair degree of unity of approach. There were, it is true, several organizations rather than one single movement of resistance to Dutch overlordship, and there were obvious differences over strategy and tactics. But there seemed at first to be few really fundamental differences separating the several elements. While self-government or independence were shadowy and distant goals there was no need for different groups to define closely their exact positions; and to avoid definition was to avoid division. Nevertheless, the surface unity of a great deal of nationalist thinking in fact did conceal important divisions. Some of these were ideological – between Islamic nationalism and the young communist party in the early twenties, for example. Others were tactical – between those who were willing to co-operate with the Dutch and those committed to an uncompromising non-cooperation. But there were also deeper fissures which were in time to reveal themselves to be fundamental. By the 1920s they were discernible, and though often concealed by alliances and re-groupings, they survived to bedevil the political alignments of independent Indonesia.

Several lines of potential cleavage may be discerned. Some arose from the ethnic diversity of the archipelago and from the cultural variety which accompanied it. Others arose from religious differences – those between Muslims, nominal Muslims and non-Muslims, or the old and continuing conflict between Islam and *adat*, or custom. Again, within the world of Islam itself there was the tension between the reformist and modernist on the one hand, and on the other the conservative *ulama*, whose roots lay as much within an older customary tradition as within Islam.

Some of these divisions overlap. Of particular importance in this picture of ethnic, religious and cultural diversity is the special position of the Javanese as the largest single ethnic group, forming approximately half of Indonesia's total population. Add to this the strength of Javanese traditional culture, its animistic village beliefs overlaid by Hindu–Buddhist civilization, and the consequent fact of Islam's comparatively superficial penetration of that society, and one can discern a particularly deep gulf cutting across the nation. The tension between *santri* and *abangan* within that society is, as we have seen, an important division, but more important is the general opposition between the Javanese as a whole and the rest of Indonesia. Add the special character of the Javanese world-view with its mysticism and its inward-looking tendency and compare it with the different temper of societies whose interests have been maritime and commercial over the centuries, which have been more susceptible to Islam and more active in entrepreneurial activity, and the gulf becomes deeper. Add again the fact of deeper Dutch penetration in Java over three centuries. One observer has attempted to generalize this difference in illuminating terms as an opposition between two chief political cultures – Javanese–aristocratic and Islamic–entrepreneurial – a dichotomy which sums up a series of largely coinciding lines of cleavage – ethnic, cultural and economic – which underlie the Java–Outer Islands opposition.[38] Other observers have spoken less sharply of *alirans* ('streams') within Indonesian society reflecting these different traditions: *santri* and *abangan* in Java, Javanese and non-Javanese, Islam of modernist or conservative colour.[39]

However defined, the significant thing is that there were basic cultural divisions in Indonesian society, separating one element from another, not merely by differences of interest or programme, but representing more fundamental contrasts of loyalty and outlook. In 1912 and the following years these divisions had yet to assert themselves. For the time being Western education had provided something of a common outlook for the élite; for the masses the messianic elements of nationalist ideology commanded support from Muslim and non-Muslim, from Javanese and non-Javanese alike. But the latent conflicts were there and were in time to give a particular sharpness to political conflict within the nationalist movement, and later still to the politics of independent Indonesia. They were to pose problems for the nationalist leadership and were to demand great qualities of conciliation and synthesis.

38. H. Feith, *The Decline of Constitutional Democracy in Indonesia*, Ithaca, 1962, p. 31. These categories are not sharply defined. For example the *santri* of Java belonged to the Islamic–entrepreneurial category rather than to the Javanese–aristocratic. And there are other groups, in other parts of the archipelago which do not fit – Christians in Ambon, Minahasa and Tapanuli, Hinduism in Bali, etc.

39. In modern Indonesia the term *alirans* has come to refer not merely to broad cultural streams, but more specifically to the political organizations and sub-organizations which have grown up on the basis of broad cultural groupings.

It was to be Sukarno's task to grapple with these divisions, attempting to draw diverse traditions together and to pursue the goal of ideological unification of the nationalist movement, subordinating its tributary currents to the supreme goal of resisting the Dutch and creating an Indonesian nation. His move to Surabaja in 1916, though he would not have known it, represented the first step along that path. In Surabaja he was to find himself in a new and exciting world, and indeed in the very heart of it in the home of Sarekat Islam's magnetic leader, Tjokroaminoto. The city was, at that time, Indonesia's nationalist headquarters. It was the centre of Sarekat Islam's organization and its working-class concentration made it also the headquarters of the Indies Social Democratic Association. In this environment Tjokroaminoto was to be, for Sukarno, a master-craftsman in political action – a model for the high-school boy from the provinces.

# 3

Apprenticeship in Nationalism –
Surabaja and Bandung 1916–26

The fifteen-year-old youth who came in 1916 from his parents'
home in Modjokerto to high school in Surabaja was representative of a recognized pattern of education. The opening of Dutch
primary schools to Indonesians made it possible for some of
them, in due course, to go on to a Dutch secondary education,
though such opportunities were very limited. Indonesian families
had to be able to meet the tuition fees for their sons, but even
when they could do so the number of places available was far
below the demand for them. It required social position and influence to secure admission and in practice it tended to be only the
sons of the *priyayi* who could obtain the privilege.

The move from a small country town to a large commercial city
must have been disturbing as well as exciting for Sukarno, and his
high hopes were no doubt tinged by anxiety as he embarked on
his new experience. Surabaja was the second largest city in the
Indies; as a port and clearing house for the exports of East Java
and as a centre for a limited amount of industrial development it
possessed a varied population. In common with other urban
centres of the Indies it was going through a period of unprecedented growth, its population more than doubling between 1905
(150,000) and 1930 (342,000). In addition to its Dutch community
and its thriving Chinese population, its numbers were swollen by
migrants from the countryside seeking employment as unskilled
labourers in the docks and in small industry, or in the numerous
other servile positions created by urban growth. In this setting
Sukarno was to be exposed not only to Western thought and to
the modernizing influences of a Dutch secondary education, but
also to the complex forces of social change and the consequent
stirrings of open and organized protest which were present in a
more dramatically positive form in a great city than they had been
in Modjokerto's more sheltered environment.

There were however other, more traditional, overtones to his
experience. If Sukarno's progress from rural Dutch primary

school to urban Dutch secondary school is to be regarded as a modern feature, shared by others on their way to membership of the new Indonesian élite, it bore a certain resemblance also to a common pattern of education in traditional society. A Javanese boy in his adolescence would often leave his father's house to live, perhaps with a relative, or perhaps in an *asrama*, or in the house of a religious teacher, whether a Muslim or a *guru* representing a pre-Islamic tradition. In this way, according to one scholar, 'adolescent males were "removed" from society and "prepared" for their re-emergence into it by means analogous to the transmogrification of caterpillars to butterflies . . . . The *guru* himself consecrated the boy's life and led him back again to the boundaries of everyday society when he and the times were ripe.'[40] This experience of removal from home liberated the boy from the established pattern of his childhood life and gave him an opportunity of drawing upon the wells of a deeper and more spiritual order. In going to Surabaja Sukarno was not, of course, removed from society. He was plunged into it. But it was a different society from the one he had left and there were certainly elements of the *asrama* setting in his membership of Tjokroaminoto's household. There were elements, too, of the *guru*-pupil tie in his relationship with Tjokroaminoto himself, even though the initiation was not into Javanese or Islamic mysticism but into nationalist thought and activity. Tjokroaminoto was the first and perhaps the greatest of several masters who were to shape him over the next ten years.

There were elements of tradition too in the disturbance of the times themselves. The Javanese world view, with its emphasis on stability, hierarchy and order, had a clear place for the opposite pole of the spectrum – for times of disorder and instability when established values were forgotten and when chaos replaced harmony. Such times aroused the messianic expectation of a just ruler who could set the world to rights again. In 1916 this sense of a society shaken loose from its traditional moorings gave an added dimension to the experiences Sukarno was about to face.

Acute homesickness assailed Sukarno as he joined the other boarders – about twenty-five all told – in Tjokroaminoto's house-

40. B. R. O'G. Anderson, *The Pemuda Revolution: Indonesian Politics, 1945–1946*, doctoral thesis, Cornell University, ch. 1.

hold. His tiny dark room at the back of the house seemed a cheerless spot to him and though he settled cockily into his class at the HBS and was able enough to earn the approbation of his teachers, the playground posed its own challenges. As one of about twenty Indonesians among about three hundred Dutch pupils he felt again the sting of discrimination which had been familiar to him at Modjokerto. Occasional scuffles and exchanges of blows were bad enough. The cool and spontaneous segregation of students into two distinct, racially-defined groups was worse, and through it he experienced directly the fundamental humiliation of colonial subjection. During his first year he made vacation visits home to Modjokerto. In 1917 his father was transferred to Blitar which was also within reach, though funds were insufficient to allow very frequent visits. Sukarno was supported by his sister's husband, a Public Works inspector, as well as by his father, and he was comparatively well off. He was better dressed than Ibu Tjokroaminoto's other boarders[41] and in his autobiography he confessed to being the proud possessor of a bicycle. But this was a comparative affluence only, and he had to use his allowance with care.

His loneliness drove him at first into study. Through his father's connections he was able to draw on the resources of the Surabaja Theosophical Society library. He became an omnivorous reader and, shut away in his room, he introduced himself with growing excitement to a wide range of political thought – to Jeffersonian democracy, to the Fabianism of the Webbs, to Marxism. All of these contributed in different ways to the shaping of his thought. In philosophy, so he claimed, he sampled Hegel, Kant and Rousseau. He read Voltaire. One can only guess at the precise way in which he applied his reading to the world about him. Such classic Western problems as the proper role of the state in economic life or the respective limits of authority and individual liberty would hardly have seemed relevant to him. Aware of colonial rule and able to perceive the facts of its economic domination of the Indies, his concept of freedom was of national emancipation rather than of the liberty of the individual,

41. Author's interviews with Harsono and Anwar Tjokroaminoto, July 1969.

and he began to feel the stirrings of passion as this goal began to define itself. It is significant that in his study of history he was attracted by two themes: by accounts of national struggles for freedom and by the history of working-class organization in Europe.

The withdrawn character of his life at this time accentuated the romantic strain in his temperament. He lived to a great extent in a vivid world of his own imagination. As he moved about the streets of Surabaja he identified himself with Washington and Abraham Lincoln, with Danton and Mazzini and Garibaldi, and in his mind he transferred to the Indies the essence of their resistance to oppression. The experience left its mark. In later years a contrast was to emerge between Sukarno's intellectual style and that of other leaders who had been able to complete their education in Holland, within the liberal environment of Dutch universities. His intellectual growth was more untidy and eclectic and no doubt less disciplined than theirs, but it was also more passionate and more alive to the drama of politics. In Surabaja he came to discover that there was drama to be found not only in his books but in the real world surrounding him. His absorption in new ideas was complemented by his gradual initiation into the exciting possibilities of action provided for him by Tjokroaminoto's household.

In 1916 Sarekat Islam was four years old and it was moving into the period of its greatest expansion. Though its real numbers undoubtedly fell far below the two and a half million members it claimed in 1919 its character was nonetheless that of a mass organization and it succeeded, as did no other nationalist organization of the time, in finding a broad base of popular support in the countryside as well as in the towns. In the poverty and conservatism of the Javanese village it could tap the visionary streams of peasant culture which had formed a continuing element in prenationalist movements of agrarian unrest. It gave an answer to peasant needs not so very different from that provided a hundred years before by Diponegoro, or by the Banten peasant revolt of 1888, or more recently, by the Saminist movement which had been of concern to Dutch authority in the closing years of the nineteenth century. In the new and more fluid patterns of the city it could rally those who had drifted from their village setting to form part of the new working class.

It was not the only movement of political significance with its headquarters in Surabaja. The formation of the Indies Social Democratic Association (ISDV) in 1914 represented a more radical trend within developing nationalism. Despite their very different goals there were links between these two movements as indeed there were between Sarekat Islam and other organizations such as Boedi Oetomo. In the absence of firm party discipline it was common for individuals to belong to more than one organization simultaneously. As a case in point, the young Semaun was simultaneously Secretary of the Surabaja branch of Sarekat Islam, and Vice-Chairman of the Surabaja branch of the ISDV for a period. When Sukarno arrived in Surabaja Sarekat Islam was hospitable in this way to a variety of outlooks and could happily enrol among its numbers even those whose primary loyalty lay to the ISDV – the Indies Communist Party in embryo.

The diverse character of Sarekat Islam was reflected in the variety of persons who moved in Tjokroaminoto's circle, and his household was justly described as a 'cradle of all the ideologies'. Here Sukarno came into contact with men who contributed to his political awakening. He met the cosmopolitan Muslim intellectual leader, Agus Salim. He met Soewardi Soerianingrat who, under the name of Ki Hadjar Dewantoro, became the founder of the educational reform movement, Taman Siswa (Garden of Students) – a movement which reflected his fear that Western education was undermining Indonesia's sense of its own identity and which attempted to fashion curricula in terms of both Montessori's ideas and of Java's own culture. (When Sukarno first met him in 1917 Suwardi had just returned from exile in Holland.) He also met the founders of the Indies Communist Party: the Dutchman Hendrik Sneevliet (later, under the name of Maring, to serve as the representative of the Comintern in China), his lieutenant, Adolph Baars, Semaun, who in the twenties was to attempt to keep the PKI on the Comintern line, Musso, who helped to lead the deviation from that line and who was also, in 1948, to play a leading part in the PKI revolt against the government of the embattled Republic, and Musso's partner in deviation,

Alimin, described by Sukarno as 'the man who introduced me to Marxism'.[42] The list was almost a *Who's Who* of early Indonesian nationalism. And, of course there was Tjokroaminoto himself, a man in his early thirties, moving to the peak of his political career. Tjokroaminoto was *priyayi* by birth and had been trained for government service, but he had chosen instead to engage in commercial activity, and he had also been involved for a time in a travelling *wayang* show. As an intellectual who had turned ultimately to political action he was representative of the new political élite which was to form the spearhead of nationalism. Sukarno observed his mode of leadership and learned much from it – his ability to unite differing elements impressed the young man. So did his oratory, which formed a model for Sukarno.

Between them these people represented the main currents of Indonesian nationalism as it was at the time: its Islamic elements, conservative and reformist, its Marxism and even, in the person of Ki Hadjar Dewantoro, its links with Java's pre-Islamic cultural heritage. Ki Hadjar was, no doubt, an exception. Most of the leading figures of Sarekat Islam saw themselves as belonging to the modern world and as attempting to free themselves from the yoke of tradition, which to a great extent they were. Some observers have argued that Sarekat Islam, and even the Indies Communist Party in its early days, were proto-nationalist rather than truly nationalist movements, belonging rather to the tradition of inchoate agrarian unrest than to that later group of movements which were inspired by a perception of an Indonesian nation.[43] Such a judgement overstates the contrast between the early and later stages of Indonesian nationalism. The pages of Sarekat Islam's official newspaper, *Oetoesan Hindia*, were full of radical comment and demands for independence.[44] Nevertheless,

42. *Autobiography*, p. 40. Cf. Willard A. Hanna, *Eight Nation Makers: Southeast Asia's Charismatic Statesmen*, New York, 1964, pp. 7–8.

43. H. J. Benda and R. T. McVey (ed.), *The Communist Uprisings of 1926–27 in Indonesia: Key Documents*, Ithaca, 1960, p. xi.

44. See, as one typical example, a leading article entitled *Kemerdekaan* ['Freedom'], *Oetoesan Hindia*, 12 July 1920, and the editor's note which argued that political independence was not enough if the dominance of foreign capital were to continue. As another example, see the attack by Musso on Boedi Oetomo in *Oetoesan Hindia*, 12 August 1920.

though Sarekat Islam was groping towards a formulation of ideas which could properly be called nationalist, it was a very different formulation from the more specifically nationalist thinking to be achieved a decade later, and the change was, to a great extent, the work of the student Sukarno who absorbed the atmosphere of Sarekat Islam's headquarters.

Sukarno was not content simply to sit at the feet of his masters listening to their discussions of Indonesia's predicament, of revolutionary movements elsewhere, of strategy and tactics for the local situation. He came soon to play his own part in their debates and from discussion he moved gradually to a more direct participation in the group's activities, though still in a very junior role. His first positive steps as an active nationalist were taken in the Surabaja branch of the youth organization Tri Koro Dharma ('Three Noble Objectives') formed in 1915 as a subsidiary organization of Boedi Oetomo. As we have noticed, Boedi Oetomo could fairly lay claim to recognition as Indonesia's first nationalist – or quasi-nationalist – organization, though its goals were cultural rather than radically political. Tri Koro Dharma was also primarily cultural in its aims. It was formed to minister to the needs of secondary school students living away from their homes, and as well as providing a forum for social intercourse it sought to educate its members in their own cultural tradition and to inculcate in them a perception not of an Indonesian nation but at least of a Javanese unity, embracing the Sundanese and Madurese as well as the ethnic Javanese.[45]

As a reflection of this goal the society changed its name in 1918 to Jong Java ('Young Java'). Jong Java offered a comparatively unimportant forum for Sukarno but it was at least a beginning. From there he graduated to the senior league – in particular to his first steps in journalism as a contributor to *Oetoesan Hindia*.[46] He also began to test his skills of oratory, and he gradually

45. R. Van Niel, *The Emergence of the Modern Indonesian Elite*, The Hague, 1960, p. 169.

46. Not, it would seem, under the pen name of Bima, the bold but blunt warrior of the *Mahabharata*. He later claimed that he used 'Bima' as a penname at this time, but *Oetoesan Hindia* contains no articles over that signature.

discovered in himself the power to hold an audience. He had already acquired a reputation for public speaking in a school debating society and confirmed it by his performance in Jong Java where he became identified with, among other things, the ideals of the Djawa Dipa movement which advocated language reform. Sukarno was well aware of the political significance of language. On one occasion he urged the introduction of Malay and Dutch into Jong Java's publications;[47] on another he provoked the chairman of a meeting by speaking in *ngoko* (low Javanese) rather than in Dutch or in the high Javanese used by the essentially aristocratic members of the society.[48] The chairman ordered him to speak in Dutch. Sukarno, claiming that no reason was given for the ruling, declined to continue his speech. At the Jong Java congress in Bandung in June 1921 he made a more thoroughgoing defence of his views, arguing that low Javanese was better suited, as a language, for the promotion of unity and equality than were the different levels and the feudal overtones of the Javanese language as a whole.[49]

Through activities such as these Sukarno gradually became aware of his political capacities, but it must not be assumed that he sprang immediately to prominence. Two comments need to be made about this stage of his development. Though gaining some experience in the profession of political activism he was not yet driven by the demands of a compelling and clearly formulated ideology. Ideas gained from his reading and from listening to those who passed through Tjokroaminoto's house had only just begun to arrange themselves in a clear pattern and they had not yet drawn him to work out for himself a programme of action. For the time being his participation in nationalist activity was provoked by the sheer excitement of action almost as a goal in itself. In his Surabaja setting it would have been surprising if he had escaped that attraction; nevertheless he was still heavily dependent upon others and in this sense it is appropriate to regard this period as an apprenticeship.

47. *Oetoesan Hindia*, 21 March 1921.
48. ibid., 7 February 1921. See also Dahm, *Sukarno and the Struggle for Indonesian Independence*, Ithaca, 1969, p. 40.
49. ibid., 16 and 17 June 1921.

This leads to the second comment. In Indonesia at this time youth was not a bar to prominence and independent standing as a political activist, and it is perhaps surprising that Sukarno was no more than an apprentice. Semaun became secretary of the Surabaja branch of Sarekat Islam at about sixteen, and vice-chairman of the Surabaja branch of ISDV at seventeen. Tan Malaka began to establish himself in his early twenties and before he was thirty he had been exiled to Holland and had run as a communist candidate in a Dutch parliamentary election. At sixteen Hatta was treasurer of the Padang branch of the Jong Sumatra Bond and a year later was its Djakarta treasurer. At twenty, in Rotterdam, he became treasurer of Perhimpunan Indonesia, the union of Indonesian students in Holland, and at twenty-three its chairman. Sjahrir made his mark in Perhimpunan Indonesia before he was twenty, and in his early twenties was prominent in nationalist activity in Djakarta. By contrast Sukarno, despite the exceptional opportunities open to him as Tjokroaminoto's protégé in 1916, was to wait another decade before he entered the political arena as a figure in his own right, by which time he was already in his mid twenties. Was this because he was ambitious enough, and establishment-minded enough, to put the completion of his formal education before a precarious political career? Or was it because his own particular slant on events had not yet developed? The two perhaps went together.

The events taking place in Sukarno's vicinity as he began his initiation into politics were certainly significant enough. As they unfolded they were gradually to define the future character of Indonesian nationalism. Though Sarekat Islam seemed to be dramatically successful in establishing itself as a major mass movement the diversity of its higher echelon membership and also, no doubt, the diversity of motivation of the masses who were attracted to it gave it, in fact, an experimental character. How far was it really representative of the hidden forces within Indonesian society? How effectively was it able to formulate and express unspoken aspirations? These questions could only be answered by the test of practical politics. For the next few years the central issue was the control of Sarekat Islam itself – an issue fought out between the movement's own leadership and the communist minority within the party. Concealed within that struggle were other issues: the relevance of competing ideologies, the role of Islam as a means of channelling popular feelings, the question of co-operation with the Dutch versus non-cooperation, the place of the emerging intelligentsia in shaping goals and strategies, the appropriateness of mass parties as against élitist parties. Within ten years some of these issues had defined themselves or been resolved by circumstances. Sarekat Islam had by then lost its momentum, the communist bid for leadership had been crushed and a new type of secular nationalism had come to occupy the centre of the stage. But these developments were still hidden in the future.

Sarekat Islam's original programme of action was couched in very general terms. It announced its loyalty to the government and put forward a series of economic and cultural aims, the development of indigenous commerce, the promotion of Islam and so forth. So far it professed no radical political platform. The reaction of the Indies government to its formation was tentative; it granted recognition to the local branches of the movement but withheld recognition from the central organization.[50] However, within a few years the organization, partly because of the left-wing membership to be found particularly in its Semarang branch, began to assume a more radical colour.

As the headquarters of the Railway Workers' Union (VSTP) Semarang was a natural centre for radical thought and it was from this base that Hendrik Sneevliet founded the Indies Social Democratic Association (ISDV) in Surabaja in 1914. Over the next couple of years the ISDV developed what was eventually to become an orthodox communist tactic in underdeveloped countries – the tactic of making alliances with what were held to be progressive, anti-imperialist forces. Such alliances, according to Leninist theory, were to be temporary alliances, adopted in the common struggle against imperialism pending the ripening of the

50. Whether this decision was motivated by a desire to weaken and control the movement or to protect it is a matter for debate. See Van Niel's suggestion (p. 96) that Governor-General Idenburg feared that the central organization might not be able to accept effective responsibility for its local branches and might therefore find itself in legal difficulties.

historical situation to the point where communist parties could move independently to bring about their own revolution. The Second Congress of the Communist International in 1920 was to underwrite such a strategy, though not to the point of prescribing whether such alliances should be achieved by co-operation between separate and independent parties or by the infiltration by communists of nationalist organizations where they would form a 'bloc within'. In Indonesia Sarekat Islam appeared the obvious candidate for the role of progressive, anti-imperialist party and the multi-party membership, so common among Indonesian nationalists, made the 'bloc within' tactic the natural one for the ISDV to follow. Many of its members, as we have seen, were already members of Sarekat Islam and they made their presence felt in the first and second congresses of the party, in 1916 and 1917. At the latter congress in particular radical pressure was successful in leading Sarekat Islam to adopt a much more revolutionary programme than it had espoused hitherto. It committed itself to the goal of independence for the Indies and called for a programme of social reform. In particular, while still suspicious of atheistic communism, the congress went so far as to adopt a condemnation, not of capitalism in general, but of what it called 'sinful' (i.e. foreign) capital.

The radical trend was further illustrated in 1918 after the opening of the first session of the Volksraad, created by the Indies Government to allow some voice to local opinion, both Dutch and Indonesian. The ISDV members of Sarekat Islam urged a boycott of the Volksraad on the grounds that its creation was merely a sop to secure Indonesian co-operation with Dutch authority. Sarekat Islam resisted their pressure and decided by a narrow majority to advance candidates for election. Once there, however, the Sarekat Islam representatives joined the 'radical concentration' in the Assembly and associated themselves with attacks on the Government and with demands for more far-reaching political and social reforms. In the industrial field also Sarekat Islam took a more decisive line, seeking to establish its control over a variety of trade unions.

The honeymoon with the left-wing elements was not to continue unchecked. ISDV success in influencing Sarekat Islam policy stopped short of control over the organization as a whole and, in fact, was quickly to prove counter-productive. The conservative elements of the movement, centred particularly in the Jogjakarta branch, gathered their forces to resist left-wing pressure. In May 1920 the ISDV transformed itself into the Indies Communist Party (PKI) and at the end of the year joined the Comintern. At the end of 1921 a special congress of Sarekat Islam at last came to grips with the problem created by the presence of a tightly organized party within its ranks and adopted a resolution preventing Sarekat Islam members from belonging simultaneously to any other party. The resolution was resisted by Tan Malaka who urged that an exception should be made for members of the PKI. In the face of his opposition the party discipline resolution was carried and it represented, in effect, an expulsion of the communist enclave.

Sukarno was little more than an observer of these events. The successive Sarekat Islam congresses, the issues that were fought out in them and the growing tension within Tjokroaminoto's circle must have formed part of his day-to-day life and, having enjoyed contacts with a diversity of political figures, he must have felt torn as they fell out among themselves. His observation of these divisions, together with his reading in the history of European social democracy, impressed on him the evils of faction-fighting and the necessity for unity, but for the time being he remained principally a secondary school student who engaged in political activity as an extra-curricular interest.

A sign that he was nonetheless held in warm regard by Tjokroaminoto was his marriage, in 1920 or 1921, to Tjokroaminoto's daughter, Sitti Utari. It was what was known as a 'hung marriage' (*kawin gantung*) – a marriage contract whose consummation was delayed (in this case because of the youth of one of the partners) – and there is some inconsistency in the accounts given of the reasons for the match. One version is that the initiative came from Tjokroaminoto himself, who selected Sukarno as his son-in-law and perhaps his heir apparent as leader of Sarekat Islam as well. In Sukarno's account the decision was his own, but was based on a suggestion made by Tjokroaminoto's brother. After the death in 1919 of Tjokroaminoto's wife, Suharsikin, the rest of the family, together with the boarders, moved to a new address and it was suggested to Sukarno that it would be a relief to Tjokroaminoto if provision could be made for Utari through a suitable marriage.[51] In either case Utari was a girl of fifteen and Sukarno's first marriage was by no means a love match. It was rather a symbol of his close tie with his patron and it was to be dissolved within a couple of years when that tie weakened. The story reflects simultaneously Sukarno's personal development to maturity and the changing circumstances with which he was gradually learning to deal.

In 1921 Sukarno's secondary schooling came to an end with his graduation from Surabaja HBS.[52] He now faced an important decision. Theoretically several courses of action were open to him. Had his family been able to afford it he might have joined that tiny band of Indonesian students who were able to pursue university studies in Holland itself. Failing that he could seek higher professional qualifications in Indonesia, preparing himself for government service in a School for Native Administrators (OSVIA), attending a teachers' training school or proceeding to the newly established Technical College (THS) at Bandung. Or he could follow what might have seemed the logical consequence of his recent political association and commit himself to a career of political activity. It is interesting to notice that, in his own account of his thinking, the latter possibility was simply not mentioned. The only alternatives he gave as having entered into his consideration were those of study in Holland and entry to the Bandung THS.[53] Overseas study was probably ruled out on the grounds of expense, though he mentioned the fact of his mother's opposition as the primary reason for the decision against it. Instead he enrolled as an engineering student at Bandung.

The THS at Bandung had only just been established as the first step towards the creation of a university in the Indies. Pres-

51. *Autobiography*, pp. 46–7.

52. Not 1920 as stated by Nasution, *Penghidupan dan Perdjuangan Ir. Sukarno*, Djakarta, 1951 (p. 17) and taken over by Hanna and others. See *Oetoesan Hindia*, 11 June 1921, and Dahm, op. cit., p. 43.

53. *Autobiography*, p. 50.

sure for a local university had been growing for some years and had been supported by Indonesians and Eurasians who suffered from the high cost of undertaking tertiary education in Holland. The idea was also supported, at least so far as advanced technical training was concerned, by private business, which felt the need for a greater number of trained people drawn from the local community. In fact it was on the basis of private subscription that the THS was first established in 1919. Two years later the government recognized the *fait accompli* and accepted responsibility for what was to be the first faculty of the future University of Indonesia. (A law school was created three years later and was followed by the conversion of STOVIA, the school for training native doctors, into the Faculty of Medicine.)

In June 1921, Sukarno arrived in Bandung outwardly confident and, at twenty, a very different person from the hesitant schoolboy who had made his way to Tjokroaminoto's home five years earlier. Tjokroaminoto had arranged accommodation for him in the house of a friend, Hadji Sanusi, who met him on arrival and carried him off to see his new home and, more significantly as it turned out, his new landlady. Sanusi's wife, Inggit Garnasih, was much younger than her husband. Then in her early thirties, she was a singularly attractive woman who could not help but stir the feelings of a young man bound in the frustrating ties of a hung marriage. It is not clear whether Sitti Utari followed quickly on Sukarno's heels to Bandung, or whether he brought her back with him a year later after his return visit to Surabaja. In either case it was inevitable that Inggit's attractions should awaken the desires of her handsome and vital young boarder as he began to experience his new freedom as a college student. Her presence was to trouble him increasingly in the months ahead.

During those months Sukarno was still finding his feet in a new world. If one accepts the idea put forward at the beginning of this chapter that his Surabaja period under Tjokroaminoto's tutelage was a variant on a˜traditional Javanese mode of preparing an adolescent for adult life, his move to Bandung and his entry into the THS should represent his return to the world as a man, with a new degree of independence. The record suggests, however, that the butterfly had not burst fully winged from its cocoon. The early years in Bandung were still a period in which Sukarno was feeling his way, concentrating on his studies and sampling the city's political activity only as a sideline. He gradually extended his participation in public affairs, but still without making a position for himself as a leader of a clearly visible strain of Indonesian nationalism. At this stage he had not yet severed his Surabaja ties and the developing character of his activities during the early twenties may be best interpreted in terms of his changing relationship with his father-in-law. It was to be a year or two before he had broken his dependence upon Tjokroaminoto and was free to establish his own individuality.

Sukarno had only been in Bandung for a couple of months when an event occurred which put to the test the strength of his links with his patron. The event in question was the arrest of Tjokroaminoto in August 1921, to which Sukarno responded quickly as a loyal and dutiful son-in-law. It all arose out of events which had been troubling government authorities and Sarekat Islam alike for two years, and which had come to be known as the 'Afdeling B Affair'.

In 1919, in Garut in West Java, opposition had been growing to the forced delivery of rice to the government. One peasant family chose to reject government demands and proposed to resist authority by force. Troops were called in to deal with the situation and several lives were lost. The incident bore some of the signs of traditional peasant revolt, including some magical elements such as the sale of charms guaranteed to confer invulnerability on their possessors. It all seemed a trivial affair at first, but the subsequent investigation uncovered – or appeared to uncover – the involvement in the incident of a secret sub-organization – Afdeling (section) B – of Sarekat Islam. It is not at all clear how deeply Section B was really implicated in the Garut affair, or if it was implicated, whether it was acting with the knowledge and approval of Sarekat Islam's central organization. It could easily have been that a spontaneous movement of revolt, planning violence against the Dutch, had sought to act under the cover of Sarekat Islam's name, though there was evidence that some members of the national leadership knew of the secret section's existence. In any case the Garut incident, following as it did hard on the heels of an outbreak of violence in Toli Toli (Celebes), caused great alarm in government circles. The Toli Toli incident had been connected with a visit to the area by Abdul Muis, vice-president of Sarekat Islam, and the thought that a large organization such as Sarekat Islam might be supporting violent resistance to authority alarmed the government and also shocked moderate members of the organization itself. The findings of the inquiry into the Section B Affair were followed by a number of arrests and led to a sharp decline in Sarekat Islam membership and, for a time, to increased influence for the left wing of the movement. The right wing, centred on the Jogjakarta branch, rallied its forces and it was against the backdrop of this widening division that the discipline resolution, to which we have already referred, was brought forward and adopted at a special congress of the party in October 1921, leading to the expulsion of PKI members.

These developments were of great importance to Tjokroaminoto himself. During 1920 and early 1921 it became clear that his own peculiar style of charismatic leadership was not equal to the demands of the situation. Despite his efforts he was no longer able to bestride the factional divisions of the party and to retain control of it. His own connection with the Section B incident was not clear, but his arrest on a charge of perjury in August 1921 reflected the continuing concern of the government with what it regarded as the radical drift of the movement he led.

For Sukarno the news of the arrest posed an acute moral problem. Should he break off his studies and return to Surabaja to give what moral and material support he could? Or should he leave that task to others who were closer at hand? It was a difficult decision for him. Tjokroaminoto's imprisonment might have been prolonged indefinitely, and for all Sukarno knew a departure from the THS might have been permanent, spelling the end to his expectations for advancement through a Dutch tertiary education. But he resolved the question quickly, putting loyalty to Tjokroaminoto above his academic ambitions. He hurried back to Surabaja, where he found employment as a railway clerk and supported the Tjokroaminoto family from his meagre earnings. Fortunately things were to work out much better than he feared. In April 1922 Tjokroaminoto, having been convicted of perjury, was released pending an appeal (he was ultimately acquitted) and Sukarno was free to return to Bandung to resume his interrupted course of study.

It was not simply a matter of taking up where he had left off, however. Changes were beginning to occur in Sukarno's handling of his own personal world. One of these, as has been suggested, was the obvious weakening of the old close tie with Tjokroaminoto. Though he had rallied to the cause in August 1921, for reasons no doubt both of duty and piety, the old magic had begun to fade. The mere fact of separation was one element in the change. Sukarno was no longer under the daily influence of the older man and was more capable of viewing him in a detached light. Important, too, was his growing feeling for Inggit and its implications for his own marriage. Boarder and landlady were thrown closely together in Bandung and their growing attachment to each other forced Sukarno, shortly after his return in 1922, to take stock of his position and its obligations. He decided at last to resolve his problem by divorcing his girl wife which, in Muslim law, merely meant pronouncing the three-fold 'Talak, talak, talak,' and returning her to her father. Within a short while Sanusi agreed to divorce Inggit. She and Sukarno were married in 1923 and were for a long time a devoted couple. She was often with him at meetings and at private discussions with other students or with leading political figures of Bandung. She was in herself a simple but lively person and lived to some extent in the magical world of tradition— one of her interests was the making of *djamu*, a powder to be used cosmetically but possessing curative powers. She certainly supported Sukarno emotionally, and in the memory of colleagues who knew him at this time her support was of tremendous importance to him. Later when he became an active political leader in his own right she was a good hostess for him. Sukarno, oddly, is remembered by many from these days as a shy man. He could speak with confidence before large audiences, but in the presence of only a handful of people he did not speak easily and it was often Inggit's responsibility to stimulate conversation and to supply assurance.[54]

54. Author's interview with Inggit Garnasih, July 1969.

Tjokroaminoto accepted the fact of Sukarno's divorce from Utari and the decision was not allowed formally to alter the relations between patron and protégé, but it was a sign that Sukarno was drifting away from the master. The drift was accentuated further, no doubt, by the change in Tjokroaminoto's own political fortunes. Not only had he lost his command over Sarekat Islam as the rift developed between the right and left wings of the party, and as the party's centre of gravity moved from Surabaja to Jogjakarta, but the movement's own force had declined sharply after the Section B Affair. The split with the PKI accelerated this decline and the following years saw a fierce competition between the two parties for control over local branches. By 1923 Sarekat Islam had lost forever its leadership of Indonesian nationalism and Tjokroaminoto himself was no longer the central figure of the movement. To say that these facts contributed to the weakening of Sukarno's friendship with Tjokroaminoto is not to suggest that the former was an opportunistic, fair-weather friend. It was merely that Tjokroaminoto was no longer, and could not again be, the central figure in Sukarno's world, either politically or personally. Sukarno was in a new environment and surrounded by new activities. His divorce and re-marriage, the change in the political situation and the opportunities open to him in the life of Bandung, all combined to ease him a little further along the path to his own personal independence.

He engaged in a certain amount of speech-making in Bandung and in some political writing. Early in 1923 he attended a rally organized by the 'Radical Concentration'[55], a broad front of political and quasi-political organizations; he spoke in militant terms and was interrupted by the police.[56] A little later he was present at a PKI congress in Bandung in 1923 and spoke from

55. To be distinguished from the Radical Concentration in the Volksraad in 1918.

56. Dahm, *Soekarno and the Struggle for Indonesian Independence*, Ithaca, 1969, p. 49, is in error in saying that there is no record of this episode in contemporary sources. It was reported in *Pahlawan*, Volume I, No. 2, 21 January 1923, though without reference to Sukarno's being removed from the podium by the police, an incident he describes in his *Autobiography*, p. 65. Cf. also Nasution, op. cit., p. 24.

the floor in defence of Tjokroaminoto against an attack by Hadji Misbach. Known as 'Red Hadji', the latter was a fiery figure. He had been a member of the predominantly Eurasian party Insulinde, and an advocate of violent resistance to feudal services. He was noted particularly for his attempts to reconcile Marxism and Islam. On this occasion his fieriness was matched by Sukarno's and the younger man's defence of Tjokroaminoto led Misbach to make an apology.[57] Through activities such as these Sukarno was gradually extending his contacts with leading figures of the nationalist movement in Bandung, and was finding there a very different world from that of Surabaja.

Bandung in the early twenties was fast becoming a centre of nationalist thought and action. The ideas which flourished there were radical in character. At the same time they were less ideological in flavour than those represented either by Sarekat Islam or by the PKI. They emphasized independence and the forging of an Indonesian nation, but were less concerned with the shaping of the society or with the nature of the independent state which was ultimately to emerge. Bandung's intellectual atmosphere thus differed markedly from that which Sukarno had left behind him. Indeed, it is interesting to notice how far Indonesia's political activity throughout this whole period turns on rivalry between its main urban centres. From 1916 to 1921 the rivalry was between Surabaja, the headquarters of Sarekat Islam, on the one hand, and Semarang, the centre of Marxist thinking, on the other. From 1921 to 1923 the moderate wing of Sarekat Islam in Jogjakarta became increasingly important and a triangle of relationships was established between Jogjakarta, Surabaja and Semarang. But Bandung was beginning to establish its own claim to be a centre of secular nationalist thinking and in this centre Sukarno moved in a small circle of active people, taking part in their discussions on the nature of the colonial situation, the bases of Dutch power and the alternative ways of mobilizing a challenge to it.

Among others he came to know the dedicated Eurasian leader, Ernest F. E. Douwes Dekker (later to be known as 'Setiabudi') and his ally, Dr Tjipto Mangunkusumo, and he developed further

57. *Oetoesan Hindia*, 9 March 1923.

his earlier contact with Ki Hadjar Dewantoro (Soewardi Soeri-aningrat).[58]

Tjipto – 'my Chief' as Sukarno was later to call him – was one of the older school of nationalist leaders. Born in 1885 he was trained as a doctor and as such he entered government service. He had helped to found Boedi Oetomo though he was more radical in his views than most of its members. He resented his exclusion from European society and was uncompromising in his criticism of the colonial tie. In 1912 he had been associated with Douwes Dekker and Soewardi Soerianingrat in the formation of the Indische Partij (Indies Party), which had sought to lay the foundations of co-operation between Eurasians and Indonesians; thereafter the three men formed a closely-knit trio.

Douwes Dekker was one of the more curious and interesting figures in the history of Indonesian nationalism.[59] He was a grand-nephew of Eduard Douwes Dekker, the nineteenth-century Dutch civil servant who, under the pseudonym of Multatuli, wrote a damning indictment of the administration of the Culture System in his novel *Max Havelaar*. He had volunteered on the South African side in the Boer War. He was really the prime-mover in the formation of the Indies Party and the shaper of its platform. The Party took its stand on the proposition that residence in and commitment to the Indies, rather than racial origin, should be the basis of nationalist struggle – hence its appeal to Eurasians. Unlike Sarekat Islam, formed just a few months earlier, it adopted a radical programme demanding complete independence for the Indies, and in consequence it was refused recognition by the government. Its Eurasian membership was largely captured by the new Eurasian party, Insulinde, but Douwes Dekker himself, and his co-founders, Tjipto and Soewardi, were tried (for 'journalistic excesses') and exiled from the Indies in 1913. They were

58. In 1959, when asked which Indonesians had most influenced him, these were the men he named. (I am indebted for this information to Professor George McT. Kahin who generously made available to me the notes of his interviews with Sukarno.)

59. For a brief sketch see Paul W. van der Veur, 'E. F. E. Douwes Dekker: Evangelist for Indonesian Political Nationalism', *Journal of Asian Studies*, Vol. XVII, No. 4, August 1958, p. 551.

allowed to serve their exile in Holland, returning at various times, Tjipto in 1914, Soewardi in 1917 and Douwes Dekker in 1918. On his return the latter formed close ties with Sarekat Islam and with ISDV leaders, and he also joined Insulinde and tried unsuccessfully to lead it in a more radical direction. Finally he broke away to form his own more revolutionary, but short-lived, organization, the National Indies Party. In the early twenties Douwes Dekker withdrew from active political participation and devoted himself in Bandung to working in the educational field as an alternative way of serving his ultimate goal. He founded the Preanger Educational Institute which sought to create independent primary schools, with curricula similar to those offered by the Dutch-language primary schools. He was thus one of the promoters of the 'wild' schools movement which was an important development in Indonesian nationalism in the twenties. His friend Soewardi, now known as Ki Hadjar, was similarly engaged with the formation of his Taman Siswa movement.

The careers and ideas of these men were an important influence on Sukarno. In particular Douwes Dekker's approach to the whole Indies situation, and his possible remedies for it, differed fundamentally from that of the leaders with whom Sukarno had so far been in contact. Despite Douwes Dekker's close ties with Sarekat Islam and with communist leaders he rejected the Islamic base of the former and the doctrinaire socialism of the latter, and thought in terms of an independent nation, multi-racial in composition but bound by its common allegiance to its homeland and ready to struggle for its freedom. The creation of such a nation was more important in his view than the details of its social structure. He was, in short, a secular nationalist before secular nationalism had become the mainstream of nationalist thinking. Though his dreams of Eurasian–Indonesian partnership were to be dashed, the cast of his ideas was to be reflected in Sukarno's political activities in the late twenties.

Another figure on Sukarno's horizon at this time was that of Tan Malaka, though here the influence was indirect. The son of a Minangkabau village head, Tan Malaka had studied in Holland from 1913, returned to Sumatra in 1919, moved to Java in 1921 and joined the young PKI. He became its chairman for a short period, but was arrested for his part in a pawnshop workers' strike in 1922 and was exiled.

Like others he was permitted to serve his exile in Holland where, shortly after his arrival, he ran as a communist candidate in the parliamentary elections of 1922 – successfully, until it was discovered that he was too young to qualify for a seat! He then moved to Moscow and was subsequently sent out once more to Southeast Asia as a representative of the Comintern in the region. He was thus away from Indonesia during most of Sukarno's Bandung period. In his short tenure of the PKI leadership, Tan Malaka had shown himself to be less cautiously orthodox than was Semaun, urging the party to more effective and active opposition to the government, though as Comintern representative in Southeast Asia in the mid twenties he was to urge new leaders of the party to act cautiously and in accordance with Comintern orthodoxy. Nonetheless he was a somewhat romantic figure whose mass appeal, and whose vigorous interpretation of Marxist theory in its application to the Indies situation, made him an attractive model for the aspiring Sukarno. (His long-term importance in this story lies in the fact that, twenty years later, he was the one person who might have challenged Sukarno's pre-eminent position as the symbol of Indonesian nationalism.)

Under such influences as these Sukarno's political ideas began to arrange themselves in some kind of order. His reading in the history of European socialism and his experience in Surabaja had given him a theoretical and an immediately practical appreciation of the dangers of division. His thinking was therefore directed to the problem of securing unity and of defining correctly the elements of the struggle for which unity was so necessary. From Tjokroaminoto he had learned the techniques of conciliation and from Ki Hadjar he had drawn the idea of synthesizing Western and traditional currents of thought. Though he stopped short of accepting the totality of Marxist theory, the Marxism of Alimin and Semaun had given him at least some perception of imperialism as a system of power, a sense of the inherent unlikelihood of genuine Dutch concessions of autonomy to the Indies, and a recognition of the need for struggle. It also gave him a technique of analysis. In his writing and in his speeches he developed a distinctive mode of rebutting opponents. He would ascribe their differences with him to their 'misconceptions', and in order to brush them aside he would insist that a problem must be seen in what he asserted to be its right (i.e. largely Marxist) conceptual framework.[60] From Tan Malaka he caught something of the romance, and perhaps the unpredictability, of revolution. From Douwes Dekker he drew the concept of the primacy of nationalist revolution, overriding all other considerations of social conflict, and binding the people of the Indies into a whole.

It is possible that another element in his later thinking also had its origins in this period: his concept of 'Marhaenism', which attempted to adapt the Marxist concept of a proletariat to the social circumstances of an agrarian society. As he was to say in a speech thirty years later, the concept of 'proletariat' was hardly relevant for Indonesia.

'The proletariat are the workers who do not participate in ownership of the means of production. But our nation, Brothers and Sisters, is composed of tens of millions of people not all of whom are covered by the term proletariat. There are great numbers indeed who are not labourers, very many who do not sell their labour-power to others.'[61]

These were the masses who, despite their grinding poverty, did have rights of ownership, whether of ploughs, of hoes, of buffaloes, or of wares they sold at their street stalls. They were the 'little people', poor but not proletarians. Any social doctrine, he argued, should give a central place to the presence of such people and to their needs, instead of borrowing an arid concept from a totally different situation.

Sukarno used the term 'Marhaen' to epitomize the 'little people'. According to his own story the name originated in a meeting with a peasant farmer near Bandung. He saw the farmer tilling his field and engaged him in a conversation which is worth reproducing in its broad outlines:

'Who owns this field?' asked Sukarno.

---

60. See Dahm's illuminating discussion of Sukarno's method of handling 'misconceptions' and 'misunderstandings'. pp. 70–77 and 93–100.

61. Sukarno, 'Marhaen and Proletarian'. Speech to 30th anniversary meeting of the PNI, Bandung, 1957, published in translation by Cornell Modern Indonesia Project Translation Series, Ithaca, N.Y. 1960.

'I do,' replied the farmer.

'And the hoe, who owns that?'

'I do.'

'Those tools, who owns them?'

'I do.'

'The crop on which you are working, for whom is it?'

'For me.'

'Is it sufficient for your needs?'

'There's barely enough to keep us alive.'

'Do you ever sell your labour?'

'No. I must work hard, but my labours are all for myself.'

'But brother, you live in poverty.'

'That's right, I live poorly.'[62]

'I thought to myself,' said Sukarno, 'this man clearly and certainly is not a member of the proletariat, he is a pauper, he is poor, he suffers much, he has not enough to live on, but he is not a member of the proletariat, for he does not sell his labour-power to another without participating in ownership of the means of production. His rice field is his own property, his hoe is his own, his sickle is his own, his rake is his own. Everything is his own property; the crop of his rice field is for his own use. But still he is a pauper, he is poor. Nevertheless he is not one of the proletariat, he is a small farmer, a very poor farmer, barely making a living.'

He then asked the farmer his name and was told 'Marhaen'. Sukarno decided then to use that name to describe the 'destitute people of Indonesia'.

Thus goes the official version. It has been suggested by some that this conversation never took place – that Sukarno invented it and made it a part of the official legend.[63] But the story is a simple and entirely plausible one and it really does not matter greatly whether it is true or not. The important thing is that the concept of Marhaen resolved for Sukarno a problem which had been worrying him over the years. In 1921, at a Jong Java congress in Bandung, he spoke of the inevitability of class-struggle

62. The conversation as reconstructed here is based on two of Sukarno's accounts of it: see 'Marhaen and Proletarian' and *Autobiography*, pp. 61–2.

63. See *Daulat Ra'jat*, No. 12, January 10 1932 for an article which claimed that the term 'Marhaen' had been in regular use since 1927 and was really no more than the Sundanese equivalent of the Javanese term *kromo*.

within Indonesian society.[64] He was never happy with that view, however, and the concept of the Marhaen enabled him to put the struggle more into national than into class terms. It also represented an appropriate theoretical concept for Indonesian circumstances.

By 1926 Sukarno was ready for a wider stage. In retrospect he was to claim, in highly coloured and heroic terms, that he was already a significant political figure long before completing his THS studies. After his arrival in Bandung he emerged, he says, a 'full-fledged political fighter. With Inggit at my side, I stepped forward to keep my date with destiny.'[65] The reality was more prosaic. It was pardonable no doubt for Sukarno, Great Leader of the Revolution and President for twenty years, to read back into his student days a political role which he only came to assume later. In fact, despite his claims, and despite the undoubted fact that from 1922 onwards he did begin to stand more on his own feet, his emergence as a leader was still a gradual process compared with that of others who stepped decisively into the nationalist limelight in their teens or early twenties. He was chairman of the Bandung branch of Jong Java when he was at the THS, but in general such political activity as had engaged him while a student was subordinated to his engineering studies. He tells in his autobiography of Professor Klopper's warning to him after he had made his inflammatory speech at the rally organized by the Radical Concentration in 1923. If he wished to continue at the THS, he was told, he must be first and foremost a student, and must avoid entanglement in politics.[66] Sukarno promised to devote more time to his work and to refrain from addressing mass political rallies. If true, and it could well have been, this exchange between teacher and wayward student was obviously more consistent with the view that politics was still a hobby rather than an obsession.

His slow movement towards political maturity was partly due to circumstances. In Sukarno's student days the nationalist movement was represented primarily, as we have seen, by mass

64. *Oetoesan Hindia*, 16 June 1921.
65. *Autobiography*, p. 60.
66. *Autobiography*, p. 65.

movements based ideologically on Marxism or Islam. This environment was of tremendous importance in the fashioning of Sukarno's political temperament and in giving him an insight into the nature of the political life, but it was not an environment in which he could play a central role. In part his slowness was due to his uncertainty about his ambitions – education could open doors to a career in government service and he may well have wished to keep his options open. In one of the chapter headings in his autobiography he called Bandung a 'Passport to a White World', and that may indeed be an accurate title. He had still to commit himself to a political career.

If his own role in the early twenties was more limited than his later memories would allow, his motives were also less pure and high-minded. His autobiography portrays him as drawn to politics by a selfless dedication, and indeed as having acquired well before 1926 the presentiment of leadership and a certain sense of proprietorship in the nationalist struggle as a whole. 'The burning desire to set my people free was beyond mere personal ambition. I was consumed with it. It permeated my whole being. It filled my nostrils; it coursed through my veins. It's what a man serves his whole lifetime for. It was more than a duty. More than a calling. For me it was a – religion.'[67] The rhetoric was in character, but a more sober judgement would suggest that the real appeal of the political life for Sukarno was the appeal of excitement and the attraction of using techniques in which he excelled, as well as devotion to the service of an ideal. He made no secret, for example, of his delight in testing his oratorical talents and in demonstrating his ability to establish a quick *rapport* with an audience. (After Professor Klopper had warned him off such recreations he played at speech making in the privacy of his bedroom.)[68] To make this judgement is not to scoff. Politics is a profession as well as a vocation and the picture of the young Sukarno drawn as a junior participant into the fringes of nationalist activity, intoxicated by the excitement of it, and attracted by the romance of revolution, is truer and not really less worthy than his own picture of a prophet inspired by the sufferings of his

67. *Autobiography*, p. 69.
68. *Autobiography*, pp. 65–6.

people and devoted only to relieving them from their oppression by the hated Dutch. From this mixture of motives he was drawn at last, at the end of his apprenticeship in 1926, to the career of politics.

Yet, having said all this, there is perhaps a sense in which Sukarno's account of the call of destiny was not so far from the truth. When he made his decision in 1926 he was dedicating himself to political action as a way of life and thereafter it was indeed his overwhelming preoccupation. When he became President of Indonesia nineteen years later it was not through accident, or through the circumstances of the time, or through his skill in grasping an opportunity as was the case, for example, with his successor – it was because he had been heading that way for more than twenty years. Even before he made his final choice of a political career his romanticism had made him see himself as a great leader, moving the masses, providing a national ideology and in the forefront of the struggle against the oppressor.

# 4

# First Steps as a Nationalist Leader:
# The Search for Unity 1926–9

The THS course of studies was normally of four years. In Sukarno's case the interruption caused by his return to Surabaja for seven months during his first academic year had forced him to take an additional year over the course, but he completed it at last with a dissertation on harbour design, and graduated in 1926 as an *Ingenieur*.[69] He was now free to commit himself, if he wished, to a political career, but the decision does not seem to have been a completely foregone conclusion. He spent a little time considering the possibilities open to him. The logical conclusion to his education would have been entry as a technical graduate to the ranks of government service, but this would inevitably have closed the doors to political action. Alternatively he could have tried his hand as an architect in private practice while continuing, as a sideline, to indulge his appetite for politics. Or he could engage in politics as a full-time profession. He received an offer of government employment in the local Department of Public Works and another of a similar kind from the city of Bandung. He refused both. To support himself for the time being he accepted a post in the Ksatriya Institute School run by his mentor, Douwes Dekker, but according to his own version his inflammatory style of teaching history brought him up sharply against a visiting Education Department Inspector and led to the termination of his appointment.[70] Finally he opened an engineering and architect's office in partnership with one of his THS contemporaries, Anwari. His restlessness merely concealed the fact that his real vocation had by now begun to establish itself. Within a year he was to remove himself effectively from the architectural profession and to take his place as a recognized leader of one of the main currents of Indonesian nationalism. The next few years formed his first great period of political creativity. It was a time

69. *Jaarboek van de Technische Hoogeschool te Bandoeng*, Bandung, 1927, p. xxix.

70. *Autobiography*, pp. 71–2.

in which he saw his goals with absolute clarity, and in his pursuit of them he changed the world about him.

The political life that Sukarno had sampled in Bandung during his student days had consisted in part of occasional meetings and rallies of the Radical Concentration type, in part of contacts with a variety of separate organizations – with Sarekat Islam, with Jong Java (of which he was chairman in Bandung) and others – but more typically of political discussion in small private groups. In this sort of setting Sukarno had been influenced by Tjipto and Douwes Dekker. Gradually his own home became a centre for talk and argument among Bandung's leading political activists. He came to know students who had recently returned from overseas, and who were anxious to play their part in political movements at home. In this setting common ideas began to shape themselves and Sukarno began to feel his way towards his own formulation of them.

The springboard from which he was to project himself into the nationalist leadership was the Algemeene Studieclub ('General Study Club') which he helped to found early in 1926, shortly before his graduation. Sukarno served as secretary to the Club and was one of its prime-movers. The Study Club idea was itself part of a wider ferment in political circles. In broad outline its organization followed the model set two years earlier by Dr Sutomo, at that time a medical teacher in Surabaya. Sutomo in his medical student days had been one of the original members of Boedi Oetomo. He had later been employed in the government's medical service and had then pursued graduate studies in Holland where he had had a considerable influence on the thinking of the increasingly politically-conscious group of Indonesian students there. In 1923 he returned to a teaching appointment in Surabaja. The cultural ideas of Bóedi Oetomo had remained with Sutomo, and in 1924 he resigned from his post and founded the Indonesian Study Club, not as a political society but with the aim of developing cultural self-consciousness and an understanding of social and also political problems among educated Indonesians. The idea caught on, and similar groups were founded in other large cities – in Batavia, Semarang, Solo and Bogor – as well as in Bandung. Sukarno's General Study Club, however, though ostensibly based on Sutomo's example, had its own distinctive flavour. It was emphatically political rather than educational and the ideas of its members were radical rather than moderate. It looked to independence as the goal of nationalist endeavour and rejected the view that this could be achieved gradually by co-operation with the Dutch. It placed its emphasis on the necessity for struggle. This was Douwes Dekker's political teaching rather than that of Sutomo.

In helping to launch the Study Club venture Sukarno was in fact endeavouring to lead a new departure in Indonesian resistance to colonial rule. He saw about him the fragmented state of the movement. The rift between the PKI and Sarekat Islam was but one example of its fissiparous character. Outside Sarekat Islam there was a patchwork of smaller, ethnically-based groups – Jong Java, Pasundan, Jong Sumatra and others as well as religious organizations such as Muhammadiyah. Sukarno deplored these divisions. He saw the necessity for unity and began to feel his way towards the idea of an all-embracing mass organization as a means of developing a power which could challenge that of the colonial régime. The exact method of doing so was still to be worked out in detail, but by 1926 Sukarno had grasped the central idea that a reworked and sharpened concept of nationalism might be used to appeal to all sections of the politically-conscious Indonesian community.

'Nationalism' is a vague term which has meant widely differing things to different people. In its European context the notion had its links with the radically democratic elements of French revolutionary thought, but it also had obvious authoritarian overtones. For some political thinkers it has carried the implication that the individual could only find himself in the national collectivity. In Afro–Asia nationalism has been the product of societies in upheaval. For them, as we have seen, it has appeared as an integrating idea, increasingly important as customary values seemed to lose their binding force. The vision not merely of independence, but of a new political order based on a sense of national identity, however hazily it might be perceived, offered a focus of loyalty which might override family, ethnic, or other traditional ties. This perception defined itself only gradually. In

Indonesia the term 'nationalist' was loosely applied to all of the intelligentsia-led political organizations which developed in the last forty years of colonial rule, despite their differing aims and differing tempers. With the formation of the General Study Club in Bandung it began to acquire a narrower, and perhaps a clearer, expression.

Sukarno, certainly, condemned the exclusiveness and chauvinism of European nationalism and contrasted it with his own nationalism which, he said, was based on love of all humanity. But his own concept was narrow in a different sense. A programme freed alike from Islam and from Marxist theories of socialist revolution, emphasizing the primacy of the political struggle for independence and ignoring questions about the form of the state and the type of society to be built when independence came, reflected a purer 'nationalist' conception from those which had gone before in Indonesia. As a starting point Sukarno, basing himself on Renan, argued that a nation was not defined by race or language or religion or boundaries. It was 'a soul, a fundamental outlook' arising from a common history and from 'a desire, an urge to live as one'.[71] Moved partly by passion and partly by considerations of political utility, Sukarno was quick to see this as a potentially unifying idea which could be used to bring together opposing factions. He had observed at close quarters in Surabaja the divisions which had separated the leaders of one anti-Dutch organization from those of another, and he had since, at a greater distance, watched Sarekat Islam tearing itself apart. His political instinct led him to believe that he could bridge these divisions. His eclectic inclinations fitted him for the task and led him, in his own elaboration of nationalism, to draw on a variety of intellectual sources. He could apply a Marxist analysis of imperialism or make use of Muslim hostility to infidel domination, but in so doing he was concerned to develop the central idea of the nation as an entity which could reconcile conflicting elements in Indonesian society and subordinate them to an over-

71. 'Nationalism, Islam and Marxism.' This article has been reprinted in Sukarno, *Dibawah Bendera Revolusi* ['Under the Banner of Revolution'], Vol. I, 1959; there is an English translation in the Cornell Modern Indonesia Project's Translation Series, Ithaca, 1970.

arching ideal. In this way he was at last beginning to identify himself with a consistent and distinctive point of view.

The General Study Club produced its own journal, *Indonesia Muda* ('Young Indonesia')[72], and in its pages Sukarno expounded his maturing ideas. An article 'Nationalism, Islam and Marxism', published over three issues in 1926, may be regarded as the first important statement of his own position and an early expression of the ideas of the new secular nationalism in general. After referring to the diversity of elements to be found in Indonesian nationalism, and to the three dominant ideas which had motivated different parties – nationalism, Islam and Marxism – he posed what was, for him, the central question: 'Can these three spirits work together in the colonial situation to become one great spirit, the spirit of unity? The spirit of unity which can carry us to greatness.'[73] His answer was naturally in the affirmative. Indeed only in this way – only by combining these diverse forces – could success be achieved. 'The ship which will carry us to free Indonesia is the ship of unity.' But the manner of his argument is interesting.

The essay, structured to deal in turn with nationalism, Islam and Marxism, appears to treat them as separate currents within the general stream of Indonesian political activity. Sukarno appealed to each in turn, urging them to sink their differences and to co-operate with each other. Nationalists who refused to work with Marxists, he argued, misunderstood the direction of history. Marxism's origins in Indonesia were the same as those of nationalism – a common resistance to a common oppressor. Muslims, for their part, should overcome their fear of Marxism and recognize it as an ally. Capitalism, the enemy of Marxists, was also the enemy of Islam, and the new Marxist tactic was to work with genuine Islamic movements of nationalism in Asia. Muslims should not be alarmed by Marxism's hostility to religion since this was in essence a hostility to Christianity. Finally he called on Marxists to co-operate in the common struggle. Marxism

72. Not the *Suluh Indonesia Muda* [Torch of Young Indonesia], which was founded a year later by the merging of *Indonesia Muda* and *Suluh Indonesia*, the organ of Dr Sutomo's Indonesian Study Club.

73. 'Nationalism, Islam and Marxism'.

was not an unchanging dogma; it was in the process of adapting itself to new circumstances and in colonial countries it had recognized the necessity of fitting itself to the needs of different local situations. In a country like Indonesia, where Christianity had been the faith of those on top and Islam the faith of those underneath, Marxism and Islam ought to be natural allies. Sukarno distinguished between the philosophical materialism and the historical materialism of Marxist theory, and pointed out that the latter did not depend upon the former. There was no need therefore for Marxism as a social theory to be anti-religious.[74] Marxism must recognize that Islam, in supporting the struggle of those who were downtrodden, could be a progressive and not a fanatically conservative force and its efforts must, in some respect, parallel those of Marxism. (He added, it should be noted, a very strong rebuke to those Marxists who failed to co-operate with Muslims. Those who ignored unity, 'those whose theory is conservative and tactics out of date . . . such Marxists should not feel their honour slighted if they are called the poison of the people'.)

But the three currents were not really, in Sukarno's mind, simply variants, equal in status and complementary to each other. The way in which he developed his argument suggested implicitly that nationalism was the central current. It was because Islam was the religion of the underdog that it must be nationalist. It was because capital in Indonesia was foreign capital that the Marxist struggle against capitalism must be a nationalist struggle. The goal was unity between nationalism, Islam and Marxism, but it was the nationalist content of Islam and Marxism that made unity possible. Nationalism was the over-arching ideology

74. Dahm (*Sukarno and the Struggle for Indonesian Independence*, Ithaca, 1969, pp. 75–6) scoffs a little at Sukarno's attempt to brush aside the clash between religion and Marxism and at his view that the clash arose from a 'misconception' about Marxism. 'Sukarno believed he had found the key to solving the problem [of uniting belief in God and Marxism] in the difference between philosophical and historical materialism,' says Dahm and he takes Sukarno to task for separating the two. But Dahm is unfair here. Whatever Lenin may have said about the importance of philosophical materialism as a basis for Marxist sociological thinking, there is no logical connection between the two and, in logical terms, it was perfectly open to Sukarno to argue that one could believe in a 'creator-god' and accept a Marxist sociology simultaneously.

which could channel the different currents into the one stream.

In arguing his case he displayed his easy handling of the wide variety of ideas he had sampled in his student days. Allusions were made to Ernest Renan and H. G. Wells, to Marx and Engels, Kautsky and Radek, Sun Yat-sen and Gandhi, Sismondi and Blanqui, to the Koran and to Mohammed Abduh. (An unkind critic might suggest that some of this name-dropping was intended to demonstrate that he who had not been overseas was, nonetheless, at home in modern thought.) He digressed to expound the labour theory of value and showed his attraction to Marxism as offering a systematic explanation of why things happened as they did in the world. At the same time his essential Javanism showed through. As a superficial sign of it the very first sentence of the article contained a *wayang* allusion – a reference to Bima, who was evoked as an example of struggle against powerful enemies. More profoundly, the basic assumptions of the article were Javanese in temper. Not only was there the traditional emphasis on harmony and accommodation between conflicting points of view, but there were also hints of the very Javanese idea that a great leader was one who could hold such conflicting ideas in harmony. Sukarno was able to argue for the possible unity of all currents of nationalism because he felt *himself* to be a Marxist and a Muslim simultaneously. This capacity could, in Javanese terms, sustain a claim to power.

Such a conclusion should not be over-stressed. The argument advanced by Sukarno in this essay was primarily tactical. Nationalism was seen as a minimum programme on the basis of which diverse elements could work together. He had not yet gone far in his attempt at actual synthesis – at building an ideology which would combine features of all Indonesian points of view. His article was nonetheless a first attempt at synthesis and his eclecticism in 1926 foreshadowed the Sukarno of the future who would seek for a more intimate blending of different streams of thought.

The ideas of Sukarno and his Study Club fell into a responsive environment. The events of the previous few years had discredited the ideologically-based mass parties and paved the way for a more emphatically urban movement reflecting the growing numbers, and the growing alienation, of the intelligentsia. The forces combining to swing the course of nationalist activity into new channels were in part negative – the destruction of earlier movements – and in part positive – the emergence of new currents of thought. The change in circumstances needs some examination.

In October 1921 Sarekat Islam's adoption of its discipline resolution had brought its alliance with the PKI to a formal conclusion. Torn by factional divisions and uncertain of its goals, Sarekat Islam was by this time fast losing its central place in the nationalist movement. From the PKI's point of view, however, its expulsion from Sarekat Islam posed crucial theoretical problems. Leninist theory held that in colonial situations the time was not ripe for communist parties to seek hegemony over the nationalist struggle. They should therefore ally for the time being with the national bourgeoisie and co-operate with revolutionary nationalist organizations in the struggle against imperialism. On the face of it Sarekat Islam appeared to be such a party, and in 1921 the PKI therefore found itself faced with an uncomfortable set of choices. Should it moderate its revolutionary drive and seek to repair the breach with the Sarekat Islam leadership so that its members might once again be admitted as a 'bloc within' the larger party? Or should it accept the fact of its exclusion by seeking, nonetheless, to support Sarekat Islam's struggle, co-operating with it as a 'bloc without'? Or should it take the view that Sarekat Islam was no longer a revolutionary party and enter into direct competition with it, forming a rival organization at the grass roots level, drawing Sarekat Islam's membership under its own control and making its own bid for the leadership of a mass movement? Similar questions agitated communist movements elsewhere, and in groping towards a solution the Indies party was both experimenter and subject in the gradual evolution of Comintern theory.

There were differences of opinion in PKI ranks on these issues of theory and practice and the matter was complicated by the fact that not all Sarekat Islam branches were willing to follow the discipline resolution of the central organization.[75] There was thus

75. For the best account of these issues see R. McVey, *The Rise of Indonesian Communism*, Ithaca, 1965.

an opportunity for the PKI to compete at the grass roots level for control of Sarekat Islam members. This it did with some success though Semaun, who returned in May 1922 from a six months' visit to Moscow, argued that the PKI should avoid all radical programmes of direct action and seek to co-operate once more with non-communist nationalism. Unfortunately for his argument a further Sarekat Islam congress of February 1923 confirmed the discipline resolution and ended any hope of reconciliation.

Thereafter the story was one of intense competition between Sarekat Islam and the PKI for control of local branches. The PKI began to establish its own rival organizations at the local level and it seemed at first to be winning the tussle. Sarekat Islam's strength declined and PKI membership grew. But the Indies government was moving at the same time to exercise a closer control over popular movements. In 1924 it began to impose repressive measures, arresting some leaders and placing restrictions on the right of assembly. In the face of these pressures the PKI began to have doubts about its attempt to create a mass movement so quickly. It recognized that such a policy might dilute the party's proletarian character and revolutionary fervour and make it a less effective instrument of revolutionary action and it therefore returned to the ideas of class and doctrinal purity. In so doing it began to overestimate its strength and it became impatient with the cautious prescriptions of Semaun and the Comintern. Instead it began to espouse more radical policies, promoting, in particular, a series of strikes by the labour unions under its control and deciding to plan a more general insurrection. It is not necessary to trace the complexities of the party's unhappy domestic debate or to inquire into the tangled story of its relations with the Comintern. In December 1925 a conference of party leaders at Prambanan resolved to push the new radicalism to its logical conclusion and to prepare for open revolt.

During 1926 the party continued on its path of leftward deviation. Alimin and Musso were despatched to Moscow to solicit Comintern approval for the party's plans of rebellion. Their mission was unsuccessful and they found instead a firm opposition to the idea of insurrection. But plans for revolt had gone too far to be checked entirely. In the event the half-hearted revolts which did break out – in West Java in December 1926 and in West Sumatra in January 1927 – were inevitably small affairs, unco-ordinated and deplorably planned, and they were easily crushed by the colonial authorities. They ended not only the party's revolutionary deviation but, for the time being, its very existence.

The unhappy fate of the PKI in 1927 was no doubt on the cards from the very beginning. Its failure was in part due to bad leadership, mistaken strategy and appalling execution; but no strategy could conceivably have succeeded. In fact the PKI was in a totally impossible position after October 1921. Having been excluded from Sarekat Islam it could not follow an orthodox strategy of alliance with a progressive anti-imperialist movement, nor could it succeed in a course of independent revolutionary action. In Indonesia, as in China during the same period, Comintern orthodoxy and deviation to the left alike were totally out of line with local circumstances.

In retrospect these events stand as a clear watershed in Indonesia's nationalist history, and also as a critical point in the career of Sukarno. The decline of Sarekat Islam and the crushing of the PKI rebellion cleared the ground for a new type of movement based on a more narrowly defined form of nationalism – narrowly defined in the sense that it eschewed social issues and focused simply on the goal of independence. Sukarno's General Study Club, making a most opportune appearance, was an early representative of the new secular nationalism, but it was not the only sign of the changing temper of thought and it needs to be seen in a wider context of nationalist development. Of growing importance in the mid twenties was the influence of Indonesian students who, like Sukarno, had enjoyed the benefits of a Dutch-language education in the Indies but who, unlike him, had been able to cap it with the experience of tertiary education in the Netherlands. The rebellions of 1926 and 1927 were a negative factor in changing the direction of nationalist thinking. A positive element was provided by this new group of university-educated leaders.

A trickle of Indonesian students had been making its way to Dutch universities since the early years of the century, but after

World War I a change could be observed in their character. The post-war students were young men who had experienced the political stirrings of their homeland before leaving for Europe and their political consciousness was further developed in Holland. For many of them it was an unexpected revelation to mix there with others from all parts of the Indies, and to perceive for the first time the possibility of an Indonesian nation. Those who had been active in Jong Java or Jong Sumatra were suddenly brought to see beyond these ethnic limitations, and many years later they came to look back on this shift in outlook as a sharply felt experience.[76] Men like the law student Sartono (later to be Speaker in the Indonesian parliament), Ali Sastroamidjojo (later Prime Minister), Iwa Kusumasumantri (a minister in several governments of the Republic), Mohammad Hatta (future Vice-President), and a little later Sutan Sjahrir (Prime Minister during the early years of the revolution) were a distinguished generation, well fitted to play an important part in the intellectual development of the new nationalism. The bite of this student group was seen in 1922, when the old society of Indies students in Holland ('Indische Vereeniging') was reorganized and rechristened the Perhimpunan Indonesia ('Indonesian Union' – PI). The Indische Vereeniging had been essentially a social club; Perhimpunan Indonesia saw itself as a political organization, and the use of the name 'Indonesia' was a token of its nationalist spirit.

The environment of Dutch universities was a liberating experience for Indonesian students. In the Hague, Rotterdam, Leiden or Utrecht, they enjoyed an acceptance which Dutch colonial society in the Indies had denied them. They acquired a solid discipline which was to mark them out in the future leadership of independent Indonesia, and they fed on a variety of intellectual sources. They observed parliamentary democracy in action and drew upon the springs of the Western European democratic tradition. Some of them moved in Dutch communist circles and their revolutionary tendencies were strengthened by contacts with exiled or itinerant Indonesian members of the PKI, such as Tan Malaka and Semaun. Others moved in a liberal socialist environment. From these varied influences there was to develop

76. Author's interviews in 1969 with members of the early PNI.

a distinctive strain in Indonesian political thinking, demanding radical action to break the colonial tie but emphasizing the importance of individualist and broadly humanist values. For many of these students the experience of being steeped in Western thought resolved in an unexpected way the crisis of personal identity which had confronted them at home. Sjahrir, as we have noticed, was later to regard himself as bound more closely to the world of European philosophy than to the values of his own society, and others shared that measure of westernization.

Politically, as expressed through Perhimpunan Indonesia, the programme of these students rejected the old Ethical Policy ideal of Dutch–Indonesian partnership and scouted the possibility of obtaining substantial concessions by co-operation with the Dutch in such institutions as the Volksraad. Their goal was the creation of an independent Indonesian nation, and this could be achieved, in their view, only through the efforts of Indonesians themselves.

In the mid twenties returning PI members sought to play the part in Indonesian nationalism for which they felt their education fitted them, and it was natural that they should be attracted by the Study Clubs among whose strong student membership they found men of their own kind. (Indeed, the PI executive in Holland had been planning the formation of a Study Club in Bandung at the time that Bandung students were forming it.) To this extent the Study Club movement should be seen almost as a local Indonesian channel of PI thinking. But there were differences too, between the two groups. As the returning students made their contacts with political circles at home they quickly became aware of the force of Bandung's new personality and no doubt they and Sukarno measured each other warily.

PI students possessed, by and large, a more disciplined approach to political and social thought than was represented, for example, by Sukarno's easy eclecticism. They felt themselves to be internationalist in outlook and they tried to fit their Indonesian nationalism into that broader context. They were also more Western, by comparison with the strong Javanese element in Sukarno's make-up. While they were experiencing the intellectual conflicts of Europe Sukarno was drawing his own experience from a Javanese setting. It was, in its way, as broadening an experience as theirs, for in Tjokroaminoto's household he was in the very power-house of Indonesian political activity – he was not viewing the local ferment from a distance. These differences in outlook were permanent, and in the future they were sometimes to divide Sukarno from other nationalist leaders. But in the meantime there was common ground; those who had studied in Holland were, like Sukarno and his colleagues, nationalists in the strict sense, and his Study Club therefore offered a meeting place for these two distinct tributaries. The coming together of 'Bandung nationalism' and that of the overseas students provided the general setting for Sukarno's first period of political creativity.

The new nationalism, if it was to become an effective force, required more than the academic forum of the Study Club. It required an organization directed specifically to political action and the time was ripe for the formation of one. Some preliminary thinking along these lines had already been done, in Holland by the PI leadership and in Indonesia by a 'Committee for Indonesian Unity', formed in September 1926 by representatives of a variety of nationalist or quasi-nationalist organizations, but reflecting in particular the view of the General Study Club. The Study Club's ties with Perhimpunan Indonesia on the one hand, and its links with other organizations in Indonesia on the other, made it the obvious body to take the initiative and Sukarno the obvious person. Indonesian political activity was chronically fragmented but while Sarekat Islam, the Surabaja Study Club, Tjipto and Douwes Dekker were in some degree warring with each other, Sukarno maintained his own individually good relations with all of them and thus gave his Study Club the opportunity, unilaterally, to be the driving force in securing the co-operation of all other individuals and groups. His conciliatory position was indicated by the fact that at the end of 1926 he had resumed his relationship with Tjokroaminoto by co-operating with him in a new Sarekat Islam paper, *Bandera Islam* ('Banner of Islam'). Sukarno was to see to the nationalist side of the paper while Tjokroaminoto looked after its religious content.

From this base of operations the way was open for the formation of a broadly representative nationalist party. The next step was taken in April 1927, when a group consisting of Sukarno, Iskaq Tjokrohadisurjo, Dr Tjipto Mangunkusumo, Budiarto and Sunarjo formed themselves into a preparatory committee to consider creating such an organization. There was no particular chairman at the meetings of this group. It worked rather as a close and informal collection of associates. Its senior member, Tjipto, was dubious about the whole enterprise and warned of the danger of government action to suppress a specifically organized nationalist party; but the rest decided to go ahead, and finally, at a further meeting on 4 July, the new organization, Perserikatan Nasional Indonesia ('Indonesian Nationalist Association' – PNI), was formed. It was thus essentially an Indonesia-based initiative. Though the idea of a new nationalist organization had been discussed among Indonesian students in Holland the actual formation of the PNI stemmed from the work of the Study Club rather than from that of Perhimpunan Indonesia.[77]

PNI's platform reflected the ideas whose growth we have been describing. Central to the party's whole position was the idea of *merdeka* – political independence for Indonesia – and embedded in that principle was the idea of an Indonesian nation which would be welded together through participation in the common struggle for independence. As a corollary to the concept of struggle there was present also the principle of non-cooperation with the Indies Government. It is important to notice, too, what was absent: there was no concern with the political forms which Indonesia might adopt after independence, nor was there a commitment to any particular social programme. Either, as with Douwes Dekker, such matters were to be left to look after themselves after independence or there was no real appreciation of them. Yet there was virtue, too, in the limited character of the PNI's programme and in its silence about the future. In helping to cast its programme in this form Sukarno was following his own instinct. He recognized the great potential power of nationalism as an ideal and he realized that an attempt to spell out the details of the future would obscure that ideal and would cause division rather than unity. This approach had been foreshadowed in his

77. Author's interview with Mr Sunarjo, 10 June 1969.

'Nationalism, Islam and Marxism' article, and it was the right approach for 1927.

The formation of the PNI was not merely an important new step in Indonesia's nationalist endeavour. For Sukarno it meant a new recognition. It gave him at last an organization in which his leadership skills could be tested and developed. His growing stature was recognized clearly enough in his election as chairman of the party's executive; he had been only secretary of the Study Club, but by 1927 he was generally recognized as the obvious man to chair the party. Iskaq was secretary-treasurer. The other leading members included his close associate and fellow engineer Anwari, and a group of ex-PI members, the lawyer Sartono, warm-hearted but fundamentally cautious, the reflective and scholarly Sunarjo, also a lawyer, Budiarto, who had been a member of the original committee, and Samsi Sastrowidagdo. His standing among these men reflected his political coming of age.

Sukarno undoubtedly enjoyed his new position and responsibilities. From the vantage point of the PNI chairmanship he could survey the nationalist scene and attempt to re-order it in his own way. He was confident, and with some justice, that he was fitted for the position as no other would have been. Not only was he a man of presence and possessed of commanding powers of oratory – a person who could attract followers and fire them with a vision of the future; also important at this stage of nationalist organization was that characteristic which was to establish itself more and more as an integral part of his political style – his concern to smooth over differences, to promote harmony, to draw together diverse people and conflicting ideas. In the months following the PNI's foundation its task was to pick up the fragments of Indonesia's shattered anti-colonial movement and in so doing to find for itself a popular basis on which its élite leadership could operate. It was to this task that Sukarno set himself. The search for unity as he saw it called simultaneously for negotiation with possible allies outside the PNI and for a major effort of indoctrination on the part of the new nationalism. Indeed, for Sukarno, aware of the direction in which his own skills lay, the two went inseparably together. With a political point of view of his own to propagate, and with a party committed to that point

of view behind him, he could give full rein to his talents of persuasion and exhortation. The next two years were to provide a test
of that approach.

An early opportunity of mobilizing nationalist sentiment was
provided by the news of action taken by the Dutch authorities, in
June 1927, against PI leaders in Holland. Their rooms were
searched and some of them were subjected to interrogation. In
September Hatta and others were arrested, but before that – on
14 August – Sukarno and Iskaq addressed a protest meeting in
Bandung. This was followed by public meetings in other centres
at which Sukarno showed his qualities as the PNI's chairman and
confirmed his position as the organization's central figure. It was
at this period that the fervour of his oratory and his open and
almost careless challenges to Dutch authority earned him the
nickname 'Lion of the Podium'. More familiarly he was known
simply as 'Bung Karno', a name whose use he encouraged, perhaps a little self-consciously, in order to cast aside his high standing as an *ingenieur* and to assert his egalitarianism. (*Bung* –
brother or comrade – a common form of address between men,
became an affectionate style of address for nationalist leaders,
both before and after the attainment of independence.) He always
wore a *pitji* (the black velvet cap often associated with Islam) and
helped to make it almost a part of the uniform of nationalism.

In December 1927 Sukarno appeared at a mass meeting in
Batavia organized by the Batavia branch of PNI and gave an
extensive account of PNI principles. By the end of the year he
could feel that things were at last moving in the direction he
wanted – he himself was widely known, he had charted a new
course for nationalist endeavour and expounded its principles,
and the response to his words seemed encouraging. The PNI still
had to draw a mass following, but the party was there as a focal
point, expressing the ideas and the energies of a newly emerging
leadership and attracting the attention of politically conscious
Indonesians and Dutch authorities alike.

The climax to Sukarno's year's activities came in December
with the formation of what looked like a united front of nationalist organizations. As a result of his initiative an agreement was
reached at Bandung between the PNI, Sarekat Islam, Boedi

Oetomo, Pasundan, Sumatra Bond, Kaum Batawi and Dr Sutomo's Surabaja Study Club to form an organization with the unwieldy name of Permufakatan Perhimpunan-perhimupanan Politik Kebangsaan Indonesia (Association of Political Organiza tions of the Indonesian People – fortunately abbreviated to PPPKI). This was a diverse group of organizations but, on the face of it, it seemed a new and promising development. Earlier attempts to achieve nationalist unity had aimed to entice followers to enlist under the banner of a dominant ideology – first Islam and then Marxism. The PPPKI sought rather to federate existing groups, making no ideological demands beyond acceptance of the idea of struggle for Indonesia's political independence.

To Sukarno, this seemed a practical way of applying his own belief in the essential community of interests of the different streams of the Indonesian resistance to the Dutch, and in the forum of the PPPKI he showed his ability to conciliate others and to persuade quite different groups to work together for a common goal. While leading the PNI in a radical and non-cooperating direction he was able to act moderately towards the moderates who thought that adequate concessions would be won by co-operation with the Dutch. That this was a quite remarkable achievement must be emphasized strongly. To the nationalists of the twenties and early thirties the issue of co-operation versus non-cooperation was not a mere matter of alternative tactics about which there could be an honest difference of opinion. It was a dominant question which divided friends from foes. Feelings ran so high on the question that even forty years later surviving members of Sukarno's PNI remember with vividness their inability even to talk to co-operators.[78] In these circumstances Sukarno's success in creating the PPPKI and in holding it together was a personal *tour de force*.

There was, of course, a price to be paid for it. Too broad a united front could not be expected to act decisively. In fact the PPPKI was the loosest of federations and its unity proved in the end to be illusory. Its core consisted of a temporary understanding between the PNI and Sarekat Islam and its driving force was that of Sukarno and the PNI. Without his presence it fell apart.

78. Author's interviews in 1969 with members of the original PNI.

But this is to anticipate. In December 1927 it seemed to Sukarno that his new movement was gathering momentum and was demonstrating the correctness of his view that *merdeka* was the slogan to bridge the divisions separating Muslim and Marxist, Javanese and Minangkabau, westernized liberal and Javanese traditionalist, and to bring them all together in a common sense of Indonesian nationhood. The euphoria of 1927 promised bright prospects for the following year.

In March 1928 the newly found nationalist unity was supported by events altogether outside Indonesia. The Perhimpunan Indonesia leaders, Hatta, Ali Sastroamidjojo, Mohammad Nazir Pamontjak and Abdul Madjid Djojo Adhiningrat, who had been arrested in September 1927, were brought to trial in The Hague and, under the leadership of Hatta, made the occasion an opportunity for an exposition of Indonesian nationalism. Hatta's defence speech carried the battle into the very nerve centre of Dutch authority. He argued that Indonesia's interests were in fundamental conflict with those of the Netherlands and that nationalism could not be served by co-operation with Dutch power. Co-operation was, in any case, only possible between equals, and imperialism was, by its nature, a relationship of inequality. He sketched the character of imperialism as a system of power which could only be challenged through the mobilization of the power of a united people. The role of the intellectual leadership was to uncover and to serve the spontaneous power of the masses. It was an uncompromising speech, and, delivered as it was, in the publicity of a Dutch court by a man who could assume the role of a martyr in the nationalist cause, it gave a new thrust to the PI–PNI programme.

Against this background the PNI prepared for its first congress, which assembled in Surabaja at the end of May. After the first day of the congress, when Sukarno addressed a gathering of over a thousand, the meeting adopted a fuller statement of aims covering political, economic and social fields. These were inevitably couched in general terms, for the party's need was still primarily that of consolidating its own organization. A change in name from Perserikatan Nasional Indonesia ('Indonesian Nationalist Association') to Partai Nasional Indonesia ('Indonesian Nationa-

list Party') reflected its recognition of its organizational purposes.[79]

The congress gave a new stimulus to the PNI and the succeeding months were a period of even more intense activity for
Sukarno. He seemed to be almost continuously on the move from
end to end of Java, fulfilling a speaking engagement here, encouraging the faithful there, and working effectively with Sartono to extend the organizational machinery of the party. In July
he was speaking at Pekalongan, the end of August found him at
Gresik, and immediately afterwards in Surabaja for the first
PPPKI congress. PPPKI affairs claimed him again later in
September in Batavia and in early October in Bandung, where the
local section of the PPPKI organized a general meeting of the
member organizations. Then he visited Semarang for more
speech-making before returning to Bandung where another
general meeting of the PPPKI was in preparation. And so the
round continued into 1929. He found time in the midst of all this
for journalistic activities as well. In July 1928, following a decision
taken at the first congress, the PNI established its own paper,
*Persatuan Indonesia* ('Indonesian Unity'), under the joint editor-
ship of Sukarno and Sunarjo. At the same time he continued to
write for other papers – for *Suluh Indonesia Muda* for example,
the magazine formed in 1927 by the merger of the Bandung Study
Club's *Indonesia Muda* and the Surabaja Study Club's *Suluh
Indonesia*, and for *Banteng Priangan*, the organ of the Bandung
branch of the party. Articles entering into controversy over
population pressure and agrarian policy,[80] giving a moving
tribute to Tjipto Mangunkusumo when he was exiled in 1928,[81] expounding theories of imperialism,[82] criticizing the change of heart
of his old mentor, Adolph Baars,[83] commenting at length on the
release of the PI leaders in Holland and on the implications

79. 'Partai Nasional Indonesia' is literally 'Indonesian National Party',
but in fact it is always translated as 'Indonesian Nationalist Party' and this
was certainly what the name meant to its members.

80. *Suluh Indonesia*, 1927, published in Sukarno, *Dibawah Bendera Revolusi*, p. 25.

81. *Dibawah Bendera Revolusi*, p. 41.

82. ibid., p. 51.

83. ibid., p. 57.

of their acquittal for the movement in Indonesia[84] and discussing nationalism's attitude to pan-Asianism[85] followed each other regularly. Together they represented a consistent and coherent body of nationalist comment – the products of a pen whose style and message were becoming widely known.

In addition to his public appearances and his appeals through the pages of *Persatuan Indonesia* and elsewhere, he also made his contribution to the task of developing the organizational side of the party. The main initiative here was that of Sartono rather than Sukarno. The party attempted to link itself with the existing pyramid of territorial divisions of the Dutch administrative system in the Indies. Its aim was to establish regency branches and from these to extend organization down to the village level. Section organizations were created in sub-districts (*ketjamatan*) and 'locals' at the village (*desa*) level, and where appropriate, further sub-groupings within the *desa*.[86] But work in the *desa* was difficult since political activity at that level was easily detected by the government administrative service. The real interest of PNI leaders lay in the urban branches where they could more easily awaken a response. Plans were made for the creation of a legal advice bureau, for co-operative activities and for literacy courses all to be available to the public at large.

In Bandung some efforts were directed to the education of potential leaders as well as to the mass rallies and the dissemination of party propaganda. As part of that effort Sukarno was involved in the work of a small cadre school in Bandung. It met four or five times a week at his own house and comprised about fifteen members. Among them, representative of one type of person who was drawn to the PNI, was the young Maskun. Maskun was largely self-educated in political matters. He had read magazines and local newspapers and had gradually become acquainted with some of the writings of PI members. He suddenly became

84. ibid., p. 63.

85. ibid., p. 73.

86. See recollections of Gatot Mangkupradja, Secretary of the Party after the 1928 congress, in 'The Peta and my Relations with the Japanese in Indonesia', *Indonesia*, Cornell Modern Indonesia Project, No. 5, April 1968.

politically conscious, joined the PNI and was attracted to Sukarno as its leader. He came to board with him and was later to be arrested with Sukarno at the end of 1929. The basic course material for the cadre classes was prepared by Hatta and Ali Sastroamidjojo, who were still in Holland, and by Iskaq. These three were responsible for devising courses in Economics, the History of Nationalism, and Public Administration respectively. Sukarno was responsible for Economic History, but he was also the leader of the class and the expositor, and it may be assumed that even in the other courses he did not limit himself to the recapitulation of prepared material.[87]

The demands of political action did not leave a great deal of time for the leaders of the party to pursue an active intellectual life of their own. Sukarno was naturally preoccupied by the politics of the moment, and his day-to-day conversation was directed to immediate tactics rather than to general theories and ideas.[88] But there was room, in more relaxed moments, for ideological discussion too. There was talk of nationalism, its meaning and its particular characteristics in Indonesia. Was it like German nationalism? Or Japanese nationalism? There was talk of Marxist theory and its relevance to the Indonesian situation; there was philosophical argument about the utility of dialectics as a tool of thought. (In these discussions Sukarno saw Indonesian nationalism as a dialectically-produced opposite of Dutch nationalism.)[89] On all these questions there was a high measure of agreement amongst the members of the Bandung group. In particular Renan's concept of nationalism, quoted by Sukarno in his 'Nationalism, Islam and Marxism' article, served them all as an acceptable basis for action, and it was given specific expression at a youth congress held in Batavia on 27 and 28 October 1928. The congress was composed of representatives of the main youth organizations – Jong Java, Jong Bataksbond, Jong Sumatra, Jong Islamieten Bond, Jong Celebes, and others. It thus leaped over narrow ethnic divisions and it produced the famous 'Youth Pledge', which stressed Indonesia's common history and its

87. Author's interview with Maskun, 30 June 1969.
88. ibid.
89. Author's interviews with Ali Sastroamidjojo and Sunarjo, June 1969.

common desire for nationhood and which looked to the forging of national unity on the basis of 'one land, one people and one language'.[90]

Involvement in these varied activities made for an exacting life but also for an exhilarating one, for Sukarno had clearly found his *métier*. It was not without its anxieties. The widening scope of the PNI's activities brought it the unwelcome attention of the police, but in fact members of the party operated fairly openly, sheltered by the comparative permissiveness of Governor-General de Graeff's administration. (In his autobiography Sukarno no doubt exaggerates the extent to which conspiratorial and cloak-and-dagger behaviour – secret meetings in brothels or in the back seat of a car – was called for.[91]) Nonetheless, the possibility of sudden police action to break up a meeting, raid headquarters or arrest a group of leaders was always present. Another cause of anxiety was the simple matter of livelihood – the party's own funds were certainly not extensive. Sukarno refers to Inggit's contribution to the budget through the sale of her home-made cosmetics and to his own earnings through occasional pieces of paid journalism, but there was also aid from wealthier individuals.[92] Gatot Mangkupradja, for example, party secretary after the first congress, was a man of some substance with income from rice fields, real estate and taxis inherited from his father, and it seems that he contributed much of it to the cause, impoverishing himself in the process.[93] People like Ali Sastroamidjojo, Sartono, Iskaq and Sujudi who had resources from their legal practices, clubbed together to pay Sukarno's salary of seventy-five guilders a month. (This was in theory. In fact the salary did not always come.) The pooling of resources in this way was not uncommon, for the movement created a sense of camaraderie among its members which they were later to recall with nostalgia.

In May 1929, when a thousand delegates gathered in Batavia for the second congress of the party, two years of effort appeared to

90. *Persatuan Indonesia*, 1 November 1928.
91. *Autobiography*, pp. 82–3. Cf. Gatot Mangkupradja, op. cit., p. 110.
92. *Autobiography*, pp. 86–7.
93. Gatot Mangkupradja, op. cit., pp. 108–111.

have produced real achievements. The party had seven full branches, Bandung, Batavia, Jogja, Surabaja, Malang, Pekalongan and Palembang, together with several candidate branches, and it claimed ten thousand members. As with the membership claims of other Indonesian parties, these figures must be treated with some reserve. Membership varied widely from one area of Java to another. Of the ten thousand, six thousand were from the Priangan. Many were merely nominal adherents taking no real part in the party's activities, and one authority gives the total as only about half the claimed number.[94] Nonetheless, there was a growing framework of organization and an energetic leadership working through that membership and making a widening impact both on the new Indonesian élite and on urban and rural society. The issue of *Persatuan Indonesia* which preceded the congress was able to give an impression of the party's educational and social as well as political achievements.[95]

The two years of activity had also been of importance in Sukarno's own personal growth and in the development of his political skills. He had shown himself to possess some organizational gifts and, more noticeably, great powers of rhetoric. He could capture mass audiences and fire them with a sense of nationalist identity and purpose. Through his oratory and his writing the elements of his ideological position had gradually defined themselves.

There were several distinctive features to be noticed in Sukarno's thought. First of all, and of fundamental significance, was his ideal of nationalist unity to which attention has been drawn. He was concerned to stress the essential coincidence of interest between the several streams of nationalist thought. He was moved here partly by tactical considerations. The only advantage that the Indonesians had against the Dutch was the advantage of numbers, but the use of that advantage depended on unity. Nationalist solidarity was thus a partial answer to Dutch skills

94. Dahm, op. cit., pp. 110–11, gives a membership of about 5,000 in September 1929 (2,740 in the Priangan, accounting for over 50% of the whole membership), but refers to a sharp increase over the next three months leading, perhaps, to a doubling of the membership.

95. *Persatuan Indonesia*, 15 May 1929.

in playing upon differences and applying a policy of divide and rule. But Sukarno's approach also included the common Javanese values of tolerance and harmony – the belief in the desirability of consensus through deliberation. Islam in particular he felt to be the main obstacle to consensus and much of his appeal to unity was directed to that quarter. In the true *abangan* tradition Sukarno saw Islam, not as it was, but as he thought it ought to be – a part of a unified Indonesian totality. Such a view was, of course, inevitably opposed to the thorough-going Islam of the *santri*. It was important, nevertheless, that a leader like Sukarno should act as though that gulf was less deep than it was, and should argue that a synthesis of ideas was possible.

Secondly there was his insistence on the idea of non-cooperation, not merely as a tactic but as a matter of principle. He stressed the futility of moderation, the impossibility of compromise with the imperialist enemy and the clarity of opposition between *sini* and *sana* – between 'our side' and 'their side'.

But every effort which makes the demarcation line more perfect between us and them is good for our struggle. The more obvious the line between our people and the overlords, the sharper the division appears between our side and theirs, that is, the clearer that antithesis can be seen and felt, the purer and cleaner too becomes the manifestation of our struggle in consequence, thus imparting character to our struggle.

Because for us, the Indonesian nationalists, the problem of our struggle is the problem of power. The matter is not a question of justice, the matter is not a question of rights.[96]

As a corollary there was the concept of mobilizing the power of the people for the struggle. An awakened national consciousness and an organization to give it expression were the foundations of the people's might. Non-cooperation and self-reliance were the methods which would lead to success.

There may seem to be a paradox here. The sharpness of his insistence on non-cooperation may seem to run counter to his search for unity and his emphasis on tolerance. How could it be reconciled with his conciliation of the moderates within the

96. Sukarno's message to the first PPPKI congress in 1928, in *Dibawah Bendera Revolusi*, p. 83 ff.

PPPKI? But unity, for Sukarno, was not to be achieved through narrowing the movement to exclude all doubters. He sought the unity of *all* of 'us'. Among 'us', admittedly, there were people who were prepared to co-operate with 'them'. They must be persuaded to change. Sukarno was seeking the non-cooperating unity of the *sinis* against the *sanas*. In the meantime the co-operators must be handled gently.

Thirdly there was his concept of Marhaenism. The idea of the 'little people' may not seem to constitute a particularly profound contribution to political thought but in fact it represented a fair assessment of the nature of Indonesian society. Marxism had given Sukarno his most systematic tool of social analysis, and in his examination of the nature of colonial domination he spoke pretty much in the terms of Lenin's analysis of imperialism. He was, not, however, misled into attempting to apply a Marxist social analysis rigidly to Indonesian circumstances, and his perception of the absence of a proletariat and of the importance of the poor, but property-owning, masses was significant. It went along with his view of the anti-imperialist struggle. He saw that struggle not as containing elements of class tension as the PKI had believed, but as a simple struggle of the Indonesian people as a whole against the Dutch. By the same token his nationalism looked to independence but contained no very clear picture of the social changes to be worked for after independence had been achieved.

Finally there was an apocalyptic strain running through his speeches and articles which had a direct appeal to his Javanese audiences. A particular expression of this in 1928 and 1929 was his occasional prophetic reference to the rise of Japan and to the coming of a Pacific war which would enable Indonesia to obtain her freedom. This was a shrewd prediction but in the circumstances of Java in the late twenties the prophecy had a special appeal, for it was quickly linked with traditional expectations arising from the prophecies of Djoyoboyo. (Djoyoboyo was a twelfth-century king of Kediri who, according to legend, had prophesied that Java would be occupied by yellow-skinned conquerors who would stay for the lifetime of the maize plant. When the maize ripened and was ready for harvest the conquerors

would leave and Java would be free.[97]) Though it was uninten-
tional on his part, Sukarno's reference to a Pacific war encouraged
popular hopes that this would see the fulfilment of the prophecy.

These elements of Sukarno's thought and method of action
were to remain unchanged in their essentials over the years. They
reflected a consistent view of the world, and they were largely
independent. He had drawn heavily on Western thinkers in his
intellectual development, but he had not bound himself to any
single Western framework of ideas: instead he reshaped his
borrowings to serve his own purposes and tried to fashion a series
of attitudes which were related to Indonesian realities and which
could serve as a basis for united action. The real problem for a
political leader in Indonesia was that of making contact with the
masses, arousing a sense of national identity and a will to resist.
Sukarno understood this and his idea of making the PNI a mass
party, though unsuccessful in the end, was practical and reasonable.

It has been argued by one scholar that Sukarno's political
thinking in fact failed to take account of Dutch power, that the
slogan '*Merdeka* now' was not backed by any realistic sense of
ways and means, and that his posture as a revolutionary leader,
challenging the might of the colonial régime, was therefore lacking in practical substance. Sukarno, the criticism runs, while
conceding that the colonial problem was not a moral problem but
a problem of power, confused might and right and seemed almost
to assume that the government's strength would fade before the
growing might of the organized people.[98]

This does him less than justice. Sukarno was a romantic revolutionary, and perhaps he did miscalculate his own strength and
that of the movement he had created. Time was indeed to show
that the PNI was no match for Dutch power. But the idea of
creating a mass movement based on non-cooperation with the
Dutch was a realistic way of going about a nationalist struggle.
If a large party could be built up, and if it really could command

97. See Dahm, op. cit., pp. 6–7 for an interesting discussion of the hypothesis that the historical figure of Djoyoboyo became associated with anti-
foreign prophecies and with the *Ratu Adil* myth only in the mid eighteenth
century.

98. Dahm, op. cit., pp. 93–4 argues in these terms.

mass support and inspire mass enthusiasm, would it not pose problems of control for colonial authority and, in the long run, might it not strain Dutch resources and weaken Dutch strength? For the foreseeable future, certainly, the authorities possessed the power to take effective repressive action, and the goal might therefore prove to be distant and the road a painful one to follow. In terms of practical politics, nonetheless, it was at least a possible road.

That criticism of Sukarno, however, does raise other interesting questions about his cast of mind. How far at this time did he see man as the plaything of history and how far as the maker of history? His Marxism might, perhaps, have encouraged him to emphasize the power of impersonal forces and to believe that human action could only be effective if it fitted into the trends of historical development, but as a political leader he could not but believe that events had a certain openness of texture and that they could be shaped by the power of the human will. Judgements of this kind must also take account of the traditional component of Sukarno's thinking. There are elements in the Javanese worldview that stress the impotence of the individual in the interplay of cosmic forces, and the need to fit in with those forces. But there is also the belief in the spiritual power (*kesaktian*) of exceptional persons. The 'voluntarism' of Sukarno's political thinking, if it can be called that, was a departure from fundamentalist Marxism and it fitted without any sense of paradox into Javanese thought.[99] It may also have carried with it the typically Javanese assumption that power is a concrete, finite and strictly limited commodity which, if it is increased in one place, must be decreased in another. To build up the power of the PNI would in itself be to decrease Dutch power. This kind of assumption might have played its part in encouraging Sukarno to miscalculate his own strength.

Sukarno's efforts in rallying the fragmented nationalist movement to the banner of the PNI were only partially successful. Divisions continued to exist. The PNI's insistence of non-cooperation with the Dutch was at variance with the more moderate approach of such people as Hadji Agus Salim, Dr

99. cf. Schram's account of the voluntarism of Mao Tse-tung. See Schram, *Mao Tse-tung*, Penguin Books, 1966, pp. 125–7, 277, 293–5.

Sutomo and Ki Hadjar Dewantoro, who were willing to work within the framework of the Volksraad, to press there for modifications of policy on particular matters, and to look towards the ultimate concession by the Dutch of wide powers of local autonomy for the Indies. Again, the Sukarno approach did not satisfy the more devout Muslims who wanted Islam to be the basis of the struggle against the colonial authorities and who suspected Sukarno of making a religion of nationalism. Hadji Agus Salim on one occasion warned Sukarno against his implied deification of the nation when the latter spoke of 'Mother Indonesia' (*Ibumu Indonesia*).[1] The co-operation between the PNI and Islam within the PPPKI was maintained only with difficulty. Even Islam itself was divided. After the purging of the Communist element within Sarekat Islam, rifts had appeared between the forward looking modernist and reformist elements on the one hand and the more conservative rural *ulamas* on the other. In 1926 the tension between the two led to the formation of Nahdatul Ulama ('Council of Muslim Theologians') which was to remain thereafter a distinct grouping within the house of Islam, more closely linked with the Javanese tradition.

These were deep divisions and Sukarno cannot be blamed for his failure to bridge them. It was to be a permanent failure, but it was due to the intransigent nature of the divisions themselves. Sukarno may have underestimated the basic character of these fissures within the movement, and his nationalism, claiming to offer a synthesis, in fact came to be but one stream of nationalist thought among the others. But he did see certain things very clearly. He saw that the Dutch could never be *persuaded* to give up their stake in the Indies, but that an awakened nationalism might *force* them to do so. He saw the necessity for nationalist unity if the movement was to have any chance of ultimate success, and he believed that an adequate base for it existed in spite of deep ethnic and cultural division. 'The political atmosphere of Indonesia is full of hope for unity,' he had written in the introductory editorial of *Persatuan Indonesia*.[2] 'Every national party

1. Hadji Agus Salim in *Suluh Indonesia Muda*, August 1928. See also *Persatuan Indonesia*, 1 September 1928.
2. *Persatuan Indonesia*, 15 July 1928.

urges "unity". . . . It is the wish of the times.' Sukarno gave his
hearers a vision of that unity, and though it was never quite to be
achieved in practice neither was it ever again entirely lost to
view. He felt the fact of colonial rule, with all its attendant humiliations, to be a fact of such overwhelming importance that all
other things must pale into insignificance beside it.

But in following this path Sukarno was not the epitome of
Indonesian nationalism. There were other important figures and
other points of view beside his own within the movement.
Sukarno however, as the PNI's ideologue, was uniquely able to
project a compelling vision to his listeners, and his leadership of
the party constituted something of a watershed in the evolution
of nationalist thinking. He could appeal to a wide variety of
elements. To the élite he could give a promise of effective and
radical action – before 1927 it was easy for Indonesian intellectuals to be associationist in outlook without having a bad conscience, but after it was more difficult – and for the ordinary Javanese he could touch the messianic vision of totality and harmony,
of a re-united kingdom and a new golden age. He reached out also
beyond the élite and beyond the Javanese, attempting to awaken
a sense of identity and an awareness of the evils of colonialism
amongst the masses of the Indies population as a whole. This was
a tremendous undertaking, but people who were once awakened
to nationalist consciousness never lost it. What the PNI had
achieved by 1929 was largely the achievement of Sukarno, and
his synthesis had become the outlook of the central stream of
Indonesian nationalism. The 1929 congress confirmed his leadership and seemed to promise further successes in the future.

Sukarno opened the congress with a speech asserting confidently the party's ability to overcome any obstacles which the
government might put in its way.[3] Though dealing with momentous matters in a momentous manner his remarks were laced also
with homely touches, as of a father speaking to his children. He
had by this time developed the assurance that he was *the* leader of
the movement, the one to whom the people looked. In speaking
of the disappointment of those for whom there was no room in
the congress hall, he said that he had heard them cry: 'Bung

3. *Persatuan Indonesia*, 1 June 1929.

Karno, we want to come in. Bung Karno, we want to come in.'
He pointed to this as proof of the existence of a popular movement, but the assured use of his own name was a common device
in his speeches. He was the one to whom the excluded would call,
and who would give expression to their hopes. This assured
assumption of his central position went along with his insistence
on neatness in dress and daring in manner – these were his ways
of awakening a feeling of nationalist self-respect as a reaction to
the innumerable humiliations, individual and collective, of
colonial subjection. He was concerned to appear to his followers,
down to the humblest villagers, as an embodiment of their idea
of what a great leader should be. His perception of his standing as
leader of the party was underlined by the adulatory terms of
*Persatuan Indonesia*'s reports of the meeting. Sukarno was always
referred to in the party paper as 'the PNI buffalo'. 'The PNI
buffalo rises from his resting place,' said one of its reports of the
congress, and it went on in terms that caught something of
Sukarno's manner of establishing contact with an audience before
speaking: 'He stands for a minute, silently surveying those
present. All is deadly quiet, so that one could hear a pin drop.
Then as if he had finished drawing together his creative powers he
opens quietly but with his voice gradually becoming more re-
sounding.'

Sukarno's opening speech was followed by those of Soenarjo
and Ali Sastroamidjojo, recently returned from overseas, who
linked the PNI's activities with those of Perhimpunan Indonesia
in Holland. Other speakers gave their attention to more specific
aspects of Indonesia's colonial situation. Euphoria was the order
of the day and for the time being the party's momentum seemed
likely to continue unchecked. After the congress Sukarno resumed
his round of engagements. In July celebrations were held in
Batavia and Bandung to mark the party's second anniversary and
he was the star speaker at each, stressing the growth of Indonesia's national awareness and re-affirming the PNI's goal of
complete independence. A fortnight later he and Iskaq addressed
a meeting of a thousand members at Pekalongan and a week
after that he was in Surabaja helping to celebrate the fifth anniversary of Sutomo's Study Club.

Behind the optimism of these months, however, there was a gathering threat to the PNI's progress. The Dutch authorities felt increasing concern at the rise of nationalism and at the growing popularity of its chief exponent. Over the past two years the Indies Government, though alive to the activities of the PNI, had quietly held its hand. Governor-General A. C. D. de Graeff was a tolerant and humane man; he had been an associate of Idenburg and of other exponents of the Ethical Policy. By contrast with his heavy-handed predecessor, Fock, he was a model of enlightenment and his appointment in 1926 had seemed to herald a return of the ideals of the ethically-inspired administration of Van Limburg Stirum, of which he himself had been a member some years earlier. He had had to deal on his arrival with the communist rebellions, and he had done so sternly, but in his desire to improve relations between Indonesians and the government he was not disposed to adopt a repressive attitude to the new nationalism which had followed. However, proconsular patience was not unlimited and apart from his own inclinations de Graeff found himself under strong pressure from elements of the colonial community, both within the Government and outside it, to restrict the PNI's freedom of action. Why, they asked, should its leaders be free to preach rebellion from one end of Java to the other? As Sukarno's speeches became more inflammatory the Governor-General found it increasingly difficult to resist those who were urging him to act.

In July the first sign of declining permissiveness was given by the arrest of Iwa Kusumasumantri for his political activities among plantation workers in the East Coast Residency in Sumatra. The immediate reaction of the PNI was to turn the action to its own ends, as it had done two years earlier after the arrest of Hatta and his associates in Holland. Protest meetings were held in Batavia, Bandung and Surabaja involving the other associations within PPPKI as well as the PNI itself. Meanwhile Sukarno carried on his other political activities as before. But the rashness which had stirred his audiences for so long was now increasingly risky.

In December he was scheduled to speak at the second PPPKI congress, to be held in Solo from the 25th to the 27th. He took his leave of Inggit and set off by road in company with Gatot Mangkupradja to keep his appointment. From the congress he went on to address a meeting at Jogjakarta on 28 December. The meeting broke up at midnight and Sukarno and Gatot Mangkupradja retired to the house of Sujudi, a lawyer with whom they were to stay. There, in the early hours of the morning, came the inevitable knock at the door. A Dutch officer demanded admittance and with a party of Indonesian police he strode through the house, identified his victims, and arrested Sukarno and Gatot Mangkupradja. The prisoners were hustled off without ceremony to the police station where they were kept in cells for twenty-four hours until, early the following morning, they were placed on the train for Bandung under heavy guard. There they were taken to Bantjeuj Prison, their final place of confinement. The following day they were joined by two other members of the party, Maskun and Supriadinata.

The arrests were part of a large-scale move against PNI leaders. Most of them were released after a short time, but Sukarno and the other three were held for interrogation and subsequent trial. The PNI's period of comparative immunity had come to an end and the court proceedings, when at last they were held, were to be a trial of the new nationalism as well as of its leaders.

# 5
## The Fact of Division 1930–32

Bantjeuj Prison was an old institution and Sukarno later recalled its discomforts – his tiny cell, the primitive toilet arrangements and the misery of isolation.

'It was a shattering experience. I am a sybarite. I am a man who gratifies his senses. I enjoy fine clothes, exciting foods, love-making, and I could not take the isolation, rigidity, filth, the million little humiliations of the lowest form of prison life.'[4]

It was some time before he was allowed a visit even from Inggit and his human contacts were limited to those with his warders and with the police interrogators.

The interrogations seemed pointless to the prisoners. Under Netherlands legislation of 1919 the Indies government possessed the power to deal summarily with cases like this. It could have detained Sukarno and his colleagues without trial, or it could have sent them immediately into exile as it had done with other political prisoners from time to time. Why, on this occasion, had it decided to go through the formalities of a public trial, with all the risks that this would entail? Was there not a danger that formal court proceedings would enable the prisoners to cast themselves in the role of martyrs? Might they not, in this way, win greater popular sympathy than they had achieved through their direct political activities?

A letter from Governor-General de Graeff to Van Limburg Stirum just after the opening of the trial suggests that a mixture of motives was present. A trial gave the government the opportunity to show itself as just – as bound by proper judicial procedures – rather than as arbitrary in its suppression of opposition. It was also felt that the formality of a trial would bring home more sharply to nationalist leaders the dangers of extremism and the desirability of moderation in their future behaviour.[5] But such

4. *Autobiography*, p. 97.
5. S. L. van der Wal, *De Volksraad en de Staatkundige Ontwikkeling van Nederlands-Indië*, Vol. II, Groningen, 1965, pp. 94–5.

advantages were at best speculative; there was equally the possibility that a court might display more clearly the hostility and power of the government and thus strengthen nationalist feeling, or that it might emphasize the futility of moderation. Certainly reflections of this kind determined the nature of the defence Sukarno proposed to adopt.

Formally the prisoners were supposed to be represented by Sujudi, chairman of the Central Java branch of the PNI and Sukarno's host on the night of his arrest, Sartono, a former PI member and now the PNI's vice-chairman, Sastromuljono and Idi Prawiradiputra. But Sukarno, certain in his own mind that he would be convicted, brushed aside their professional assistance and their counsels of moderation. With the example of Hatta before him he decided to conduct his own case and to turn the trial into a political event. It gave him a platform from which the nationalist case could be presented in sharp and dramatic terms. Eight months were to elapse from the time of their arrest before the four men were brought to trial and, day after day, for a good part of that time, with ink and paper supplied from outside and with his toilet box as a desk, he laboured at his defence speech. What emerged was not a defence but a challenge – a rejection, not so much of the court's authority, but of the whole colonial situation of which it was a part. When the case eventually came to trial he was ready with a long oration, loosely structured, wordy and repetitive at times, but passionate, and typical of the rhetorical style he had made his own.[6]

The trial opened at the Bandung District Court at 8.15 on the morning of 18 August 1930 under the presidency of Mr R. Siegenbeek van Heukelom. Its hearing of evidence was spread over twenty-seven days, lasting until 29 September. The four prisoners were charged under Articles 153 *bis*, 169 and 171 of the Penal Law Book. Article 153 made it a crime to contribute by speaking or writing, directly or by implication, to the disturbance of public order; 169 prohibited organizations which encouraged their members to commit offences, and 171 dealt with lying re-

6. Though the speech was delivered in Dutch it has also been published in an Indonesian version, 'Indonesia Menggugat' ['Indonesia Accuses'], Djakarta, 1951.

ports deliberately designed to disturb public tranquillity. The blanket terms of 153 alone would seem to cover any nationalist activity and might be held sufficient to render Sukarno's actions illegal without any further need to establish conspiracy.

The trial opened on a general note. During the first days the President questioned Sukarno on matters relating to the formation of the PNI and the character of its nationalism. What was the meaning of the revolution which Sukarno had predicted? What sort of revolution was it to be? What was the nature of the party's organization? How were its funds spent? What sort of message did it give its followers? How were its leaders trained? Mr Siegenbeek pursued this line of questioning for several days but as the hearing proceeded the inquiry moved to a consideration of more particular issues. Since Article 153 had originally been aimed specifically at the PKI the prosecution attempted to establish links between the PNI and the communist party. Mr Siegenbeek, without much positive result, probed the question of whether the PNI had taken over many old members of the PKI, and whether the PNI's teaching was not similar to that of the PKI. On the ninth day of the trial the prosecution pushed this inquiry further through the examination of its star witness, Police Commissioner H. H. Albreghs of Bandung. Even Albreghs, however, was not able to produce any convincing evidence to support the view that there was any link between the two parties. Then, with an eye to Article 171, the prosecution made a great deal of play with the prediction of Sukarno, and of the PNI in general, that Indonesian freedom would eventually come as a result of a Pacific war which would shake the foundations of the old European empires and give nationalism its opportunity. Attempts were made to show that the PNI had looked to the outbreak of this war in 1930 and that in so doing it had fed the mystical expectations of the populace that 1930 would be a year of great happenings.

Much of the evidence of the last few days of the trial concentrated on this point. A wide variety of witnesses was called, many of them humble village members of the party representing varying degrees of sophistication and political consciousness. They were asked what sort of indoctrination they had received and what their view of the party was. Their evidence did, in fact, suggest that it was the apocalyptic elements of PNI propaganda rather than its more coherent and analytical examination of capitalism and imperialism which had struck answering chords in the popular mind.[7]

To Sukarno this preoccupation of the court with such aspects of his speech-making over the last three years seemed trivial and beside the point. When on 1 December he came to make his own defence he did, towards the close of his speech, give specific attention to these questions, but for the most part the speech was on quite another level. It surveyed, in broad terms, the nature of imperialism, stressing its systematic character, tracing its impact on Indonesia and attempting to place the PNI in that historical context.

Sukarno opened with some observations on the court itself. Arguing that the purpose of his speech was to show the court the character and purpose of the PNI, he referred to the elastic character of the clauses under which he was charged and he warned his judges against the use of the law as a political weapon. From this he plunged into his exposition of the nature of capitalism and imperialism.

Central to his analysis was a distinction between the old and the new imperialism. There were similarities between the two. All imperialism, whether ancient or modern, involved the control by a metropolitan power over the economies of other people. There was, however, an important difference, he argued, between Portuguese or Spanish imperialism or the operations of the East India Companies of Britain and Holland in Southeast Asia on the one hand, and the kind of impact made by the imperial powers from the closing years of the nineteenth century on the other. Modern imperialism was the child of modern capitalism. Quoting extensively from a motley collection of sources – from the Dutch socialist, Troelstra, from H. N. Brailsford, from Otto Bauer, from Engels, Schumpeter and Thomas Moon – he built up his view that

7. See extracts from the trial proceedings given in H. A. Notosoetardjo, *Bung Karno dihadapan Pengadilan Kolonial* ['Bung Karno before the Colonial Court'], Djakarta, 1963. *Persatuan Indonesia* also carried very full reports.

all forms of modern imperialism, whether expressed through the mandate system, the establishment of protectorates or the annexation of full colonies, were products of economic necessity – of the need for markets or for special privileges of investment. In the past the search for trade advantages had led to imperial rivalries between Britain, France, Spain, Portugal and Holland in all parts of the globe – in America, India, the Far East and Southeast Asia. But with the development of modern capitalism the search for avenues of investment and for opportunities for the exploitation of colonial peoples had added a new compulsion to the insatiable drive for empire. Britain in particular had been concerned to block and limit the expansion of her rivals, planting her flag in new parts of the globe, though still without satisfying her desire for possessions. Imperialism had become world-wide in character. It was a hungry process. There might, perhaps, be beneficial by-products to this expansion which might bring knowledge, progress and civilization to underdeveloped peoples, but these were not the basic purposes of empire. The basic purpose was profit.

A good deal of this analysis was couched in Marxist terms. From his account of capitalism as a system which separated labour from the means of production Sukarno moved, without any closely argued connection, to the view that imperialism was a consequence of the export of capital in order to avoid falling interest rates at home. Thus far he marched with Lenin's *Imperialism*. He drew also on under-consumptionist explanations of empire and emphasized the drive for new markets. None of this analysis was tightly constructed and all of it was derivative; his readiness to quote from such a variety of authorities was itself characteristic of his unsystematic approach to the question. However, this was a forensic occasion, not an academic seminar, and the sheer sweep of Sukarno's exposition of imperialism spreading over the surface of the globe and bringing rivalry, conflict and exploitation in its train had a certain grandeur about it.

Having analysed the dynamics of imperialism in general, Sukarno turned to consider its role in Indonesia. He sketched briefly the East India Company's search for commercial monopoly, its policies of extracting forced deliveries from Indonesian cultivators, and its divide-and-rule method through which principality after principality was enslaved. He went on to describe the horrors of the Culture System and finally came to the age of modern imperialism which was born when surplus Dutch capital needed a new outlet. The door was opened to the private investor in 1870, communications were expanded, new enterprises sprang into being and Indonesian wealth was drained from the country on a larger scale than ever before. Indonesia became a source of raw materials for European industry, a market for the products of European industry, a region for exploitation; and the increasing wealth of the country was therefore accompanied by the increasing misery of its population. Was it any wonder, he asked his judges, that a nationalist resistance should spring up?

He then turned to consider that movement, the product of the awakening of the Indonesian people. 'The Indonesian giant, unconscious and lifeless until recently, has now risen and has gathered up its strength.' He pointed out that this was not an isolated and purely Indonesian awakening. Nationalism was to be seen in Egypt, in India, in China and in the Philippines. It was a general movement and the growth of nationalist organization was the product, and not the cause, of this popular awakening. 'The sun does not rise because the cock crows: the cock crows because the sun rises.' Here Sukarno linked the growth of organized nationalism with the deep and unsatisfied longings of the people. 'Why do the people always believe in the coming of a *Ratu Adil*? Why do they still place such faith in the prophecies of King Djoyoboyo? Why are there constant rumours of messianic figures appearing in this or that village?' The reason was simply that 'the weeping people endlessly, unceasingly, wait and long for the coming of help as a man in darkness endlessly, every hour, every minute, every second, waits and wonders when, when will the sun rise'. 'The people's movement is the product of the people's suffering,' and the influence of their leaders was also a product of that suffering. 'We only show the way.'

This was the context in which Sukarno sought to place the PNI and to develop his argument that it was not a movement of an illegal kind. The PNI was concerned to press for independence. Unlike other parties it saw independence as a prerequisite for social development, not as a result of it. Further, because of the essential conflict of interests between imperialists and their subjects the PNI argued that independence could be achieved only by struggle. But what sort of struggle? Here Sukarno moved to the second – and perhaps the more dubious – part of his defence. He wished to insist that the PNI was a revolutionary party leading the struggle for independence; but if that point were established it would be tantamount to an admission that its activities were illegal in terms of the penal code. He had therefore to argue that its revolutionary character stopped short of illegal actions. The party was revolutionary, he said, not in the sense of using bombs and dynamite and insurrection to oppose the power of the State, but only in the sense of wanting radical and swift change. Its method was to build up its mass support and to develop thereby the people's strength (*machtsvorming*). And, said Sukarno with very Javanese rhetoric, spiritual strength was much more important than physical strength and action. 'As if there were no weapons more potent than knives, bombs and dynamite. As if there is not a weapon more powerful than tens of warships, hundreds of aircraft, thousands, hundreds of thousands, millions – of soldiers. As if there is no longer the weapon of the spirit, which if conscious and aroused, burning the hearts of the people, is more powerful than a thousand rifles, a thousand cannon, yes, a thousand armadas and a thousand armies, fully equipped and armed.' The PNI's task was to mobilize this weapon of the spirit, to create unity, to build a mass movement, to give it consciousness and to prepare it for the struggle – but not to make a rebellion. The distinction might have seemed a fine one to the court. To the possible argument that the building up of the people's power would ultimately lead to rebellion Sukarno replied that the future could not be known. European developments might change things. Capitalism might be overthrown in Holland, for example. Holland might cut the imperialist tie herself. These things could not be foreseen. For the moment the important thing was that the PNI had remained within the law.

And so to Sukarno's defence of his own actions as a PNI leader. The PNI was a legal party and sought to operate by legal means. If there was unrest among the people there were reasons for it – all of them pre-dating the formation of the PNI. The party was not the cause of the unrest but rather a symbol of it. Though the PNI was concerned to shape and mobilize popular feeling it did not incite its members to commit crimes. And what of the charge that he had spread lying reports calculated to sow disaffection? His statements about the coming of a Pacific war were supposed to fall into this category. But, he argued, he had not predicted that such a war was about to occur – only that it would occur at some future time. The clash of interests of the imperialist powers was such that a conflict of this kind was likely.

The speech lasted for two days and altogether it was a marathon performance. Sukarno had ranged from highly theoretical exposition to detailed legal argument. He slipped from passionate oratory to readings of tedious excerpts from his authorities. Throughout it all he spoke within the framework of a broadly coherent point of view and gave, in effect, a statement of the PNI's whole intellectual position. He was adamant on one point – that independence was the goal and that it was the prerequisite for other things. Exactly how it was to be achieved was far from clear, and what sort of society was to follow was shrouded in Sukarno's own poetic imagination; he saw merely 'a brightly beckoning future'. 'Indonesia's future appears now only as an aura, beautiful as the approaching dawn. It is a voice of promise, like the far off music of the gamelan on a clear moonlight night.'

As a rhetorical exercise the speech revealed his own tricks of style and phrase. There was much repetition, though usually in slightly different forms, of words, phrases and ideas, as he built them up to his points of climax:

'There is no people who can attain greatness without national independence, there is no country that can be firm and strong without being free. Conversely, no colony can attain glory; no colony can attain greatness. Therefore every colonial people desires freedom so that it can attain greatness. Every people which lacks freedom, every people which because of that is unable to control its own affairs in its own interests and for its own happiness, lives in an unsettled atmosphere . . .

'The PNI takes up the inner essence of the colonial question, tackles the colonial question directly in its fundamentals, takes up the basic philosophy of the colonial question, that is to say – let us repeat – that in every colonial system there is a conflict of interests between the imperialist and the native people.'

There was repetition too in the sense of echoing the words and ideas developed hours before. Again and again, for example, he returned to his phrase about bombs and dynamite. Again and again he referred, and in the same words, to the essential conflict between colonial rulers and their subjects.

As a propaganda occasion, Sukarno's defence served its purpose. It failed to impress his judges however. Hatta, in the more liberal setting of the Netherlands, had managed to secure his own acquittal, but the colonial atmosphere of Bandung was another matter. On 22 December the prisoners were convicted. Sukarno was given a four-year gaol sentence. His companions escaped with lighter terms – Gatot received two years, Maskun twenty months and Supriadinata fifteen.

The prisoners were sent to serve their sentences in Sukamiskin prison near Bandung. (It is said that Sukarno, during his brief period of practice as an architect, had worked on the plans for Sukamiskin, just as he had drawn the perspectives for that tasteless symbol of colonialism, Bandung's Grand Preanger Hotel.) Again he felt the horrors of isolation, tempered only by contact with other prisoners at meal and exercise times. Inggit was allowed to visit him twice a month. In a letter from prison he described his employment making notebooks in the prison's printing works and being allowed, at the end of the day, only six minute's bathing to clean his grease-covered body.[8]

It was during this period of imprisonment that Sukarno embarked on a closer study of Islam than he had made before. Books could be brought into him after careful inspection but political books were not allowed and the resources of the prison library were very meagre. However, the Koran, the Bible and works of religious commentary were available to him, and Sukarno describes himself as finding Islam for the first time. It was hardly a conversion. Sukarno was never to embrace Islam in the whole-

8. 17 May 1931. 'Keadaan Dipendjara Sukamiskin, Bandung' ['The Situation in Sukamiskin Prison, Bandung'], published in Sukarno, *Dibawah Bendera Revolusi*, p. 115.

hearted and doctrinally complete way demanded by leaders of Indonesia's Muslim organizations. Rather he deepened his appreciation of Islam and added it to the other ideological influences he had made his own. He espoused it, that is to say, in the syncretistic fashion of the Javanese *priyayi*, and though he saw himself as continuing to seek a synthesis of secular and religious thought, the real *santri* would continue to regard him with suspicion.

Early in 1931 his lawyers lodged an appeal against his sentence. The appeal was heard by the Supreme Court of Justice in Batavia, which on 17 April gave its decision upholding that of the Bandung District Court. However, the authorities, in part as a political gesture, and in part because it was believed that the trial and its outcome had successfully served the purpose of warning Indonesian nationalists of the possible consequence of their agitation, decided to reduce the sentences. It was announced that the prisoners would be released in December 1931.

On 31 December Sukarno stepped out from Sukamiskin a free man. As he turned to resume his leadership of Indonesian nationalism he found the movement in sad disarray.

The mass arrests of PNI leaders in December 1929 had caught the party surprisingly unprepared, both psychologically and organizationally. It would seem, in retrospect, that the outward success of the party in 1928 and 1929 had lulled the leadership into a false sense of security. The ease with which new branches had been formed, the ready emotional response of the audiences which had gathered to hear Sukarno and other leaders and the apparent tolerance of the Government towards the party's activities had combined to conceal the fragility of nationalism's new-found unity, and to conceal also the material weakness of the movement. This optimism was rudely shattered on 29 December 1929, and, though the whole burden of the PNI's propaganda had stressed the intransigence of imperialism and the consequent need for struggle, the party seemed to have had no plans to deal with what should have been an expected contingency. Apart from a PPPKI rally there was hardly even a murmur of protest at the arrests.

In the immediate crisis Sartono assumed the role of acting-chairman and under his cautious leadership the remnants of the executive decided to suspend, for the time being, all of the party's activities. This decision was taken ostensibly in order not to prejudice the prospects of the prisoners, but there was undoubtedly also a recognition of the danger of further political action. If the purpose of the government in swooping on the leaders of the party had been to curb its activities, it was tremendously successful.

With the conviction of the prisoners a year later the new leadership could no longer delay the formulation of a longer-term policy for the party. After its year of quiescence should it again seek to mobilize its forces, protesting against Sukarno's imprisonment and attacking the government on other issues? Or should it seek to preserve itself by the pursuit of moderation? The resolution of these questions turned a great deal on personalities, but the debate about alternative courses of action also gave an airing to the critical and long-standing tactical dilemmas of the nationalist movement. The old issue of co-operation versus non-cooperation was among the most important. There were those who drew from Sukarno's arrest the moral that radical demands for independence were futile in the face of overwhelming Dutch power and who argued that moderation, and a willingness to work with constituted authority, offered the only hope of gaining results in the long run. The pursuit of limited objectives within the forum of the Volksraad would secure gradual concessions more effectively, they argued, than political rallies and mass action. There were others who drew the opposite lesson: that the action taken against the PNI leadership had, in effect, made the party illegal, thus underlining the futility of co-operation and the necessity for struggle. Closely connected with this issue was the question of whether mass parties or élitist parties were more effective. If co-operation versus non-cooperation had been the major issue in the late twenties the question of mass action versus cadre training was to be one of the main issues of the early thirties. Finally there was the question of what long-term strategy should be: conspiracy and planned insurrection or prolonged and unspectacular preparation for a struggle far in the future.

These were crucial questions, but the interesting thing about the discussion of them was Sukarno's own growing significance as the absent leader. The spectacle of his trial with its echoes of martyrdom had focused attention on him as nationalism's central figure. In prison he remained the symbol of conciliation – the person who could resolve conflicts and concentrate attention upon the imperialist enemy. His standing was enhanced, in particular, by comparison with the caution of Sartono, and the inaction of the party in the months following his arrest stood in sharp contrast to its earlier vigour. With the PNI paralysed other less provocative nationalist groups moved to the centre of the stage. Dr Sutomo, for example, sought to give political expression to the ideals of his Surabaja Study Club through a new party, Persatuan Bangsa Indonesia ('Association of the Indonesian People'), founded in October 1930. A month earlier the Partai Rakjat Indonesia ('Indonesian People's Party' – PRI) had been formed in Batavia to press for an extension of political rights for Indonesians within the framework of Dutch rule, with the ultimate goal of an autonomous Indonesia under the Dutch crown. While these new organizations urged moderation and constitutional action, the PNI's own leadership remained confused and silent.

No revolutionary party could survive indefinitely on these terms, and it was, perhaps, only to be expected that the PNI's executive should at last decide, immediately after the Supreme Court had upheld the conviction of the four leaders on 17 April 1931, to dissolve the party. This decision was taken at an extraordinary congress on 25 April and it was quickly followed by a further decision to create a new party, uncompromised by an adverse judicial decision and therefore, in theory, able to make a fresh start. In this way Partai Indonesia (Partindo) came into being under Sartono's leadership on 29 April.

Sartono's rationale in dissolving the PNI and replacing it by Partindo was essentially legalistic. He took the view that Sukarno's conviction was a direct consequence of his activity in the PNI and that it meant that the PNI was, automatically, illegal. To change the party into a new one was to create a new legal entity which was not automatically under that ban. His reasoning did not appeal to all members of the party. There were many who complained that the dissolution of the PNI had been a minority decision, prompted by a handful of intellectuals and not really representative of the wishes of the party as a whole. There was criticism, in particular, of Sartono's failure to consult branches. More basically there was opposition to what was felt to be a change in the very character of the PNI, going beyond a change of name and legal personality. Though the new party hoped to capture the PNI's membership, and though its objectives were, on the face of it, broadly similar to those of the PNI, Partindo seemed to many to be a timid party by comparison. It appeared to be anxious to pursue its goals through the existing framework of Dutch rule and therefore to be on an equal footing with such groups as the moderate PRI.

Among the weightier critics of the change was Hatta, who was still in Holland but who kept a close eye on Indonesian developments. Hatta characterized Partindo as an imitation PNI. His views, made known through letters to the nationalist press, were that the dissolution of the party represented a failure in the leadership. He argued further that such a failure would be likely to recur if the government decided again to act against nationalist activities as it had done in December 1929 – merely to form a new party would not resolve the problem. To meet the permanent danger it was necessary to follow a different course altogether – to train a larger corps of leaders so that arrests could never again paralyse the organization as a whole. This was a long-standing view of Hatta's. As early as 1929 he had said it was necessary to produce thousands of Sukarnos and not just to applaud the one.[9] His criticism, repeated in 1931, was tremendously important for it focused the spotlight very clearly on the kind of personal contribution Sukarno, for good or ill, had made to Indonesian nationalism. The PNI had not been founded by him alone but he had, by the force of his personality, put his own stamp upon it and shaped it as a mass party. Hatta's criticism made the individual nature of Sukarno's contribution very clear, but he did not grasp, as Sukarno had done, the importance of mass support and action. He was concerned essentially with organization, whereas with

9. *Persatuan Indonesia*, 1 and 15 February 1929.

Sukarno it was not so much the party which was important as the movement.

Under the influence of Hatta's views a number of organizations critical of Partindo, and seeking a more radical leadership sprang up in different parts of the country in mid 1931. Some of these groups joined to form the Golongan Merdeka ('Freedom Group') which founded its own newspaper, *Daulat Ra'jat* ('People's Sovereignty'), to serve as its mouthpiece. At a meeting in Jogjakarta in December the Golongan Merdeka and other like-minded groups decided to merge into a new organization: the Club Pendidikan Nasional Indonesia ('Indonesian National Education Club'), to be known as the Club PNI or the PNI Baru – 'New PNI').[10] The name of the new organization was deliberately intended to carry echoes of the old PNI, but one of its main aims was the training of leaders as Hatta had urged, so that there would always be a number of people to step into the shoes of those removed by government action. This was the group with which Hatta and Sjahrir decided to associate themselves when they returned to Indonesia from Holland. Sjahrir returned to the Indies in late 1931 or early 1932 and immediately assumed the chairmanship of the new PNI.[11] Hatta replaced Sjahrir when he returned on 24 August 1932.

In this way the unity of Sukarno's nationalism was broken. The united front represented by the PPPKI had disappeared. The PNI was dissolved. Its more cautious members had found a new home in Partindo, which sought mass membership but which looked to action within the law rather than outside it. Radical opinion was turning in the direction of the New PNI. This was broadly the situation which had established itself towards the end of 1931 and which awaited Sukarno on his release in December.

Sukarno had watched the emergence of the new alignments from prison. He had been distressed by the collapse of the PNI, but he kept to himself his views about the merits of the new par-

10. *Sin Po*, 28 December 1931.

11. Sol Tas, 'Souvenirs of Sjahrir' (translated by R. McVey), *Indonesia*, No. 8, October 1969. A translator's note (footnote 12) states that Sjahrir returned in February 1932, but *Daulat Ra'jat* listed him as its Editor in Issue 12, 10 January 1932.

ties which had come into existence in its place. Which of them should receive his support? This question preoccupied him as he awaited his release, but it was natural that he should decide to keep all factions in the dark for the time being about the trend of his thinking. He was out of touch with the exact details of the situation and his mind was not made up. It would have been foolish to commit himself to one or other group before he had savoured the new situation at first hand and made his own assessment. But there were also less tangible considerations. At the point of his release Sukarno, quite consciously, was exemplifying a common theme in the Indonesian tradition – that of withdrawal and return. As Ardjuno, the hero of the *Mahabharata*, had undergone a period of trial and abstinence in order to build up his spiritual power (*sakti*), or as Airlangga had withdrawn for a long period of meditation and religious exercise before emerging to create his kingdom of East Java, so Sukarno, removed from the world for a time by his imprisonment, carried a special authority on his return. In the eyes of the Javanese it was a mystical authority and Sukarno was quite aware of the role he was playing. He saw his time in Sukamiskin as a retreat in the course of which, by meditation, he could draw on supernatural sources of power. In more practical terms his very hesitation at this point underlined his own central importance. It drew all eyes to him as his followers, seeing him still as the great unifier, waited anxiously for him to declare himself.

This pattern of behaviour with its blend of mystical and pragmatic elements was to be repeated on other occasions in Sukarno's career. Again and again he was to stand aside from events – leaving the country or simply withdrawing from the capital for a time – and then returning with renewed strength to resolve conflicts. It should not detract from the symbolic character of the occasion in December 1931 to suggest that Sukarno played the drama to the full. He withheld his final decision as long as possible, waiting upon events almost until the decision made itself.

Sukarno's release was indeed a dramatic occasion. In prison he had heard, during a visit from Husni Thamrin, of plans to give

him a massive welcome as he stepped from the gates of Sukamiskin. Supporters from near and far were to gather at the prison
early on the morning of his release, and were to conduct him in
triumph into Bandung. While moved by the news he felt that such
a mass reception would be inappropriate, and on 14 December he
wrote to Sartono to discourage the plan.[12] There would be ample
opportunity for his friends in Bandung to meet him at home
during the course of the day. For others of his comrades his intention of attending the forthcoming *Indonesia Raya* ('Great Indonesia') congress, called by Sutomo at Surabaja, would make
possible further reunions.

Despite this request, and despite the action of the police in
stopping a cavalcade of welcome before it reached the prison
gates, Sukarno's release did become something of a triumphal
progress.[13] His relatives and friends greeted him at Sukamiskin
and a procession of eight cars, under police surveillance, was
waiting to take him home. In Bandung there were crowds to cheer
him, and all through the day, still under the eyes of the police, he
was busy receiving a continuous stream of visitors coming to pay
their respects. For one as dependent as Sukarno upon popular
recognition it was a moving experience.

Nor was there to be any respite for the moment. Early next
morning he boarded the train for Surabaja for the welcome
planned for him by Sutomo. He was seen off by a large gathering
and at each stop – at Tjibatu, Kroja, Jogja, Solo, Madiun, Kerto-
sono – crowds gathered to cheer him. A crowd of six thousand
was waiting when the train pulled into Surabaja in the evening.
He was carried shoulder high from the station to cries of 'Long
Live Sukarno' and the singing of 'Indonesia Raya'. At the Hotel
Muslimin another great crowd was waiting to welcome him. He
was given only a few minutes to bath and change and was then
taken to the congress where, within an hour of his arrival in Surabaja, he was on the platform listening to the waves of applause of
delegates from a wide variety of nationalist organizations. Sutomo
made a short speech of welcome. Sukarno's response was brief

12. *Dibawah Bendera Revolusi*, p. 119.
13. Accounts of it can be found in Sutomo's paper *Soeara Oemoem*, 31
December 1931 and 2 January 1932.

but charged with emotion. The applause, he said, was not for him as a person but as a leader and a symbol of Free Indonesia. He felt like the hero Kokrosono, newly descended from meditation and self-denial and ready to take up the struggle. But he was saddened to see the movement divided. He concluded his remarks by leading in the singing of 'Indonesia Raya' while all stood (except the representatives of the Indies government who were there to keep an eye on proceedings and who stayed firmly in their seats).

On the following day he spoke to the congress at greater length, making a moving appeal for unity and stressing the importance of passion in the struggle for freedom. 'Give me a thousand men and with them I will move Mount Semeru; but give me ten youths of spirit, burning with love for their native land and I will shake the earth.'[14]

With the emotion of this welcome to sustain him Sukarno returned to Bandung to take up again the vocation of political action. His main preoccupation was, of course, the divided condition of the movement, and one of his first tasks was the redrafting of the PPPKI's constitution as a step towards reviving this now moribund coalition. More than this was needed, however. In stressing the need for unity in his speech at Surabaja on 2 January he had referred quite specifically to the rivalry between Partindo and the New PNI, and now he was forced to come squarely to grips with the problem. Which of the two should he join? Partindo contained most of his old associations and its general approach, on the surface at least, seemed closest to his own. But the New PNI could not be dismissed. It had responsible and respected leaders. It could, with some justification, claim to be more radical than its rival and Sukarno was drawn instinctively to radical rather than to cautious thinking. Both groups, he believed, were genuine nationalist organizations with the interests of Indonesian independence at heart. It seemed to him that the differences between them over principles and tactics were not fundamental enough to be the cause of division between them, and his earnest desire was, therefore, to unite them. This was the course of action most suited to his own skills of conciliation and persuasion. From the point of view of his own ambitions it was

14. *Soeara Oemoem*, 5 January 1932.

also sound practical sense. A united movement – a movement united indeed by his own efforts – would give him a central position in the struggles of the day. A divided movement would leave him merely as a faction-leader.

This mixture of idealism and political common sense quickly determined for him his immediate course of action. Partindo leaders came to him to persuade him to join their party, arguing that it was indeed the old PNI. He refused. For the time being he could not align himself with either side because to do so would only confirm and prolong the division. If he was to mediate he must keep his independence. At the root of his attempt at conciliation was his old conviction that a straightforward nationalist doctrine would enable competing groups to submerge their differences, a belief which had seemed to be justified when he had constructed the PPPKI in 1927. Now he attempted to repeat the miracle. In the following months he negotiated with the leaders of Partindo and the New PNI and addressed their branches, but this time the miracle seemed slow in coming and finally Sukarno was forced to admit failure.

The failure was due in some measure to the fact that circumstances had changed since 1927. The secular nationalist idea had been an adequate rallying point for the splintered nationalist movement after the crushing of the communist revolts; it had seemed to offer a new and hopeful approach to the problem of imperialism and colonial status. But once radical nationalism itself had come under the ban of the government the optimism it had engendered vanished quickly. In the early 1930s, therefore, there existed a more sober assessment of realities – a recognition of the power of Dutch authority and of the inevitable slowness of the progress towards independence. This more pessimistic atmosphere made Sukarno's magic less effective. But of importance too was the fact that in 1932 he had to deal with new men – men whom he could not easily dominate and who had their own very definite views about the best strategy to adopt. The most significant of them were, of course, Hatta and Sjahrir. Hatta, as we have noticed, was still overseas, but his influence on Indonesian developments through his writing and also through Sjahrir was very close. Sukarno's experience with the pair made him aware of the presence of a new leadership, quite different in temper from his own, but perhaps of comparable force. His negotiations with them in 1932 laid the basis of a future (somewhat ambiguous) relationship of co-operation and suspicion – a relationship of opposites held together in reciprocal tension – which was to be a continuing theme in Sukarno's political career even after Hatta and Sjahrir had disappeared from active political life.

How far was the difference between Sukarno and the Hatta–Sjahrir combination a matter of ideas and how far of personalities? In 1932 it was Sukarno who made the conciliatory moves. He went to Sjahrir and his colleagues – not they to him – and attempted to convince them of the need for unity. To Sukarno there seemed to be no serious issue of principle at stake. In terms of policy Sjahrir and Hatta, as we have seen, wished to concentrate on the leadership problem and lay the foundation for the future by training cadres. Sukarno, on the other hand, was aware of the danger in what seemed to him to be an élitist approach – it might shield the leaders of nationalism from life-giving contact with the people at large. By contrast he wished to move back immediately to the mobilization of mass action. But was this difference, after all, so great? Could not cadre formation be combined with mass action? Was the gap between the two points of view really so wide as to rule out that sort of compromise? To Hatta, long critical of Sukarno's leadership, it did seem that a fundamental question – a whole style of political behaviour – was in the balance. He was contemptuous of what had been achieved so far by action in the Sukarno manner. The course of events had demonstrated, he believed, the ineffectiveness, and indeed the unreality, of mass organization. Even the kind of unity represented by the PPPKI, he argued, was a superficial unity – a mere stringing together of diverse bits and pieces with no genuine ties, a *persatèan* rather than a *persatuan*. (*Persatuan* means a union; *persatèan* is derived from *saté* – small pieces of meat grilled on a skewer – and the term, by extension, meant a superficial unity.) For both Hatta and Sjahrir it was wrong to gloss over genuine differences between the main elements within the nationalist movement, for doing so would in the long run weaken its effectiveness. Rather it was important to support the correctly based courses of action and to fight against the incorrect. It was important, that is to say, actually to promote struggle within the movement. What had been for Sukarno a mere difference of emphasis was thus transformed by Hatta's famous inflexibility into a difference of principle.

Though the discussion between Sukarno and the leaders of the New PNI was conducted in the language of strategy and tactics, in the end the failure of negotiations was probably due to basic differences of personality. The two sides were indeed very different from each other. Hatta's cast of mind was drier, more analytical, less volatile and less ebullient than that of Sukarno. As a person he seemed colourless by contrast with Sukarno's quicksilver manner. He could not sway large audiences and probably even felt that to play upon the emotions of a crowd through the use of tricks of rhetoric was slightly dishonest. His private life was controlled and austere. These qualities were heightened by his academic training in Rotterdam. For him, words and ideas should be handled in a disciplined fashion and not used in a calculated way for emotive purposes. For Sukarno, on the other hand, words and ideas were agents of passion, and passion should lead to action.

These very basic personality differences naturally inhibited the attempts of Sukarno to negotiate an agreement with Hatta's followers for a reunified nationalist movement. The tactical arguments in which both sides engaged were in fact rationalizations rather than reflections of genuine differences of principle. Or rather, principle and temperament went together. Sukarno by temperament saw the possibility of moving mountains by faith and possessed the skills with which, just conceivably, he might have achieved the miracle. But it was a fragile position and, with his sense of destiny, he needed to be taken seriously. He depended on the enthusiastic response of others and his self-esteem was easily punctured by the direct criticisms of Hatta and the casual superciliousness of Sjahrir. They exposed his underlying insecurity. For this reason there could be no easy co-operation between the three leaders, though in fact the nationalist movement needed the passion of the one as much as the discipline of the others.

When at last it became clear to him that Partindo and the New PNI could not be joined, Sukarno's own course of action had more or less determined itself. Partindo by this time had committed itself to a policy of non-cooperation. This was still an important issue with Sukarno, and caused a public dispute with Hatta when the latter was invited in November 1932 to accept nomination as a candidate for election to the Dutch parliament. Hatta did not proceed with his candidacy but in considering the proposal seriously he laid himself open to attack by Sukarno for his willingness to abandon the principle of uncompromising opposition to the Dutch.[15] Partindo was also attempting, with some success, to be a mass party, having enrolled seven thousand members by October 1932. In its whole character it was the nearest existing organization to the old PNI. In the circumstances it was natural that Sukarno should decide to cast his lot in that direction. At the end of July he announced his decision to join Partindo, and was subsequently elected to its chairmanship. His own account of his decision did not touch the basic elements of incompatibility in the situation. In a statement written for public consumption and published in his own journal *Fikiran Ra'jat* he recalled his passionate desire for unity on his release from Sukamiskin. He had attempted tirelessly to close the gap between the two parties, he said, to cool heat, to end misunderstandings, and during this period he had been careful not to lean to either side. Having failed, he had now to commit himself to one party or the other in order to carry on his own struggle. Both parties were concerned with the interests of the people; in selecting Partindo he was simply exercising his right to choose.[16]

15. See 'Djawab saja pada Saudara Mohammad Hatta' ['My Reply to Friend Hatta'] in *Dibawah Bendera Revolusi*, p. 207. See also Dahm's excellent treatment of the content of the discussion, *Sukarno and the Struggle for Indonesian Independence*, Ithaca, 1969, pp. 158–62.

16. 'Maklumat dari Bung Karno kepada Kaum Marhaen Indonesia' ['Announcement from Bung Karno to the Indonesian Marhaen'], *Dibawah Bendera Revolusi*, p. 167.

# 6
# Exile

Sukarno's decision to join Partindo set the seal upon a continuing division in Indonesian nationalism. The division, never clear-cut, had been incipient for several years – indeed ever since the coming together of PI leaders and the leaders of Bandung's nationalist youth to form the PNI in 1927. Under Sukarno's chairmanship the potential uneasiness in the relations of the two groups had been avoided. With his arrest there was an opportunity for their differing approaches to political action to express themselves more clearly. Sukarno's release, coinciding roughly with the return of Hatta and Sjahrir from Holland, provided leadership for the two elements and crystallized the division.

The rivalry between Partindo and the New PNI is sometimes seen as a rivalry between radicalism and moderation, or between left and right. In the early thirties such antitheses were not applicable. Partindo, with its emphasis on non-cooperation, self-help and mass action, certainly bore the closer resemblance to the old PNI, but the New PNI could by no means be called moderate, and indeed with its emphasis on the gradual preparation of genuine leaders, it might with justice have claimed to be more radical than Partindo which was attempting to mobilize the might of the masses.

With his assumption of Partindo's chairmanship Sukarno slipped rapidly back into his leadership style of 1928–9. His life consisted once more of rounds of speeches and a certain amount of political journalism, plus a little desultory architectural practice in partnership with *Ir* Rooseno as a means of earning a modest income. The columns of *Fikiran Ra'jat* carried his articles – discussions in the Marxist vein of the unreality of bourgeois political democracy in the absence of economic democracy, lessons on non-cooperation and mass action, somewhat polemical exchanges with Hatta, a classical statement of his distinction between Marhaen and proletarian, and other writings of a similarly didactic kind.[17] He also conducted, as a regular feature, a question-and-answer column in which his ideas could be developed in a popular form.[18] Questions were varied, ranging from practical inquiries ('Where can I buy Jaures' *French Revolution*, and for how much?')[19] through questions relating to his own writings and speeches ('What language is *machtsvorming*, and what does it mean in Indonesian?')[20] or to the local political scene ('What are the parties which are combined to form PPPKI?')[21] to questions of general political theory ('What is the meaning of imperialism?'[22] 'What is the difference between Fascism, Nazism, Marxism and Communism?').[23] Some questioners were referred to articles in earlier editions of *Fikiran Ra'jat* or *Suluh Indonesia Muda* for fuller discussions of the points raised. Others received pithy, off-the-cuff definitions of complex points. This regular column enabled Sukarno, by repetition, to drive home his own assessments of events. 'Q. Is it true that PPPKI has become a brake on the nationalist movement? A. No. Not very radical, but not a brake.'[24] A regular question was whether any difference of principle separated Partindo and the New PNI, to which Sukarno always replied that in his view there was no significant difference.[25]

For the most part his essays and his answers to questions showed no great change in the ideas he had developed before his arrest. The same themes recurred: the essential coincidence of interest of the different streams of nationalism and the necessity therefore of unity; the concept of Marhaen; the ideas of *machtsvorming* and mass action; the principle of non-cooperation and the belief in the sharpness of the antithesis between ruler and ruled. One of his answers summed it all up in a couple of sentences: '. . . we can only expect improvement when we have

17. A selection of his writings from this period appears in Sukarno, *Dibawah Bendera Revolusi*.

18. A collection of extracts from this column have been published under the title *Primbon Politik* ['Political Divining Manual'], ed. H. A. Notosoetardjo, Djakarta, 1963.

19. *Primbon Politik*, p. 127.
20. ibid., p. 141.
21. ibid., p. 143.
22. ibid., p. 135.
23. ibid., p. 173.
24. ibid., p. 159.
25. e.g. ibid., pp. 74–5.

enough strength to demand that improvement. The other camp will not be willing to make this or that improvement if they are not *forced* to do so by our own *strength*.' But some additions to his earlier thought, or at least some modifications of emphasis, can be seen.

Sukarno's most significant piece of writing during this period was an essay entitled 'Achieving Independent Indonesia'[26] which was the fruit of a few days' holiday at Pengalengan, a mountain resort to the south of Bandung, in March 1933. The essay bore a strong family resemblance to 'Indonesia Accuses'; its opening pages contained the same distinction between the old and the new imperialism and the same view that surplus capital was the cause of empire, the draining of colonial wealth its consequence. The same sort of figures were marshalled to prove the point and again the mobilization of popular power was advanced as the means to combat imperialism. But as the essay unfolded it revealed a new perception of further goals of nationalism lying beyond mere political independence. Indonesia was once free, Sukarno argued, rejecting the view that the period of Indian influence had been a period of Indian imperialism, but the people themselves had never been free. Before their subjection to Dutch capitalism they had been subjected to the feudalism of the Hindu kingdoms. From this argument Sukarno moved to the view that independence would not of itself bring freedom and justice to the ordinary man. Independence was merely a 'golden bridge' to a just society – a prerequisite, but not the ultimate goal in itself.

Towards the end of the essay he returned to his distinction between political and economic democracy:

> Our democracy ... must not be a democracy *à la* Europe and America, which is just a 'portrait of parties', a political democracy only ... but a political and economic democracy which gives one hundred per cent sovereignty to the people in the ordering of their political and economic affairs.[27]

Nothing very specific was said about the way in which the just society was to be achieved once the golden bridge had been

26. 'Mentjapai Indonesia Merdeka' (published in *Dibawah Bendera Revolusi*, p. 257).

27. *Dibawah Bendera Revolusi*, p. 320.

crossed, but acceptance of the idea of social transformation as a further goal to be sought after independence was, if not a new element in his thinking, at least given a fuller exposition than before, and his discussion of the question contained one of his very rare references to the need for class conflict – not between proletarian and capitalist but between Marhaen and capitalist. The carriage of victory as it crossed the golden bridge, he said, must be in the hands of the Marhaen. 'Across the bridge the road divides: one way goes to the world of Marhaenist welfare and the other to the world of Marhaenist misery.' The Marhaen in control of the carriage must see that it did not take the second road leading to Indonesian capitalism and an Indonesian bourgeois society.[28] The evils of capitalism were a continuing part of Sukarno's thinking, certainly, but the idea that Indonesia's little people might have to fight against Indonesian capitalists was not.

The essay also showed a greater concern with the facts of Dutch repressiveness than Sukarno had shown himself to possess as PNI chairman. At least, he now seemed to be aware of the fact that more than mere *machtsvorming* was needed if the power of the colonial régime was to be shaken. We find, in consequence, an exposition of the need for a more conscious and determined fighting role for a nationalist party. Mass action is useless without leadership and direction. The function of a revolutionary party must be to supply that direction. It must be a vanguard. In this concept of the party as a vanguard there were echoes of Lenin, as there were in the further idea that a vanguard party must be organized on the principles of democratic centralism. But perhaps there were more immediate echoes of Hatta and Sjahrir. Sukarno's emphasis on the structure and function of a revolutionary party was his answer to their argument that oratory and inspiration were no substitute for planning and the careful preparation of continuing leadership in the mounting of effective political action. This idea of a mass-plus-vanguard party seemed to be a new development in his thinking.

Yet was this really as much of a change as it seemed to be? Or was it merely a matter of words? There was indeed self-delusion still in Sukarno's analysis. The idea of a vanguard party was never

28. ibid., p. 315.

translated into political reality – there proved to be insufficient time for that, in any case – but even the vision remained misty. It was described by Sukarno in rhetorical rather than in practical terms and it did not really fall in with the approach of the New PNI. In fact a vanguard concept, if it was to be effective, would inevitably involve the division of the movement – the expulsion of doubters and the doctrinally unsound. This, indeed, was just what Sjahrir wanted. But Sukarno in speaking of a vanguard still romantically expected it to embrace all factions, still stressed the Javanese principle of harmony.

'Achieving Indonesian Independence', though a representative statement of Sukarno's views at the time, was to be of comparatively limited influence for it was banned by the Government before it could circulate very widely. These were not the permissive days of the late twenties and the seizure of the pamphlet was a sign that the Government was not prepared to allow Sukarno – or any other leader – the same rights of organization and propaganda as it had permitted before. On 1 August 1933, as he left an executive meeting in Batavia, Sukarno was arrested for the second time.

It was certainly a testimony to Sukarno's quality that Partindo had flourished under his leadership. In less than a year its membership had more than doubled. The two dozen-odd branches of October 1932, comprising about seven thousand members, had risen to seventy-one branches with about twenty thousand members at the time of his arrest.[29] But the survival-power of the party proved to be little greater than that of the old PNI. For all Sukarno's talk of the role of a vanguard party and his apparent awareness of the hard political realities of his environment, he had not managed to create an instrument which could ride out a period of government oppression. He could hardly be blamed for that. The political realities were indeed hard and until Dutch power had been shattered by the Pacific War, whose coming Sukarno had foreseen, it was more than a match for any conceivable movement of Indonesian resistance. Whether led by Sartono

29. Dahm, *Sukarno and the Struggle for Indonesian Independence*, Ithaca, 1969, p. 158.

or Sukarno, or by Hatta and Sjahrir, any nationalist enterprise was bound to be too light for the counterpoise of so great an opposition. Sukarno's arrest proved to be the beginning of decisive government action which was to subdue and control the nationalist movement for the remaining years of colonial rule.

The whole atmosphere surrounding the arrest was in sharp contrast to that of 1929. Colijn, who was now Prime Minister of the Netherlands, had long been an opponent of Indonesian nationalism and his views had their effect on the Indies Government. Governor-General de Jonge, the instrument of Holland's hard line, did not in any case share the liberal sympathies of his predecessor, and there was to be no nonsense this time about a public trial. Summary justice and the exercise of executive discretion seemed a far more effective way of proceeding. Sukarno was at first imprisoned once more in Sukamiskin, but this was merely a temporary place of confinement; it was the Government's intention to remove him from further political action by exiling him from Java.

Before this happened Sukarno, at the end of November 1933, cast a bombshell into the midst of his followers by resigning from Partindo. His letter of resignation stated that he was no longer in full agreement with the party's policies. The public reaction to the news was one of shock. Was he, the great opponent of compromise, about to become a co-operator himself as his critics claimed?[30] The Dutch-language Press had the story of his resignation first, which in itself seemed significant. He was said by some to be no longer a revolutionary leader and his picture was taken down from the walls of Partindo's headquarters. The motives for his resignation are not clear. Was it an act of despair at his new confinement, or an attempt to secure gentler treatment and therefore a sign of a lack of moral fibre? Or did it represent a real change of attitude about the practicalities of political struggle and was it therefore, as Dahm has suggested, a coming to grips with reality and, as such, 'his *first revolutionary deed*'?[31] One cannot

30. 'Tragedie Soekarno'. Editorial (by Hatta) in *Daulat Ra'jat*, No. 80, 30 November 1933. See also *Oetoesan Indonesia* for an indication of the heat of the controversy.

31. Dahm, op. cit., p. 172. (The italics are Dahm's.)

know for sure since Sukarno was given no opportunity to become a co-operator. Early in 1934 he was whisked off by train to Surabaja and, together with Inggit, her mother and Ratna Djuami, her niece, he was put on board the KPM vessel *Van Riebeeck* for the island of Flores where, in the remote village of Endeh, he was expected to make his home for the foreseeable future.

Having seized Sukarno the Government moved against other leaders. In February 1934 Hatta and Sjahrir were arrested and exiled, also without trial, to the notorious Tanah Merah prison camp at Boven Digul in West New Guinea. (They were transferred to rather better circumstances in the Banda Islands in 1936.) These repressive moves forestalled the New PNI's experiment in the training of leadership cadres. Hatta and Sjahrir were seized before they had had adequate time to implement their proposals and others followed them. Even so the New PNI did manage to survive more effectively than did Partindo. It may not have done very much by way of resistance to Dutch power but its members retained their sense of identity as participants in a living organization right through the thirties. This was small comfort however. Both branches of radical nationalism were now deprived of their most effective leaders and the nationalist movement thereafter was compelled to follow the paths of moderation and co-operation rather than those of *machtsvorming* or the training of an uncompromising élite. A new party, Parindra, rather than Partindo represented the norm of political action under the new dispensation by the mid and late thirties.

Founded in 1935 by a combination of such groups as Boedi Oetomo, Persatuan Bangsa Indonesia and other smaller nationalist organizations, and reflecting the views of more moderate leaders such as Thamrin and Sutomo, Parindra (Partai Indonesia Raya – 'Greater Indonesia Party') favoured working within the framework of the Volksraad. So did a number of other groups including a breakaway Muslim group, which, under the leadership of Hadji Agus Salim, had split away from the non-cooperating Sarekat Islam (or Partai Sarekat Islam Indonesia – PSII – the name adopted by the party in 1929). There were, it is true, some attempts to revive a more radical approach – the 'illegal PKI' for instance, which was set up in 1935 by Musso who had managed to slip back secretly into the Indies. But this was so weak and ineffective an effort as to be to all intents and purposes non-existent. Musso's return was brief. He had to flee again before he had taken more than the first steps towards re-creating the PKI. Insofar as there was any degree of radicalism at all in the nationalist movement, it was to be found not in Indonesia but in Holland, where the communist affiliations of the Perhimpunan Indonesia leaders, Setiadjit and Abdulmadjid, turned the Union's policies in a sharply leftward direction. Their line, however, aroused no response within the Indies.

Sukarno, in isolation at Endeh, could only watch helplessly as the nationalist movement changed its direction. Its willingness to compromise the principles he had expounded inevitably added to the frustrations of his exile. In a way Flores was perhaps more galling for him than Sukamiskin had been. He had some freedom of movement and was allowed a certain degree of contact with other people, but the very limited character of that contact underlined day by day the contrast between his present circumstances and the hurly-burly of political action and sharpened his sense of impotence. Like his first imprisonment his exile could be viewed as another example of withdrawal, of *semadi* – the search for spiritual renewal through meditation – and Sukarno could take that view of it when it suited him. But deeply rooted though he was in the tradition of Java, he was not Javanese enough to use a retreat from the world to achieve serenity. In Endeh, and later in Bengkulu, he felt caged and confined rather than liberated by meditation.

However, if the psychological consequences of exile were severe, the material circumstances, comparatively speaking, were not. He was much better off in Endeh than were other exiles whose lot was to be imprisonment in Boven Digul. Indeed it is necessary to ask why it was that he should be favoured in this way while Hatta and Sjahrir and many others were sent to face the horrors of Tanah Merah. Sukarno's own answer, given in his autobiography, was that the Government wished to separate him from other political prisoners lest he organize a resistance movement in New Guinea. There was little chance of that happening, but his importance as a political prisoner may have made it seem prudent to separate him from the others. Or perhaps, on the contrary, he was, in the eyes of authority, less dangerous than others – a mass leader but not an effective practical plotter against the regime. There is, however, some evidence to suggest a less creditable reason: that he begged not to be exiled, and agreed to abstain from political activity if he were allowed to remain at liberty.[32] If so, his earlier resignation from Partindo falls naturally into place.

Certainly Sukarno was a privileged exile rather than the reverse. He gathered a circle of friends about him from the humble ranks of Endeh's small society – peasants, artisans, traders – and he amused himself by organizing dramatic performances with them. He could enjoy a family life, though the death in October 1935 of his mother-in-law, with whom he had had an extraordinarily warm relationship, was a particular blow. He had too some contacts with the outside world; he was allowed to correspond with friends and to write on politically neutral topics for the Indonesian-language Press. He translated from the English a life of Ibn Saud[33] – 'an immense man, tremendous, vital, dominant'. Sukarno noted that Ibn Saud had not fully freed himself from a feudal outlook but still he saw him as 'towering above all Muslims of his time'.[34]

During these years Sukarno returned again to the study of Islam, and discussed its problems in an extended correspondence with the theologian T. A. Hassan of Bandung, to whom he gave glimpses of his circumstances and his feelings.

'I am in good spirit thank God. I am continuing my study of Islam but lack of a library is unfortunate; I have devoured all the books I have. After working in the garden, and chatting with the family to cheer them up, my daily work is just to read. I alternate between sociology

32. I am indebted for this information to Mr John Ingleson, who bases it on his researches in the Netherlands State Archives.

33. Probably H. C. Armstrong, *Lord of Arabia: Ibn Saud*, London, 1934 to which Sukarno made reference in his *Pantja Sila* speech of 1 July 1945.

34. Letter from Sukarno to T. A. Hassan, 12 June 1936. *Dibawah Bendera Revolusi*. p. 337.

and works on Islam – the latter by Muslims themselves, in Indonesia and elsewhere and by non-Muslim scholars.

'In Endeh itself there is nobody I can refer to – they have little knowledge as usual and are very *kolot* [conservative]. They all just repeat the faith without themselves understanding the principles. There are one or two who know a little – but not enough for me . . .'[35]

Hassan supplied him with books and Sukarno, in reply, commented on them and expressed his feelings about the condition of Indonesian Islam in general. He condemned the preoccupation of Muslim teachers with the Koran and the Tradition and with questions of Islamic law and jurisprudence. The law, in his view, was the destroyer of the spirit and soul of Islam – again and again he returned to this theme. To Hassan he urged the introduction of Western learning in Islamic schools, since Islam could only be understood in the context of wider scientific knowledge.[36] He ridiculed the tendency of Muslims to set the stamp of 'infidel' on everything: Western knowledge – *kafir* ['infidel']; radio and scientific medicine – *kafir*; trousers, neck-tie and hat – *kafir*; spoons and forks and chairs – *kafir*; Latin writing – *kafir*; yes, everything connected with peoples who are not Muslim – *kafir*![37] All of this was theologically superficial, no doubt, and for an obvious reason. Sukarno was simply not interested in theological subtleties. His concern with Islamic questions remained from first to last a political concern. His reiterated condemnation of the *ulamas* was, really, the product of his desire that Islam should play its part in Indonesia's nationalist awakening. Muslim leaders, he said, should develop a feeling for history.[38] Why should Islam constantly go back to the period of its past greatness, long ago, instead of playing its role in the present?[39] Holding up Kemal Ataturk as his example he insisted that 'Islam is progress'. This slogan, which was repeated in other letters, was a political

35. Sukarno to Hassan, 17 July 1935. *Dibawah Bendera Revolusi*, p. 328.

36. Sukarno to Hassan, 22 April 1936. *Dibawah Bendera Revolusi*, p. 335–6.

37. Sukarno to Hassan, 18 August 1936. ibid., p. 340.

38. Sukarno to Hassan, 14 December 1935. ibid., p. 332. (The date is given as 1936 but the order in which the letters are printed suggests that that is a misprint.)

39. Sukarno to Hassan, 22 February 1936. ibid., p. 334.

battle-cry. While wanting Islam to modernize itself he was not a 'modernist' in the religious sense, and his interest in Islam did not amount to a sort of conversion as has been suggested.[40] His way of handling Islam was consistent with the attitude he had always maintained and his letters to Hassan reveal no more than an attempt to include Islam more effectively in his synthesis.

As always when Sukarno put pen to paper his writings from exile were didactic in tone – handing down ideas to his followers, not really arguing about them. It was not in his nature to reveal the subtler workings of his mind as Sjahrir did in his letters from exile. Sukarno conveyed his thoughts by straightforward assertion; Sjahrir was reflective and introspective, examining his own thoughts and attempting to probe deeply into his own character. But Sukarno's letters in their own way were moving, suggesting as they did the frustration of inaction and revealing the temper of his spirit:

'Present day Islam is half dead, has no life, spirit or fire, because Muslims drown themselves in the book of *Fiqh*, instead of flying like the *garuda* bird in the sky of living religion. Anyway that's my situation in Endeh – I want to learn but have no guide. I go back to the books that I have. But even books written by authorities on Islam have parts which just don't satisfy me, sometimes my mind and memory just won't accept them. In a more lively place, it would certainly be easier to spread my wings . . .'[41]

Early in 1938, after Sukarno had suffered a severe bout of malaria, it was decided to remove him to a healthier place of exile. He was brought back from Flores to Surabaja. There was no tumultuous welcome for him however. With his escort he paused in Java only long enough to be taken from one end of the island to the other, to Merak on the Sunda Straits. From there he was shipped to Bengkulu in South Sumatra. Bengkulu, once the site of Fort Marlborough, the Sumatra station of the British East India Company,[42] was a somewhat larger place of confinement

40. Dahm, op. cit., p. 184.
41. Sukarno to Hassan, 17 July 1935. *Dibawah Bendera Revolusi*, p. 328.
42. Bengkulu, or Bencoolen as it is normally spelt in English references, was founded as a British East India Company station in 1685 and remained such until it was handed over to the Netherlands by the Anglo–Dutch treaty of 1824.

than Endeh, but it was still isolated and remote enough to keep Sukarno quite out of political circulation.

As in Endeh, he had to be content with a small circle of contacts among the local population – the local schoolmaster, members of the small local trading community, Muslim teachers, farmers and so on. Sukarno always possessed the common touch and when he put himself out to make friends he could do so quickly and with ease.[43] But in Bengkulu one person in particular was to become very important to him: his eye was caught by Fatmawati, the daughter of the local leader of Muhammadiyah. Sukarno had accepted from her father the offer of a teaching position in the local elementary school and his friendship with the father brought him into contact with the daughter. She later became a boarder in the Sukarno home and a regular companion of the exile on his walks around Bengkulu. By his own account they discussed many things, including Muslim marriage law.[44]

At Bengkulu Sukarno kept up his occasional journalism, confining himself, of necessity still, to 'safe' subjects, though these were not narrowly defined. The political situation in the Indies was out of bounds for him, naturally, but he was permitted to expound in general terms upon world political developments. The rise of fascism in Europe, its ideological features and its basic character were subjects on which he was able to comment.[45] But mainly he wrote on Islamic matters. It was perhaps his teaching post in a Muhammadiyah school which opened to him the columns of *Pandji Islam*, the Muhammadiyah journal published in Medan, the capital of Sumatra's East Coast Residency. In its pages he advocated, as one might have expected, the modernization of Islam, but as in his letters to Hassan, it was the political

43. See photographs in *Dibawah Bendera Revolusi* of Sukarno both in Endeh and Bengkulu surrounded by unidentified groups with the captions: 'Sukarno and his friends.'

44. *Autobiography*, pp. 140–41.

45. See, for example, articles which appeared in *Pandji Islam, Pemandangan* and *Pembangun* in 1940–41, and are reprinted in *Dibawah Bendera Revolusi*: 'Bukan Perang Ideologi', p. 361; 'Indonesia versus Fasisme', p. 457; 'Djerman versus Rusia, Rusia versus Djerman!', p. 515; 'Beratnja Perdjoangan Malawan Fasisme', p. 547; and 'Fasisme adalah Politiknja dan Sepak Terdjangnja Kapitalisme jang Menurun', p. 589.

role of Islam which really concerned him.[46] This was not his only outlet. He was also a contributor to the Djakarta paper, *Pemandangan*, and it was in *Pemandangan* that he gave his public, in 1941, an attempt at self-analysis: 'Bung Karno: Sukarno by Sukarno himself' ('Bung Karno: Soekarno oleh Soekarno Sendiri').[47] Despite the promise of the title the article was not, after all, written in a genuinely introspective vein. It was essentially a political tract, concerned to give what Sukarno felt to be an appropriate public image rather than to probe his inner self. If it is revealing at all of Sukarno as a person, it is in its indication that he always tended to see himself in such public and heroic terms – the nationalist crusader fighting for the welfare of his people. 'Sukarno by Sukarno himself' returned to his old theme of synthesis and reconciliation of the three streams of nationalism, Islam and Marxism. But he went a little further than his well-established insistence on the necessity for such reconciliation by staking a claim to be himself the symbol of synthesis, uniting within himself the main streams of Indonesia's identity. 'What is Sukarno? A nationalist? An Islamist? A Marxist? Readers, Sukarno is a mixture of all these isms.'[48]

As his days passed in these activities his private life presented increasing perplexities. His friendship with Fatmawati had become a great deal more than friendship and its character could not be hidden from Inggit. Her natural jealousy and resentment made themselves plain and finally brought the situation out into the open. Had Sukarno had his way he would have taken Fatmawati as a second wife under Muslim law, but Inggit, with passionate anger, rejected such an arrangement – a reaction not so very unlike that of Fatmawati herself when confronted with a new rival fourteen years later. Sukarno's own justification of his desires and behaviour – that after seventeen years of marriage Inggit had not borne him any children – was, no doubt, only part of the story. It does less than justice to his own passionate nature and to the fact that Inggit was some ten years older than himself.

46. See, for instance 'Me-"Muda"-kan Pengertian Islam', *Pandji Islam*, 1940; *Dibawah Bendera Revolusi*, p. 369.

47. *Dibawah Bendera Revolusi*, p. 507.

48. ibid., p. 508.

But the striking thing is the stability, hitherto, of his marriage to Inggit. In view of his later well-earned reputation for sexual licence his monogamy over seventeen years is a matter for comment. In any case his desire to take a second wife was not out of line with the customs of the religion which he formally accepted, though Inggit did not see it in quite those terms.

This personal crisis was still unresolved when events in the outside world brought Sukarno's exile to an end and swept him back to the centre of the political stage.

During the later thirties Indonesian nationalism continued to be contained within moderate bounds. This was as much a matter of necessity as of choice. Events were confirming Sukarno's prediction that political concessions would never be granted as a reward for nationalist co-operation with Dutch authorities. In 1936 the Volksraad, by a clear majority, adopted a petition requesting that a conference be called to discuss plans for the introduction, over a ten-year period, of autonomy for the Indies within the framework of the Dutch constitution. This was not a particularly radical demand. It resembled, in some measure, American plans for the concession of self-government to the Philippines, and it was wholly in line with the kind of programme hinted at by many Dutch spokesmen during the heyday of the Ethical Policy. Nevertheless, the Soetardjo Petition received a cool reception in The Hague. It was shelved for the time being and eventually, two years later, it was formally rejected. This was a crushing blow to the hopes of the moderates but no other course of action was really open to them.

In the permissive environment of the late twenties the power of the mobilized people and the importance of unremitting struggle to grasp independence from the hands of the reluctant Dutch had seemed credible concepts. The repressive atmosphere of the thirties showed them to be otherwise. At that stage for those nationalists who were still at large it was either moderation or nothing. In any case the changing pattern of European politics forced Indonesian intellectuals to take a slightly different view of the course of their own struggle. The rise of European fascism had led the more radical of them – Amir Sjarifuddin, Wikana,

Muhammad Yamin and others – to see colonial independence for the time being as a secondary goal. Their own struggle was caught up in the wider resistance to fascism within Europe and Asia. This point of view was expressed in 1937 in the formation of a new party, Gerindo, (Gerakan Rakjat Indonesia – 'Indonesian People's Movement'). Gerindo was more radical than Parindra had been, but while stressing the importance of Indonesian independence, it placed its primary emphasis on Indonesian co-operation with Holland against Germany in Europe and against Japan in the Pacific.

In 1939, against the background of these shifts of emphasis, a further attempt was made to unite the diverse elements of Indonesian nationalism into one broad front after the style of the defunct PPPKI. Gapi (Gabungan Politiek Indonesia – 'Federation of Indonesian Political Parties') comprised eight organizations, including Gerindo, PSII and Parindra. Its programme united the goals of anti-fascist struggle and ultimate Indonesian independence; its nationalist content was expressed in the holding of a broadly based congress in December 1939 which officially adopted Indonesian as the national language, the red and white flag – the *Merah-Putih* – as the national flag, and the song 'Indonesia Raya' (Great Indonesia) as the national song.

Shortly afterwards the Volksraad once again attempted by resolution to urge the Netherlands Government to take gradual steps towards the granting of Indonesian autonomy. The Wiwoho Resolution, like the Soetardjo Petition of over three years earlier, envisaged self-government as soon as possible without breaking the ties with the Netherlands. It was passed, however, five months after the outbreak of the war in Europe and in the immediate future the government of the Netherlands was to lose control of its relations with its colony. In May 1940 the German armies overran the Netherlands and it was a Dutch Government in exile which eventually replied to the Wiwoho Resolution postponing any political reform until after the war. In September 1940 the Indies Government did however set up a committee under the chairmanship of F. H. Visman to consider political, social and economic developments in the Indies. The committee considered various proposals for future political reforms and on 30 July 1944 the Netherlands Government in exile, speaking through Queen Wilhelmina, looked forward to a revision of the Netherlands constitution after the war which would, amongst other things, change the relationship between metropolis and colony. But no specific proposals were advanced and the promises were to be overtaken by events.

Sukarno watched these developments from a distance, commenting sometimes in his articles upon their broad ideological aspects. In interpreting them he took up a position which, in some respects, was in line with the internationalist outlook of orthodox socialism – with the ideas of Gerindo for example, or of Hatta and Sjahrir. There were highly significant differences, however. Sukarno deplored the horrors of fascism, its concentration camps, its oppression and its cruelties.[49] He followed the fashion of regarding fascism as the product of capitalism in decline[50] and rejected it as contrary to the Indonesian spirit – as opposed to the principles of deliberation and consensus, which were rooted in Indonesian custom.[51] But at the same time he tended to scoff at those who saw the outbreak of the Second World War in ideological terms, regarding it as a conflict between fascism and democracy. Bourgeois democracy was not, in his view, real democracy, and there was not all that much to choose between these so-called opposing ideologies. The war, like all wars, was a conflict of interests, not a conflict of ideas. It was therefore not a war in which Asian countries should necessarily feel committed to take sides.[52]

In the long run it was not the European war which really mattered to Indonesia. More important were to be the developments in the Pacific whose coming he had predicted so frequently over a decade earlier. To this extent Sukarno was at least as prescient as those who had seen the rise of fascism in Europe as the main threat to the march of progress and as the prime concern of the Indonesian nationalist. He had his own sense of history and it proved as relevant as theirs – as events were soon to show.

49. e.g. article in *Pemandangan*, 1941; *Dibawah Bendera Revolusi*, p. 559.
50. Article in *Pembangun*, *Dibawah Bendera Revolusi*, p. 589.
51. Article in *Pandji Islam*, 1940; *Dibawah Bendera Revolusi*, pp. 457 ff.
52. 'Not a War of Ideologies', *Pandji Islam*, 1940; *Dibawah Bendera Revolusi*, pp. 361ff.

Japan's bid for empire in Asia was a remarkable story. In retrospect it is not easy to say whether it was the result of clear-sighted preparation and deliberate planning or of skilful opportunism from time to time – the opportunism of Premier Ito at one time, of Foreign Minister Kato at another, of the Kwantung Army at another. On the basis of her amazing industrial revolution she had made herself a power to be reckoned with by the early twentieth century; certainly her expansion – Formosa in 1895, the southern part of Sakhalin in 1905, Korea in 1910, mandates over Germany's Pacific island possessions after World War I, Manchuria in 1931 – had all the appearance of careful deliberation. There were, it is true, occasional reverses – Western intervention after the Sino–Japanese War of 1894–5 which secured the retrocession of the Liaotung Peninsula, for example, or the diplomatic defeat which, at the Washington Conference in 1922, had robbed her of the gains extorted from China through the Twenty-One Demands. And there were undoubtedly differences within Japan about the speed and direction of her advance – between army and navy, between civilian and military leaders, between younger officers and older ones, between a variety of clan-based military factions. But the continuing presence of a sense of imperial mission seems too obvious and too strongly embedded in Japan's increasingly nationalist ideology to be merely a matter of occasional caprice.

Indonesia's place in Japan's plans was not defined with any degree of clarity until the very end of the thirties, but Japan's view of herself as the divinely appointed leader of Asia against European imperialism undoubtedly had implications for all Southeast Asian dependencies of European powers. In the twenties and thirties Japan was concerned to expand her trade with Indonesia and, despite Dutch efforts to restrict the flow of manufactured goods, her economic offensive was remarkably successful. During the years of the depression her trade drive enabled her, for a time, to contribute as much as thirty-one per cent of the imports of the Indies – a higher proportion than that contributed by Holland itself.[53] She also expanded her direct role in the retail trade of the Indies. Japanese nationals established themselves in

53. M. A. Aziz, *Japan's Colonialism and Indonesia*, The Hague, 1955, p. 101.

both urban and rural trade, selling Japanese goods at low prices and purchasing maize, rubber and copra in return.[54] The Indies government, through quota agreements, licensing regulations and immigration restrictions, checked this offensive in some measure, but Japan's interest was by then too well established to be rooted out easily, and as far as Indonesians were concerned Japan's cheaper goods and her trading competition with the unpopular Chinese made her representatives welcome. In other fields, too, she sought to make her preparations for the future – Indonesian students were encouraged to study in Japan, plans were made for the publication of a Japanese-sponsored Indonesian-language newspaper and Japan even developed an interest in Islam to the point of organizing an Islamic world conference to which an Indonesian delegation was invited.

These activities began to fit more clearly into a wider plan when, in 1940, Japan formulated her scheme for bringing Southeast Asia into her Greater East Asia Co-Prosperity Sphere. Her blueprint did not lay down in precise terms the relationship which the various parts of the Co-Prosperity Sphere were to bear to Japan herself, but the preparations were made for an advance into the region despite the risk of conflict with Britain and America. After the fall of the Netherlands in 1940 Japan sent a delegation to Batavia to negotiate directly with the Indies government, hoping to by-pass the Dutch government in exile in London and to acquire the sort of domination she wanted by direct dealings with the Indies. The negotiations dragged on into 1941 but by that time Japan had come to recognize that she would have to use force to realize her ambitions in the Indies as in other parts of Southeast Asia.

Whether or not Sukarno had read aright the detailed signs of Japanese policy over the years, he caught at least the main drift of events. He saw, in historic terms, the coming clash of empires and he felt in his bones the importance of that clash for Indonesia's nationalism. During the thirties the Dutch had shown themselves to be firmly in control of their Indonesian colony and more than a match for the unaided efforts of popular resistance. That hold was now to be broken from outside.

54. ibid., p. 102.

On 7 December 1941 came the Japanese attack on Pearl Harbour. The following weeks saw the massive southward sweep of her armies and the collapse of the seemingly impregnable bastions of imperial power. On 10 Janauary 1942 the first Japanese forces landed in the Netherlands East Indies. They hoped to take possession of the islands without opposition and for that reason Japan had refrained from declaring war on Holland. However, the Dutch had declared war on Japan and their forces in the Indies prepared to defend themselves. It was a weak defence. The Dutch air and naval forces had some successes against the Japanese (though at considerable cost) in the weeks before the landings, but once Japan turned her offensive directly against the Indies after the epic battle of the Java Sea she met with no effective resistance and within two months had acquired control of the colony. On 7 March the military government was formally created. In the eyes of many Javanese it seemed that Djoyoboyo's prophecy was on the verge of fulfilment.

# 7

# Collaborator or Patriot?

The Japanese conquest and occupation of the Indies was an event of cataclysmic proportions for the nationalist movement as a whole, as well as for Sukarno himself. It shattered the continuity of Dutch power and shaped the forces of Indonesian nationalism in new and unexpected ways. For Sukarno it ended his exile, presented him with difficult political and moral problems, and brought him back to the centre of political life – no longer in opposition but with formal standing as a representative of nationalist opinion. It was during the Occupation that Sukarno became the unchallenged leader of his people.

It could be argued that the significance of these developments for Sukarno's personal evolution was less than their significance for the nationalist movement as a whole. The Occupation was something that happened to him, not something that he created. He responded to it and manipulated the situation it brought into being, but he did not make that situation as he had made the PNI and was later to make the political order of guided democracy. Such a judgement would underestimate the creative character of Sukarno's response to the challenge of the Occupation. The new situation was to prove well suited to his particular talents – much more so indeed than the environment of Dutch empire had been. The Japanese ruled in a highly political manner, through mass organizations, grand rituals and ideological indoctrination. This was very different from the apolitical or anti-political style of the Dutch and allowed much more scope for an agitator such as Sukarno. He believed that Indonesian independence could be achieved in some way or other through the Japanese occupation, and held to this view even when Occupation policy became more and more oppressive and when the Japanese seemed quite determined to resist all concessions. Much faith was needed during these years, but, in its broad outlines, his vision was to prove correct in the end. His efforts to contain Japanese power and his single-minded conviction that through it he could ultimately

reach his goal justify the judgement that this was one of the
periods in which Sukarno knew fairly well where he was going
and in important ways was shaping the world about him.

As the first Japanese landings took place in Sumatra the Dutch
were implementing hasty plans to evacuate as many of their
nationals as possible to Australia. It was a race against time, and
in the event, only small numbers managed to escape. Sukarno,
as an important political prisoner, was to be evacuated too and at
short notice he and Inggit were ordered to prepare themselves for
the rugged cross-country journey from Bengkulu to the nearest
embarkation centre – the west Sumatran port of Padang.

The story of his flight under the care of a small Dutch escort
is told in heroic terms in his autobiography. The first part of the
journey was made by truck, the last part by foot over jungle paths.
The party arrived wearily at Padang to find their convoy gone,
the Dutch administration in ruins, and the city left pretty much
to its own devices. In the interregnum between the collapse of
Dutch power and the arrival of the first Japanese forces, looting
was rife and the town was gripped in a mood of uneasy expectancy. Sukarno and Inggit sought shelter with Waworuntu, a
friend from Bengkulu, and it was in his house that he was staying
when, a few days later, Japanese troops entered the town.

The exact stages of the next part of the story are not clear
though Sukarno has given his own account of them.[55] He was
known to the Japanese authorities in Padang and shortly after
their arrival an officer of the Sendenbu (propaganda department)
made contact with him. This approach by the Japanese requires
no elaborate explanation. Though in some areas Dutch police
were used initially by the Japanese to maintain order, the intern-
ment of Dutch officials left the military authorities with the
necessity of laying the foundations of a new administration and
for this purpose it was necessary for them, in Indonesia as in
other territories they seized, to identify and come to terms with
acceptable authorities among the indigenous population. In the
case of Indonesia it was obvious common sense to establish a
working relationship with the leaders of the pre-war nationalist

55. *Autobiography*, chapter 18.

movement who might be persuaded to regard the Japanese as liberators, and whose mediation was necessary if popular acceptance of Japanese rule was to be secured. They had their tabs on Sukarno and he was an obvious quarry.

The initial approach was followed by an invitation to visit Bukit Tinggi, the local command headquarters of the 25th Army, the Occupation force in Sumatra. The Japanese occupation, it should be noticed, led to a *de facto* division of Indonesia into three separately administered zones: Sumatra under the 25th Army based in Singapore, Java under the 16th Army based in Batavia, and east Indonesia – Borneo, Celebes, the Moluccas and the Lesser Sundas – under the Japanese navy. Sukarno's invitation came from the Sumatran commander, Colonel Fujiyama, and he decided to accept it. A few days later, he was ushered into Fujiyama's presence for the interview which was to determine his actions for the next three years.

According to Sukarno, Fujiyama opened their discussion by referring to the role of the Japanese as the liberators of Southeast Asian countries from Western domination. Sukarno seized the implication of these remarks – that the ultimate goal of Japanese rule would be a free Indonesia. He pressed the point on Fujiyama. Was this a correct inference? 'The pause was no longer than a heartbeat. "Yes, Mr Sukarno. Perfectly correct." '[56] In the light of this exchange he listened to the proposition that he should work for the military administration, providing a link with the Indonesian people and seeking to secure Indonesian acquiescence in Japanese rule.

This was not by any means a hopeless proposition in 1942. Japan's pre-war propaganda proved to have been effectively devised – even some nationalist leaders had been attracted during the thirties by the image Japan had managed to convey of herself.[57] With the invasion of the Indies there was a widespread predisposition to welcome the invaders and in some places they were given a joyous welcome in the streets.[58] There was a good deal of

56. ibid., p. 160.

57. Sjahrir, *Out of Exile*, New York, 1949, p. 112.

58. M. A. Aziz, *Japan's Colonialism and Indonesia*, The Hague, 1955, pp. 149–50.

gay fraternization with the troops and for a time the red and white flags of the nationalist movement sprouted at house fronts side by side with Japanese flags (until the former were banned within a few days of the beginning of the Occupation). The welcome was to be short-lived and it was not long before many Indonesians came to see the Japanese as harsh and arrogant; but for the time being the new rulers were anxious to present a smiling face and Sukarno's ability to command mass support might enable them, in the beginning, to find some sort of popular consent for their régime.

From Sukarno's point of view there were both pros and cons to be considered as he sat in Fujiyama's room. On the one hand there was the danger of earning a quisling's reputation. What would his own people feel if Japanese rule grew more and more unpopular? Would they accept his authority if it were based on Japanese power? But, on the other hand, there could be great opportunities: it was clear that the Japanese needed someone like him and that there was no other Indonesian who could rally the population so effectively. He could therefore surely ask a high price for such assistance as he could give to the Occupation authorities. There was a prospect, if he accepted, of softening the pressure of Japanese rule and, with luck, of hastening the eventual coming of independence. These were important possibilities, but there was, perhaps, an even more compelling consideration in his mind, touching his most fundamental assumptions about the Indonesian struggle – his deep anti-Western sentiment. For the time being, Sukarno and the Japanese had a common foe. He had yet to experience the power of Japanese imperialism, but he knew well the power of Dutch imperialism, and this loomed in his mind as the greater danger to his cause. The hold of the West must be totally broken. With these considerations in mind he did not need to balance the alternatives for very long. He had already thought about the issues and now his mind was quickly made up. He decided to accept Fujiyama's offer without much real hesitation.

Some of the consequences of his decision became apparent immediately. He had come to Bukit Tinggi by train with a Japanese escort. He returned to Padang in a Buick which was made available for the time being for his personal use. In Padang he played his appointed role without running into any insuperable crises of conscience. He helped the local Japanese authorities to handle the difficult problem of rice distribution. He interceded on behalf of Indonesian prisoners arrested for sabotage, though at the same time he had to use his influence to prevent such subversion in the future. He toured nearby rural areas combining his appeals for co-operation with the Japanese with nationalist propaganda of a general kind.

In due course the Japanese completed their conquest of Java. Landings at the beginning of March 1942 found the same crumbling of Dutch resistance and within eight days Bandung was captured. Its fall was followed by the formal surrender of the whole Netherlands East Indies. Though Java was under a different command and became a separate military administration from that of Sumatra it was obviously still the centre of government and, in fact if not in theory, its administration was superior to that of the 25th Army in Bukit Tinggi. Thus, when Lieutenant-General Imamura, commander of the 16th Army, established his military government in Djakarta he requested the services of Sukarno, and Fujiyama complied. Sukarno was despatched with a safe conduct, and though held up for a time in Palembang he was in the end able to find a small motor boat to take him across to Java.

There was no public and triumphal welcome for him on his arrival on 9 July after a four-day crossing. He landed at Pasar Ikan and quickly made contact with Anwar Tjokroaminoto and Hatta who, with two or three others, hurried down to greet him. They carried him off to Hatta's house where he was to spend his first night. (Later he moved to a comfortable but comparatively modest Dutch bungalow in Menteng, which was to be his home for the duration of the occupation.) At Hatta's he was able to meet other leaders of the movement – those who had survived the repression of the thirties – such as Yamin, Subardjo and Soenario, and others who, like Hatta and Sjahrir, had had their spell of exile until the outbreak of the Pacific war had moved the Dutch to release them. On the following day he made an orientation tour of Djakarta, visiting government offices and having his first brief meeting with Lieutenant-General Imamura. In the course of the day he had the opportunity of making one speech to a small gathering and in it he recalled the remarks made after his release from prison ten years earlier – that given a thousand, a hundred, even ten young men with the right spirit, he could throw the whole world into an uproar.[59]

Sukarno's reunion with Hatta had its own overtones. Their last contact, nine years before, had been marked by rivalry and even by bitterness. Now, in the Occupation crisis, there was no room for the differences which had separated Partindo and the New PNI in 1932 and 1933. The two men, different in temper still, now had to work closely together, and they quickly settled down to devise the plan of action which was to carry them through the next three years. The question of co-operation with the Japanese authorities or resistance to them was settled quickly. Hatta was already an adviser to the Occupation régime and it was agreed that the two men would together follow the course of action Sukarno had already chosen. They would hold office under the military administration, serving the Japanese, softening the harshness of their rule where possible, and using whatever opportunities were offered for keeping nationalist hopes alive. Others, including Sjahrir, would work to develop an underground network capable of organizing resistance to Japanese authority. Sjahrir would listen to Allied radio stations and maintain contact with Sukarno and Hatta, informing them of underground developments and helping them to develop their own strategy. They in turn would keep him apprised of Japanese plans and purposes. How far this was an explicit agreement from the beginning may be a matter of doubt. Sukarno's account of the conscious formulation of the plan follows that of Sjahrir;[60] Nonetheless it is possible that the division of labour between the 'collaborators' and the underground emerged in practice rather than by a specific plan. The details of the way the agreement was reached do not matter. It was 'such a simple formula', says Sukarno,

59. The details of Sukarno's return and of his first day in Djakarta are to be found in *Asia Raya*, 10 and 11 July 1942.

60. Sjahrir, op. cit., pp. 245–6. Sukarno is here referred to as Abdul Rachman and Hatta as Hafil.

'that when re-examined two decades later, it almost seems profound'.[61]

Did Sukarno make the right decisions, first in Bukit Tinggi and later, together with Hatta, in Djakarta?

One must consider first, if only to dismiss it quickly, the view that, despite his talk of serving his people, Sukarno was really motivated by a desire for the large cars, the comfortable accommodation, the immunity from harassment and the other perquisites of authority.[62] Having been imprisoned twice and then exiled was he returning to Djakarta determined never to experience a fugitive existence again? The later Sukarno certainly enjoyed luxury and the appurtenances of office, both for themselves and for what they implied – that he was *the* leader of the Indonesian people. Nonetheless to judge his 'collaboration' in these terms would be to judge crudely and inaccurately. Such an interpretation would be inconsistent with the Sukarno of the twenties and thirties and with the Sukarno of the years of revolution and independence, even taking account of the defects of his leadership in the early period and of his sybaritic tendencies in the later. It is true that Sukarno could falter on occasion as was shown by his fear of exile and his resignation from Partindo, but to see him merely as a time-server would ignore his revolutionary romanticism and his intensely political nature. Whatever elements of material self-interest may have been in his mind were undoubtedly buried beyond the range of his conscious deliberations, and it is these which are involved in a judgement of overt motives.

But even moving to the level of political principle, the collaboration issue is not a simple one. Was his decision out of character with his long-established emphasis on the principle of non-cooperation with alien authority? Was it really in the best interests of the movement and was it recognized as such by others? The question of whether he chose rightly was one which, despite the confidence of his own account of it, was in fact to trouble him

61. *Autobiography*, p. 173.
62. See, for example, Willard Hanna's description of Sukarno as an enthusiastic collaborator, in *Eight Nation Makers: Southeast Asia's Charismatic Statesmen*, New York, 1964, p. 32.

in the future. He found himself again and again required to perform tasks for the Japanese which were to torture him at the time and which haunted him for a long time after. His part in providing forced labour for service outside Indonesia was the task which shamed him most, but once the original decision had been made there could be no turning back, no luxury of deciding that some duties performed on behalf of the Japanese were permissible and others not.[63] Like so many choices about ends and means it was all or nothing, and Sukarno could only hope that others beside himself would judge that the end really had justified the means. Before examining his role during the Occupation it is worth looking further at his dilemma and his resolution of it.

Sukarno's defence of his decision perhaps oversimplifies the complexity of the moral and tactical issues facing him. For him, as for Hatta, the moral question – which course of action was right – and the tactical – which course of action was expedient – were inextricably linked, and any attempt to separate them here must necessarily be artificial. On the moral level it could be argued that the charge of collaboration which was to be levelled against Sukarno by Dutch critics after the war was totally irrelevant.[64] Sukarno had no reason to be loyal to the Dutch – the reverse was the case. The Dutch had imprisoned and exiled him and there was no earthly reason why he should, on their behalf, have opposed the Japanese invasion and occupation. His goal was Indonesian independence and any steps that might help to bring about that goal were morally justified. He had opposed co-operation with the Dutch on principle, but temporary co-operation with the Japanese seemed to promise better results and he was now ready to accept that argument from expediency.

Such an argument is all very well as far as it goes. The important point, however, is that the moral component of the collabora-

63. See Cindy Adams's account of Sukarno's sharp reaction to her questioning of him on this point in *My Friend the Dictator*, Indianapolis, 1967, p. 203.

64. See, for example, the scathing account of P. S. Gerbrandy, wartime Prime Minister of the Netherlands, in his *Indonesia* (London, 1950). Sukarno is described as a 'so-called nationalist' (p. 51) and a 'lickspittle of the Japanese' (p. 53).

tion issue was an important question within nationalist circles both during and after the war. Many Indonesians came to condemn as collaborators some of those who accepted office under the Japanese. The first cabinet of the Republic failed to command confidence for the very reason that it contained many such people.

The hostility to collaborators on the part of many nationalists was part of a total outlook. It was of a piece with views on questions of social order and political strategy, and indeed, with more fundamental ideological perspectives. It went hand in hand with ideas about the nature of capitalism, the causes of imperialism, the role of colonial nationalism and indeed the course of history itself. The Indonesian socialist of Dutch education, or the Marxist, tended in the thirties, as we have already noticed, to see fascism as *the* enemy. Gerindo, more ideologically radical than the other major parties of the time, had established its priorities quite frankly in these terms, and had subordinated the struggle for independence to the anti-fascist struggle. Hatta and Sjahrir thought in the same way; Japanese imperialism fitted easily into their interpretation of European fascism. Sjahrir had noticed with misgiving the growing popularity of Japan in Indonesia in the thirties.[65] When news of the Spanish civil war reached him in Banda Naira he saw it as another step in 'the triumphal march of fascism throughout the world,' and he added that the Far East also had 'a supernationalism in the form of Japanese fascism, with its vast reserves of human cannon fodder'.[66] To him 'the Axis was a more dangerous threat to Indonesian freedom than existing Dutch colonialism'.[67] Indeed by 1938, he spoke of the necessity to 'take a stand in the same camp as Holland'.[68]

There were emotional overtones to this view. Indonesians who had studied in Holland saw the Dutch in a totally different perspective from those who had stayed in the Indies. They saw them not as insensitive and complacent colonial overlords but as including men of humanity and liberality. They respected their Dutch teachers and exchanged ideas with Dutchmen who thought as they did about world problems. For them it was not the Dutch as

65. Sjahrir, op. cit., pp. 186–7.  66. ibid., pp. 115–16.
67. ibid., p. 219.  68. ibid., p. 211.

such who were the enemy, but the system of imperialism in which Holland had participated and which was itself linked with the rise of fascism.

Sukarno's anti-Dutch feelings had never been softened in that way and intellectually he was much less committed to the systematic world-view from which the outlook of Hatta and Sjahrir was derived. He had condemned the evils of Nazism, certainly, and Sjahrir was later at pains to stress his anti-fascist outlook.[69] Nevertheless Sukarno's whole position was different in emphasis. In his writings in 1940 and 1941 he had stressed not the historical battle between fascist reaction and socialist progress but rather the international conflict between rival empires. His prophesies about a Pacific war were somewhat apocalyptic in flavour rather than being based on a closely argued view of history, but ever since the late twenties Sukarno had seen Indonesia's salvation as coming from the clash of empires in the Pacific which would break the hold of the West. In consequence, he did not have initially the same kind of moral inhibitions about using the Japanese for nationalist purposes.[70] More positively his opposition to Western imperialism was more firmly fixed than his opposition to Japanese imperialism. The West was the real enemy. Japan was an enemy too but she could be used for Indonesia's purposes. To this extent his collaboration was willing, a fact which made him very different from Hatta, who hoped for independence ultimately through negotiations with the Dutch. There was also, perhaps, some confusion in Sukarno's mind about the likely trend of events. For a time he seemed to believe in the likelihood of a Japanese victory, and saw collaboration as the only means of working for a degree of Indonesian autonomy. In either case, though he had opposed co-operation with the Dutch on principle, the question of co-operation with the Japanese was, for him, primarily a matter of strategy.

69. ibid., p. 246.

70. In this he was perhaps not so far removed from the position of Indonesian Muslim opinion. Muslim leaders on the whole felt no strong ties of loyalty to Western liberal values and their attention had been caught by Japan's apparent interest in Islam. See H. J. Benda, *The Crescent and the Rising Sun*, The Hague, 1958, pp. 94–5.

The decisions of Sukarno and Hatta in 1942 were thus made within different intellectual frameworks. It would probably be fair to go further and to say that Sukarno's consideration of the whole complex problem was conducted within a less strict and austere moral climate than was that of Hatta. It was not just that his values were different but that he was less aware of all his assumptions, less self-conscious in arguing to himself the finer points of his position. He saw instinctively what his response should be, and to that extent his decision, quite characteristically, was made with less agony. Undoubtedly he experienced a strong feeling of exhilaration once the choice was made. Some months earlier he had been isolated and impotent. Now he was back in the thick of great events, enjoying a new prominence and in direct touch again with his people. Almost immediately after his return to Java a tour of the island gave him the thrill of contact with mass enthusiasm and the knowledge that he, the great nationalist leader, was not forgotten. With such a change in his position it was not surprising that the Japanese occupation should present itself, not as a disaster to be handled as well as might be, but as a great opportunity.

For Hatta it was very different. It was not so long since he had published a widely-read article in *Pemandangan* urging opposition to Japanese aggression and arguing 'it is better to die standing than to live kneeling'. It was specially difficult for him therefore to bow to the needs of expediency, even though, paradoxically, it had been he who had always argued during the colonial period that co-operation with the Dutch was not a matter of principle but a matter of tactics. Sjahrir, in looking back over the question after the end of the war, argued that Hatta had been compelled to accept a position under the Japanese by *force majeure*.[71] It is significant that he did not advance the same justification for Sukarno.

71. Notice, too, the coolness of Sjahrir's comment on Sukarno as compared with the warmth of his comment on Hatta. It expresses itself in particular in the rather abrupt statement of the end of their association when Japanese policies became oppressive. 'There was no longer any immediate reason for Rachman [Sukarno] to see me and I lost touch with him until just before the proclamation of our independence.' (*Out of Exile*, p. 247.)

Before we leave this question it is worth raising an interesting speculation: Had the Japanese won the war would Sukarno have continued to co-operate with them? Would he have been to a Japanese régime as Thamrin was to the Dutch – working with them in the hope of securing a greater degree of autonomy for Indonesia? There is obviously no evidence – one can only judge by the picture one develops of Sukarno. It is possible that, in his forties, he was reaching the age of corruptibility. But it would seem unlikely that he could have borne indefinitely the frustration and humiliation inherent in such a role. The probability is that he would have reverted to the non-cooperation of the twenties and early thirties, and there lies part of the explanation of the apparent inconsistency in his different attitudes to the Dutch and to the Japanese. It was the very permanence of Dutch rule which made co-operation wrong in principle. It was the hoped-for transience of Japanese rule which made co-operation a matter of tactics rather than principle.

To guess at what Sukarno would have done in the event of a Japanese victory, however, is to speculate. To judge him in 1942 it is necessary to inquire into his motives, as we have tried to do, and to assess his actual performance, which has yet to be considered. What real chance did he have to serve his cause under the Japanese?

The temper of the Japanese occupation to which Sukarno pledged his support established itself only slowly and, even in retrospect, its real nature remains something of a puzzle. Western observers have had no difficulty in characterizing Japanese imperialism as one of the most naked and cynical in history. According to this view Japan concealed her real intentions during the twenties and thirties behind a mask of fair words about building a new order in Asia while simultaneously laying her plans for Asian conquest, to be carried out by the most savage and brutal means if necessary. This was not necessarily the way it appeared to the colonial subjects of the European powers. Ever since her defeat of Russia in 1905 Japan had been a symbol of Asia's ability successfully to resist the West, and in the succeeding decades her propaganda, stressing her role as the liberator of Asia, had had considerable success even when it had become associated in the thirties with a highly mystical and racist ideology. Were Japan's 'new order' professions merely rationalizations of a determination to seize the resources of other countries? Or did they contain elements of a programme of reciprocal benefit which might reasonably command support in Southeast Asia?

The main areas in which Japan's professions could be judged before World War II were Formosa, Korea and Manchuria. In none of these were any real concessions made to the local population. Economically all three were opened to Japanese capital investment and their development was subordinated to metropolitan interests. Culturally they were subjected to intensive programmes of Japanization. Politically they were colonial dependencies effectively governed from Tokyo. It may be assumed that had she been successful in her plans for extending her new order in Southeast Asia Japan would have established a similar paramountcy in the countries concerned.[72] But Japan's capacity for self-delusion was considerable; her ultra-nationalist ideology of the thirties was not just a cynical justification of empire, if 'cynical' means that it was consciously devised to conceal an unpleasant reality. Japanese patriots of the period accepted their own propaganda and there was an element of sincerity in their belief that the Greater East Asia Co-Prosperity Sphere would bring benefit to its Southeast Asian members and be acceptable to them. When Japan talked of bringing freedom to Asia it was not conceived as freedom for individuals, or for nations, but as freedom for Asia as a whole against the imperialism of the West. Such a freedom would, in consequence, recognize Japanese leadership and the superiority of Japanese civilization.

There were, of course, many shades and differences of opinion on the part of individual Japanese, including those entrusted with the task of carrying the Co-Prosperity Sphere southwards. General Yamamoto, for example, was determined to make Indonesia serve Japanese interests. Admiral Maeda, by contrast, had a certain sympathy for Indonesian nationalist aspirations. As

72. For a consideration of Japan's plans for Indonesia in the light of her record elsewhere, see M. A. Aziz, op. cit., and W. H. Elsbree, *Japan's Role in Southeast Asian Nationalist Movements*, New York, 1953.

liaison officer between army and navy in Djakarta, Maeda secured for himself a special position of confidence in Indonesian nationalist circles during the war through his ability to understand the nature of nationalist hopes and to see a proper place for their fulfilment within the broader plan for the Co-Prosperity Sphere.

But no doubt he was an exception. In fact the temper of Japanese rule in the Indies was harsh, and its immediate objective, naturally enough, was to subordinate Indonesian interests to Japanese war needs. Though the authorities from time to time did show signs of willingness to make concessions to Indonesian feelings, it would seem to have been for reasons of expediency rather than of principle. During the years of the Occupation there were distinct changes of mood as concessions, or promises of concessions, were replaced by efforts to wring the last ounce from the Indies in support of the Japanese war effort, and as these in turn were replaced by renewed relaxation in the hope of securing more willing Indonesian co-operation.

In such an environment Sukarno had to judge with care the limits within which he had freedom to move. He had some leverage; having put almost every Dutchman in the Indies into prison camps, the Japanese were forced to rely on Indonesians to fill many of the positions formerly filled by Dutch officials and, for a time, these people enjoyed a tremendous access of confidence as they discovered their ability to exercise the administrative responsibilities from which the Dutch had excluded them. In the territorial administration the Japanese continued to rely, as the Dutch had done, on the *priyayi* administrative corps. At the same time Japan was anxious to secure the support of political leaders who could persuade the population at large to accept their régime. This was the part assigned to Sukarno and Hatta. They, together with Ki Hadjar Dewantoro (Suwardi Suryaningrat) and, as a representative of Muslim opinion, Kiyayi Mansur, chairman of Muhammadiyah, came to be known as the 'Four-Leaved Clover' (Empat Serangkai), and were, at first informally and later formally, used by the military administration as the representatives of Indonesian mass opinion.

Despite these apparent steps towards co-operation with the

Indonesian leaders Japan was nevertheless determined to keep power firmly in her own hands. Nationalist leaders were given prestige but no executive authority and there was no intention of allowing any real concessions to Indonesian aspirations. One of the first actions of the military administration was to ban independent political activity, and, shortly afterwards, to dissolve all political organizations. Even such simple manifestations of nationalist sentiment as the flying of the nationalist red and white flag or the singing of 'Indonesia Raya' were forbidden. The Japanese flag was to be flown on appropriate occasions. The Japanese calendar was adopted. Dutch street names were replaced by Japanese names. Steps were taken also to reshape the educational system in order to give effect to the conqueror's guiding principle of Japanization. In these circumstances Sukarno had to move circumspectly. In public speeches he extolled the Japanese nation and promised Indonesian support in the struggle against Western imperialism. At the same time he sought to keep alive a vision of the Indonesian future. 'Long live Japan' became a familiar conclusion to his speeches but he added also 'Long live the Land and the People of Indonesia'. If he could sometimes get away with sentiments which went well beyond Japanese wishes it was because he continued to be useful to the authorities and was able to fit himself to some extent into their policies.

In the field of political mobilization the Japanese felt their way gradually. They were concerned to create an officially sponsored front-type organization to serve as a substitute for the organizations they had proscribed. In April 1942 they inaugurated the AAA (Triple A) movement which was planned as a united front of all political forces. Its purpose was to inculcate the concept of Japanese leadership of Asia – a goal which was implicit in its title since the three A's stood for the three slogans: 'Japan the Leader of Asia', 'Japan the Protector of Asia', 'Japan the Light of Asia'. Sukarno and Hatta held themselves aloof from this movement and it was hardly surprising that the Japanese should soon feel the necessity of devising more subtle methods of maintaining contact with both the political and religious leaders of the people and of securing some measure of co-operation from them.

The need to conciliate Islam seemed particularly great. The

vigorous activity of secular nationalism in the late twenties and early thirties and the comparative quiescence of Islam in the political sphere after the decline of Sarekat Islam had combined, during the closing years of Dutch rule, to conceal the tremendous political potential of religious feeling. In fact no secular nationalist party, whether the non-cooperating PNI, Partindo, the moderate PRI or Parindra had ever succeeded in stirring the massive ground-swell of popular support which had once carried Sarekat Islam into a dominant position, and though Islam had withdrawn from politics in the thirties it was still an important force. It was also less affected by the influence of Western liberal and democratic thinking and was thus less likely to be automatically hostile to Japan as a fascist power. Given the concern of the Japanese before the war to woo Muslims in Indonesia and elsewhere, there was at least the possibility in 1942 that Indonesian Islam might be manipulated so as to provide some basis of support for Japanese rule. Islam was deeply divided in a number of ways – between conservative and reformist, between rural *ulama* and urban *santri*, between politically active Muslim organizations and those concerned with social rather than political goals. The aim of Japan's Islamic policy was to bridge these divisions and create a single organization under the influence of the military administration and able to speak for Muslims with a united voice.

It was a difficult aim to achieve and, in the event, the Japanese adopted several simultaneous courses of action. They made a direct approach to the simple and conservative *ulamas* of Java. The Japanese head of the Religious Affairs Department of the military administration made a sweep through Java in May 1942 visiting rural centres of Islam. This was followed by an invitation to representative Muslim teachers to visit Djakarta where they were fêted and flattered in a manner unheard of under the Dutch. At the same time the Japanese at a different level reconstituted the pre-war MIAI ('Islamic Council of Indonesia') which had been dissolved along with other organizations in July 1942. Finally in November 1943 a new Islamic federation was created – Madjelis Sjuro Muslimin Indonesia ('Consultative Council of Indonesian Muslims') abbreviated to 'Masjumi'. Unlike the

MIAI, Masjumi embraced both Muhammadiyah and Nahdatul Ulama.

By these several methods the Occupation appealed to different elements within the Islamic community and in so doing it gave to Islam as a whole a political importance that it had not enjoyed for twenty years. This policy paved the way for Islam's independent position within the future Republic of Indonesia. However it did not succeed in creating the acquiescent Islam desired by the Japanese. A permanent gulf was fixed between Japanese doctrines of the divine origins of her empire and the equally absolute claims of Islam. The Japanese requirement, for example, that Indonesians bow in the direction of Tokyo at the beginning of meetings offended Muslims through its very resemblance to their own ceremonial and was in due course dropped, but the hostility it had aroused remained. Though Masjumi may have given the Occupation an appearance of Muslim support, that support was temporary and uncertain.

The Japanese attempt to win Muslim opinion was balanced by the simultaneous wooing of other forces and in particular by the attempt to secure the support of leaders of secular nationalism. Here Sukarno was on his home ground. If Japan wished to organize a more effective degree of popular co-operation than the Triple A movement then she would have to associate the nationalist leaders more closely with it. This fact gave weight to Sukarno's proposal that a new all-embracing political party should be formed, able to represent the nation as a whole. The Japanese authorities recognized the expediency of going along with the suggestion, though they were probably taken by surprise when Sukarno, in a premature announcement of the proposed organization, discussed its functions as being to harden the masses in preparation for a future struggle and to forge the Indonesian people into a single unity.[73] Here was an example of one of his common tactics. In public statements he was often able to commit the Japanese to promises they had not quite made, but from which it was then a little difficult for them to withdraw.

There was some delay in securing approval from Tokyo for the

73. Article in *Asia Raya*, special issue 7 December 1942 (2602), and a speech on the following day published in *Asia Raya*, 9 December 1942.

creation of the mass organization but eventually the first anniversary of the completion of the conquest of Java – 9 March 1943 – was chosen as its inauguration date. The movement was to be known as 'Putera' (an abbreviation of Pusat Tenaga Rakjat – 'Centre of the People's Power'). Sukarno was appointed chairman and his colleagues, Hatta, Ki Hadjar and Mansur, together with an equal number of Japanese, formed its Advisory Council.

In his speech on the occasion Sukarno once again placed the emphasis as much on the development of Indonesia's popular strength as he did on the function of the movement as an aid to the Japanese struggle against the West. He referred to the fact that the acronym 'Putera' was an Indonesian word with its own meaning – son. '*Putera*, the name which recalls to each son of Indonesia that he is a Son of his Mother, with the responsibility to honour her so long as blood still flows in his veins and a soul still lives in his body.'[74] His closing words had, perhaps, a double meaning for his hearers: 'Long Live Japan! Long Live Indonesia! Long live the new movement of Pusat Tenaga Rakjat! Long Live the great assembly of Putera!'

The formation of Putera seemed, on the face of it, to be a victory for Sukarno. It gave a boost to the nationalist leadership which offset to some extent the improved position of Islam under Occupation rule and it provided a base for the pressing of further demands. It gave a formal standing to Sukarno himself and it provided him with an organization through which, with luck and an adequate degree of Japanese permissiveness, he could reach out to the people as a whole. The Japanese, of course, saw it in rather a different light. In forming such an organization they were not really intending to make a genuine concession to local opinion. Despite the Indonesian elements in Putera's Central Council and in the local branches of the movement the military authorities allowed it no real power. In practice Putera was used to mobilize a semblance of support for the Japanese war effort through the cooperation of Sukarno and the other accepted leaders of the nationalist movement, and among other things it was harnessed to the service of the forced labour (*romusha*) programme of the

74. *Asia Raya*, 9 March 1943 (2603).

Occupation. The conscription of Indonesian labourers to serve the Japanese army, not only in Indonesia but in other parts of Southeast Asia, was one of the harshest and most resented aspects of Occupation rule. The *romushas* were pressed into labour battalions and used for road-making or plantation-maintenance or for the many other tasks involved in supporting the Japanese war machine. Though no certain figures exist whereby the impact of the programme can be precisely determined it is estimated that well over a quarter of a million such labourers were sent overseas, and that only about seventy thousand of them ever returned to Indonesia.

There was indeed a delicate balance of moral issues, with no easy way of determining whether the chairman of Putera was more effective in serving his own people or in helping the Japanese. Sukarno's actions were in part determined by his judgement about the likely outcome of the war. In early 1943 he was visited by three young men, the medical students, Soedjatmoko and Soedarpo, and Soebadio, a law student. The three were acting on their own initiative and they wanted to make a personal protest about the style of Sukarno's collaboration. They confronted Sukarno at his office and indicated that they would wait there until he agreed to see them. Sukarno began to handle them with practised skill, explaining the difficulties of his position and the needs of the situation as he saw it. Sensing that the initiative was slipping away from them and that the interview might be over before it had properly begun, Soedjatmoko made a bid to catch and hold the attention of the older man. He did so by bursting out with 'We have come to renounce our allegiance to you, Bung.' This did stop Sukarno and made him listen more carefully to them. A long argument developed in which Sukarno put his view that the Japanese were likely to win the war. From their clandestine radio sources the young men believed otherwise and they argued that Sukarno's actions should be based on the expectation of an Allied victory.[75]

They left him unconvinced, no doubt, but by early 1944 Sukarno had come to agree with them. During 1943 and 1944 the

75. Author's interview with Soedjatmoko, July 1969. Sukarno's account of the incident is given in his *Autobiography*, p. 193.

worsening of the war situation led to a series of marked oscilla-
tions in Japan's attitude to nationalist pressure. Some concessions
were made to local feeling, then Occupation control was tightened
up again, and finally Japan moved gradually towards a policy
more seriously designed to create an independent Indonesia.
Sukarno adjusted himself quickly to each of these changes.

The first phase opened on 16 July 1943 when in a speech to the
Diet the Premier of Japan, General Tojo, foreshadowed a shift in
policy in some of the occupied areas of Southeast Asia. Referring
specifically to Java he spoke of the intention of associating the
local population more directly with the processes of government.
In July Tojo made a personal visit to Djakarta in the course of
which he repeated his promise that opportunities would be given
to Indonesians to participate in government. But there were signs
of fundamental differences of view. Dahm points out that whereas Sukarno in his contribution to the exchange of speeches
referred in his usual way to 'Indonesia', Tojo pointedly referred
only to 'the Southern Regions' and the 'Natives of Java', thus
implicitly rejecting the nationalist concept which was integral to
Sukarno's plan.[76] Sukarno made his own point clearly enough by
contrasting the visit of Tojo, bringing 'love to the Indonesian
people', with the 1941 visit of the Dutch Minister of the Colonies,
who came only to strengthen colonial rule, and he emphasized
the Japanese decision to give the people of Indonesia a share in
their own government.[77] Even so, there was little in the exchange
to encourage Sukarno in his hopes that extensive concessions
would be made towards limited self-government.

In September the creation of a hierarchy of deliberative bodies
seemed to offer some fulfilment of the Japanese promise. In
Djakarta a Central Advisory Council was established, again
under Sukarno's presidency, and local councils were set up in
each residency and in the municipality of Djakarta. Side by side
with this development a number of Indonesians were appointed
to positions within the administration – to the Departments of
General Affairs, Education, Justice, Propaganda, Religious

76. Dahm, *Sukarno and the Struggle for Indonesian Independence*, pp.
250–51.

77. *Asia Raya*, 8 July 1943 (2603).

Affairs and Public Works – and similar appointments were made to the regional administrative services.

Despite Sukarno's brave hope, expressed as he opened the first meeting of the Central Advisory Council, that 'Today we begin a new era',[78] the whole system of councils seemed in some ways almost a reconstitution of the council system established by the Dutch in the twenties and thirties. The Central Advisory Council bore a strong family resemblance to the Volksraad. Twenty of the forty-three members were nominated by the Commander-in-Chief of the 16th Army and the remainder were elected by the local councils. Like the Volksraad it was essentially an advisory body, but one important difference was that the Volksraad gave its members a forum in which they could debate genuine issues and criticize government policy even though they could not change it. The Central Advisory Council allowed no such freedom of debate. Yet, within the context of the Occupation, the creation of the Central Advisory Council did mark an important advance from the Indonesian point of view. Meeting every three or four months, its real function, admittedly, was to provide for the Japanese the appearance of Indonesian co-operation and to give them an indication of local feeling on such questions as rice levies or the *romusha* system.[79] But by the same token the Council had an opportunity to bring pressure to bear on the military authorities to modify some aspects of unpopular policies. More important in the long run was the fact that it gave Sukarno an additional position of prestige which, with care, he could turn to his own ends. As with Putera, his chairmanship of the Central Advisory Council enabled him to reach out, as their leader, to the population of Java as a whole. Every new symbol of representation and autonomy was important in creating a vision of future independence.

In addition to the council system other important measures were adopted during this 1943 period of Japanese conciliation. Efforts to win the backing of Islamic leaders were complemented by attempts to tap a further reservoir of support in the ranks of Indonesian youth. From the beginning of 1943 a series of youth organizations were set up for this purpose, offering a simple train-

78. *Asia Raya*, 17 October 1943 (2603).
79. See Aziz, op. cit., Part II, Chapter IV.

ing in the elements of military drill and providing the authorities with the means of inculcating pro-Japanese ideals. One of the more important of these organizations was the Seinendan, directed towards the village people of Java; later ones were aimed at the urban youth, including high-school students. Such organizations had a considerable attraction for young men tossed out of their traditional place in society by the turbulence of the times; they offered a corporate existence with values markedly different from those of the older nationalist leaders of Indonesia. Some elements of Japanese militarism inevitably rubbed off on those who were introduced to it in this way – they were attracted by the authoritarian values of the Japanese young officer class, by its belief in spiritual power (not so very different from the Javanese idea of *semangat*), by the values of austerity and courage and by the use made of theatrical ritual. They acquired a fascinated respect for the manifestions of power – and an acceptance of violence almost as a virtue in itself. More importantly, the experience gave some of these young men a prospect of direct participation in the affairs of the nation when the time came. In due course this was to make 'youth as such' – the *pemudas* – an independent element in nationalist politics and to affect the setting in which Sukarno's own part was to be played.[80]

In September 1943 this sort of policy was carried a big step forward when the Japanese agreed to the formation of a volunteer military force to be composed of, and officered by, Indonesians, but trained by the Japanese. The idea of an Indonesian force had been suggested in a number of quarters. It had the support of the nationalist leadership as represented in Putera, and later in the Central Advisory Council. In October 1943 the creation of the force, to be known as the 'Volunteer Army of Defenders of the Homeland' (Sukarela Tentara Pembela Tanah Air, abbreviated to Peta) was announced.

From the Japanese point of view Peta was a means of preparing an Indonesian defence against possible Allied landings. From the Indonesian point of view its function was different: in giving a

80. See B. R. O'G. Anderson, *Java in a Time of Revolution: Occupation and Resistance 1944–1946* (Ithaca, 1972), chapter 2, for an account of Peta's emotional function for Javanese youth.

military training to Indonesians it gave nationalism the possibility of something it had never had before – armed force.
Though it was under Japanese supervision, and though its access
to arms was kept under strict control, it was an Indonesian force
under Indonesian officers and its leadership was chosen from
among men of the nationalist-minded intelligentsia. In its rank
and file were many of those who had been enrolled in one or
other of the youth organizations, and though the force as a whole
was subject to a good deal of Japanese indoctrination in the
course of military training, Sukarno and his associates were able
to argue to the Japanese that nationalist fervour was important
if such a force was really to play a part in defending the homeland
against Allied landings. The nationalist leadership was therefore
able, through propaganda and through its influence on the selection of officers, to expound its own ideas within Peta's ranks and
Peta was in due course to emerge as the core of the army of the
Republic of Indonesia. Even during the Occupation some sections of it showed their revolutionary fervour by staging revolts
against the Japanese authorities, as in the Blitar Revolt of
February 1944.

Taken together, the prestigious position given to nationalist
leaders, the formation of the advisory council system, and the
establishment of Peta added up at least to a limited Japanese
recognition of nationalist aims and Sukarno was the beneficiary
of this policy. His own personal life at this time had undergone
some readjustments during the year. In 1943 his relations with
Inggit reached a crisis which was resolved by divorce. Fatmawati
was still in Sumatra but in June he married her by proxy and
brought her shortly afterwards to Djakarta. In the following year
his eldest son, Guntur, was born.

In November 1943 Sukarno, with the aura of his office as
President of the Central Advisory Council about him, led a small
delegation consisting of Hatta and Ki Bagus Hadikusumo to
Tokyo to express the thanks of the Indonesian people for the
concessions granted them. It was a formal visit; the party was
fêted and its members were decorated by the Emperor. For
Sukarno the visit was of tremendous importance, for it was his
first experience of the world outside the Indies. Unlike Hatta,

Sjahrir, Sartono and many others whose names studded the rolls of nationalist leadership, Sukarno had not had the opportunity of travel and overseas study. He had not visited Holland and, until his visit to Japan, he had never seen an industrialized society. The impact must have been considerable.

In retrospect his visit represented the end of Japan's first wooing of the nationalist leadership. By this time the emphasis of Occupation policy had begun to shift.[81] The authorities felt, perhaps, that the concessions made to Indonesian opinion during the course of the year in the form of Putera and the council system had served nationalist rather than Japanese ends. The pressure of the Pacific War to which the Occupation authorities were reacting had led to the emergence of contradictory counsels. Some pointed to the vital importance of trying to enlist Indonesian support for the war effort and stressed the importance of ensuring that the local population should side with the Japanese in the event of Allied landings in Indonesia. Others saw a need for greater ruthlessness in directing Indonesian manpower and resources to war needs. By the end of 1943 the latter voices were beginning to prevail, and steps were taken to check further advances towards an expansion of Indonesian autonomy and to bring the existing organs under Occupation control. Putera was dissolved and replaced by a new 'People's Loyalty Organization' to be known as the Djawa Hokokai.[82]

The Djawa Hokokai was officially inaugurated at the beginning of March 1944. It differed markedly from Putera. The announcement of its formation made no bones about its purposes; the old

81. Dahm, op. cit., gives May 1943 as the date for a marked shift in Japanese policy. He points out that Yamamoto's appointment was followed by Japan's decision to incorporate Indonesia within the Japanese empire (pp. 245–8). But the Japanese, too, were feeling their way and there was still room after May for Sukarno and his colleagues to manoeuvre. Their efforts to make Putera serve nationalist ends were countered by Japanese actions to control it, certainly, but against Dahm's argument must be set the formation of the Central Advisory Council and of Peta. The Central Advisory Council was intended to serve Japanese interests it is true, but in some measure, as Dahm points out (pp. 254–5), it was successfully used by Sukarno for nationalist purposes. There are thus some grounds for dating the real 'crunch' for Sukarno and his colleagues as coming later than May.

82. *Asia Raya*, 9 January 1944 (2604).

formulae about 'co-operation' between Indonesians and Japanese were absent and the emphasis was placed firmly on the mobilization of all efforts towards winning the war. The tentacles of Djawa Hokokai penetrated more deeply to the base of village society from the central organization down to neighbourhood associations within the village or urban *kampong*. The maintenance of regional and village branches was compulsory – thus enabling Japanese control to be imposed at all levels. Sukarno remained as chairman of the new organization but he worked more closely under the supervision of the military government than he had as head of Putera, and his freedom of action was thus much reduced.

If the formation of the Djawa Hokokai was a sign of growing Japanese desperation in the face of their declining fortunes in the war, a further shift of policy occurred in the course of 1944. As Japanese reverses made themselves still more apparent, voices urging greater concessions to Indonesian nationalism once again became influential. On 7 September 1944 Tojo's successor, Premier Koiso, announced to the Diet that independence would be granted to the Indies in the near future.

When this promise was announced with banner headlines in *Asia Raya*, Sukarno, in a Press interview, looked back to his own 1942 decision to work with the Japanese military government and felt that his choice had been the right one. Lasting freedom could only be obtained through sacrifice, he said. He still called on the Indonesian people to support Japan's struggle for a Greater East Asia, but the sacrifice to which he referred included for him and his hearers, no doubt, the hardship and humiliation which the Occupation had imposed.[83]

The Koiso Declaration changed the whole setting of political action in Indonesia. Certainly its wording was indefinite. No date was set for the fulfilment of the promise and Japanese commanders in the area were informed that it was not intended to set a

83. *Asia Raya*, 8 September 1944 (2604). Dahm (pp. 225–6) notices Sukarno's habit of looking for dramatic moments when decisions were made – in this case his meeting with Fujiyama in 1942 'at the entrance to Ngarai' – the wild gorge on the outskirts of Bukit Tinggi. It should be added, however, that he began to use this phrase after the event, when the gamble had succeeded.

definite date for the time being.[84] In the event it was to be six months before positive steps were taken to set up an Indonesian preparatory committee to explore the means by which the transition to independence could be effected, and several more months before Japan moved decisively towards the fulfilment of the promise. By that time she had lost the ability to complete the task. But the promise itself, and the expectations it aroused, released new forces in Indonesia. The new situation as it emerged in the closing months of the war, and Sukarno's role in manipulating it, are worth separate consideration. Before turning to this new phase of Sukarno's political career we must return to the questions posed earlier in this chapter. In the light of the record of 1942, 1943 and early 1944 can one assess his collaboration more accurately? We have looked at his initial motives. What of his actual performance?

Sukarno's co-operation with the authorities brought him the chairmanship of Putera and of the Djawa Hokokai and the presidency of the Central Advisory Council. These posts were important in shaping him as a leader. After years of opposition, non-cooperation, imprisonment and exile, he suddenly had position and responsibility. At the same time he was involved in the performance of unpopular tasks. He had to mobilize support for the Japanese war effort; he used extravagant pro-Japanese slogans; he played his part in the *romusha* programme and in controlling village production for the army's needs. Undoubtedly the Japanese benefited enormously from his co-operation – it served abundantly the purpose for which they had brought him back to Java. Sukarno's justification of himself was that even while doing these things he was serving the long-term interests of Indonesian nationalism. His speeches may have been cleared by the propaganda department but a close study of them, he said, would reveal that 'seventy-five per cent of them were pure nationalism'.[85]

It would be hard to check that quantitative claim but there is

84. Anderson, *Some Aspects of Indonesian Politics Under the Japanese Occupation 1944–45*, Ithaca, 1961, p. 2.

85. *Autobiography*, p. 178.

much evidence to support it. His articles and speeches contained much praise of Japan's leadership of Asia and of its challenge to the power of Western imperialism. Only a Japanese victory could 'cleanse' Asia from imperialist influence, he wrote in an article to celebrate the first anniversary of the attack on Peal Harbour.[86] He was ready, on all occasions, to attack the Allies and his famous – or notorious – phrase '*Amerika kita setrika. Inggeris kita linggis*' ('We will iron out America and knock down the English') became a familiar refrain in his oratory. But he did keep before his audiences the idea of 'Indonesia'. Despite Japan's administrative division of the region he spoke on occasion of his voice spreading through all the islands of the archipelago,[87] and his perorations appealed again and again to his listeners to temper themselves 'in order to obtain what we desire'.[88]

There was a common pattern in his speeches and articles. The words uttered for the benefit of the Japanese were followed by exhortations of a different temper. It is interesting to notice how often in his speeches he used the word 'harden' (*gembleng*)[89] and resorted to images of steel and of welding and forging in urging his people to prepare themselves for the future. There were other times when he had to coax his listeners to follow Japanese wishes in the hope of receiving future benefits, as when he opened the first meeting of the Central Advisory Council and pointed out that more extensive concessions of autonomy would depend on the success of the present experiment. Yet he finished with his usual touch of independence. 'This is not a test imposed merely by the government,' he added. 'It is a test of History. Let us set ourselves to face this test of History with spirit. . . .'[90] Sometimes it is possible to detect a note of desperate apology as he tried to convey a sense of the difficulties of the position in which he was placed. In a Lebaran speech in 1943 he said: 'We are on the side of Japan, we stand behind Japan. We do this because we are sure

86. *Asia Raya*, special issue, 7 December 1942 (2602).

87. *Asia Raya*, 9 March 1943 (2603).

88. Article written to celebrate the Emperor Meiji's birthday, *Asia Raya*, 6 November 1942 (2602).

89. See e.g. *Asia Raya*, 7 and 9 December 1942 (2602) and 6 October 1943 (2603).

90. *Asia Raya*, 17 October 1943 (2603).

that such an attitude is the only way to secure the welfare of our country and our people in the future.'[91] But it was significant that as usual he went on to make other points. On this occasion he hailed Peta as a first step in the welding of an Indonesian nation – the force 'will be based on the Indonesian people, our own people'.[92]

In these ways he attempted to maintain his double game. His argument to his critics, as he remembered it years later, ran: 'To me, giving the Japanese what they want in return for more concessions that I need is the positive way to freedom.'[93] It was a matter of keeping his position at all costs and preventing nationalist feeling from expressing itself in anti-Japanese terms until the time was ripe.

This particular justification was made long after the event and Sukarno could appeal, in support of it, to the fact that independence had indeed been successfully achieved. Even so, it is not easy to make out a balance sheet of the rights and wrongs of his collaboration, and the task becomes more difficult if one rejects the benefits of hindsight and attempts to recapture the hopes, fears and uncertainties of the Occupation period itself. One authoritative judgement – that of Kahin – follows closely the terms of Sukarno's own defence (or was Sukarno following Kahin?). Putera, said Kahin, was for Sukarno and his colleagues primarily a means of spreading nationalist ideas. If they also helped the Japanese war effort it was 'only to the minimum extent necessary in order to allow the furtherance of their own long-term nationalist aims'.[94]

'Only to the minimum extent necessary'? Perhaps. But in the light of his record of vigorous support for the Japanese in 1942 and 1943, taken with the elements of servility and the oppressive policies that had to be defended, it would seem that Sukarno did go beyond that minimum. He does seem to have sacrificed much, to have compromised himself a very great deal in keeping himself acceptable to the Japanese authorities. He went further, much further, than the co-operators of the thirties whom he once

91. *Asia Raya*, 5 October 1943 (2603).
92. *Asia Raya*, 6 October 1943 (2603).      93. *Autobiography*, p. 193.
94. Kahin, *Nationalism and Revolution in Indonesia*, Ithaca, 1952, p. 107.

criticized so vigorously. They, of course, so it seemed to him, were co-operating fruitlessly with a firmly established colonial power which could only be overthrown by struggle. He, on the other hand, was co-operating with a temporary invader who could, in the end, be used for nationalist purposes if only the nationalist leadership could ride out the storm of military occupation. So it was to prove in the end. In the meantime the moral price was high. Was it really worth it? Would not independence have come in much the same way without Sukarno's collaboration? Was not underground resistance to the Japanese a more effective way of working for *merdeka*?

These will undoubtedly continue to be controversial questions for historians, but two points can be made here. First of all, the effectiveness of Indonesia's underground organizations during the Occupation was extremely limited. Before the final victory of the Japanese in 1942, Amir Sjarifuddin, one of the leaders of Gerindo, received funds from Dutch sources for the purpose of establishing an underground organization, but the vigilance of the *Kempetai* ('military police') kept its activities to a minimum. In 1944 a number of its members were executed and Sjarifuddin himself was saved from death only through the intervention of Sukarno. There were a number of other so-called underground groups, more or less informal in character, overlapping each other to some extent and comprising, for the most part, a comparatively youthful membership. Some were composed of students as was the case, for example, with a group based on the medical students' *Asrama* at Prapatan. Others had strong links with the Japanese authorities. One such group was based in the Asrama Angkatan Baru, set up in Menteng by the Propaganda Department of the Japanese military administration. Another group was located within the Asrama Indonesia Merdeka.

The Asrama Indonesia Merdeka was essentially a Japanese creation, the brainchild of Rear Admiral Maeda, Liaison Officer in Djakarta between the 16th Army and the naval administration of the eastern islands based in Makassar. It was intended to give a radical training to selected Indonesian youths. The motives of Maeda and his aides, Nishijima and Yoshizumi, are a matter for debate but they seem to have included an element of genuine sympathy for Indonesian nationalist aspirations.[95] The Asrama was under the general leadership of Subardjo, chief of the political affairs research bureau of the Japanese naval liaison office in Djakarta, aided by Wikana as warden. The lecturers in its courses included Sukarno, Hatta and Sjahrir and the emphasis of its curriculum was strongly nationalist. The important thing, however, about this medley of assorted groups was that neither individually nor collectively did they constitute an underground organization of the kind which existed in Occupied Europe. The Indonesian underground organizations maintained between them, no doubt, a rough kind of intelligence service, they listened illegally to foreign broadcasts and passed on information about developments within Indonesia. They also channelled anti-Japanese propaganda in key places. But they lacked the organizational coherence and the technical resources to maintain a continuing resistance to Japanese authority. Many of their members had an important part to play in the early months of the revolution. They were not, however, the makers of that revolution.

By contrast, Sukarno's role during the Occupation was of first importance in the making of the revolution. He had achieved significant tactical goals. The creation of Peta was of enormous importance for the future in providing a material basis of strength for the struggling Republic. The formation of the system of local councils provided a framework for local government which was to carry over into the revolution and to provide machinery through which the government of the Republic could extend its authority. The extended use of Indonesian as a national language was also of incalculable importance in consolidating a sense of nationhood. These were the fruits of Sukarno's own manoeuvring and bargaining and they reflected his mastery of political skills, going beyond his gifts of inspirational oratory.

There were other still more personal achievements: his very presence as the formal representative of the Indonesian people within the military régime helped to strengthen the mass awareness of him as the leader of his people and to create an awareness,

95. See Kahin, op. cit., pp. 115–21 for an alternative hypothesis. See also Anderson, *Some Aspects of Indonesian Politics Under the Japanese Occupation 1944–45*, pp. 50–51.

too, of his proclaimed goals. Sukarno might not really have preached pure nationalism quite as courageously, nor have stood as firmly against Japanese authorities as he claimed, but during these years he possessed channels of communication to the masses that had simply not existed for himself or for other political leaders in the past, and his use of them created a new electorate for the future. The opportunity to make speeches on formal occasions, his freedom to travel throughout Java, and, more significantly, the extension of radio communication throughout village Indonesia were of tremendous importance; his ability through the use of *wayang* allusions or other forms of private symbolism enabled him to by-pass official censorship to a great extent, and to reach out directly to his Javanese audiences. The provision of village radios – 'singing trees' as they were known – was for the purpose of informing the Javanese of the wishes of their conquerors. In practice they also made known the ideas and the person of Sukarno.

Sukarno's mode of working within Japanese policy may have seemed less than admirable to his critics, but his achievement in creating this new electorate was to be of crucial importance in the future. It helped to lay the foundation for a revolution, which would be experienced by those who took part in it as a natural climax to years of national effort in which differences were unimportant beside the overwhelming fact of being one nation. This was, no doubt, a romantic view of the history of the nationalist movement of the twenties and thirties. It was, nonetheless, of importance in sustaining the final struggle for independence. Though Sukarno, for the time being, was working within a Japanese-created situation and under the ultimate control of Japanese power, he was beginning to forge viable bases of alternative power which would stand when Japanese authority was withdrawn.

These were important achievements and they went far towards justifying the choice that Sukarno made in 1942. It is wrong to argue, as some have done, that the collaboration issue does not arise in a judgement of Sukarno. Of course it arises, and if one holds the view that willing co-operation with an occupying power is of itself cowardly and weak, then Sukarno does not emerge too well from a study of the Occupation. But the criterion is very severe. Equally one should notice the assurance with which he made his choice and the confidence with which he swept through the following years, handling the Japanese and his own people and turning events where he could to the advantage of the nationalist cause. This ability and its achievement must command admiration.

The consequences were important for himself as well as for Indonesia. From his first experience of political organization and leadership through the publicity of his trial and the martyrdom of his imprisonment and exile, Sukarno had gradually established a central position for himself in the nationalist movement, but these years of Occupation were the years in which he became the ostensible leader of an Indonesian nation.

# 8

# The Proclamation of Independence

For Sukarno the Koiso Declaration was the light at the end of the tunnel. It marked the opening of a new phase in the Japanese occupation and created a situation in which he could escape, bit by bit, from the humiliations of the past two years and begin to act with a more satisfying degree of independence. But, paradoxically, the new situation had its restricting as well as its liberating features for Sukarno. As the leader of Putera and Djawa Hokokai he had been a national figure embodying the hopes of all Indonesians, albeit within a Japanese power structure. After the Koiso Declaration politics became a little more open and various forces began to manoeuvre against each other. There was some irony in the fact that Sukarno, in spite of his efforts to continue to bestride all factions, tended, as in the late twenties and early thirties, to become associated with one particular element in the political amalgam rather than act as the representative of them all.

The essence of Japanese occupation policy had been balance. The military administration, as we have seen, maintained an equilibrium between distinct and possibly rival groups. It had wooed rural Islam and cultivated the support of modernist Islamic opinion too; it had sought to bind *priyayi* officials and other customary leaders of society to its own purposes in much the same way as the Dutch had done and it gave prestige and prominence to the secular nationalist leadership. In pursuing these parallel policies Japan was also altering and reshaping the essential forces of Indonesian nationalism. The use of Indonesian civil servants in minor positions, though limited, had given a new confidence to members of the élite. The politicization of Islam had given form and content to a latent and powerful political force. The youth organizations and the creation of Peta had given 'youth as such' a sense of its own identity and a perception of a bold and revolutionary role for it to play. As long as Japan asserted ultimate power a balance could be artificially maintained between these forces, but with the promise of independence a new sharpness of rivalry made itself felt.

In the event Sukarno and his colleagues were to be the first beneficiaries of Occupation policies. The secular nationalist leadership had used well its opportunity to establish itself firmly during 1942 and 1943, so that after September 1944, when the last phase of the Occupation began to run its course, its superior strength was apparent. Masjumi, its most effectively organized rival for power and influence, was strangely quiescent in the early months of 1945. It managed to avoid being absorbed into the Djawa Hokokai but, though it kept its separate identity and though its leaders regarded with suspicion Sukarno's attempts to construct a national synthesis, in fact the balance of forces maintained by Japanese policy was gradually tilted in favour of the secular nationalists.

Nevertheless the very circumstances of 1945 did place a premium on harmony. With independence apparently within reach at last, there was obvious advantage in avoiding division and conflict in nationalist ranks and therefore much justification for Sukarno to assume that he was the representative of all groups. As in the late twenties, and again in 1932, this was the position to which he most aspired. His position during the Occupation had enabled him to convey to the population at large a new sense of a common Indonesian identity and he could justly be said to have created the mass basis on which the Indonesian revolution was to be built. In August 1945 he was the indispensable figure without whom a declaration of independence could not be made.

The main setting for Sukarno's political activities in the closing months of the Occupation was an 'investigating body for the preparation of Indonesian independence' (Badan Penjelidik Usaha Persiapan Kemerdekaan Indonesia – usually abbreviated to BPKI), a committee established by the Japanese to consider all aspects, political and administrative, relating to the creation of an independent Indonesia. The decision to establish the BPKI was announced on 1 March 1945 after several months in which nothing had been done to implement the promises of the Koiso

Declaration. It was in doubt whether the Japanese seriously intended the committee to chart a course of positive action or
whether they regarded it as a possible diversionary tactic. It was
to be merely an advisory body, but its terms of reference were
wide and it is probable that the Japanese expected it to become
bogged down in undirected discussion of which the only consequence would be an exposure of the factional differences of its
members. If so, their hopes were to be disappointed, for the
committee's deliberations, partly as a result of Sukarno's own
contribution, proved to be disciplined and effective.

The announcement of the decision to create the BPKI was
followed by a further delay of two months before its membership
was finally determined. On 28 April, a list of sixty names was
published. Apart from the Indonesian chairman, Dr Radjiman
Wedioningrat, and the two vice-chairmen (one Indonesian and
one Japanese), there were to be sixty ordinary members drawn
from the main ethnic groups of Indonesia and from the chief
currents of nationalist thought and organization. There were also
to be seven Japanese observers. Though it was in some ways a
widely representative body the committee was heavily weighted
on the side of age rather than youth and on the side of secular
nationalism rather than Muslim opinion.[96] Sjahrir and Hatta
were members, of course, and they, together with other political
leaders who could be described as secular nationalists, comprised
almost thirty-four per cent of the total. Representatives of the
territorial administrative corps formed another sixteen per cent.
By contrast, representatives of the Islamic élite made up only
eleven per cent and Islam was thus strikingly under-represented.
This imbalance gave Sukarno a forum favourable to himself and
enabled him to impose the stamp of his own personality on its
proceedings. For the time being, under his leadership, secular
nationalism was able to stake its claim to constitute the vanguard
of Indonesian nationalism.

After a preliminary meeting early in May the BPKI eventually
gathered on 28 May for its first plenary session. For Sukarno
there was perhaps some amused satisfaction in the choice of

96. For an analysis of the membership see Anderson, *Some Aspects of
Indonesian Politics Under the Japanese Occupation 1944–45*, p. 18 ff.

locale – the heavily imperial building behind whose sturdy pillars the Volksraad had once carried on its deliberations. Proceedings were opened with much ceremony by the commander of the 16th Army, General Nagano, who was followed by other inaugural speakers. Even when the opening formalities were over the committee was slow in getting down to serious business and the session was in danger of losing its way in formal rhetoric when Sukarno, on 1 June, seized the opportunity to make his own intervention. In a speech which proved to be one of the great occasions of his career he drew the meeting together, smoothed over the differences for the moment, and aroused a sense of united purpose. He did so by giving a new and passionate statement of the ideas which had formed the core of his political thinking over twenty years, and which he now advanced with some additions and some new emphasis, in the form of five fundamental principles, his *Pantja Sila*.

Sukarno saw his *Pantja Sila* as providing a philosophical basis for nationalist action and for the future republic to which it was leading. The principles were devised in a form which would, he hoped, embrace the separate currents of nationalism and make possible the unity he so desired.[97]

The five principles were nationalism, internationalism (or humanitarianism), democracy (or consent), social prosperity and belief in God. Together Sukarno saw them as bringing together the fruits of Western thinking and the traditional values embedded deeply in Indonesian society. They contained, he said later, 'the essence of the Indonesian spirit'.[98] Each was expounded at some length.

It was not surprising that nationalism should be Sukarno's first principle. He explained that it should be understood not in the narrow sense of freedom from foreign rule but in the positive sense of making a self-conscious people. Renan's definition of nationalism in terms of a desire to be together was no longer sufficient for him since it could be used to justify the ethnic nationalism of small groups of people. The Indonesian nation by

97. The speech was published as 'Lahirnja Pantja Sila' and in translation as 'The Birth of Pantja Sila', Djakarta, 1950.

98. Independence Day speech, 17 August 1956.

contrast must reach out beyond ethnic communities and comprise 'all human beings who, according to geopolitics ordained by God Almighty, live throughout the entire archipelago of Indonesia from the northern tip of Sumatra to Papua!' He saw the unity of Indonesia as based on the glorious past – in the realms of Srivijaya and Madjapahit – but clearly to recapture that sense of nationhood required positive action. Nationalism 'in the fullest sense' meant 'neither Javanese nationalism nor Sumatran nationalism nor the nationalism of Borneo, or Celebes, Bali or any other, but the Indonesian nationalism which at one and the same time becomes the principle of one national state'.

Nationalism needed to be seen together with his second principle, that of internationalism. Nationalism was in danger of becoming petty patriotism and needed to be balanced by respect for other peoples, by the principle of internationalism. But internationalism itself needed to be distinguished from mere 'cosmopolitanism' which did not recognize nationalism. On the contrary, it should be 'rooted in the soil of nationalism', and thus the first two principles were dovetailed together.

Similarly, democracy and social justice were closely linked in his mind. Democracy (or representative government, or consent) would enable fair play for different forces which could compete with each other within the framework of representative government. But political democracy would not guarantee prosperity for all. In Western democracies, he claimed, the capitalists were in control and there was no social justice or economic democracy.

Finally came his insistence that the state should rest on a belief in one God, though this principle must have room for tolerance and mutual respect. 'Not only should the people of Indonesia have belief in one God, but every Indonesian should believe in *his own* particular god. The Christian should worship God according to the teachings of Jesus Christ, the Muslim according to the teachings of the prophet Mohammad, Buddhists should discharge their religious rites according to their own books, but let us all have belief in God.' (Christ and Mohammad, he added, both showed tolerance to other religions.)

Having elaborated his five principles Sukarno attempted to show them all to be part of the one whole. 'The two first principles, nationalism and internationalism, nationalism and humanitarianism, I press down to one, which I used to call *socio-nationalism*.' Similarly with democracy 'which is not the democracy of the West but politico-economic democracy, together with social justice'. This is also 'pressed down to one' and called socio-democracy. Finally – belief in God. 'And so what originally was *five* has become *three*: socio nationalism, socio–democracy and belief in God.' But these three could again be gathered together to form one principle. In establishing an Indonesian state all should be responsible – 'all for all'. Therefore:

'If I press down five to get three, and three to get one, then I have a genuine Indonesian term – *gotong rojong* [mutual co-operation]. The state of Indonesia which we are to establish should be a state of mutual co-operation. How fine that is! A *Gotong Rojong* state!'

In this remarkable statement Sukarno's search for synthesis and one-ness received its ultimate expression.

In its intellectual content the *Pantja Sila* speech did not add a great deal to Sukarno's early ideas. Nationalism was not, on this occasion, dealt with as the overriding principle, able to reconcile competing attitudes; but in stressing the importance of social justice and a belief in God as basic principles for the revolution he was, nonetheless, echoing the argument of his old 'Nationalism, Islam and Marxism' essay. With the compression of his five principles to three and from three to one he was stressing the indigenous character of them all and claiming that they fell squarely within the Indonesian tradition. As a whole the speech opened a grand vision of unity and it was greeted with thundering acclamation. It contained, it is true, nothing in the way of a plan of practical action. There was no consideration of the urgent and specific details involved in the transition to independence; but ideas and feelings were of practical importance too. After the last three years of enforced service to the interests of Japanese propaganda Sukarno's speech came as an inspiration to his hearers. In the setting of the Occupation it was revolutionary, and this sort of stimulus was vitally necessary if the élite was to be nerved to the task ahead. For Sukarno too the response was an inspiration. This was an occasion when his desire for unity was exactly in line with the feelings of his audience: he could move them with his vision and they could inspire in him the confidence on which he depended.

In the end, of course, and after the emotional euphoria had died away, its success as a unifying doctrine proved to be limited. Sukarno intended the speech to provide a state philosophy. 'This philosophical basis is the fundamental, the philosophy, the underlying reason, the spirit, the deepest desire on which to build the structure of a Free Indonesia, enduring and age-long.' In the years to come quite diverse groups were to use it to justify their attitudes and actions. Nevertheless its appeal was less than universal. It did not bridge effectively the main divisions of Indonesian nationalism and it tended to be not a state philosophy but the philosophy of one constituency. Muslims, in particular, under-represented in the BPKI, were offended at the fact that Sukarno regarded Islam as but one religion among many. He claimed that he himself was a Muslim: 'If you open my breast and look at my heart, you will find it none other than Islamic.' But his real attitude was made abundantly clear when he rejected the idea of an Islamic basis for the state and told Muslims bluntly that their path to influence should lie only through the support they could command within a representative assembly.

'The House of Representatives, this is the place for us to bring forward the demands of Islam. . . . If we really are Islamic people, let us work hard, so that most of the seats in the People's Representative Body we will create are occupied by Islamic delegates . . . then the laws made by this representative body will naturally be Islamic laws.'

Even though in this passage he spoke of 'us' bringing forward the demands of Islam in the House of Representatives, it was clear from the context that he meant 'them'. He was too concerned with his desire for a consensus embracing different groups ever to want to see Muslims in such a position of strength that they would dominate the consensus.

He went on to suggest even more bluntly that in fact Indonesia was not an Islamic country. 'We say that ninety per cent of us are Islamic in religion, but look around you in this gathering and see what percentage give their votes to Islam. . . . To me it is a proof that Islam does not yet flourish amongst the masses.' Hardly a fair proof, given the mode of selection of the BPKI! Sukarno's conclusion might, of course, have been correct, but in any case his remark was a challenge and it underlined the fact that his synthesis was not really all-embracing but was distinctly partisan.

For the moment, however, in a forum which was so heavily weighted on the secular nationalist side, he carried conviction and his personal dominance was reflected in the willingness of the BPKI to leave him in charge of the next stages of its work. Before bringing this first – and largely hortatory – session to a close the committee provided for its deliberations to continue in a more detailed fashion at the sub-committee level, and it established a small group under the chairmanship of Sukarno to consider proposals for the constitution of an independent republic. The sub-committee included such figures as Hatta, Kahar Muzakkir, Soebardjo and Hadji Agus Salim, and, a little later, Mohammad Yamin. It thus represented Islam as well as secular nationalist opinion.

After the close of the full session the committee proceeded to consult widely with both official and unofficial groups and it invited suggestions from all quarters on the subject of Indonesia's constitutional needs. In its formal sessions its main activity was the drafting of a form of words to serve as the preamble to the constitution, and here again Sukarno was concerned to reconcile differences and to woo his possible opponents. The sub-committee's document, which came to be known as the Djakarta Charter, seemed to move much further towards satisfying Muslim opinion than did the *Pantja Sila* speech. The crucial passage stated that Indonesia would be a republic founded not only on the bases of unity, a righteous and civilized humanity, democracy and social justice, but also on 'belief in God, with the obligation of practising the laws of Islam for the adherents of that religion'. The meaning of this passage was ambiguous. Did it impose obligations only on devout Muslims or on all who were nominally adherents of Islam? Was the fulfilment of the obligation to be left to each individual Muslim or was it to be enforced by the state? Did it mean separate laws for Muslims and non-Muslims? These problems were not resolved and many Muslims remained disappointed at the failure of the preamble to provide specifically for an Islamic state. It was to require all of Sukarno's tact and persuasion to secure the BPKI's acceptance at its next session of what was, in the end, clearly a compromise wording. The controversial passage was finally to be dropped from the preamble before the formal adoption of the constitution, but a dozen years later the Djakarta Charter was again to be a matter of considerable controversy when the Constituent Assembly of the Republic, elected to draft a permanent constitution, discussed its status and its meaning as a constitutional document.

The constitution itself was considered at the second session of the BPKI which assembled on 10 July. Once again Sukarno played a major role though not the only one; he was a lenient chairman who made no claims to be a constitutional lawyer. Though he was later to insist that the 1945 constitution was an ideal document for Indonesian circumstances it would be wrong to see it, in 1945, as reflecting particularly his own political feeling. A good deal of the detailed work had been done by a small group working with Hadji Agus Salim at his own house. Under Sukarno's chairmanship the committee as a whole accepted the principle of a unitary rather than a federal state, with a powerful presidential executive. Ministers were to be chosen by the president and were to be responsible to him and not to an elected assembly. Provision was made for a 'People's Deliberative Assembly' (Madjelis Permusjawaratan Rakjat) which was to be the repository of popular sovereignty, which would elect both president and vice-president and determine the main lines of state policy, but which was not designed to exercise very much control over the president once he had been elected. It was to meet at least once every five years. It could meet more often, certainly, but it obviously was not intended to maintain a continuous check on presidential authority. The legislative body, the Dewan Perwakilan Rakjat ('People's Representative Council') was subject to a presidential veto and had no power to direct the executive. Even its legislative powers could be by-passed through the use of the president's emergency powers to issue regulations.

More important as a forum for policy-making was a 'Supreme Advisory Council' (Dewan Pertimbangan Agung) but it was to be chosen by the president and its powers were advisory. Of course, while the outlines of the constitution appeared to provide for an almost dictatorial president, the wide dispersion of power in Indonesia was likely to tell against any heavy-handed exercise of authority. Any president would, in practice, have to conciliate pressure groups.

A further question debated at the second session of the BPKI concerned the territorial limits of the republic; it is worth some attention, since the debate on the matter appeared to show Sukarno as a man of expansionist tendencies. In view of his later adventurist foreign policy it is important to clear away possible misconceptions on the point.

The territorial issue was pressed most strongly by Mohammad Yamin who, in due course, was to become one of the more flamboyant ideologues of Sukarno's Indonesia. Yamin, calling on ethnic, historical and geopolitical considerations, argued that the republic of Indonesia should go well beyond the boundaries of the Dutch colony of Netherlands India and should embrace the former British colonies and protectorates in Malaya and Borneo. This was the area from which the Indonesian people had been drawn, Yamin argued, and he demanded that 'the Motherland of the people be transformed into the territory of a state'. Sukarno aligned himself on this occasion firmly on Yamin's side. Indeed, he went further and confessed to his past dreams of a 'Pan–Indonesia' stretching as far as the Philippines, but he recognized that Philippine sovereignty would have to be respected. In the case of Malaya, he believed that nationalist sentiment there would favour union with Indonesia. A state built on that basis would be in line with Indonesia's past glories and the God-given facts of geography.

> God in his wisdom has mapped out this earth. Everyone looking at the world map will understand what God has ordained as shown on the map. God has determined that certain parts of the world should form units – the British Isles as one and likewise the Hellenic islands, and India surrounded by the ocean below and the Himalayas above . . . and when I look at the islands situated between Asia and Australia and between the Pacific and the Indian Oceans I understand that they were meant to form a single entity.[99]

99. Yamin, *Naskah Persiapan Undang-undang Dasar 1945* ['Text of the Preparation of the 1945 Constitution'], 1959, Vol. V. pp. 206–7.

When a vote was taken a substantial majority (thirty-nine out of sixty-six) supported an Indonesia including Malaya, Britain's Borneo territories and West New Guinea.

Sukarno's words on this occasion persuaded some later observers to see the presence of a basic Indonesian imperialism which was to find its expression, in due course, in the opposition of Sukarno's Indonesia to Malaysia. Even at the time it aroused doubts among the more cautious. Hatta, for example, was much more modest in his expectations and in his view of what was right. He warned the BPKI against demands which could be regarded as imperialistic and which might become insatiable. His own preference was to confine the future republic to the territories of the Dutch colony, leaving Malaya as a separate and independent state – unless its inhabitants themselves wished to join Indonesia. Too much should not be made of this difference of opinion. The BPKI debate took place within a particular historical context. The European empires in Southeast Asia had fallen, and in the closing months of the war there seemed a possibility of reshaping boundaries along 'natural' lines, freed from the distortions of European colonialism. The situation seemed fluid and to look to a 'greater Indonesia' in mid 1945 was not necessarily to look beyond the bounds of practical politics. There was some radical Malay opinion which looked in the same direction. For Sukarno to think in these terms did not necessarily imply an ideology of expansion. In 1963 his responsibility for Indonesia's hostility to Malaysia was to be clear and direct as will be seen, but it would be a mistake to see the seeds of that future policy in his views of 1945.

The deliberations of the BPKI were conducted against the background of a growing restlessness in Indonesian society at large. There was a feeling of heightened expectations – a sense of troubled times and of the approach of great events. To some extent this feeling sprang from deeply flowing currents of the Javanese messianic tradition – the idea of *merdeka* itself contained something of the idea of a return of a golden age. At a more practical level the coming defeat of the Japanese would obviously herald enormous changes for the Indonesian people at large. The feelings of youth had already received violent expression in the February revolt of Peta forces in Blitar, and less violently in other ways – in the activities of the Japanese-sponsored youth organiza- tion Angkatan Muda ('Young Generation') in Djakarta, Bandung and Surabaja as well as in the ferment of Djakarta under- ground circles and in the formation of a new youth organization, Angakatan Baru ('New Generation') in January 1945. Japanese sponsorship of youth organizations did not ensure a quiescent membership and the authorities found it increasingly difficult during the course of 1945 to control the monster they had created.[1] In Muslim ranks, too, though Masjumi was less voci- ferous than might have been expected, preparations were made for the coming struggle. Early in 1945 a Muslim military corps, Hizbullah – the 'Army of Allah' – was formed as an auxiliary of Masjumi. Like Peta, its members received an initial training under Japanese auspices. Those trained were in turn entrusted with the formation of local Hizbullah groups all over Java – units which were to play a significant role in the early months of the revolution. In July an attempt was made to form a new front organization under Sukarno's leadership. This body, Gerakan Rakjat Baru ('New People's Movement' – GRB), embraced both the Djawa Hokokai and Masjumi, but from the Japanese point of view it failed in its object of curbing popular hopes. Rather it provided a new forum for their expression. It was be- coming increasingly difficult for the Japanese to keep the lid on Indonesian feeling. Sukarno himself felt the pressure, though his role for the moment was to contain it.

So the War moved gradually towards its conclusion. Late in July the Japanese Government decided to take immediate steps towards the creation of an independent Indonesia and in its last desperate moments, on the eve of Hiroshima and Nagasaki, began to implement the decision. To this end it announced the forma- tion of a new body – a committee to prepare Indonesian indepen- dence (*Panitya Persiapan Kemerdekaan Indonesia* – PPKI). On 8 August in a radio speech hailing the formation of the new committee Sukarno spoke jubilantly of the rapid approach of

1. See, for example, Anderson, *Some Aspects of Indonesian Politics Under the Japanese Occupation 1944–45*, p. 18 ff.

independence and made his first famous reference to the old Djoyo-boyo prophecy. Indonesia must be free, he said, before the maize bore fruit.[2] On 8 August 1945 Indonesia's leaders were summoned by Marshal Terauchi, Commander-in-Chief of Japan's Southern Expeditionary Forces, to meet him in Saigon. Sukarno, as he flew out of Djakarta on the following day accompanied by Hatta and Radjiman Wedioningrat, had reason to be in a triumphant frame of mind. The goal he had set himself twenty years before was about to be achieved, and he personally had established himself as the recognized leader of his country. He could feel himself, therefore, and not entirely without justice, to be the agent of victory. Certainly Hatta was there to share his triumph and Hatta, too, could perceive with justice the significance of his own part in two decades of struggle for independence. For the moment the two men could enjoy their triumph together.

In Dalat on 11 August Sukarno, still in ignorance of the cataclysm which had laid waste Hiroshima three days earlier, learned from Marshal Terauchi that the PPKI would be inaugurated on 18 August and that independence would soon be granted, though still under Japanese guidance, to a republic exercising authority over the former territory of the Netherlands East Indies. They were assured that the way was open and that the next step was up to them.[3] As the party flew back to Singapore on 13 August its members knew that the end was in sight for Japan and that any talk of Japanese guidance of an independent Indonesia was bravado. Indeed, within a day or two, Japan might no longer be in a position to fulfil any of her promises. If so, it would be left to Indonesia herself to seize independence. But Sukarno still hoped that a peaceful transfer of power might be safely arranged before the final Japanese collapse. After a brief stopover in Singapore the party flew into Djakarta on 14 August.[4] Before being driven off to

2. *Asia Raya*, 8 August 1945 (2605).

3. Author's interview with Hatta, 24 June 1969.

4. During the course of his journey Sukarno had had a meeting in Taiping (Malaya) with the leader of the Union of Peninsular Malays (KRIS), who were interested in associating with Indonesia's declaration of independence. It is a significant commentary on the depth of Sukarno's 'Greater Indonesia' ideas that despite that expression of interest he gave no more thought to such an association. After his return to Djakarta his preoccupation was solely

the Gunseikan's palace for a celebratory ceremony, Sukarno conveyed to the waiting crowd the news of his mission, referring once again to the Djoyoboyo prophecy: 'In my radio speech a short while ago I said that before the maize bore fruit Indonesia would be free, but now I can say that before the maize blossoms Indonesia will already be free.'[5]

The final steps were not to be quite so easy however. Sukarno quickly discovered that he had returned to a complex political situation in Djakarta. The city was alive with rumours of a Japanese surrender or impending surrender, and for the various groups of nationalist leaders this posed questions of tactics. How was Sukarno to handle this situation? Should he and his colleagues – the senior representatives of Indonesian nationalism to whom the Japanese had been planning to transfer authority – simply await the course of events and hope that Japan would still have time to carry out the transfer? Or might an early surrender frustrate those hopes? Should they, instead, seek to secure at least the passive consent of the Japanese authorities for an immediate declaration of independence by themselves? Or should they, as the youth leaders urged, ignore the Japanese altogether and make a bold proclamation, grasping independence courageously and in the face of possible Japanese opposition? Should the PPKI be the body to take the initiative? Designed to secure a wide regional representation as well as to contain the main currents of Indonesian opinion, its membership had been announced during Sukarno's absence in Tokyo. The secular nationalists, though a minority on the twenty-one-man committee, once again outnumbered the leaders of Islamic opinion, and the committee could be expected to be responsive to Sukarno's leadership. Should he anticipate its formal inauguration and call upon it to take matters into its own hands? Or was it, as a Japanese creation, too tainted?

These were difficult questions. If Japanese consent, active or

---

with a proclamation relating to an Indonesia narrowly conceived in terms of the former Dutch colony.

5. *Asia Raya*, 14 August 1945 (2605).

passive, were secured, might not the Indonesian government established in this way seem to the advancing Allies – and perhaps to many Indonesians – to be a puppet government? On the other hand if Sukarno yielded to the *pemuda* (youth) pressure and committed himself to a bold declaration of independence might that not lead to swift and decisive Japanese action to maintain order and to preserve authority in their own hands, as they were bound to do under any conceivable surrender terms, until they could hand over civil power to a representative of their conquerors? Sukarno spent the two days following his return in anxious negotiations on these questions with other Indonesian leaders. His own concern was with prudence and practical possibilities. He wanted to establish Indonesia's independence and for him the exact ways and means of doing so were incidental to the final end. Others, however, had strong views about the ways and means and Sukarno had to cope with two closely related but yet distinct types of pressure.

The first of these was represented by Sjahrir whose views were uncompromising. Neither he nor his followers were willing to accept any proclamation of independence made under Japanese sponsorship. For that reason he opposed a declaration made by the PPKI which was itself a Japanese creation. He argued on tactical grounds that in view of the attitudes of the Western allies this would be impolitic, but his approach to the question was all of a piece with his broader views of world history and the nature of fascism. He wanted a declaration of independence to be both anti-Japanese and anti-fascist in character.

The second type of opposition was that of the youth leaders who were less worried about such ideological niceties, but who also were concerned that the seizure of power should owe nothing to the Japanese and that it should be boldly done.

Sukarno was made aware of Sjahrir's views almost immediately on his return from Saigon. On the afternoon of that day a phone call came from Hatta to ask him whether he had yet retired for his afternoon sleep. Hatta explained that Sjahrir was with him, that he believed the Japanese were already on the point of surrender, and that he was urging the need to proceed straightaway to a proclamation. Sukarno invited them both round to his house at Pegangsaan Timur and the argument continued.[6] An immediate proclamation would be possible, said Sjahrir. Popular support would rally to a self-declared Republic and the Japanese would be unable to crush it. The youth organizations were ready with their own preparations for an uprising which would follow a declaration of independence.

His reasoning was persuasive. Hatta, however, argued that, in the eyes of the Allies, it would not really matter how independence was declared – Sukarno and he would still be regarded as

6. Interview with Hatta, 24 June 1969. The precise chronology of these August days is a matter of some disagreement. Sjahrir's account in *Out of Exile* contradicts some well-established facts. In Sjahrir's account 16 August is a 'spare-day' in which nothing happens between the night-long drafting of the proclamation (the night of the 15th to the early morning of the 16th) and the formal announcement of it on 17 August. Anderson's two accounts (in *Some Aspects of Indonesian Politics Under the Japanese Occupation 1944–45* and in *Java in a Time of Revolution*) differ from each other on the question of whether Sjahrir visited Sukarno in company with Hatta on the 14th or on the following day, having left Hatta to raise the point first with Sukarno. Dahm accepts Anderson's first account in believing that Sjahrir visited Sukarno on the 15th rather than the 14th, but differs from it in having Hatta's earlier approach to Sukarno also take place on the 15th.

Hatta's memory confirms Sjahrir's statement that the pair of them visited Sukarno immediately after the return from Saigon on 14 August. The author has checked this memory further against that of others who were involved in the discussions. Among others Mr Ali Budiardjo has a clear memory of discussing with Sjahrir the outcome of his visit to Sukarno on 14 August. This story is also consistent with the fact that a good part of August 15 was spent by Sukarno in making contact with Maeda and in trying to establish the fact of the Japanese surrender. In the view of the present writer the following table of events seems to be fairly firmly established:

14 August – the return from Saigon. In the afternoon, Sjahrir calls on Hatta and the pair of them then visit Sukarno.

15 August – Sukarno, Hatta and Soebardjo visit Maeda. In the evening Sukarno receives Wikana and his colleagues and is later kidnapped.

16 August – Sukarno and Hatta are held by their kidnappers at Rengasdengklok. They return to Djakarta in the evening and the rest of the night is spent in attempts to see the *Gunseikan*, the meeting with Nishimura and the drafting of the proclamation with a good deal of additional coming and going on the part of various *pemuda* leaders. The planned uprising is called off.

17 August – the proclamation.

collaborators. Sukarno agreed with Hatta and tended to regard the risks attendant upon an insurrection as too great. He was anxious to secure at least an unofficial understanding with the Japanese if it could be arranged. Sjahrir was by this time convinced that no proclamation would carry weight unless it was made by Sukarno, and he therefore left the meeting in considerable anger at the attitude which Sukarno had taken.[7]

On the following day, 15 August, Sukarno, together with Hatta and Soebardjo, Head of the Research Bureau of the Japanese Naval Liaison Office in Djakarta, attempted to find out from the Japanese authorities whether Japan had in fact surrendered.[8] They went first to the office of General Yamamoto, the *Gunseikan* (head of the military administration), and found the building almost deserted. Its silence and emptiness was perhaps the clearest testimony to the fact that surrender had already taken place. They went on to the Naval Liaison Office to find Rear-Admiral Maeda, whose apparent sympathy to nationalist hopes has already been mentioned. They found Maeda in his room and asked him whether the rumours of a surrender were true. Maeda bowed his head in silence for what seemed to his visitors an embarrassing time – perhaps a minute. At last as Sukarno and Hatta exchanged glances, he looked up and admitted the probability that Japan had surrendered. No official word had been received, however, and he promised that he would let Sukarno know of such confirmation. With this assurance Sukarno and Hatta decided to call the PPKI meeting for the next morning, the 16th, two days ahead of schedule. Soebardjo was asked to make the arrangements, which was easy enough since most delegates had been accommodated in the Hotel Des Indes.

There was still another crisis for Sukarno to face however. At about 10 that evening, at his house at Pegangsaam Timur, he

7. In Sjahrir's account he left this meeting believing that Sukarno had promised to make a proclamation at 5 p.m. that evening. Mr Ali Budiardjo, however, remembers speaking with Sjahrir on 14 August after his meeting with Sukarno and recalls Sjahrir's anger at Sukarno's refusal to budge.

8. This account is based on interviews conducted by the author with Soebardjo and Hatta, June 1969.

was disturbed by a knock at the door and he opened it to receive an unexpected delegation representing the youth groups of Djakarta.

Like Sjahrir the *pemuda* leaders wanted a bold seizure of independence without Japanese authority, but they were more jumpy and volatile than he, and were disposed to push their view with all the clarity and urgency of inexperience. They were convinced through the news from their clandestine radio sources that surrender had already occurred and that an immediate declaration of independence was therefore necessary before the PPKI met. Their forces were poised ready for action the moment Sukarno gave them the word and now his prudence appeared to them to be standing in the way of action. On the afternoon of 15 August, while Sukarno and Hatta were consulting with Maeda, the members of the various youth groups in the capital had been conferring among themselves, though in a somewhat disconnected fashion, about the ways in which they might bring their own influence to bear. A meeting of a variety of such youth leaders, some of them drawn from the Menteng Asrama, some of them from the Medical Students group, some from the Asrama Indonesia Merdeka, finally decided to send a delegation to Sukarno to argue their case directly with him.

These were the events which led to Sukarno's unexpected visitors, led by Wikana of the Asrama Indonesia Merdeka. Their arrival opened a new and highly dramatic phase of deliberations. Over the next hour or so a heated argument developed as Sukarno confronted his critics. To their demand for an immediate declaration Sukarno argued that precipitate action in direct opposition to the Japanese could lead to futile bloodshed and might crush the infant republic at birth. A little patience, and an understanding with the Japanese might, on the other hand, enable the republic to be proclaimed just as quickly and much more safely. Wikana replied that bloodshed would occur in any case if Sukarno would not live up to his position as nationalist leader and accept the responsibility for a declaration of independence straight away. At this Sukarno's anger revealed something of the strain he had been under for two days. 'Don't you threaten me,' he cried. 'Here. Here is my neck. Kill me now. Go on. Cut my head off. You can kill me but I will never risk unnecessary blood-shed because you want to do things your way.' Wikana was abashed. He recognized in any case that no effective declaration of independence could be made without Sukarno, but Sukarno's outburst had of itself shamed him and the argument continued on a quieter level with others gathering to take part in it. Hatta had heard what was going on and, accompanied by Soebardjo, had hurried round to Sukarno's house to lend his support to the view that a rash and premature declaration would be fatal. Wikana and his friends could make their own proclamation if they thought they could get away with it, but the older men would not take the initiative themselves at that point.

The youth leaders eventually withdrew, defeated for the moment but reluctant to concede their defeat. At a midnight meeting with their colleagues, in which Chaerul Saleh and Adam Malik took a leading part, it was decided that one further and more drastic attempt should be made to force Sukarno's hand. Kidnapping a leader, not to harm him but to impress upon him the sincerity of the kidnappers and to try to influence his actions by moral suasion, became a not unfamiliar tactic in Indonesia during and after the revolution, and this was the course of action the youths decided to adopt. Between four and five in the morning two cars pulled up at Pengangsaan Timur 56. Sukarno was roused and he, together with Fatmawati and their infant son, Guntur, was hustled into one of them. The kidnappers then moved on to collect Hatta, and the party drove on through Djakarta's outer suburbs and out along the Tjirebon road. Their destination was the remote village of Rengasdengklok. In a house vacated for the occasion by a Chinese trader the argument continued, with Sukarno and Hatta firm in their passive opposition to their kidnappers and with the latter the prisoners of their own plan. They could not proceed without Sukarno's support to launch the coup against the Japanese which they had planned for that day. Hatta chipped his captors about how their own revolution was faring. 'What is the news from Djakarta? Has your revolution begun? Are your forces in control yet?'

In Djakarta, in the meantime, the disappearance of Sukarno

and Hatta threw into confusion the several groups who were seeking a proclamation of independence, and also the Japanese who were keeping in touch with them. Admiral Maeda, who had hitherto maintained a continued contact with Sukarno, made efforts through his aide, Nishijima, to find out where the Indonesian leaders were. Some of the youth leaders were meeting at the office of the Navy's Political Affairs Research Bureau in Prapatan, but they were reluctant to disclose the whereabouts of their prisoners. Eventually it was agreed that Soebardjo, the head of the Research Bureau, would be conducted to Sukarno, and that he would try to arrange for the return of the prisoners to Djakarta. As the party set off in Soebardjo's car he was kept in ignorance of their destination. He at first thought of Bogor, but when the car turned left at Djatinegara, he thought it might be Purwokerta or Subang. Then the turn left at Krawang made him realize that it was Rengasdengklok. The party arrived late in the afternoon and Soebardjo was able to convey the firm news of the Japanese surrender and to promise at least Maeda's complicity in a declaration of independence.

At about 10 p.m. the Rengasdengklok party had returned to Djakarta and ultimately to Maeda's house, which the Admiral agreed to make available for the meeting of Indonesian leaders. Meetings elsewhere were likely to be broken up but the Admiral's house had a certain 'extra-territoriality' status *vis à vis* the military administration. Soebardjo was asked to call the PPKI together at that rendezvous. While he was doing so a final unsuccessful attempt was made to secure the authority of the military government for a proclamation. That it was unsuccessful was hardly surprising, since the military government was now legally bound to oppose any change in the *status quo* until their surrender had been received by the Allies. The *Gunseikan* refused, by telephone, to receive Sukarno, Hatta and Maeda. Nishimura, head of the general affairs office of the military administration, did meet them however and Sukarno used the kidnapping incident to show him how acute the pressures of the situation were. He pointed to the danger that things might get out of hand and an unco-ordinated rising take place. Nishimura refused to sanction formally any independent Indonesian action, but he did at last allow the possibility that a proclamation might perhaps be made without his knowledge. Maeda, with this nod, was prepared to encourage Sukarno and Hatta to go ahead and to rely on his own ability to persuade his army colleagues to turn a blind eye. In these circumstances about thirty Indonesian leaders gathered to make the final preparations. They included members of the PPKI and some of the youth leaders such as Sukarni and Chaerul Saleh. They did not include Sjahrir.

While a group of youth leaders, accompanied by Nishijima, moved hastily through Djakarta streets to call off the uprising arranged for that night, the meeting at Maeda's house spent the remainder of the night in hammering out the terms of a proclamation. A small group gathered about Sukarno in the living room of the house to prepare a draft while a larger crowd milled about in the big dining-room at the front waiting for the results. Maeda himself had retired to bed and there was no further consultation with the Japanese as the drafting process proceeded. The result was a brief, bare statement. It was not couched as Sjahrir would have had it in strong, anti-Japanese terms. It did not even demand immediate action to seize the machinery of power as the youth leaders wanted. It simply stated:

We, the people of Indonesia, hereby declare Indonesia's independence. Matters concerning the transfer of power and other matters will be executed in an orderly manner and in the shortest possible time.

It was signed by Sukarno and Hatta.

The party eventually dispersed at about 7 a.m. It was now the morning of 17 August. Sukarno went home to snatch an hour or two of sleep but at 10 o'clock he was ready for the formal announcement of Indonesia's independence. After some confusion about the place of the declaration (a plan to have it in Djakarta's central square was hurriedly altered to avoid the danger of a clash with Japanese troops) the simple ceremony was performed in front of Sukarno's house at Pegangsaan Timur. A comparatively small crowd of people collected there. The principals in the case must have felt somewhat exhausted and be-draggled after two days and nights of practically continuous action, tension and debate. Sukarno, nevertheless, appeared sprucely dressed as always, and, flanked by Hatta and Lieutenant Latief of Peta, he read the words of the proclamation. The red and white flag of the Republic, made for the occasion by Fatmawati, was run up an improvised flagpole and those present sang 'Indonesia Raya'. Indonesia had begun her revolution.

# 9
# Chairman of the Revolution

A superficial observer of Sukarno's career might expect the proclamation of independence to be the climax of his biography. During these August days Sukarno was the central and necessary figure, the only person who could take on himself the responsibility of making the proclamation. For the moment he was, as he had always tried to be, the symbol of a united nation. With the proclamation, despite the years of struggle ahead, he had reached the goal that he had been seeking for twenty years, and 17 August was in great measure his own achievement.

That picture contains much truth, yet it does need some qualification. In a soberer judgement 17 August, and the story of events leading up to it, show Sukarno in rather an ambiguous light – or rather the several stories, for there are at least three distinct ways of looking at the bare facts as they are known. One might call these the Sukarno version, the Hatta version and the Malik version respectively. Sukarno's account sees himself as in control of events throughout, knowing the best course of action to take and resisting those who tried to divert him from the safest path to independence. Hatta's story is of a less assured Sukarno, but his version would agree with Sukarno's in arguing that the kidnapping of 16 August in fact postponed the proclamation by a day. The PPKI meeting was called for the morning of the 16th. Had Sukarno and Hatta been there to lead it, a proclamation would then have been made. The third version – that of Adam Malik – holds that without the kidnapping there would have been no proclamation.[9] Sukarno trusted Terauchi too much. He was so anxious to get Japanese authority, and so sure that he would get it, that he would have procrastinated until it was too late. Only the kidnapping brought him to see the necessity of a speedy proclamation.

9. *Story and Struggle concerning the Proclamation of Indonesian Independence, 17 August 1945 (Riwajat dan Perdjuangan sekitar proklamasi kemerdekaan Indonesia, 17 Agustus 1945)*, 1948.

A consideration of these alternative interpretations must raise, first of all, a question concerning Sukarno's method of handling a critical situation. As he came face to face with the youth of the capital, anxious to play a direct role in the disordered and unstructured situation which was expected to follow a Japanese defeat, Sukarno was tentative and pragmatic. In the discussions on the night of 15 August and during the day of his capture he resisted firmly enough the rashness of the young men and kept his lines of communication to the Japanese open. Throughout he acted closely in concert with Hatta, whose sober pragmatism he normally despised. His caution was at first due to his belief that it might still be possible for independence to come through the Japanese plan of transferring authority to an autonomous local government. He did not share the view that this would taint the Republic, and it appeared to be the only way to avoid a conflict which could destroy all hopes of independence. When this seemed no longer possible he still wished, in the interests of safety and order, to have at least an informal Japanese blessing for an Indonesian seizure of power. But it remains doubtful whether his actions through these few days were the result of a clear perception of the realities and possibilities of the situation – did he play his cards decisively and with skill or did he temporize until the issues had sorted themselves out? Neither was out of character for Sukarno, but it seems clear that, on this occasion, his actions were marked by uncertainty rather than by decisiveness. His later account of August 1945 was characteristically self-assured. It gave a picture of a leader seeing the possibilities and the dangers of the situation more clearly than his hot-headed critics. In fact, it was a time of agony and doubt for him as he gradually felt his way forward.

Does the evidence allow a conclusion on the question of whether his hand was forced by the kidnapping? On balance it probably does support Malik's view rather than that of Sukarno and Hatta. Had the kidnapping not occurred it is doubtful whether the PPKI would have been anxious to move to a proclamation of independence on 16 August, or even whether it would have been permitted to do so by the Japanese. Certainly, Sukarno himself was waiting for a word from the authorities at that time.

Even on the night of the 16th, after the return from Rengasdeng-klok, he made his eleventh hour attempt to secure Japanese consent. Only when that attempt failed was he prepared to fall back on Nishimura's apparent nod of complicity and go ahead with the proclamation.

This points to a second way in which the August days were revealing. They posed clearly the problem of Sukarno's future relations with a new element in the situation – the *pemuda* leaders. A good deal more was at stake here than mere questions of tactics – these concealed a more fundamental difference in perceptions of what the revolution was about. Sukarno was a member of an older, pre-war group of leaders who, whether co-operators or non-cooperators, had been engaged in the practicalities of the struggle against the Dutch. This was also the generation which had been represented in Putera, the Central Advisory Council and the Djawa Hokokai. Later, as President, Sukarno was to evolve his philosophy of 'continuing Revolution' and to emphasize flux and turmoil almost as qualities in themselves. In 1945, however, he was in a sense a conservative. Brought up within the framework of Dutch rule, independence to him simply meant the transfer of the apparatus of the state from Dutch (or Japanese) hands to those of himself and his colleagues. The *pemudas*, by contrast, were representatives of new channels of power and they saw Sukarno as the leader of a nationalist establishment from which they were excluded. They had become an organized force under Japanese rule and they had been moulded to some extent by Japanese methods of controlling the Indonesian population. Many of them had been attracted by the expressive and ritualistic character of the devices by which the Japanese had mobilized mass sentiment. In some measure they had been influenced by Japanese authoritarian values and even captivated by Japanese ruthlessness and cruelty. In August 1945 they sensed the possibility of political action outside the traditional framework of orderly government and administration.[10]

As part of these differences of temper there were conflicting concepts of revolutionary virtue. In the months following August

10. This contrast is sharply drawn by B. R. O'G. Anderson in *Java in a Time of Revolution: Occupation and Resistance 1944–1946*, Ithaca, 1972.

1945 the efforts of Sukarno and his colleagues to lay the foundations of government and to reach an understanding with the
British occupation forces, and later with the Dutch, ran counter
to the *pemuda* view that struggle was almost virtuous in itself. The
very circumstances of the time placed a premium on direct action.
The Republic in fact was born in a situation which quickly came
to border on anarchy as independent groups and organizations
sprang up to struggle for *merdeka*. Some were comparatively
large and well organized and were based often upon the structures
created by the Japanese themselves to mobilize support for their
rule. Some were led by youths who had had training in the
Occupation's para-military organizations such as the Heiho, the
Seinendan or Peta. Others were informally organized groups of
youths, gathered about a charismatic leader.

These 'struggle-organizations' (*strijdorganisaties*) as they were
called, gave a mass insurgency character to the revolution and
were a living expression of the *pemuda* ethic that direct participation in the common effort was indeed the essence of revolution.
Revolution was to be experienced rather than soberly planned,
and in the struggle men could fulfil their highest nature. These
spontaneous movements were of tremendous importance in
giving the revolution momentum and in providing an immediate
basis of strength in which power could be seized, as it were, with
bare hands. But they also meant a dispersal of power and a threat
to order. To Sukarno and the leaders of the revolution the task
was to mobilize power so as to establish a *de facto* government.
It was of the utmost importance that they should impress the
allies with their capacity to keep order. This meant, among other
things, bringing the struggle-organizations under control. Thus
an opposition quickly developed between the policies of negotiation and struggle – between *diplomasi* and *perdjuangan* – which
was to be a continuing theme of the revolution.

In the longer term these differences in the perception of the
nature of the revolution were to become part of the legitimizing
mythology of Indonesia, important in sustaining the authority of
competing forces. Different groups developed their own sense of
property in the revolution. Adam Malik's account of 1945, for
example, stressed the role of youth in the events of August, and

the importance of the struggle-organizations in the months that followed. The members of such organizations, he believed, could give more accurate expression to the deepest yearnings of the Indonesian people than could the older leaders who were divorced from popular feeling and confused about the proper course of action. He criticized the moderation of the governments over which Sukarno presided and their policies of negotiation rather than struggle. But it was Sukarno, in the end, who managed to appropriate the symbols of the revolution for himself.

The gulf between Sukarno and his *pemuda* critics was patent in August 1945. Other tensions were concealed for the moment but were soon to show themselves. It might have been thought that the Indonesian élite, in confronting an external enemy, could not afford the luxury of domestic politics; but in revolutions there is no legitimacy, and rivalry broke out between opposing groups even as the initial moves were being taken to resist the return of Dutch authority. As Sukarno was drawn into these conflicts – between *diplomasi* and *perdjuangan*, between government and opposition – his was no longer the directing hand. Whatever he might come to believe later on, the years of revolution were not a high point in his political career. The management of events was in large measure in the hands of others who were more skilled than he in administration and negotiation. Yet they needed his integrative skills, they worked within the framework of his formal authority and could not have managed without him. If he did not direct the revolution he at least presided over it. His presence was enough in itself to draw support to the new government at the beginning and at critical times thereafter he made his own direct contribution to the shaping of events. In Surabaja at the end of October 1945, in Jogja in July 1946 and again at the time of Madiun in 1948, he played an independent and decisive part. The important thing was that, even where he supported one group against another, and thus entered directly into the political struggle, he was able to do so as one standing above faction. None of the others could have done that. Hatta, Sjahrir, Tan Malaka, Amir Sjarifuddin – all had their individual contributions to make but none of them could have symbolized a united nation as well as Sukarno.

The reception of the proclamation must have surprised even Sukarno himself. When the *pemuda*, on the afternoon of 17 August, seized the Domei radio headquarters and broadcast the news to the nation at large their announcement aroused passionate enthusiasm across the country and triggered a series of spontaneous moves against Japanese authority. Within a short time this mass response organized itself through the formation of the first struggle-organizations, whose members seized public buildings in the major cities. From the end of August in Djakarta, Surabaya, Semarang and Bandung, key buildings were taken, sometimes only after heavy fighting with Japanese forces, and a semblance of republican authority was established in varying degrees. In some cases steps were taken by the struggle-organizations to seize Japanes arms.

While these steps represented the 'revolution in being' Sukarno and his colleagues in Djakarta faced the less spectacular tasks of creating the formal machinery of government. The immediate steps were quickly taken. At its meeting on 18 August, the day following the proclamation, the PPKI approved, with some amendments designed to remove any suggestion of a special constitutional position for Islam, the draft Constitution of the Republic. It adopted regulations providing for an interim government, and acting under these transitional regulations it moved to the election of a president and a vice-president. There was no controversy about the election of Sukarno and Hatta to these offices.

On 23 August Sukarno went on the air to explain the republic's objectives and to stress the importance of earning international recognition for it. This was his first speech to the nation as President and in his opening words he appealed with emotion to 'All of my people: In Sumatra, in Java, in Borneo, Sulawesi, the lesser Sundas, Maluku, from Atjeh to Ambon', calling upon them to stand firm in the struggle for Indonesia *merdeka*.[11]

On the following days the PPKI made arrangements for regional administration and for the formation of a 'Central Indonesian National Committee' (Komite Nasional Indonesia Pusat – KNIP). The latter proved to be an action of great im-

11. Text of speech in *Merdeka*, 25 August 1945.

portance. The KNIP was intended to be an advisory body to the president but it gradually became much more than that. It was formed on 29 August when Sukarno dissolved the PPKI and reappointed its members to the new body, together with 135 others representing a wide range of ethnic and political opinion. The KNIP quickly established itself as a central forum within which a national consensus could be expressed. In practice no government could move without its support and it quickly became, in effect, the parliament of the republic.

Within this constitutional framework Sukarno moved to the formation of the republic's first cabinet. It was responsible to him as the constitution provided, and, not surprisingly perhaps, it was composed for the most part of older and established leaders, many of whom had held office during the Occupation. Amir Sjarifuddin, appointed as Minister of Information, was an exception, but as a whole the Cabinet, consisting of such people as Subardjo (Foreign Affairs), Ki Hadjar Dewantoro (Education) and Sartono (Minister without Portfolio), was not designed to secure the approval of Indonesia's revolutionary youth.

The new government appealed, successfully, to the Indonesian members of the administrative service to transfer their loyalty to the Republic. At the end of August the foundations of Indonesia's National Army were laid when a Peace Preservation Corps was established, drawing its members from the ranks of Peta and the Japanese-created youth organizations.

The creation of a body of ministers, the formation, in outline, of a civil service and the formal creation of an army were, of course, merely the externals of republican authority. The government still had to govern and this meant piecing together real control stolen from the multiplicity of separate powers which had sprung up. Even the republic's own army was a power unto itself – or a group of powers, for it was at first the loosest of organizations. The President and his government had in fact to negotiate with military leaders or with leaders of the struggle-organizations who possessed their own material strength or who had independent bases of popular support.

In this situation of potential anarchy Sukarno was the one unquestioned focus of authority. There were some who at first doubted this, Sjahrir among them. He had held himself aloof from the proclamation and from the formation of the government, but after a trip through Java he became convinced that the mass movement of revolution which was taking place did indeed look to Sukarno as the leader of the nation, and he returned to Djakarta to give him his own support. A striking test of Sukarno's stature was given on 19 September, when Djakarta's youth groups planned a mass meeting in the city's central square to be addressed by the President. The Cabinet received the proposal with misgiving for it seemed an unnecessary challenge to Japanese authority. However, since the meeting had been announced it would have seemed craven not to hold it. An enormous crowd assembled on the stated day and as they did so Japanese troops took up their positions in the square. Tension was high; an unwise move from crowd or troops might have precipitated massive bloodshed. In fact the troops held back and an anxious Sukarno made a brief speech affirming the principle of national freedom and calling upon his audience to disperse quietly. Their obedience to his command was, for the Japanese, a convincing demonstration of his authority. His popularity was confirmed further in early December when he made a tour through East and Central Java and aroused tremendous popular response.

Though warmed by the applause of the masses, Sukarno was less sure of himself as he faced the routine tasks of government. For these he relied heavily on his Vice-President, leaving many of the details to him while he directed his own talents to the task of mobilizing support. This division of labour was sensible, but it had important consequences for Sukarno's position. Hatta, and those about him, drew stature from their handling of the practical tasks of government and inevitably detracted a little from the stature of Sukarno. As small disagreements emerged on particular issues of policy an incipient rivalry seemed to be developing within the ranks of the government, but it was barely visible – power-struggle would be too strong a term. Sukarno by his willing co-operation with Hatta and the leaders of the KNIP was able to contain the competition for power and influence by a typically Javanese accommodation to it. He listened readily to KNIP's proposals and was prepared on occasion to accept its wishes even when they ran counter to his own. But partly as a result of that co-operation it soon became clear that the centre of gravity in the government had shifted dramatically.

One step in this trend was a decision to grant the KNIP co-legislative power with the President. A petition to this effect from KNIP members was presented to Sukarno and, with his agreement, the change was then embodied in a Vice-Presidential Decree of 16 October. Immediately afterwards KNIP delegated its new power to a 'Working Committee' which would be responsible to the larger body, but which could meet regularly. The Working Committee under Sjahrir's chairmanship became, as Kahin has described it 'the dynamic heart of the government'.[12]

Even before these developments, there had been significant differences between Sukarno and his colleagues on questions of political organization. Within a few days of the proclamation the government toyed with the idea of creating a single state party to mobilize popular support for the Republic. The initial steps were in fact taken towards the establishment of the Indonesian National Party, as it was to be called, carrying the familiar initials PNI. In a way this proposal represented an attempt to apply to the circumstances of the infant republic the mass mobilization techniques of the Japanese, and for Sukarno it represented a not unfamiliar method of rallying popular sentiment. The PNI, he said, would become 'the motor of the people's struggle'.[13] But others argued that a state party of this kind would carry echoes of the Occupation and that it would be authoritarian in character. The KNIP leaned rather to the idea of a multi-party system as a more democratic arrangement.

In this difference of opinion there was the seed of a basic conflict about the form and character of the state, but the conflict, on this occasion, was quickly resolved, and the resolution of it was, again, a reverse for Sukarno. The state party idea was dropped and the new party was dissolved before it had been fully established. By a KNIP decision at the end of October it was decided instead to encourage the formation of competing political parties

12. Kahin, *Nationalism and Revolution in Indonesia*, Ithaca, 1952, p. 153.

13. 23 August speech, *Merdeka*, 25 August 1945.

whose function would be to express the views of their members within the KNIP.

Such organizations were quickly formed. The name PNI was now appropriated by a new Indonesian Nationalist Party having no connection with the proposed state party or with the old PNI, except that many of the old PNI members found a home in the new PNI and the new party hoped to enjoy some of the prestige of the old. Muslim political organization expressed itself at first in the formation of the all-embracing Masjumi, based on a wide range of Muslim organizations such as the old Partai Sarekat Islam Indonesia, Muhammadiyah and Nahdatul Ulama. A socialist party was formed through the union of supporters of Amir Sjarifuddin and Sjahrir. And a Communist party – PKI – was re-established. A number of smaller parties were also formed and Indonesia's multi-party system thus sprang into existence. These developments, though accepted by Sukarno, ran counter to his instincts. He would have preferred to bring all sections of opinion into the one organization as he had attempted to do in the late twenties and again in the early thirties.

The trend reflected in these decisions was soon to be carried further and to reach a more definite resolution. During the month of October criticism of Sukarno's Cabinet, with its weighting on the side of age and experience (and therefore on the side of collaboration with the Japanese) began to crystallize around the person of Sjahrir. Sjahrir's attitudes were made clear at the beginning of November with the publication of his pamphlet, *Our Struggle* (*Perdjuangan Kita*), which contained a vigorous attack on those who had worked with the Japanese. It also contained a criticism of the undirected and potentially fascist attitude of the *pemuda* groups who lacked, in his view, an informed ideology ('their understanding must be given content . . . so that they do not lower themselves to the level of wild beasts').[14] However the pamphlet did command support among the *pemuda* critics of the government who fastened on its anti-collaborationist passages and not on its critique of pemudaism.

Sjahrir's attack on collaborators had inevitably, at least by

14. Sjahrir, *Our Struggle*, Cornell Modern Indonesia Project Translation Series, 1968, p. 36.

implication, included Sukarno. He feared that Sukarno might at any time be seized by the British as a collaborator and he felt that under a Sukarno government the Republic itself was vulnerable. At the same time Sjahrir recognized that, in the eyes of the people, Sukarno was the authentic leader of the revolution. As he saw it there could be no Republic without Sukarno, but a Republic led by Sukarno lacked standing in the eyes of the world. His solution, as embodied in a proposal of the KNIP Working Committee of 11 November, was to separate the position of president from that of chief executive. It was suggested that, though the constitution provided for a presidential system of government, the president should, as a matter of policy, agree to accept only cabinets which commanded the support of the KNIP. Through this change of constitutional convention the position of president would become largely ceremonial, while power would rest with a prime minister and a cabinet controlled by the representatives of the nation gathered in the KNIP.

At this stage Sukarno was away from Djakarta, and he knew nothing of the Working Committee proposal. Hatta however, as Vice-President, agreed to the proposal and asked Sjahrir to form a government. The original Cabinet refused to accept that decision and, for a day or two, the republic had two groups of ministers each claiming to be the legitimate government. Sjahrir turned to Sukarno to resolve the issue. He was recalled to Djakarta where, according to one report, he met members of both governments, whom he lined up opposite each other in his house at Pegangsaan Timur 56. He announced his acceptance of the idea of cabinet responsibility and indicated his willingness therefore to accept the Sjahrir government as the government of the republic for the time being.[15]

Sukarno accepted the idea of cabinet responsibility with more than a formal willingness. On the face of it this was surprising. The change confirmed the trend towards the whittling down of his authority and there were inevitably moments of humiliation for him thereafter. He had to defer to the judgement of his ministers

15. The story of the confrontation of the two Cabinets was told to the author by Soedjatmoko, who was one of the two young men sent by Sjahrir to find Sukarno and bring him back to the capital.

and at times to accept instructions only thinly disguised as requests even from quite junior members of the group about Sjahrir. He bore these slights as best he could. In fact he had good reasons. First of all he was himself at that time uneasy about his standing in Allied eyes and believed that arrest was a real possibility. He was also disconcerted by the *pemuda* criticism of him and was at a loss to know quite how to handle it. He was therefore willing to lean on others who possessed the skills of day-to-day government. There was another reason also. Sjahrir was no friend of his (in the future a fundamental quarrel was to part them finally), but Sukarno in November 1945 recognized that Sjahrir at least supported him as President, and he suspected that the other critics of the government wished to change not merely the Cabinet but the President as well. For Sukarno, this was the important thing. Even if the presidency was, for the time being, to be merely a figurehead office, it at least gave Sukarno the sense that he was *the* leader of the Indonesian people, standing above party. This was the perception he was to bring to the office for the whole of his long tenure of it. He was constantly aware of the institution of the presidency and of himself in the position. The KNIP proposal, since it supported him in his office, to that extent ministered to his own concept of himself.

This change in constitutional convention involved a clearer definition of the strengths and weaknesses of the President's own position. Narrow limitations were placed on his ability to direct events, but at the same time he had been raised above the domestic struggle. If his authority was limited it was still an independent authority. In November we see a harassed and unsure Sukarno and thereafter a Sukarno elbowed to one side. But he was still there, indispensable as arbiter and unifier when critical moments came. It was a remarkable demonstration of his personal authority that even those who had taken executive responsibility from him turned to him at such times.

Over the next twelve months three main issues commanded the attention of the leaders of the republic to the exclusion of almost all else: the arrival of the British forces whose task it was to receive the Japanese surrender on behalf of the Allies; the emergence of further sharp internal divisions within the republic itself and the opening of negotiations with the Dutch. These were not questions for Sukarno alone to consider – indeed the process of coping with them confirmed the trend, already established, for real power to be concentrated in hands other than his own. But Sukarno retained his standing through his ability to legitimize authority, to arbitrate and to reconcile differences among those about him.

As President, Sukarno could not escape defining his attitude to the *diplomasi-perdjuangan* antithesis. It was not easy for him. He had preached for so long the necessity of struggle that his image could well suffer if he now became the prophet of moderation. But for the moment his executive responsibilities counselled prudence and he had no hesitation in opposing even heroic actions if they were likely to discredit his government in Allied eyes. A major crisis confronted him in late October and early November in Surabaja.

The Surabaja conflagration was a product of the delicately balanced pattern of tensions and suspicion which developed as British forces began to land in Java at the end of September. In Indonesian eyes the British were merely a cover for the Dutch who were expecting to resume control of the Indies as a simple matter of course. Indeed the British themselves assumed at first that this would be their role. The presence of a *de facto* republican government soon made it obvious that things were not to be as simple as that. The British quickly made their own assessment of the Republic's strength and recognized it as an important factor in the situation. Certainly they did facilitate the return of Dutch forces as the Indonesians feared would be the case, but they also gave virtual recognition to the Republic, regarding it as able to exercise considerable control over its population, and they thus aroused Dutch resentment in turn.

In Surabaja British caution was not sufficient to smooth Indonesian fears. By early October the city was effectively in Indonesian hands as a result of the actions of the struggle-organizations (under the leadership in particular of the romantic figure of Bung Tomo, whose independent radio station stirred the patriotic feelings of the populace and directed its military activities). On 25

October British forces under Brigadier-General Mallaby arrived to arrange the evacuation of prisoners of war. First contacts between the Indonesians and the British were cordial enough but the British occupation of key points of the city, and an air drop of pamphlets calling for the surrender of arms, sparked two days of fighting between British and *pemuda* forces. On 29 October, as battles raged in the streets of the city, the British called to Sukarno to fly to Surabaja and to use his influence to arrange a cease fire. Sukarno came and toured the city, appearing before the *pemuda* fighters as their President and appealing for restraint and calm. Once again he was able to show the remarkable extent of his personal authority even over forces such as these which were, to say the least, only imperfectly under the control of the Republic's government. Agreement was reached that British forces would be allowed to perform the limited job of evacuating prisoners.

Unfortunately, in a confused skirmish which followed this agreement, Mallaby himself was killed and tension rose immediately. Sukarno, now back in Djakarta, went on the air to appeal once again for restraint in Surabaja. He stressed the point that all fighting must be the responsibility of the central government. On this ground 'I order that all fighting against the Allies cease. . . . We are definitely not at war with the Allies.' Once again he was listened to and for the next few days the evacuation was carried out. Then, on 9 November, with the immediate task in Surabaja completed, the British decided after all to seize the city, and for the second time they called for submission and the surrender of arms.

The Indonesian authorities of Surabaja decided to resist and from then on the government in Djakarta lost control of the situation. The British attack was launched and there followed three weeks of bitter fighting. The attackers were supported by air power, naval bombardment and superior arms but they were met by an extraordinary demonstration of Indonesian resolve and courage. Street-fighting of a guerrilla kind was directed by Bung Tomo and only after great bloodshed were the Indonesian forces defeated. Their resistance had shown the British what kind of warfare would be necessary if they were to attempt to assert their authority in other Republican-held areas. Though there was fighting elsewhere, in Bandung, Semarang and in smaller towns, it never matched the ferocity of that in Surabaja. For the British the Surabaja experience was an irresistible argument in favour of pressing the Dutch to negotiate.

For the Republic the battle of Surabaja was one of the epic incidents of the revolution. For Sukarno its significance was less clear-cut. In his visit on 30 October and in his subsequent radio broadcast after Mallaby's death, he took the risk of appearing as a tool of British authority. In fact he did not have a great deal of room for manoeuvre, for it was necessary to impress on the Allies the Republic's ability to control its forces. It was also the case that even the armed youth of Surabaja could not withstand well-trained and well-equipped troops. For these reasons Sukarno felt he had no alternative but to restrain Indonesian ardour and try to ward off an open conflict. The *pemuda* may have been convinced that only a demonstration of determination could pave the way to ultimate victory, but for Sukarno in November 1945 policy required caution and moderation.

While the battle of Surabaja was in the making, problems of a different kind were facing Sukarno in Djakarta, where there developed the first of a series of internal struggles for power which marked the history of the revolution. On this occasion opposition developed about the semi-legendary figure of Tan Malaka. It was concerned ostensibly with questions of policy. To negotiate or not to negotiate? On this question Hatta and Sjahrir and their supporters – and also Sukarno – found themselves opposed over the next three years, first by Tan Malaka's 'national Communist' followers, and then by the revived PKI. Sukarno's position in this alignment may seem surprising, since he of all men had been an exponent of the view that the real enemy of Indonesia was Western imperialism and that one could never hope for any concessions whatsoever from that quarter. In fact, as the Surabaja crisis had demonstrated, Sukarno was now clearly, even if reluctantly, on the side of *diplomasi* rather than *perdjuangan*.

It could be argued, paradoxically, that his conflicting feelings at this time were in themselves a source of strength. Where neither diplomacy nor struggle alone would have sufficed to defeat the Dutch, Sukarno's ambivalent position between Sjahrir and the radicals gave him a precarious survival-value at a time when continuity of leadership was important. Be that as it may he had come to accept the view that the Republic's survival depended on a negotiated solution, even though holding such a view had adverse political consequences for him. He was *persona non grata* with the Dutch, and the Republic's policy of negotiation was bound to strengthen those who were more acceptable to the other side – notably Sjahrir and Hatta. In Sukarno's eyes these men who had studied in Holland, who had acquired, to a great extent, European liberal values and who felt comfortable in Dutch company, were more than half Europeans. For the moment these qualities gave them political strength and made it inevitable that he himself should play a secondary role. This fact must have reminded him of the rivalries of the early thirties, but he accepted the facts and, as the challenge from Tan Malaka developed, Sukarno identified himself firmly with the government's policy of negotiation.

Tan Malaka, it seems, had returned secretly to Indonesia during the Japanese occupation after more than twenty years' working abroad in the shadowy avenues of international communist organization. During the latter years of the Occupation he had worked in a coal-mine in Banten, but in August 1945 he appeared in Djakarta under an assumed name. He presented himself unannounced one morning at Soebardjo's house and only after a moment's hesitation did Soebardjo recognize his visitor.[16] In the following months the two men established a close relationship as Tan Malaka tested his footing in the Djakarta political environment. He had hopes that he might topple Sukarno from the presidency but he found that Sukarno's support was not easily to be undermined. He made contact with Sukarno himself and persuaded him to draw up a secret political testament which would provide for the succession to the presidency in the event of the President or the Vice-President being arrested or killed. Sukarno accepted the idea of a testament but he did not make Tan Malaka his sole heir. He decided instead that the presidency

16. Author's interview with Soebardjo, 20 June 1969.

should be put into commission in the event of a crisis and named a group of three others besides Tan Malaka to share power.

As Sjahrir prepared to open negotiations with the Dutch, Tan Malaka began to gather about him some of the youth leaders, such as Adam Malik and Chaerul Saleh, and set himself to build up a mass movement committed to opposing all negotiations with the enemy. Such a programme was calculated, of course, to destroy the image of sober practicality and responsibility which Sjahrir had attempted to create in order to provide a basis for realistic give and take at the conference table. But there was much popular support for it and Tan Malaka's 'Struggle Union' (Persatuan Perdjuangan – PP) in fact drew to itself a wide range of individual organizations.

At the end of December as Dutch forces began to filter into Djakarta it was felt that the risks of maintaining the city as the seat of government were too great, and the decision was made to transfer the government secretly to Jogjakarta. Sukarno's house backed on to the main railway line out of Djakarta and, on the night of 4 January 1946, he and Hatta slipped quietly aboard a train which stopped there to pick them up while Sjahrir stayed behind in Djakarta in order to preserve his contacts with British and Dutch forces. The division of government in fact weakened the Prime Minister. His opponents were able in Jogjakarta to mobilize their opposition to him more effectively; they were re-mote from the patent evidence of Dutch strength and it seemed to them that a policy of uncompromising struggle was not un-realistic. As the PP developed its criticism of the concessions which the government was believed to be making, Sjahrir finally decided, at the end of February, to resign.

His resignation placed the immediate initiative in Sukarno's hands. It was open to him to offer a commission to the PP leaders whose opposition had led to Sjahrir's fall and this must have seemed most in accordance with the constitutional conven-tions which had been adopted in November. Instead, following his own inclination, he sought to assemble a broadly-based coali-tion of ministers which would give a voice to Sjahrir's opponents, without reversing Sjahrir's policy of seeking accommodation with the Dutch. But the PP leaders refused to put forward any candidates of their own for cabinet posts except on the basis of a programme of uncompromising opposition to negotiations, so Sukarno turned once more to Sjahrir.

Back in office Sjahrir moved against his opponents. He arrested Tan Malaka and other leaders of the PP. The arrests temporarily checked the momentum of the PP opposition but did not end the plans of some of its leading members. How far Tan Malaka was the central figure in the plotting which followed, and how far he was caught up in the plots of others, is not clear. He was still under detention when the climax came and the actual attempt was made to overthrow the government.

On the night of 27 June Major-General Sudarsono ordered the arrest of Sjahrir as he returned to Jogja after a visit to East Java. The arrest – or kidnapping – was followed by a move to confront the President with what was hoped would be a decisive opposition to the policy of the government. The plotters, however, miscalculated their strength. Sukarno immediately took emergency powers into his own hands and demanded the return of Sjahrir. In a radio speech he appealed to the people to reject those who were determined to seize power by any means. One expected the hostility of the Dutch to the Republic, he said, but more dangerous were the internal enemies who did not recognize the limits of legitimate opposition and who could not distinguish between 'opposition' and 'destruction'. 'Truly we do not fear the danger that comes from without . . . because we can see it. But still more dangerous is the threat from within, the internal adversary who scrapes away at the foundations of our Republic little by little.'[17] This speech steadied the situation and three days later, when the mass movement of support on which the plotters had counted had failed to materialize, Sukarno moved to arrest Sudarsono and others involved in the affair – Tan Malaka, Subardjo, Yamin, Iwa Kusumasumantri and Sukarni.

The 'July 3rd Affair', as it came to be known, had been a major threat not only to Sjahrir's government but to the Republic itself. It was a particularly tangled incident and not a simple challenge by a clearly organized opposition. It did contain elements, cer-

17. Radio speech of 30 June 1946, published in *Merdeka*, 1 and 2 July 1946.

tainly, of a clash between the government and its opponents over issues of policy. Tan Malaka was the rallying point for those who believed that the Dutch were untrustworthy, that the attempt to secure a negotiated transfer of sovereignty was bound to fail and that the outcome would be the extinction of the Republic. The actual course of negotiations indeed provided some evidence for the validity of such an analysis. But beyond this well defined opposition between the exponents of *diplomasi* and *perdjuangan* were other issues.

For some of the *pemuda* supporters of the PP Tan Malaka symbolized not just a different mode of struggling for independence; he was the symbol of a different kind of revolution altogether. Sukarno, Hatta and Sjahrir were seeking merely to take over the machinery of state in the first instance, leaving questions of social reconstruction to be considered later. They stood on the side of orderly change, not of revolutionary upsurge. Sukarno, in his radio speech of 30 June for example, referred quite specifically to the importance of showing to the outside world that the government could govern, thus denying the Dutch charge that Indonesia was not ripe for independence.[18] Tan Malaka by contrast appeared to promise a more fundamental change – the creation, out of the anarchy of revolution, of new channels through which popular power could flow. In exile he had been a revolutionary dreamer and now on his return he was able to crystallize the dreams of others.

But there were *pemuda* supporters on both sides of the power struggle of 1946 and it is not possible to interpret that struggle simply in terms of pemudaism as such. A further distinction to be made within the ranks of youth itself is between those whose Marxist background made them think primarily in anti-fascist terms and those who, moved by nationalist principles rather than by anti-fascist ideology, had been willing to co-operate with the Japanese during the Occupation. The former reflected Sjahrir's own pre-war analysis that it was necessary to stand with Holland in the late thirties against the challenge of Nazi barbarism. The latter had been willing to use Japanese barbarism for nationalist ends. The opposition of 1946 was drawn largely from the latter

18. ibid.

group, but it found itself opposing the figure of Sukarno in spite of the fact that he too had used Japanese power for Indonesian purposes.

Finally, there was an element simply of frustrated ambition on the part of the leaders who stood about Tan Malaka. There were hurt men who had suffered keenly from the abrasive nature of Sjahrir's attack on collaborators; there were ambiguous figures like the ascetic and idealistic Commander-in-Chief, General Sudirman, who had links with Sjahrir's supporters as well as with his opponents and there were intriguers like Yamin.

From this variety of overlapping groups and issues came an opposition willing to risk a coup against the government. In judging the coup attempt it would, of course, be possible to argue that, in the shifting alignments of the early revolution, the PP was as legitimate a force as any other, including even the government, and that, given the broadly based organizations which composed it, it was possibly more representative than the government. Such a view, however, could only be maintained by ignoring the fact that, as a movement of opposition, it could command the support of heterogeneous elements which could not have remained united had their leaders held responsibility for the formulation and execution of policy.

For the story of Sukarno the significance of the coup attempt was that it once again stressed his central position and his independence of faction. As the opposition emerged he attempted first to form a more widely representative government. After his failure he remained as the arbiter of the conflict, exercising authority after Sjahrir's disappearance and retaining his control of events until the emergency had passed. Over the following weeks he took an active part in the negotiations leading to the formation of Sjahrir's third cabinet, which his efforts made more representative than its predecessors and in which he ensured that Sjahrir's personal following was reduced. Finally, at the end of 1946 and as part of the same policy, he moved to increase the size of the KNIP from 200 members to 514, adding representatives of functional groups and regions as well as additional representatives of political parties. Here could be seen the principle of representation that he was to elaborate more fully ten years later.

The defeat of the Persatuan Perdjuangan confirmed the policy of negotiation with the Dutch. Whatever the *pemuda* organizations may have felt about the ritual importance of struggle, the government was aware of the Republic's essential weakness and saw no alternative to its policy. But negotiation certainly carried its own dangers. It is very doubtful whether the Dutch ever seriously intended to come to terms at the conference table. Early in 1946 discussions with Lieutenant-Governor-General Hubertus van Mook made it clear that, though Holland professed herself ready to grant some sort of extended autonomy to the Indies, she was not disposed to negotiate such changes with the self-proclaimed Republic, and this reluctance remained over the next three and a half years.

For a time during 1946 discussions at Linggadjati, a hill station near Tjirebon, did offer hopes for a negotiated solution. In November, by the Linggadjati Agreement, the Netherlands recognized the Republic as exercising *de facto* authority over Java, Sumatra and Madura. They also agreed to co-operate in the formation of an Indonesian federation to which sovereignty would ultimately be transferred, and in which the Republic would merely be one constituent state. The Dutch had insisted upon the federal principle ostensibly because of Indonesia's diversity. To the Republic that argument seemed merely to be a divide-and-rule tactic intended to give Holland a maximum of influence in an independent Indonesia. By contrast the Republic had demanded a unitary state formed by the transfer of sovereignty to itself. Nevertheless the Agreement as a whole did appear to contain the essentials of a solution: the Dutch conceded the all-important principle of Indonesian independence and the Republic, for its part, accepted, though with misgivings, a curtailment of its claim to represent all Indonesia.

Sukarno left the details of these negotiations to his ministers. He regarded the subtleties of proposals and counter proposals as minor matters compared with the central question of independence, and he did not seem to see that the central question depended very much upon the precise character of the individual proposals discussed at the conference table. Surprisingly for one who had always insisted that the Dutch could not be trusted he maintained a high degree of optimism that the Linggadjati promise of independence meant what it seemed to say. His optimism was premature. The Agreement was vague about interim arrangements and differences of interpretation soon left it a dead letter. It became clear, for example, that whereas the Republic expected the formation of the Indonesian federation to be a joint enterprise between itself and the Netherlands, the latter insisted that it was solely a Dutch responsibility. The Dutch began unilaterally to create a series of states on the basis of which the federation would later be established. To leave no doubt about their rights in the matter they issued an ultimatum to the Republic, demanding firstly that *de jure* sovereignty remain with the Netherlands until the transfer of sovereignty to the United States of Indonesia, secondly that authority remain vested in the representative of the Dutch crown during the interim period, and thirdly that a joint police force be formed to operate in both Dutch-controlled and Indonesian-controlled territory.

These demands placed Sjahrir in a dilemma. To reject them was to open the possibility of a Dutch attack; to accept them would lose him his support in the KNIP where a new coalition had been formed – the Sajap Kiri ('Left Wing') – prepared to lead the opposition to any further concessions. Sjahrir in fact accepted the idea of *de jure* Dutch sovereignty for the time being along with the position of special representative of the Dutch crown, but he could not accept a joint police force which would have given Dutch forces a toehold in the Republic's own territory. Even so his concessions went too far for his critics and in the face of Sajap Kiri opposition he resigned.

Sukarno once again accepted the responsibility for forming a new government. He pressed Sjahrir unsuccessfully to remain in office and then turned to Amir Sjarifuddin who managed to form a government commanding KNIP support. But Amir, like Sjahrir, had to come to terms with reality. He too accepted the first two Dutch demands and rejected the third. The concessions were not enough, however, to prevent the Dutch deciding to resort to force. On 20 July 1947 their troops launched the attack which they cynically described as merely a police action.

The Dutch were, of course, heavily committed, psychologically and economically, to their colony. Even so the decision to re-impose their control by force was taken with a remarkable degree of arrogance and self-righteousness. The conviction of so many Dutchmen in the Indies and at home that they had been good colonial rulers, that they were still loved by their former subjects and that Sukarno and his colleagues were a small and unrepresentative minority, must rank as one of the major pieces of self-deception in the annals of empire. It helped to explain the extraordinary intransigence of Dutch negotiators before and after the launching of the July attack.

As the heavily armed Dutch troops moved out into the Javanese and Sumatran countryside Indonesian forces withdrew, but they continued to maintain a heavy guerrilla harassment of the enemy. In the struggle for survival Sukarno once again became the symbol of national resistance, but there were limits to the inspirational role he could play – the main spheres of effective action at this time were on the battlefield and at Lake Success, where Sjahrir, now the Republic's representative to the UN, was very much in the limelight.

During the crisis Sukarno turned to the written as well as the spoken word to convery his message. In the midst of the conflict he was engaged in preparing a handbook for the women's movement, the title of which – *Sarinah* – recalled the name of his childhood nurse. *Sarinah* reflected much of the nature of his leadership at this time (the mere fact that he had an opportunity to write was itself significant) for despite the supposedly specific nature of his subject – the role of women in the revolution – he dealt with several general issues. The book contained a statement, memorable in places, of the nature of revolution itself. Sukarno looked beyond the present struggle to the just society of the future; the national revolution of the moment, he said, must be distinguished from the social revolution to come. There were Marxist echoes in his extended discussion of the necessity for successive stages of revolution, but there was also his familiar rhetoric as he described the nature of the task: 'a gigantic undertaking that requires the mobilization of gigantic manpower, a persevering and gigantic will, thoughts and assessments on a gigantic scale'. To accomplish both revolutions required passion:

Is it possible for a most mighty and a most difficult struggle to go on with enough élan if there are no ideals, no idealism, no romanticism! . . . Yes, perhaps this really does smell of idealism, perhaps this really does smell of romanticism. . . . But I offer thanks to God that my soul is not empty of such idealism and romanticism. I pity people who do not possess that 'Indonesian romanticism'.

The task also required unity, and this theme once again occupied a central place in his argument. 'All of the islands of the Indonesian Archipelago need one another.'

In his speech of 17 August these thoughts were given further expression. He called for the unity of all Indonesia in terms which foreshadowed his later slogan 'From Sabang to Merauke', and more particularly he accompanied his vision of a united Indonesia with a practical appeal for support for the Republic from those at present outside the area of its authority. The Republic, he said, was the leader of the struggle of the whole Indonesian nation:

'Be sure, Sisters and Brothers outside Java, and Sumatra and Madura – with the disappearance of the Republic there will disappear also, exterminated by the Dutch, the independence movement outside the Republic. . . . The Republic is not the property of the Indonesians who live in Java and Sumatra alone, the Republic is also the property of our sisters and brothers who live in Borneo, in Sulawesi, in the lesser Sunda islands, in the Moluccas, in Irian.'

While Sukarno was writing the Dutch had discovered that victory was not to be achieved easily. The first police action awakened world attention. An Australian resolution brought the dispute to the attention of the United Nations Security Council which called for a cease fire and offered its assistance to the two parties in their negotiations. The cease fire left the Netherlands in possession of substantial areas of Java and Madura, formerly under republican control, and it did not prevent further mopping up operations. When, after several months, formal negotiations were renewed under the auspices of the United Nations Good Offices Committee, the Dutch thought themselves to be operating from a position of strength. This fact was reflected in the truce which was signed on 19 January 1948 on board the USS *Renville* and which left the Dutch still in possession of the territorial gains they had made in July. Provision was made as before for an inde-

pendent United States of Indonesia, but now the principle of continuing Netherlands sovereignty in the interim period was set out
and the Republic's position in the proposed federal state was left
very much in doubt. The Dutch had continued, by setting up
their own puppet states, to move towards a federation of their
own devising and the only safeguard that the Republic could
secure was that within twelve months a plebiscite would determine whether those parts of Java, Sumatra and Madura captured
by the Dutch would adhere to the Republic or be formed into
separate states for inclusion in the federation. In accepting the
truce proposals the Republic felt itself to be doing so under strong
pressure for there seemed to be no guarantee that the Dutch
would not use their *de jure* sovereignty to reduce the Republic's
power and perhaps to destroy it altogether. Indeed, after another
year of abortive negotiations, a second Dutch police action was
launched on 18 December 1948 with the clear intention of crushing the Republic once and for all.

The Republic's problems during that year did not, however, come
solely from its external enemy. Internal division continued to
threaten its unity. The signing of the Renville Agreement on 19
January 1948 provoked immediate controversy in Indonesia and
presented Sukarno with a new cabinet crisis. Sjarifuddin resigned
at the end of January and Sukarno's skills in creating unity were
again called into play. He responded by deciding to form a presidential cabinet – a cabinet, that is to say, which was responsible
to him rather than to the KNIP. He was perfectly entitled to do
this under the 1945 Constitution, but he also knew that his action
could command strong support within the KNIP. Hatta was
entrusted with the task of forming the new government and he
succeeded in bringing the PNI and Masjumi together and in
building a strong team on their co-operation. It was not as
broadly based a cabinet as Sukarno would have liked; though an
attempt was made to include representatives of the left-wing
parties their demands for key posts were too extreme to be acceptable and the cabinet was formed without them.

As Sukarno had feared, these splits in the precariously maintained unity of 1947 were soon to open more widely. On this

occasion the challenge to the Republic was led by the PKI. Like the Persatuan Perdjuangan of two years earlier, it posed a fundamental threat since it struck at the very legitimacy of the régime and envisaged, ultimately, its overthrow by force. In so doing it gave Sukarno his first direct experience of the difficulty of making communism a part of the national consensus, though it did not destroy his faith in the possibility of such an achievement.

The strategy of the PKI during 1948 was shaped in part by local developments, but also by the changing policies of the international communist movement as a whole. During the first two years of the revolution the PKI was moved by nationalist as much as by communist aspirations, and the temper of Soviet policy allowed it to be so. In the course of 1947, however, the development of the cold war in Europe was accompanied by the collapse of united fronts and the sharpening of tensions between communists and non-communists elsewhere. The creation of the Cominform and the formulation of the 'Two Camps doctrine' changed the framework within which individual communist parties devised their tactics. In Indonesia the change came slowly, but widespread disappointment at the terms of the Renville Agreement provided a setting in which the new policy was able to find support among younger leaders of the PKI. The policy of negotiation seemed to have failed and the PP-type demand for all-out guerrilla warfare seemed therefore to have more credibility and to be capable, in consequence, of sustaining a sharper PKI initiative.

Sukarno soon felt the effect of these developments. The newly stiffened communist party made the Hatta government the target of its criticism and, by implication, since this was Sukarno's own government, the criticism was applied to him also. As the campaign developed it was made very clear to him that even his prestige was not enough to guarantee Republican unity.

The PKI strategy, like that of the Tan Malaka opposition before it, was directed to the building up of a broadly-based united front of organizations sympathetic to its aims. The 'People's Democratic Front' (FDR), as it was called, was an alliance comprising Sjarifuddin's Socialist Party, the Labour Party, Pesindo and SOBSI, the Indonesian Federation of Trade Unions and the

PKI itself. In February 1948 it demanded the repudiation of the Renville Agreement. In the following months it maintained its attack on the government, complaining that the revolution had become bogged down in negotiations and compromise and urging the seizure of Dutch property. It supported strikes designed to weaken the government's position. These were familiar attitudes and they did find a measure of popular support. Nevertheless it was clear that the government could never be toppled by constitutional means and at some stage in July or August the leaders of the FDR moved further to a decision to seek power by force if other means failed.

This shift to a more radical position was in part due to its lack of success so far. Partly it was due to a new element in its leadership – an element provided by the return from Moscow of the old PKI leader, Musso.

Musso arrived incognito at Bukit Tinggi airfield early in August posing as the secretary of Suripno, a PKI member who had been representing the Republic in eastern Europe, and he disclosed his identity at a PKI meeting in Jogja a couple of weeks later. He was immediately instated as party secretary. This was only Musso's second visit to his homeland over a twenty-year period – he had stayed in Moscow after the failure of the 1926 rebellion and had returned briefly in the mid thirties to organize the short-lived 'Illegal PKI'. He now returned to steer the PKI more decisively along the course indicated by the 'Two Camps' doctrine. His return was followed by Sjarifuddin's dramatic announcement that he also had been a communist since 1935 – a claim which was doubted by many of those who knew him closely.

Musso's leadership did not immediately set the PKI on a collision course with the government. Opposition was still confined to bold words and to the strengthening of the party by attempts to absorb the groups closely allied to it. Early in September a speaking tour by Musso and Sjarifuddin and other leaders of the PKI was designed, still within the framework of constitutional opposition to the government, to rally support to the PKI banner. Sharpened tensions had by this time created a dangerous situation. In Surakarta, where the pro-PKI Fourth Division was resisting government plans for army rationalization, fighting broke out between it and troops loyal to the government. In this tinderbox situation only a spark was required to ignite a more general conflagration. The spark was provided, unexpectedly so far as Musso and Sjarifuddin were concerned, by pro-PKI troops who, early in the morning of 18 September, seized key points in the city of Madiun and called for revolt against the government. Musso and Sjarifuddin, caught unawares hurried to Madiun where they found that they had little option but to accept the insurrection, though from their point of view it had broken out prematurely.

Like the PKI rebellions of 1926 and 1927 the 'Madiun Affair' was doomed to a quick defeat. Unlike them it was directed not against a colonial overlord but against an Indonesian government, and it thus introduced the horrors of civil conflict into the nationalist struggle. The PKI in later years was to justify its action on the grounds that the revolt was forced upon it. It was responding, it claimed, to the provocation of the Hatta government. The 'incident' in Madiun between a reactionary group in the army and a group faithful to the revolution was used by Hatta's government as a pretext to begin a white terror, said Aidit in 1955. The communists had no alternative therefore but to take up arms and defend themselves.[19] This picture of government provocation against an innocent PKI became the theme of the PKI's annual observance of the anniversary of Madiun.[20] However the government in 1948 had little difficulty in portraying the revolt as an act of treachery to the embattled Republic. In these terms, Sukarno rallied support in a radio appeal which called on the nation to choose between himself and the communists. 'Brothers, what is the true meaning of these events?' he asked, and gave his own diagnosis in terms of simple alternatives:

'The PKI under Musso's leadership is attempting to seize power in our country. Fellow countrymen, in the name of the struggle for Indo-

19. D. N. Aidit, speech of 23 May 1955, published as: *Lahirnja PKI dan Perkembangannja 1920–1955* ['The Birth of the PKI and its Development, 1920–1955'], Djakarta, 1955.

20. See, e.g., *Harian Rakjat*, 19 September 1952, 19 September and 28 September 1954, 17 September 1955, 19 September 1956, etc. See also Kahin's account (op. cit.) of the affair which is still the fullest and most balanced treatment available in English.

nesian independence . . . I want to explain to you that you must make a choice: to follow Musso and his PKI who will destroy the idea of Indonesian independence or to follow Sukarno–Hatta who, with the help of God, will lead you along the road to independence for Indonesia and freedom from all oppression.'[21]

Sukarno's appeal was accompanied by the vesting in him of absolute authority to deal with the emergency. Immediate steps were taken to arrest PKI leaders in Jogja and elsewhere and to prepare military action against the communist forces. It soon became clear that the PKI lacked the popular support to trigger a general uprising and its defeat was therefore only a matter of time. In vain did the rebels plead that they were attacking not the Republic but only the reactionary elements in the government; in vain did they insist that they were not trying to establish a Soviet government. The argument that the Sukarno and Hatta government was essentially indistinguishable from the Dutch or the Japanese government, and that it was now indeed in the process of selling out to the Dutch, did not strike echoes in the popular mind, and, either positively or passively, the nation made its choice for Sukarno rather than Musso. By the end of October, largely as a result of vigorous action by the Siliwangi Division under Colonel A. H. Nasution, the revolt was over. Musso was killed in a minor engagement and other leaders, including Sjarifuddin, were captured. (Most of them, including Sjarifuddin, were to be executed after the opening of the second Dutch police action.)

The revolt led to the elimination of the PKI for the time being. That it was suppressed so promptly was due in great measure to Sukarno's ability to stand as a symbol of the Republic's unity; the confidence of his appeal to the nation was one more illustration of his capacity to rise to the occasion. But the crisis had other meanings for him too.

First of all, he continued to regard the PKI as an authentic element in the Indonesian revolution and his condemnation of it on this occasion was a condemnation of what he believed to be its deviation from the party's proper course just as, in 1926, he had

21. *Merdeka*, 20 September 1948.

condemned Marxists who betrayed the cause of unity as 'the poison of the people'. In a pamphlet distributed shortly afterwards he placed the revolt in the context of his analysis, given in *Sarinah*, of the successive stages of the revolution.[22] The trouble with Madiun was that it was 'a social revolution that was provoked, a social revolution that was forced years and perhaps decades before its time'. 'The "Madiun Social Revolution" was an act of revolutionary-ism gone astray.' It 'did not stand on objective factors but was merely forced by the subjective passions of its leaders alone'. The same point had already been suggested in his radio appeal of 19 September. The terms of that speech had, quite characteristically, allowed a distinction to be made between the PKI and Musso's leadership of it. 'The PKI under Musso's leadership', 'Musso and his PKI', 'the PKI–Musso' – such phrases kept open the possibility that the PKI itself, under different leadership, might be a valid part of the revolution.

Secondly, he had learned – or thought he had learned – that his own stature was sufficient to enable him to control dissident elements which threatened the state. It had seemed to be so in 1946 and 1948. Again in 1949, during the second police action, a renewed threat from the national communist followers of Tan Malaka constituted no real danger. (It ended in the killing of Tan Malaka by a local military officer and the removal thereby of a romantic figure who had stood, if only in the shadows, as a possible alternative to Sukarno himself). Years later Sukarno's confidence that he could overcome all challenges allowed him to flirt with a rejuvenated PKI and lead it back to the edge of power, in the conviction that, should it again present a threat to the Indonesian consensus, he could destroy it by a word of command.

During the Madiun crisis the Dutch, under American pressure, exercised surprising restraint and did not try to turn the internal conflict to their own ends, but their final attempt to crush the Republic followed soon after. An observer of Dutch–Indonesian

22. *Kepada Bangsaku*. This consisted of the major part of Chapter 6 of *Sarinah*, together with a new section commenting on the Madiun Affair. This new section was later published, together with other works of Sukarno under the title, once again, of *Kepada Bangsaku* (Djakarta, 1962).

negotiations in November 1948 might have been pardoned for thinking himself back on the eve of the first police action. Both sides were still locked on the question of the interim government which was to precede independence. The Republic had already resigned itself to accepting the ultimate authority of a representative of the Dutch crown during the interim period. It still could not accept a Dutch demand that Netherlands forces, under the authority of that special representative, should have the right to maintain law and order. To accept that proposal, it seemed to Hatta and his colleagues, would be to invite annihilation.

Once again the Dutch, on 15 December, served on the Republic an ultimatum which seemed designed to be rejected. And early on the morning of 19 December, the Dutch launched the surprise attack on Jogjakarta which opened the second police action.

On the morning of the 19th when Sukarno awoke to the sound of the bombing of Jogjakarta airport and to the news of its subsequent capture by paratroops, there was still a short space of time in which he and other leaders could have left the capital. The question was considered at a hastily called cabinet meeting later in the morning and Sukarno listened then to the suggestion that he should take to the countryside and direct a guerrilla resistance to the Dutch attack. He hesitated, torn between the romantic appeal of such a role and the soberer counsels of those who felt that it would be better for the government to remain at its post and face capture by the Dutch. It was another critical moment for him, but unlike many other occasions when difficult alternatives faced him there was no time to temporize and to wait for the right choice to reveal itself. On this occasion to delay a decision was itself to make a decision. Actively or passively Sukarno chose to remain in Jogja, and that afternoon Dutch forces captured the President and his closest colleagues, Hatta, Hadji Agus Salim and other members of the government. Sjahrir was also seized. On the following morning Sukarno acted as president for the last time before going into detention. He rejected out of hand a Dutch request that he order the Republic to cease its resistance.

Though Sukarno was to be criticized for his choice he probably made the right decision. As events turned out, the second police action was to prove a fatal mistake for the Dutch. It shocked world opinion, jolted the UN into slightly more positive action and persuaded influential circles in America that economic aid should be withheld from the Netherlands until the Dutch showed signs of willingness to enter into serious negotiations with the Republic. In Indonesia the Dutch found that it was not so easy to eliminate the Republic from the scene and thus present the world with a rapid *fait accompli*. In Sumatra, by pre-arranged plan, an alternative government proclaimed itself under the leadership of Sjafruddin Prawiranegara. In Java Dutch armoured forces could move along roads and capture towns but they could not occupy the surrounding countryside, and continuing guerrilla resistance made nonsense of their claims that there was no significant opposition to their advance. In fact such resistance now flared up in areas on the Dutch side of the cease-fire line. There were also important reactions outside Java where the Dutch had erected an elaborate structure of fifteen semi-autonomous states over the course of the previous eighteen months. These states were supposed to form the basis of the future Indonesian federation and in establishing them the Dutch had been able to count on fears of republican Java among the local aristocracies of the outer islands. The second police action shocked outer island opinion and made it ready, for the first time, to follow Sukarno's appeal in his speech of 17 August 1947 and to see the Republic as the genuine leader of a truly national struggle for independence. In the face of these factors Holland, by mid 1949, had come to recognize that she could not impose a solution on the Indies by force.

Sukarno and Hatta were not directly part of the struggle which led to this change of attitude. On 30 December they were taken, in company with Sjahrir, Hadji Agus Salim and other members of the government, to Bangka. Here the prisoners were divided into two groups: Sukarno, Sjahrir and Salim were flown on to Brastagi, North Sumatra, and then to Prapat, the holiday resort on Lake Toba; Hatta and the others were kept in Bangka and some months later the Prapat group was brought back to join them there. They were all thus removed from the actual months of conflict. But symbols were important and even in detention Sukarno remained the embodiment of Indonesian nationalism. His final speech to the nation, prepared hastily during the first hours of the attack on Jogja, was never broadcast as planned for the Dutch managed to immobilize the radio station before it could be delivered. Nevertheless typewritten copies were later circulated, secretly in Dutch-held areas, openly outside them. The speech matched the occasion. Sukarno recognized that the Dutch might capture key points in the Republic, but he reaffirmed his faith in ultimate victory. The enemy could not smash Indonesia's fighting spirit nor crush the popular demand for independence.

Finally in June 1949, as a result of the eventual Netherlands agreement to revive negotiations, a cease fire was ordered. On 6 July a plane belonging to the United Nations Commission for Indonesia picked up Sukarno and his colleagues at Bangka and returned them triumphantly to Jogja. They were met at the airport by the Sultan of Jogjakarta, and Sukarno, with his usual eye for the drama of an occasion, handed to a special corps the original proclamation flag which he had taken with him. He and Hatta were then driven back to the city through cheering crowds to resume control of the government.[23]

But though Sukarno had preserved his standing as a national leader during the period of his confinement in Prapat this period presented him with another sort of challenge, which wounded him deeply and left its permanent mark. Immediately it concerned his relations with Sjahrir; at a more general level it illustrated a continuing contrast of leadership styles, reviving a theme which had been important in the early thirties and which was to have its significance again in the rivalries of the future independent Republic.

This outline of Sukarno's career has so far been concerned with describing his establishment of a distinctive temper and mode of leadership. On his diagnosis of the colonial situation he built his programme of mass action to resist Dutch power; by his oratory he had been able to reach out to a mass audience and instil a sense of nationhood where it had not existed before. As a crusader of nationalism he sometimes misjudged the power of the enemy, and in developing his own style he found himself, as we have seen, at odds with others of a different intellectual stamp. The collapse of the PNI vision of the late twenties was followed, in the early

23. *Merdeka*, 7 July 1949.

thirties, by rivalry with leaders who might have been more subtle than he as political analysts, but who lacked his flair and imagination and his *rapport* with the masses. It was not, at that time, a fatal rivalry.

In 1932, Sukarno on the one hand and Hatta and Sjahrir on the other had chosen to go in different directions, but they still saw themselves as taking different paths to the same destination, and they were able to come together once again under the common threat of the Japanese occupation. Their alliance lasted through the revolution. Sukarno and Hatta as President and Vice-President were the *dwi-tunggal*, the combined leadership joining Java and the outer islands, Javanism and Islam, passion and intellect. They were complementary to each other and as a pair outshone all rivals. For his part, Sjahrir during the crucial early months of revolution, was the architect of the policy of negotiation. In November 1945 and again in March and July 1946 Sukarno relied on Sjahrir's judgement and supported him against his critics. After Sjahrir's premiership had ended he was still, as Indonesia's representative at the UN, a vital adviser and negotiator for the Republic. But at Prapat Sukarno and he came to the fatal crisis in their relations.

It is not clear precisely what happened. According to one story Sukarno, during their stop at Brastagi, asked his Dutch captors for Arrow shirts and other minor comforts. Sjahrir rebuked him for making the request and argued that such a concern with trivia was unbecoming to a national leader in a time of crisis. According to another story Sjahrir is said to have told Sukarno impatiently that he was not President of the Republic at Prapat and shouldn't act as though he were still in command of events. To a man like Sukarno, who was so conscious of his position as President, this was indeed a terrible thing to say. Sukarno's own story is that Sjahrir accused him in the presence of others of political stupidity. Whichever version is true it is clear that Sukarno felt himself to have received a deep insult. Both men were, of course, under tremendous strain. After three years of struggle their arrest, and the swift advance of the Dutch, must have seemed to mark the end of their hopes, whatever words of courage Sukarno may have uttered in the text of his radio speech. In that context of frustration bitter words were easily said, and Hadji Agus Salim was later reported as saying that Sjahrir went too far in his criticism of Sukarno at Brastagi and Prapat.

This personal clash confirmed Sukarno's incipient hostility to Sjahrir and to the ideas he represented. In his autobiography he speaks a little contemptuously, but nonetheless affectionately, of Hatta. He laughs at his bookishness, at his apparent lack of interest in sex, at his coldness. But for Sjahrir he shows resentment and anger:

> He was vicious. And what actually did Sjahrir do for the Republic? Nothing except criticize me. While I was taking hammer blows on the head, his entire underground effort can be summed up by saying he sat quietly and safely away somewhere listening to a clandestine radio. . . . Sjahrir never took it on the chin like I did. He never permitted himself to be in the line of fire. All his fighting was done behind my back.[24]

If the rivalry between charismatic leadership and intellectual leadership is a sub-theme in the pre-revolutionary story of Sukarno it took on a sharper note thereafter. Even after his rivals had been effectively removed from the political arena Sukarno was driven to prove to himself, and to the world at large, that he too had a world view, and that it was more valid as a guide to action than theirs.

If Sukarno and his colleagues returned in triumph to Jogjakarta in July 1949, it was a triumph which was still tinged with anxiety. Earlier experience of the Linggadjati Agreement and the Renville truce made Republican leaders suspicious of Dutch good faith, and the Roem–van Royen agreement which had preceded the cease fire seemed, like earlier agreements, to safeguard the Dutch position rather than that of the Republic. The Dutch returned only a fraction of the territory which they had gained in the second police action, and they secured virtual recognition for the fifteen states they had created as a basis for their proposed federation. However, they did at least now recognize the Republic as one of the states which would form part of the United States of Indonesia, and it was able to exert its leadership in the final negotiations.

24. *Autobiography*, p. 210.

At The Hague on August 23 1949 delegates of the Republic and of the Federal Consultative Assembly set up by the Dutch to represent the fifteen constituent states met representatives of the Netherlands to bring the four-year struggle to an end. This 'Round Table Conference' moved quickly to arrange the transfer of sovereignty to a federation consisting of the Republic and the fifteen other states. The transfer was to be complete and unconditional. Provision was made for a Netherlands–Indonesian Union as foreshadowed in the Linggadjati Agreement, but even here there was no real Dutch control. The Union Statute provided only for voluntary co-operation and stressed the absolute sovereignty and equality of the two parties. The Union was to be of little importance and was finally repudiated by Indonesia in 1956.

All parties were so determined to reach swift agreement on the essential question – the transfer of sovereignty to Indonesia – that they were not disposed to allow lesser questions to stand in the way, even though some of these lesser questions were in themselves important. In consequence a number of issues remained to trouble Dutch–Indonesian relations in the future. Indonesian representatives were appalled at the size of the debt to be assumed by Indonesia. They held that the size of the public debt of Netherlands India at the time of transfer was due in large measure to the military operations of the Dutch against the Republic, and they saw no reason why they should shoulder that responsibility. Though a compromise figure was reached it still seemed an unfair burden to the Indonesians. Secondly, the question of West New Guinea was left unresolved: it was agreed ambiguously that the *status quo* should be maintained in West New Guinea for the time being, but that within a year the future status of the territory would be determined through negotiations. Finally, the form of the new state was a matter of controversy in some circles. To the republican leaders it seemed that the original Republic, proclaimed in August 1945, represented the whole of Indonesia. They had agreed at Linggadjati to accept the federal structure for an independent Indonesia but they continued to feel, even at the Round Table Conference, that the federation was a Dutch construction which imposed unwelcome restraints on Indonesia's autonomy. The federal solution was accepted in 1949 but only with reluctance.

These outstanding issues were solved in time in different ways. The outstanding debt was repudiated in 1956, but the question of West New Guinea remained until 1962 as a symbol of incomplete nationhood. The constitutional question – a unitary versus a federal state – was resolved much more quickly. Immediately after the transfer of sovereignty on 27 December 1949 the federation began to change its shape, in part by the decision of some of the constituent states to merge themselves into the Republic, and in part through the direct surrender, by others, of their powers to the federal government. This process was completed by constitutional amendment and the United States of Indonesia gave way to the unitary Republic of Indonesia on 15 August 1950. The change left Indonesia with a continuing problem of regionalism but it represented the essential completion of Sukarno's struggle for an independent and undivided nation.

# 10

# Figurehead President

On 27 December 1949 the Dutch formally transferred sovereignty to the Republic of the United States of Indonesia and on the following morning Sukarno took his leave of Jogjakarta, the Republic's revolutionary capital, and returned to Djakarta, the capital of the new Indonesia.[25] The two Dakotas bringing the Presidential party touched down at Kemajoran airport just after 11.30, and, preceded once more by the proclamation flag, Sukarno drove to the palace amid the welcoming crowds, feeling, as he put it, like a fish in water or like a buffalo that had returned to its *kraal*.[26]

After the pre-war years of struggle against the overwhelming power of the colonial government, the wartime humiliation of serving the Japanese and the anxieties and hardships of the revolution, his entry into the presidential palace – formerly the residence of the Dutch governor-general – was a moment of historic fulfilment. For those interested in symbols the moment carried some of the elements of the establishment of a new dynasty. Like other Javanese rulers in the more distant past Sukarno was possessing himself of the regalia which conferred power. The changes of place names in the capital underlined the rejection of the usurpers and the return of a native ruler. Batavia became once again Djakarta. The Koningsplein – the vast square to the south of the palace – became the Medan Merdeka ('Freedom Square'). The residency became the Istana Merdeka. In some ways the geography of Djakarta even reproduced, though in mirror image, that of the royal seat of Jogjakarta. The palace looked south-

25. A nice point of constitutional law was raised by Sukarno's appointment as President of the United States of Indonesia. Though he had been chosen for this office on 16 December, he did not then or thereafter resign as President of the old Republic of Indonesia, now merely a constituent state of the federation. When he left Jogja on 27 December he was seen off by Mr Assaat, who had taken office as Acting-President of the Republic of Indonesia.

26. *Aneta News Bulletin*, 30 December 1949.

wards across the Medan Merdeka (matching the *alun alun*, or large grassed square before the Sultan's palace), its back turned to the sea and its face towards the mountains, the abode of the gods. In due course Sukarno was to set up his *tugu*, his symbol of potency, in the centre of the Medan Merdeka.

The traditional symbolism was there in abundance, but for the central figure the triumph was, perhaps, less than complete. Though he occupied the limelight on 28 December, the political role assigned to Sukarno himself in the new Republic was deliberately circumscribed. This was a natural continuation of the situation inherited from the revolution. In November 1945 Sukarno had accepted the conventions of a parliamentary system in place of the strong executive presidency prescribed by the 1945 constitution. This erosion of his authority with its measure of accompanying humiliation was not imposed on him willy nilly, as we have seen. The pressure of political realities persuaded him to go along with the change and his partnership with the other leaders of the revolution thereafter had been remarkably close. By 1949, however, power lay essentially with Hatta and his colleagues who had 'managed' the revolutionary struggle. They had directed the controversial policy of negotiations with the Dutch and with UN representatives; they had been competent to bargain toughly, arguing complicated points of procedure and substance at Hoge Veluwe, Linggadjati, Kaliurang and The Hague and at the same time they had administered the affairs of the Republic under siege and had been able to defeat the challenges to their authority in 1946 and 1948. It was a matter of course that Hatta, Prime Minister of the Republic since January 1948, should be appointed to lead the first cabinet of the United States of Indonesia.

During 1950 this power balance was important in helping to determine the emphases of the new constitution. As pressure mounted to convert the United States of Indonesia into a unitary state the task of preparing a provisional constitution for the new republic, pending the drafting of a permanent constitution by an elected constituent assembly, was entrusted to a committee representing the several parts of the United States of Indonesia and the original Republic, now a member state of the federation. This committee was composed of people who were themselves parliamentary representatives, who were used to a parliamentary system and who were, therefore, not anxious to create a powerful executive and thus lessen their own authority. It was not surprising therefore that the provisional constitution should once again follow parliamentary lines.

Effective power was placed once again in the hands of a prime minister and a cabinet dependent on parliamentary support, and a mere figurehead role was assigned to the president.[27] The provisional constitution did, of course, allow certain areas of presidential responsibility. The appointment of a cabinet *formateur* was his prerogative. (Whether the constitution also required him to accept without question the proposals made to him by the *formateur* was a matter which constitutional lawyers might debate,[28] but whatever the legal position Sukarno did, on occasion, question the suitability of proposed ministers.) Provision was made, too, for the president to issue decrees on a number of matters, including the formation of a new cabinet, the dissolution of parliament, the proclamation of a state of emergency and the declaration of war. Such decrees were to be countersigned by the appropriate minister, however, and it was made very clear that the president would merely be acting on these occasions as an agent of the government. There was no provision for the formation, in a time of emergency, of a presidential cabinet, and in this important respect Sukarno's powers were more circumscribed than they had been even under the constitutional conventions of the revolutionary years.

Sukarno resented the limitations imposed on him. Some months before the formation of the unitary state, in his inaugural address as President of the United States of Indonesia, he had

27. See A. K. Pringgodigdo, *The Office of President in Indonesia as defined in the Three Constitutions in Theory and Practice*, Ithaca, 1957, for an analysis of the 1945 Constitution, the Federal Constitution of 1949 and the Provisional Constitution of 1950. Pringgodigdo's judgement is that the presidency under the 1950 Constitution was clearly a ceremonial rather than an executive office. For a further discussion of the constitutional position of the President, see Kahin, 'Indonesia' in Kahin (ed.) *Major Governments of Asia*, 2nd edition, 1964, pp. 601–4.

28. See Pringgodigdo, op. cit., p. 26. See also Ismail Suny, *Pergeseran Kekuasaan Eksekutif*, Djakarta, 1963, p. 114.

condemned the conventions of Western liberal democracy and, in words which foreshadowed his political initiatives of the mid fifties, he spoke of Indonesia's need for democracy with leadership. Here was a hint of the sort of part he really wanted to play. He did not want to be tied down to the routine affairs of government, nor did he wish to risk incurring the odium that might well follow from the exercise of executive responsibility. What he really wanted was the authority to exercise a general leadership of the nation while others attended to the details. He was conscious of his stature and felt passionately that he had a contribution of his own to make to Indonesia's development; any constitution which kept him merely as a maker of speeches, a host at official receptions and the man to whom ambassadors presented their credentials was unjust to his service in the cause of nationalism.

For the moment his dissatisfaction was muted and he seemed prepared to follow the rules of the constitutional game. It was to be six or seven years before he was ready to embark on a course of major, continuous and direct political action. But well before then he had begun to flex his muscles and to probe the restraints imposed on him. Even under the constitution he did have some room for manoeuvre. His influence could be brought into play in the complicated negotiations which accompanied the formation of each new cabinet and he had the constitutional right to be informed, which gave him an opportunity of bringing pressure to bear on the formation of policy. He might go even further: a constitution does not necessarily describe the realities of political life and in a vaguely worded document, as this one was, the power of a president might, to a considerable extent, be defined only in practice. Sukarno's power under the 1950 constitution might be said, without much exaggeration, to be what he could get away with. At times he made direct appeals to the people – over the heads and against the wishes of his governments. To his ministers such actions appeared at best to be cases of improper meddling in matters on which a president should have been strictly neutral, and at worst to be a deliberate sabotage of their authority. To Sukarno they appeared as a proper response to a deteriorating political situation. He justified his actions not in the arid terms of constitutional clauses but by an extra-constitutional view of the nature of the presidency. With some justice he saw his authority as derived not from the constitution but directly from his standing as the leader of the revolution, representative of all his people.

At first Sukarno's restiveness reflected a generalized and unfocused dissatisfaction, but gradually he became more purposive as he assessed the strength of the forces about him. The political balance of the republic comprised, in essence, three principal elements: Islam, especially as organized in Masjumi, radical nationalism as represented in the PNI and, in due course, the army, which began to establish itself as a political force in its own right. The army, in the nature of things, had to be treated with circumspection, but Sukarno had little doubt about his ability to manipulate the PNI, and his strategy as it slowly emerged was directed towards balancing and reducing the power of Masjumi.

Much of Sukarno's criticism in the first years of independence was aimed at the tone or spirit of national life now that the battle for *merdeka* was won. He expressed a widely felt disappointment. The young republic had had some grounds for optimism as it faced the future in 1950 – it had survived the internal challenges to its integrity in 1946 and 1948, and the sense of common purpose gained in resisting the Dutch might have been expected to carry over into the more prosaic tasks of independent nationhood. Within a period of five years, however, Indonesia had had as many governments, none of which could claim more than partial success in coming to grips with the urgent tasks confronting them.

Within the framework of the parliamentary system the early governments were all party-based. Indonesia possessed a multiplicity of political parties but the main elements in the shifting alignments of the early years were Masjumi and the Indonesian Nationalist Party (PNI). The PKI was only beginning to recover from the crushing defeat inflicted on it after the Madiun affair. Sjahrir's Socialist Party (PSI) was important for its intellectual influence on the élite as a whole and was strongly represented in the higher levels of the bureaucracy and the army, but it did not seek to build up mass support for itself. Smaller organizations such as the two Christian parties, Katholik and Parkindo, the Murba Party (the Nationalist Communist Party led by former followers of Tan Malaka), the Sarekat Islam Party (PSII) and a number of other minor groups also sometimes supplied individual ministers, but were peripheral to the major PNI–Masjumi relationship. As these were the two leading political organizations it was widely felt that stable government should depend on a partnership between them, but co-operation was secured only intermittently and with difficulty – indeed to some extent the politics of the early fifties may be seen in terms of rivalry between the pair. The Natsir government (September 1950–March 1951) was dominated by Masjumi with the PNI in opposition. Sukiman (Masjumi) and Wilopo (PNI) managed in succession to lead coalitions embracing the two parties (the Sukiman cabinet, April 1951–February 1952, and the Wilopo cabinet, April 1952–June 1953), but only at the cost of opening up deep fissures between opposing wings within each of the two parties. From July 1953 to July 1955 Ali Sastroamidjojo's first cabinet was led by the PNI and excluded Masjumi. In mid 1952 Masjumi's strength was greatly undermined by the secession of Nahdatul Ulama, an organization whose strength lay in its influence over village religious leaders in Java. Masjumi could no longer claim to be overwhelmingly the authentic voice of Islam.

These party rivalries seemed to Sukarno to be petty divisions eroding the unity which he felt a single party might have preserved. Nevertheless the early governments of the Republic, of whatever complexion, tackled the tasks of independence with serious determination. The construction of a unitary state was quickly and smoothly effected by Hatta. The task of demobilizing and reorganizing the armed forces was not so easy and remained to trouble his successors. Central control had to be exerted over the semi-autonomous organizations which had existed outside the Republic's regular army during the revolution and the foundation had to be laid for a trained, unified, modern professional army. Internal security was a continuing worry. The secessionist 'Republic of the South Moluccas' and the Darul Islam rebellions under Kartosuwirjo in West Java, Kahar Muzakkar in South Sulawesi and, a little later, under Daud Beureuh in Atjeh, proved difficult to contain.

Economic policy was particularly crucial for the young republic.

The early governments were pragmatically disposed, even at the risk of some unpopularity, to assist foreign investment rather than to follow the alternative path of seeking an 'Indonesianization' of the economy. The results were disappointing. The Korean war boom disguised for a time the essential weaknesses of Indonesia's economy, but thereafter falling export prices reduced foreign exchange earnings. Foreign exchange problems in turn accentuated regional rivalries, for the export-producing regions of the Republic lay outside Java and felt that densely populated Java was existing parasitically on the produce of the Outer Islands. The resentment was expressed in the early fifties in the growth of smuggling between Sumatra and Singapore and between Sulawesi and the Philippines, often under the sponsorship of local military commanders.

These factors, together with continuing budget deficits, helped to start the spiralling inflation which plagued successive governments until the mid sixties. The first few governments of the Republic attempted with only limited success to control public expenditure. A major concern of all of them was the growing size of the public service, but no government could face the unpopularity which would attend any serious attempt at retrenchment.

While successive premiers tried with some degree of success to cope with the pressure of these practical problems, Sukarno was depressed by what seemed to him to be a loss of national purpose. After the self-sacrifice, the heroism and the unity of the struggle for independence the reality of *merdeka* with its party rivalry and its faction-fighting was an anticlimax. His 17 August speech in 1952 drew a contrast between the hopes of 17 August 1945 and the results which had been achieved since, and he called on his listeners to recover the spirit of 1945. In 1953 he allowed himself to reflect on the defects which had made themselves apparent in the workings of parliamentary democracy. In 1955, in a speech to students of the Technical Faculty of the University of Indonesia he looked back over the first years of independence and complained that 'as soon as the armed revolution was completed we quickly lost the "*élan* of 1945"'. A new super-faith was needed, he argued, to replace the lost ideals.[29]

29. *Merdeka*, 11 February 1955.

While many of his public utterances were at this level Sukarno's concern with the spirit of the nation nonetheless had practical political implications. It was hardly surprising that he should gradually align himself with those he felt to be kindred spirits and to oppose those whose style was contrary to his own. He began to see Indonesian politics in terms of broad ideological differences – between those who were attracted by his expressive approach to politics and who believed that independent Indonesia still needed both an awareness of encompassing enemies in order to be united and a sense of national purpose in order to achieve great goals, and on the other hand those whose more prosaic concern was with day-to-day affairs, and who believed that the revolution was now over. There was some point in this dichotomy: Hatta and those who shared his values believed that the revolution had been completed and that the task of the government was now to tackle practical problems in a sober way; to Sukarno the revolution had merely lost its momentum as the national cohesion of 1950 was replaced by party and factional strife.

Sukarno's first testing of his position came very soon after the formation of the unitary republic in August 1950. Over the course of the following few weeks he found himself very much at odds with the Natsir government over issues both of policy and procedure. The issue of substance which divided them was the West Irian question, and in making known his own views on the matter, and in thus drawing attention to the fact that they differed in important respects from those of his government, he posed for the first time the question of how a president should behave under Indonesia's provisional constitution.

West Irian was a natural issue for Sukarno to make his own. It meant for him a continuance of the struggle – the national revolution would not really be complete in his eyes until the territory withheld at the time of the Round Table Conference had been transferred to Indonesia. But there was a further element of conscious calculation. Later commentators were to argue that the West Irian issue was used by Sukarno over the years as a means of diverting popular attention from domestic discontents. As a master of the mechanics of mass mobilization Sukarno saw it not quite in those terms, but certainly as a means of arousing the national will and contributing to the growth of a sense of national identity. In conversation with a visitor in 1953 he spoke of the way in which the revolution had drifted from its true path and he went on to argue, with specific reference to West New Guinea, that 'a nation always needs an enemy'.

He devoted a major part of his 1950 Proclamation Day speech to West Irian. 'This is not a small question,' he insisted. 'The Irian question is a question of colonialism or not, a question of colonialism or freedom. . . . Because we have sworn that we will go on fighting till doomsday so long as there is one part of our country, be it one tiny island, be it no bigger than an umbrella, that is not yet free.' He went on to express the hope that the territory would be returned to Indonesia within the year, but warned that, if no settlement was reached, a major conflict would develop. This seemed almost to be a statement of national policy presented to the Natsir cabinet when it took office early in September. In a sense it was not an issue on which Indonesians disagreed amongst themselves. The nation at large understood the relevant section of the Round Table agreements as involving a Dutch promise to transfer West Irian to Indonesia after negotiations relating only to the time and manner of the transfer. As it became clear that the Netherlands was intending to keep the territory Indonesians of all parties felt betrayed. But this did not mean that all demanded immediate and forceful action to recover the territory; in fact Natsir and his colleagues believed that there were more urgent problems awaiting their attention, and also that the handling of the West Irian question was best conducted quietly through the ordinary channels of diplomacy. Such a method appealed to their own sober approach to the problems of the day. In Sukarno's public stand they sensed the danger of a return to the techniques of *machtsvorming* that had marked the struggle of the old PNI against colonial rule, and they felt that this was no way to conduct foreign policy. Sukarno disagreed. A few years later he himself frankly used the term as he called for an all-Indonesia congress to overcome divisions in the nation and to 'organize strength' to recover West Irian.[30]

30. *Merdeka*, 18 December 1954.

Formal negotiations with Holland were opened in The Hague in December 1950. The conference ended without agreement and the failure of these initial negotiations seemed to lend force to Sukarno's view that the New Guinea question required a forceful Indonesian stand. He urged the government to abrogate the Round Table agreements and to adopt some form of economic sanctions. The cabinet refused and conveyed to him its view that as constitutional president he should refrain in future from taking up public positions which varied from those of his government. Inwardly angered Sukarno accepted the decision and the implied rebuke with as good a grace as he could muster, but it was a humiliation for him and he moved to recover ground in a way which illustrates well his skill in evading the restraints placed upon him. His next remarks on West New Guinea appeared, in some ways, to fall in with the wishes of the government, but, taken as a whole, they were in fact barely more restrained than his earlier comments had been.

Sukarno chose a gathering at the palace of members of a Journalists' Union conference to explain his position. He referred to his earlier statements that before the sun rose on 1951 West Irian would have become part of Indonesia. Obviously smarting at the fact that 1951 had dawned without any change in the situation he said that if his previous remarks were regarded by the Indonesian people as a promise – now an unfulfilled promise – rather than as a call to action, he would be willing to lay down his office. He pointed out that in a system of cabinet responsibility to parliament a president could not publicly hold a different opinion from that of his government; but he argued that West Irian was by the constitution part of Indonesia and he had taken an oath of loyalty to the constitution. He concluded by saying that it was not enough to talk of rights and justice; political struggle could succeed only if it was based on strength. If the Indonesian people really based their demands for West Irian on genuine strength they would recover that part of their territory before the beginning of 1952.[31] Taken in conjunction with his remarks about the constitutional limitations on him, these words represented a new challenge rather than a retreat from his earlier position.

31. *Merdeka*, 16 January 1951.

No progress was made on the West Irian question over the next few years. Sukarno continued to demand that diplomacy be backed by action, until at last the PNI-led government of Ali Sastroamidjojo in 1954 did begin to take more positive measures by allowing limited military incursions to take place on the fringes of the territory. To that extent Sukarno had been successful in shaping official policy. However, his original differences with the Natsir cabinet had implications for him beyond the West Irian question itself. Firstly, they represented Sukarno's initial testing of his position as a constitutional president and showed him that he did in fact possess a certain area of independent action. The cabinet at least had been unable to control his words. Secondly, the differences contributed to the development of his political sympathies. He became aware, in particular, that important elements in the PNI shared his view that some sort of direct pressure should be brought to bear on the Netherlands, and like-mindedness on West Irian was associated with like-mindedness on other questions. Masjumi's willingness to assist foreign investors, the pro-American tendency of its foreign policy and its links with the younger reforming officers within the army reflected attitudes which went against Sukarno's predispositions. By contrast he felt that in the PNI there were at least some people who shared his concern at the drift of events.

These sympathies should not be overstressed. There were elements within the PNI with whom Sukarno did not see eye to eye, as was soon to become apparent, and he had at least some allies within the ranks of Masjumi. Oddly enough it was the conservative Sukiman wing of the party that was much more favourable to him than were Natsir's supporters. During the premiership of Sukiman, who succeeded Natsir in April 1951, Sukarno found himself at odds with the government on a number of issues – he disapproved of the decision to sign the Japanese peace treaty; the acceptance of American aid under the US Mutual Security Act (which sought to make the giving of aid dependent on the willingness of recipient states to align themselves with the broad goals of American foreign policy) also went against the grain and a mass round-up of communists ordered by the government in April 1951 reflected a general fear of left-wing activity which he did not share. Nevertheless Sukiman was much more ready than Natsir to allow a fuller measure of presidential freedom of speech on political questions, and in return Sukarno was prepared to give public support to the policies of the government even where he was not entirely happy with them. Yet despite this accommodation with Sukiman, Sukarno found that the PNI's approach to issues of policy was much more congenial to him, and, as these affinities began to define themselves in the early fifties, one could detect the outline of a general strategy which, at first, was perhaps not even clear to Sukarno himself. His concern now was not merely with the 'spirit' of the nation, with its *élan* or its revolutionary temper. After his experience at the hands of Natsir a more positive element in his thinking was a growing hostility to Masjumi as a political party and, by extension, a growing suspicion of Islam as a component of the political scene.

Over the years, Sukarno, in his search for a synthesis, had spoken again and again of the proper role of Islam, drawing attention to the fact that it had its own place in the national consensus. He claimed to be a Muslim himself and in 1955 he made the pilgrimage to Mecca. But somehow his appeal seemed never to evoke a proper response from organized Islam itself. The militant Muslim seemed to want more than a place in the consensus – for him there could be no compromise since the demands of religion were absolute. He talked therefore of the necessity for an Islamic state, though the nature of that state might never have been very clearly defined. Sukarno could never really understand this absolute commitment; his insistence that only a foolish obstinacy stood in the way of a political accommodation between Muslims and non-Muslims reflected a fundamental inability to enter the mind of the former. In the circumstances Islam gradually came to represent, in his mind, a serious political threat to national unity, a feeling which was made increasingly apparent after 1952.

In January 1953, during a visit to South Kalimantan, Sukarno gave voice to his suspicion of Islam. In a speech at Amuntai he spoke of the essential unity of Indonesian nationalism. This was a familiar enough theme, but on this occasion he allowed his words to reflect his fear of Muslim extremism, for he referred to the Muslim demand for an Islamic state and pointed out how divisive it was. What was wanted was a nation which would embrace Muslim and non-Muslim alike.

Whether he expected it or not, reports of the speech aroused a furore among Islamic leaders in Java and their reactions emphasized more clearly than ever before the depths of the gulf separating Islam from Sukarno's own idea of a nationalist synthesis. For once Muslim ranks were closed and the President was openly accused of supporting secular nationalism. One needs to see the Amuntai speech against the background of the mounting militancy of Masjumi's wild man, Isa Anshary, the chairman of the West Java branch of the party. Anshary's extremism was offensive even to many moderate Muslims and it intensified Sukarno's fear that Islam was potentially a powerful political force and a threat to Indonesian unity. The Amuntai speech was therefore not so much an example of Sukarno's tendency to take sides as an appeal to Islam to curb itself and fit into the Indonesian consensus he was anxious to achieve. In this it was unsuccessful and, inevitably, the effect of the speech was to bring more clearly into the open one of the major divisions cutting across Indonesian society; politically, it confirmed the President's alignment with the radical wing of the PNI against Masjumi.

Sukarno's political preferences and antipathies defined themselves more clearly during the PNI-led government of Wilopo. There were, indeed, signs of a departure from presidential neutrality when he performed his constitutional functions in the negotiations which brought the Wilopo government into being. After the fall of the Sukiman cabinet in February 1952 the sharp differences which had by this time established themselves between Masjumi and PNI, and between different factions within both parties, made the task of forming a new government unexpectedly difficult. Sukarno commissioned two cabinet *formateurs* – Sidik of the PNI and Prawoto of Masjumi. In a sense it was an impeccable choice. Sidik belonged to the radical element in the PNI with which Sukarno found himself in sympathy, Prawoto belonged to the Natsir wing of Masjumi with which Sukarno had already had his troubles. It might have been hoped that between them they would produce a government with all the virtues, combining a sober Natsir-type problem-solving approach with more than a dash of inspiration, leadership and a sense of nation-building. However, Sidik and Prawoto were so different from each other in temperament and policy that they were unable to agree on a list of ministers.

Sukarno then turned to Wilopo of the PNI, who succeeded in bringing together a group of people prepared to serve under him, but the list he eventually presented to Sukarno, though essentially a PNI–Masjumi coalition, leaned heavily on the side of members of both parties whose political style was opposed to that of the President. Sukarno hesitated – and almost precipitated a constitutional crisis. In the eyes of many the president's job ended with the appointment of a *formateur* and he was obliged to accept a proposed list of ministers without question and to give them the opportunity of testing their acceptability to parliament. Others felt that there was still a proper role for presidential influence at any stage of the negotiations preceding the formation of the government. On this occasion, after delaying for a couple of days, Sukarno decided to side-step the constitutional controversy. He accepted Wilopo's proposals and the government was formed.

Nevertheless Sukarno found it difficult to get on with his new government despite its PNI leadership. Wilopo attempted to exercise a close check on his speech-making and he cancelled a state visit to Italy which Sukarno had been about to make. Sukarno could not be completely silenced of course and he used formal occasions such as Heroes' Day (the anniversary of the battle of Surabaya) to hint at the government's failure to lead. His Proclamation Day speech on 17 August was comparatively restrained but he returned at length to the West Irian theme: 'Freedom is indivisible . . . we cannot truly feel free so long as West Irian is in the hands of others.'

These were rhetorical occasions and for the time being there was little that Sukarno could do beyond giving some indication of his feelings when exercising his ceremonial functions. As it happened however, political changes were already taking place which might produce a more congenial environment for him in the future.

Over the course of the Wilopo government's term of office there were signs of a growing understanding between the radical wing of the PNI and the reviving PKI, matching the growing gulf between the PNI and the Muslim parties. The PKI under the vigorous and youthful leadership of Dipa Nusantara Aidit and his principal colleagues, Njoto and Lukman, had recognized that it must find political friends if it was to erase the memories of Madiun and make its way back to a position of respectability. With this in mind it began to be more discriminating in its attacks on what it had formerly regarded as the reactionary forces in Indonesian politics. It called off its criticism of Sukarno person-ally and it supported his resistance to Dutch imperialism over West Irian. Sukarno was not slow to respond to the change in tone. He was predisposed, in any case, to see the PKI as a valid element in the Indonesian consensus that he was anxious to con-struct. As long as the party was loyal to the Republic, and as long as it was prepared to speak as a nationalist, as well as a commu-nist, party, he was ready to welcome it. It strengthened the type of radicalism to which he was sympathetic and, by altering the existing balance of party forces, it gave politics a greater fluidity.

For the PNI the conciliatory approach of the communists opened certain attractive possibilities. The PKI was still, com-paratively speaking, a small party. It had yet to gain the momen-tum that was to startle its opponents within a few years, and in 1953 it appeared simply to be a manageable potential ally and a useful counterwiecht to Masjumi. Masjumi had already been weakened by the withdrawal of Nahdatul Ulama from its ranks and now the parliamentary support of the PKI might enable the PNI to form a government which did not include Masjumi at all. To this extent it could be fitted into Sukarno's own political strategy.

While these shifts were still taking place beneath the surface of political life a more dramatic crisis was in preparation involving the third major element in the political situation: the army. In its own way the October 17 Affair, as it came to be known, was to strengthen Sukarno's hand still further. On the morning of 17 October 1952, the streets of Djakarta became the scene of a mass demonstration directed ostensibly against parliament. The crowd, carrying placards calling for the dissolution of parliament and for immediate elections, gathered first outside the parliament building in Lapangan Banteng. It then moved on to the residence of Vice-President Hatta and finally, shortly before ten o'clock, it gathered in front of the presidential palace. At this point the involvement of the military became apparent as a group of armoured cars and tanks drew up beside the demonstrators and trained their guns on the palace.

Confronted by the crowd at his gate Sukarno reacted in characteristic fashion, giving a convincing demonstration of his supreme confidence in the face of what seemed to be a mass challenge. He emerged coolly from the palace and walked down the steps and across the lawn to the roadway where the demonstrators had gathered. He talked to some of them and then, ignoring the threat of the guns, he returned to the palace steps to speak to the crowd as a whole. He did so as a father to wayward children. He understood their dissatisfaction with things as they were, he said, and he assured them that elections would be held as soon as possible. But he insisted that he had no desire to be a dictator and he pointed out that to dissolve parliament would be a step in that direction. He then ordered them to disperse and without any question they obeyed him.

Having thus shown his mastery of the situation he re-entered the palace and received two groups of senior military leaders who came, one after the other, hard on the heels of the demonstration. They supported the demands of the crowd and urged on Sukarno the desirability of dissolving parliament. Sukarno gave them, too, the same answer – that a dissolution was out of the question.

The meaning of the October 17 incident is difficult to disentangle but in retrospect it is clear that the President was not without his own responsibility in the events which precipitated it.[32] The affair needs to be seen against a complex background of economic crisis, the need for retrenchment in government spend-

---

32. Herbert Feith, who was an eye-witness to the incident, has given the most complete analysis of this extraordinarily complex affair. See *The Decline of Constitutional Democracy in Indonesia*, Ithaca, 1962, and also *The Wilopo Cabinet, 1952–1953*, Ithaca, 1958.

ing and the problems of army demobilization and re-organization. The latter question had occupied the attention, in turn, of Hatta, Natsir and Sukiman, who were concerned to create a modern, skilled, professional army out of the largely guerrilla-type organizations which had played such an important part during the revolution. This meant attempting to overcome local and ethnic loyalties and it also meant placing a premium on professional competence rather than on revolutionary fervour. For these reasons government policies of army re-organization aroused resistance within the army from two sources in particular: from commanders who had earned the close personal loyalty of their troops and who were threatened by policies of army centralization, and from those revolutionary veterans who thought their positions were threatened by officers with superior educational qualifications and professional skills. Many such officers were *bapakist* ('paternalistic' – from *bapak*, meaning 'father'); they had built up a paternal relationship with their men which gave them semi-independent bases of power and they were likely to be adversely affected by policies which stressed professional training and competence rather than inspirational leadership as criteria for promotion. There were elements here, too, of a rivalry between those officers who had received their initial training from the Dutch and who had served in the Netherlands Indies Armed Forces (KNIL), and those, often with little formal education, who had been trained in Peta during the Japanese occupation.

The early governments of the Republic had some success in their efforts to achieve the sort of re-organization they wanted because they enjoyed the co-operation of a group of military leaders who shared their goals. With the co-operation, in particular, of Colonel T. B. Simatupang, Chief of Staff of the Armed Forces, and Colonel A. H. Nasution, Army Chief of Staff, they laid the foundations of a new, tightly organized well-trained and disciplined modern army. There were certain ideological implications of this re-organization. To a considerable degree the army leadership accepted the principle of civilian leadership of the nation, but there were limits to the extent to which they saw the army as the neutral servant of civilian government. At the very least the new military tradition which was in process of formation saw the new army, proud of its competence and revolutionary purity, as the guardian of the revolution and therefore as having a stake in the direction of the nation's affairs. Its leaders did not think themselves entitled to interfere continuously in political matters, but they did think they were entitled to set limits to what civilian politicians might do.

The alliance between government and army leadership was maintained during the period of the Wilopo government, and Wilopo's Defence Minister, the Sultan of Jogjakarta, Hamengku Buwono IX, continued to pursue policies of modernization. But the policies were still controversial, and in implementing them the Sultan met with two distinct currents of opposition; from radical nationalist opinion in parliament, to be found particularly in the PNI ranks, and, outside parliament, from military leaders both in Java and in the Outer Islands who were opposed to the Sima-tupang–Nasution reforms. The latter pressure was perhaps more fundamental in the sense that, while the party critics of government policy were opposed to the particular group of army leaders in the saddle – to Simatupang and Nasution (and also to the Sultan and to Ali Budiardjo, the Secretary-General of Defence) – the military opposition to the High Command would have developed no matter how the latter was composed. Any Chief of Staff would, in the nature of things, have sought army centralization, and would, inevitably, have aroused the hostility of local officers who saw centralization as a threat to their own authority.

Sukarno, who was himself out of sympathy with the army reforms, had links with both these elements of opposition, and from the middle of 1952 he had allowed himself to be drawn into a particularly complex series of political manoeuvres. He first of all lent his ear to the views of dissident officers who suggested to him that Nasution be replaced as Army Chief of Staff. In July this led the Sultan, Simatupang and Nasution to confront the President directly. They called upon him at the palace to discuss his views on army re-organization. The discussion was heated and indeed almost developed into a shouting match between Sukarno and Simatupang. The incident was followed, over succeeding weeks, by intensive parliamentary discussion of the reforming policies of the army leadership. The parliamentary opposition to

Simatupang and Nasution came, in particular, from certain sections of the PNI whose sympathies lay with Peta-type, *bapakist* officers rather than with the professional, KNIL-type military bureaucrats. There were additional political overtones to the debate since the advocates of reform were regarded as socialist party sympathizers and were said to be turning the army into a PSI stronghold. Since the Wilopo government was a PNI–Masjumi coalition, the parliamentary debate was, in effect, a revolt by a PNI faction against the party's parliamentary leadership and it revealed how much at odds Wilopo was with a large section of his party, which regarded him as closer to Masjumi in his thinking than to the ideals of the PNI.

The opposition came to a head in the form of a parliamentary motion (submitted by PNI member Manai Sophian) calling for an inquiry into the whole question of army re-organization, including the higher leadership of the army and the Defence Ministry. After intensive behind-the-scenes negotiations in early October, Wilopo supporters believed they had persuaded the backers of the motion to withdraw in favour of a less drastic compromise. At this point Sukarno intervened. He summoned two of the PNI's older leaders, Iskaq and Sunarjo, to the palace and through them he lobbied for support for the Sophian motion. This was sufficient to secure its passage on 16 October and it created a major crisis for the Wilopo government.

These were the main elements in the situation which had given rise to the mass movement outside the palace on 17 October. The demonstration was in fact an army response to parliamentary criticism. Though not a coup d'état it was at least an attempt on the part of those supporting Simatupang, Nasution and the Sultan to assert their strength in an overt fashion and to bring pressure to bear on Sukarno, whose sympathy with the parliamentary opposition was well known. Against this background it is not difficult to understand his decisive, assured and constitutionally proper handling of the affair. Clearly Sukarno recognized that army pressure was being brought to bear on him and he also saw the signs of confusion and division within the ranks of those who were mounting the pressure. Despite his own dislike of the parliamentary system he recognized that the challengers to it on this occasion were essentially opponents of his own supporters in the parliamentary arena. Paradoxically a defence of parliament was thus a defence of his own political capital.

He summed up the balance of pressures with intuitive skill. Undoubtedly in rejecting the demands for a dissolution of parliament he was recognizing that there was not sufficient agreement among the military to support a general coup. His most prudent course was thus to act, as he did, with complete constitutional propriety. And since his sympathy lay with those circles, within the army and outside it, which were opposed to the army leadership – and indeed since he himself had played a direct part in organizing the opposition to that leadership from within the PNI – the prudent course was also the most advantageous.

His role did not stop there. The October 17 incident was followed by the growth, in a number of regional commands, of 'anti-October 17' movements calling for the punishment of those responsible for the affair and overthrowing local territorial commanders in East Java, South Sulawesi and South Sumatra. It is highly probable that the President quietly supported these initiatives. In December the suspension of Nasution as Chief of Staff indicated that power had ebbed away from the October 17 group.

The whole affair had marked consequences for Sukarno's political environment and opened up new possibilities of influence for him. Though the government was safe for the time being its weaknesses had been exposed. The presence of the army as a political force had been more clearly revealed than before, but so had its lack of unity. And the gap between PNI and Masjumi had widened. The political implications of the October 17 incident were extremely confused but, while the PNI saw the incident not only as a challenge to parliament but also, more particularly, as a challenge to radical nationalist thinking, Masjumi recognized in some of the military leaders an approach to the problems of independence which, in many respects, resembled their own. To that extent Masjumi and PNI were on opposite sides of the fence as the lines of cleavage began to define themselves after October. The deteriorating situation created opportunities for greater presidential intervention in the future.

In 1950 Sukarno had appeared to accept constitutional arrangements which confined his own actions. In the following years, on such questions as West Irian, he had tested the solidity of those arrangements and had also begun to distinguish friends from foes in the political arena, thus contributing to the subtle realignments taking place in party groupings. After the beginning of 1953 his desire to recover for himself the paramount position in the affairs of the nation began to express itself more clearly. As is the case with all great leaders, no doubt, the elements of dedication – the belief that only he could arrest Indonesia's spiritual decline and set it again on the right path – and of simple political self-interest were inextricably fused in his mind.

The Wilopo government eventually fell at the beginning of June 1953, but not before it had succeeded in steering an election bill through parliament. This opened the possibility of replacing the *ad hoc* parliament which had existed since 1950 with one which might be expected to reflect more closely the national will. It was still to be more than two years before elections were held, but the enactment of the law quickened popular hopes that a purer, less factional, more stable political life lay ahead.

After Wilopo's fall Sukarno found it extremely difficult to form a new government. Only after a series of *formateurs* had tried their hands unsuccessfully was a cabinet team brought together under Ali Sastroamidjojo. It was a government led by the PNI and excluding Masjumi. Sukarno was well enough pleased by the outcome. There had been some pressure initially from Masjumi and PSI ranks for a so-called presidential cabinet to be formed under the leadership of Hatta. Sukarno resisted the proposal. He had already had experience of such a cabinet and had not liked its constricting effect on his own position. He therefore made a series of attempts (five in all) to bring together another PNI–Masjumi coalition. He was not sorry when, one after another, his *formateurs* failed in their efforts. The final exclusion of Masjumi was in line with his own desires and in fact he played an active role in the last stages of the negotiations which brought Ali Sastroamidjojo to office.

The new government in effect reflected the shifts that had taken place below the surface of political life over the past twelve months. After the five separate attempts to form another PNI–Masjumi coalition the PNI had felt able to go ahead without Masjumi because it knew that it could count on PKI support. The price paid for that support was indirect. The cabinet contained no PKI representatives, though two of its members came from organizations under PKI influence. More important from the PKI's point of view were the intangible benefits to be derived from the new dispensation. By the end of 1953 the party had gone far towards rehabilitating itself, and its fifth congress, held in March 1954, was a public demonstration of its new standing. The opening reception of the congress was attended by Deputy Prime Minister Wongsonegoro, Dr F. L. Tobing, Minister of Information, Sartono, who held the office of Speaker, and other public figures. In its new confidence the party felt no need to be apologetic about its past. Among the gallery of portraits surrounding the podium – Marx and Engels, Lenin and Stalin, Mao and Malenkov – was that of Musso whose picture, boldly and without shame, was given a central position beside that of Aidit.[33] Sukarno gave his blessing to the party's rehabilitation by sending a personal message to be read at the opening session.

Though he was careful never to become unambiguously identified with the PNI, Sukarno's more or less open support of the Ali government showed itself on a number of occasions. In November 1954, for example, he used a Heroes' Day speech at Palembang to attack unnamed political leaders who, he said, were serving foreign interests and trying to bring about the fall of the cabinet.[34] When questioned further on his meaning he refused to be drawn ('What I have said is clear enough'), but the assumption was that the foreign interests to which he referred were business interests which were felt still to dominate the Indonesian economy.[35] His remarks drew an immediate and critical response from opponents of the government. Jusuf Wibisono of Masjumi said that Sukarno's speech did not suit his position as head of state and conveyed, rather, the impression that he was 'general

33. *Harian Rakjat*, 17 March 1954.
34. *Merdeka*, 10 November 1954.
35. *Merdeka*, 15 November 1954.

Chairman of a certain political party'.[36] Government spokesmen defended the President's right to make statements of this kind on the grounds that, as well as being a constitutional organ, he was also the leader of the people as a whole.[37] But his real leanings were indeed clear enough and they stood out more obviously because of the election campaign which was now getting under way.

Sukarno's partiality for the Ali government was strengthened by its initiatives in the field of external affairs, where Indonesia began to make her mark. Her participation, together with India, Pakistan, Burma and Ceylon, in the Colombo meeting of Asian Prime Ministers in April 1954 made her one of an intimate group of Asian powers which was to attempt to play a united role in the affairs of the region over the next few years. The climax to Indonesia's new foreign policy came in April 1955 with the Afro–Asian Conference at Bandung.

For Sukarno this was a tremendously important occasion. Against the background of the heat and conflict of the election campaign the Afro–Asian Conference gave him the opportunity to appear, once again, as the great unifier – as the leader of a united nation which was, itself, emerging as a leader of the third world. The conference was the brainchild of Ali Sastroamidjojo who put forward the suggestion at the Colombo meeting in 1954. His proposal for a conference of Afro–Asian leaders was at first received with some scepticism by the other Colombo powers, but it was later endorsed by Nehru who saw in it an opportunity of ending China's isolation. The contact of both India and Burma with China over the course of 1954 seemed to suggest the presence of a more conciliatory Chinese approach to the outside world, and an Afro–Asian conference which included China might well, so it seemed to Nehru and U Nu, confirm this trend.

In December a further meeting of the Colombo powers at Bogor endorsed the proposal and the detailed arrangements were made under Indonesian leadership. The original suggestion that

36. *PIA News Bulletin*, 11 November 1954.

37. See, for example, remarks of F. L. Tobing, Minister of Information, *Merdeka*, 11 November 1954.

invitations be sent to the Afro–Asian members of the UN was now extended to include other non-member countries such as Cambodia, the two Vietnams and the Gold Coast, as well as China. The Soviet Union was not included despite its control of the Asian heartland. Neither were Australia and New Zealand which sometimes made claims to be considered part of the Southeast Asian region. Finally on 18 April 1955 a quite remarkable gathering began to assemble in Bandung. Planes bearing their VIP cargoes landed one after the other at Kemajoran Airport to be welcomed with full honours, and in Bandung Prime Ministers, Foreign Ministers and their accompanying retinues jostled each other in the streets or took coffee in each other's company before sessions of the conference. Nehru and Chou En-lai between them were inevitably the chief centres of interest, but such figures as Nasser, U Nu, Norodom Sihanouk and Mohammed Ali of Pakistan commanded their own share of attention. Such a gathering provided a problem for the army of 1,700 security men who were entrusted with the personal safety of the visitors, as well as for the hospitality committee which, it was discovered, had organized a call-girl service for the benefit of the delegates.

The mere presence in Bandung of representatives of twentynine countries was a considerable diplomatic achievement. The conference, as eventually composed, included a number of countries which did not recognize each other. The motives of those who came varied widely.[38] India was concerned to bring China into the community of nations and perhaps enmesh her in a web of moral commitments which would make it hard for her in the future to interfere in the affairs of other countries. China, for her part, was attempting to present a new image to the nations of Southeast Asia and Chou En-lai was remarkably successful in conveying an impression of conciliation and reasonableness, saying he had come 'to seek unity and not to quarrel'.[39] Sir John Kotelawala of Ceylon, by contrast, warned those who would listen that there were other imperialisms besides the Western

38. G. McT. Kahin, *The Asian–African Conference, Bandung, Indonesia, April, 1955*, Ithaca, 1956, gives the best account of the diplomatic issues involved in the conference.

39. ibid., p. 40.

variety. Indonesia was seeking support for her position on West Irian.

With these varying and sometimes conflicting interests it could easily have been that issues such as Israel, Kashmir or Taiwan might have torn the conference asunder and left Ali Sastroamidjojo's grand design in ruins. In fact the congress as a whole was able to focus its main attention on the issues on which there was general, if rather vague, agreement. The final communiqué dealt in broad terms with questions of economic and cultural co-operation. It declared colonialism to be evil. It announced that its signatories were in favour of peace. At a less abstract level many of the participants, of course, used the conference to negotiate privately on matters that concerned them. Indonesia's negotiation with China on the question of the nationality of Indonesian-born Chinese was one example.

But to stress these aspects would be to miss the essentials. More significant than the high-sounding generalities of the final communiqué, and more significant even than particular and more concrete achievements, was the sense on the part of participants of a common interest as nations standing apart from the great power blocs and representing the shared experiences of alien domination and of present underdevelopment. Richard Wright's passionate account of the congress in *The Colour Curtain*[40] catches well the fundamental and elementary issues 'cutting through the outer layers of disparate social and political and cultural facts' to the level of colour and resistance to imperial domination.

For Sukarno these simple and elemental implications were the important things, and in his opening speech to the congress he gave memorable expression to them. He began with a specific reference to colour: 'This is the first inter-continental conference of coloured peoples in the history of mankind!' and went on to evoke the broad currents of history and the turbulence of contemporary change, the common experience of colonialism and the reaction against it. 'Sisters and Brothers, how terrifically dynamic is our time. . . . Yes, there has indeed been a "*Sturm über Asien*" – and over Africa too. The last few years have seen enormous changes. Nations, States have awoken from a sleep of centuries.

40. London, 1956, p. 11.

... Hurricanes of national awakening and re-awakening have swept over the land. ...'[41] But in spite of hurricanes of change and the onrush of 'irresistible forces' colonialism was still not dead and resistance to it was one of the things which bound together the nations represented at Bandung. 'For us colonialism is not something far and distant. We have known it in all its ruthlessness.' Bound by this common experience the Afro–Asian world – in the past 'the voiceless ones ... the unregarded, the peoples for whom decisions were made by others' – should demand a greater voice in world affairs than it had enjoyed hitherto.

In developing these themes Sukarno's words carried echoes of his speeches on domestic affairs. The theme of unity in diversity was expounded with passion. There was diversity in Asia and Africa because they were 'the classic birth places of faiths and ideas that had spread all over the world'. 'Almost every religion under the sun' was represented in his audience. 'But what harm is in diversity, when there is unity in desire?' Multiformity in religious life did not matter if it was recognized that 'all great religions are one in their message of tolerance'. Thus in his usual manner he brushed aside what others might have felt to be fundamental differences. To the idea of unity he added that of the mobilization of spiritual power. The nations of Asia and Africa might be physically weak but 'we can mobilize all the spiritual, all the moral, all the political strength of Asia and Africa on the side of peace. Yes, we! We the people of Asia and Africa ... far more than half the human population of the world, we can mobilize what I have called the *Moral Violence of Nations* in favour of peace.'

Altogether it was one of Sukarno's grand occasions. In the past the foreign policies followed by his governments had seemed to bind him to a comparatively conservative position in international affairs. His anger with Holland over West Irian had been silenced by Natsir. He had been associated with the attempts of the Sukiman government, in the matter of the Japanese peace treaty and in the proposal to accept American aid under the terms

41. The text of this speech is to be found in Kahin, *The Asian–African Conference*.

of the US Mutual Security Act, to strengthen Indonesian ties with America. These moves had seemed to him to be departures from the requirements of a free and active neutrality. The foreign policy of the Ali Sastroamidjojo government was closer to his predilections. The government had firmly rejected the idea of Indonesian participation in SEATO and it was now seeking to clarify and define the concept of Afro–Asia. At Bandung Sukarno himself could make his own bid for recognition as one of the major leaders of the third world.

If the first five years of Indonesian independence saw Sukarno, within the framework of the provisional constitution, gradually and tentatively feeling his way towards a more central political role, the following two years were to bring matters to a head. By the closing months of 1956 there had been a shaping and clarification of public attitudes in such a way as to allow – and indeed to encourage – his direct and open intervention in affairs.

Several factors contributed to the change of atmosphere. First, and of great importance for the future, was the emergence of the army as a clearer political force. The Simatupang–Nasution reforms, as we have seen, had helped to develop the army's corporate conception of itself as the guardian of the revolution, with responsibilities to the nation at large at least equivalent to those of the civilian politicians. However, the October 17 Affair had opened deep divisions which were only gradually overcome. In February 1955 a meeting of almost three hundred officers at Jogjakarta was a landmark in the building of a new sense of common purpose. At least the army had now closed its ranks sufficiently to present a united front when the Ali government appointed an unacceptable Chief of Staff. Its concern on this occasion was with what seemed to be political interference in its own professional affairs and its stand was a major factor in bringing about the fall of the government in July 1955.

Secondly, the mounting inflation and the spread of corruption in political and bureaucratic circles accentuated that sense of disillusionment with the fruits of independence to which reference has already been made. Finally the long awaited elections, held during the Masjumi-led caretaker government of Burhanuddin

Harahap, had provided no magical way out of the morass. Technically, and viewed as an experiment in the taking of a political choice in a largely illiterate electorate, the elections were a tremendous success. The use of party symbols as well as printed lists of names, and the careful instruction of the electorate in the meaning of those symbols, were signs of the determination and ingenuity of the country in its effort to make parliamentary democracy work. The campaign, however, opened further the divisions within Indonesian society and made the aim of securing a general consensus within which party governments could operate more difficult. The euphoria of the elections in fact contributed to the sense of anti-climax which followed them.

In some ways the results did clarify political alignments. The PNI secured just over twenty-two per cent of the votes and topped the poll by a narrow margin. Masjumi (20%) did unexpectedly badly and NU (18%) and PKI (16%) unexpectedly well. These emerged overwhelmingly as the 'big four', commanding seventy-eight per cent of the votes. Two significant features of the results deserve comment: firstly the even balance between the two major Muslim parties on the one hand (39·3% of the vote) and the two major non-Muslim parties on the other (38·7%); secondly, the extent to which party rivalry reflected regional rivalries. PNI, PKI, and NU were all shown to be essentially Java-based parties, in fact drawing their main source of strength from Central and East Java – the area of the ethnic Javanese. Masjumi's main strongholds were outside that area – in West Java and in the Outer Islands of the republic. Its rivalry with the other three was thus, to some extent, a political reflection of regional resistance to Java.

The important thing about the elections, however, was that, though they had given a clearer definition of party strengths and weaknesses, they had not changed the basic character of party alignments or altered the nature of political life within the framework of the parliamentary system. To the public in general party conflicts were still seen as petty and self-seeking and were regarded as part of the same general situation in which corruption flourished and living standards declined. The second Ali Sastroamidjojo cabinet, formed in March 1956 on the basis of the party distribution in the new parliament, consisted of a PNI–Masjumi–NU coalition under PNI leadership. To the nation at large this cabinet seemed no different in essential character from its predecessors. Lack of agreement between the two major parties inhibited the government in taking strong action on such matters as corruption, civil service retrenchment or the smuggling conducted, often with military approval, between the exporting areas of Sumatra and Sulawesi and Singapore or the Philippines, in order to by-pass the exchange control regulations of the central government. As was always the case, coalition government proved to be weak government, lowest common denominator government, unable to offend entrenched interests or to tackle fundamental problems.

The elections, in effect, confirmed and completed the popular sense of disillusionment and thereby actually increased the possibility of a political crisis. As long as elections had been expected to cleanse political life other forces were prepared to hold their hands. Their failure to change the nature of the political scene thus contributed directly to the formation of an atmosphere in which decisive action from one quarter or another – from the army, perhaps, or from the President – was possible. At the same time the revealed weakness of Masjumi (which many had expected to dominate the poll results) and of the PSI, and the comparative strength of the PNI and the PKI, meant that Sukarno's position was greatly improved *vis-à-vis* his opponents. The stage was set for new departures.

As 1956 ran its course it was clear that events were moving towards some sort of climax. The first overt sign of a tendency to direct action came from within the army – but not from its High Command.

By 1956 army unity was still only partly achieved. It was the concern of General Nasution, who had returned to the position of Chief of Staff in November 1955, to assert his authority more effectively over subordinate officers in regional commands. In doing so he was, in a sense, taking up where he had left off in 1952, but whereas in 1952 his policies had brought him into opposition to the President he now tended to see army and

President as natural allies in their custodianship of the affairs of the nation. Ironically his new approach now brought him sharply into conflict with some of his former associates, some of whom were now in regional commands and in some degree opposed to the High Command. However, despite the lack of a military consensus there were officers both at the centre and in the regions who felt that the army, its patience now exhausted, should step into the political arena to set things to rights. Their mounting dissatisfaction revealed itself in a series of actions.

In the early morning of 13 August 1956 Indonesia's Foreign Minister, Roeslan Abdulgani, was arrested on the orders of the West Java commander, Colonel A. E. Kawilarang, and with the complicity of Deputy Chief of Staff Zulkifli Lubis. The charge against him was corruption and the arrest was timed to secure maximum dramatic effect, for Roeslan was on the point of leaving for London to attend the conference on the Suez crisis. Only the direct intervention of the Prime Minister, acting through Nasution, secured his release, and he left the country later in the day on the understanding that he would return to submit himself to an inquiry into his conduct. (A cabinet committee in due course decided that there were no grounds for action against him.) Later, in early November, Colonel Lubis, who had resigned as Deputy Chief of Staff after the Roeslan affair, attempted to bring troops into Djakarta to effect a coup d'état in the capital. His plans were easily forestalled by officers loyal to Nasution, but the atmosphere of crisis was by then greatly accentuated. On 1 December Hatta, who had announced his resignation from the vice-presidency earlier in the year, finally laid down his office, thus bringing to an end the Dwi-Tunggal – the co-operation of himself and Sukarno which had symbolized in a sense the unity of Indonesia – of Java and Sumatra, of nation builder and administrator – and for some it indicated much more powerfully than anything else the inner crisis facing the country. Finally on 20 December, Colonel Husein, regional commander in West Sumatra, took over the government of the province of Central Sumatra. Two days later the North Sumatran commander attempted a similar coup in Medan, but in this case the central government was quickly able to recover control, though the succeeding months saw separatist movements in other regional commands also.

Against this background of military coup and counter-coup and of regional resistance to the centre, Sukarno began to stake his own claim to authority, independent of the parties and parliament on the one hand and of the army on the other.

During 1956 he had shown increasing independence. In a number of instances he had opposed the policies of the government and more fundamentally he had begun to criticize the very basis of parliamentary institutions. On no less an occasion than the opening of the new parliament in March he argued that the Western convention of majority rule (fifty per cent plus one) was unsuited to Indonesian society and he expressed the hope that the new parliament would conduct its operations not on that basis but with an eye to the Indonesian principle of *gotong royong* (mutual help). In subsequent speeches he returned to the idea that he had advanced in 1950 and in later years of the desirability of developing for Indonesia a system of guided democracy, or democracy with leadership, to replace the liberal democracy of the West.

Over the course of the year, Sukarno was absent from Indonesia on two state journeys. Between May and July he visited the United States and Western Europe. In America he had a triumphal progress, addressing Congress, expressing his admiration for Jefferson at Monticello, seeing – and being greatly impressed by – the industrial civilization of America (he was moved, in particular, by the sight of thousands of employees' cars parked at the Chrysler–Plymouth Corporation works at Detroit) and relaxing with his son Guntur in Disneyland. This was only his second overseas journey as President (in 1955 he had made the pilgrimage to Mecca and had followed it by a state visit to Cairo), and if it seemed that he was being seduced by the West during his American visit the impression was countered in August and September when he made visits to Yugoslavia, Czechoslovakia, Russia, Outer Mongolia and China. In October he was back in Indonesia, full of vitality and impressed on the one hand by the material triumphs of capitalist society and on the other by the social programmes of communist Russia and by the energy of China in attempting to transform and industrialize an agrarian society. Showing a new confidence, and drawing on his personal standing, he began to take the initiative from government, the political parties and the army.

The opening step in his new campaign was a speech to youth leaders at the palace on 28 October. Looking back to 1945 and to the idea of a state party which had almost been implemented then, he announced that the decision to encourage a multiplicity of parties instead had been a great mistake. Could it not be rectified? 'Do you know, brothers and sisters, what my dream is as I speak to you? ... My dream is that the leaders of the parties would deliberate together and then come to the decision "Let us now join together to bury all parties".' Shortly afterwards he announced that he had his own plan – his concept (*Konsepsi*) – for the solution of Indonesia's ills and that, if asked, he would announce it.

In these two speeches he began his frontal attack on the system of parliamentary democracy, and, for good or ill, inaugurated his third great period of political creativity.

Since the end of 1956 marks a turning point in Sukarno's political career it is a convenient place to take stock of the circumstances within which he had been operating and to assess his handling of those circumstances.

Why had the hopes of 1949 turned so sour by the mid fifties? The reasons are complex. Independence had brought some visible achievements. There had been a great increase in educational facilities; there was a sense of competence among the new administrative élite; there was pride in Indonesia's international standing. But there were disappointments, too. The pettiness of much of the country's political life seemed to betray the ideals of the revolution, as did the prevalence of corruption. Poverty remained and mounting inflation seemed evidence of governmental failure to deal with economic problems. As far as material standards of living were concerned, obviously no government, and no alternative constitutional arrangements, could have satisfied the extravagant popular expectations that had existed in 1950. There was no great surplus waiting to be redistributed once the foreign exploiter had been driven out. Alternative economic policies could, no doubt, have averted, or at least slowed down, the decline of the export economy, but no rapid increase in the living standards of the masses could have been achieved. Contrary to popular belief Indonesia is not a rich country. She has extensive natural resources, but in addition to the shortage of capital and of the technical skills required for their development, there is the fact of the enormous pressure of the population dependent upon them.

Disappointed hopes were thus an inevitable framework for all political activity. The small size of the educated élite, and the wide gap that separated it from the great mass of the peasant and urban population, did not contribute to the effective working of a party system. Party rivalries were very largely intra–élite rivalries. The multiplicity of parties made coalitions inevitable. Finally, extra-constitutional forces (such as the army) impinged on political life and affected the operation of parliamentary institutions. The President, as we have seen, was another such force acting often beyond the limits imposed on him by the constitution. In this way shifts gradually occurred in the domestic balance of forces and Indonesia's political forms became increasingly out of line with her political realities. In the early fifties the parties had been the main agents of political activity but by 1956 it was becoming clear that they no longer reflected the real distribution of power in Indonesia. The breakdown of the parliamentary system was thus only a matter of time.

Behind all of these factors lay the essentially divided character of Indonesian society, which explained the inability of all governments to mobilize adequate power to govern effectively. The geographical spread of the archipelago accentuated feelings of ethnic identity and of regional loyalty which often conflicted with loyalty to the Republic. Regional discontent was a complex phenomenon. In part it reflected regional dissatisfaction with central control and a desire for greater local autonomy; in part it involved demands for a greater share of public spending on roads, hospitals and other services in the Outer Islands; in part it arose from the economic differences between export-producing, sparsely populated areas and the densely populated island of

Java which was a net consumer. In particular there was regional resentment at the artificial exchange rate which penalized exporters and favoured consumers. These grievances were real, but were perhaps less basic than they appeared at the time. More fundamental was the fact that regional differences were associated with contrasting culture patterns – the hierarchical rice-based civilization of inland Java on the one hand and the more egalitarian, and perhaps more dynamic, commercial societies of West Sumatra or Sulawesi on the other. Religious differences fitted into and confirmed these oppositions. Apart from the difference, within Java and outside it, between devout Muslims and those whose lives were governed by an older customary pattern, there was the fact that Islam had taken deeper root in North and West Sumatra than it had in the rice civilization of Java. The major political parties reflected these older cultural currents within Indonesian society – the Java-based parties on the one hand and Masjumi, with its strong Outer Island affiliations, on the other.

Some of Indonesia's problems were of the kind that faced all new states as they attempted to modernize agrarian societies and to build representative political institutions in place of the externally based power of colonial régimes. But problems of internal division were particularly acute in Indonesia and made stable government extraordinarily difficult to achieve. Sukarno did not create these divisions, and their presence justified his claim that the task of nation-building in Indonesia was far from accomplished. They made it clear that there was still a need for his integrative skills. But was it possible that he also capitalized on the divided state of society? For all of his talk of the necessity for unity, were his efforts during these years really directed towards the conciliation of differences? Did his interference with the processes of parliamentary government in fact contribute to the loss of respect for constitutional conventions?

First of all it should be noted that, while the emphasis of this chapter has been on Sukarno's efforts to escape from the limitations imposed on him as constitutional President, in fact his political activity, if placed in perspective, was comparatively restrained after all. His constitutional functions in cabinet formation were exercised with varying degrees of discretion. On the first such occasion, in August 1950, he consulted widely among political leaders before appointing Mohammad Natsir as cabinet *formateur*. He then left Natsir to his task, coming to his aid only when negotiations between Masjumi and PNI reached the point of deadlock. When Natsir eventually formed the cabinet from which the PNI was excluded Sukarno simply accepted the result, though it ran counter to his own belief in government by the widest possible consensus. His conduct of the negotiations which led to the formation of the Sukiman government was, perhaps, a little more direct, in that he personally pressed Sukiman to accept the position of Prime Minister; but, again, his task was really confined to assisting negotiations. In the following year, as we have seen, he hesitated before accepting the list of names placed before him by Wilopo – but then he gave way gracefully. In 1953 he resisted the idea of a Hatta government and was ultimately to welcome the formation of a cabinet without Masjumi, but he did not actively engineer that result and he behaved with comparative propriety throughout negotiations. He was abroad (on his pilgrimage to Mecca) during the crucial stages of the formation of the Harahap government in 1955. In 1956 he did bring pressure to bear on Ali Sastroamidjojo to include a PKI sympathizer, but without success. On these occasions his preferences were allowed to peep through, but he could not be accused of grossly abusing the powers conferred on him.

Outside the exercise of these constitutional functions his interference with the proper processes of government was occasional, not continuous, and for the most part it took the form of public disagreements with government policies and of indirect attempts to influence decisions, rather than of an open refusal to abide by the rules of the game. His determination to retain his freedom of expression on the West Irian issue has been described. He disliked some aspects of the army re-organization plans pursued by Natsir and Wilopo and in 1952 he played his part in encouraging the opposition to the army leadership. He was embarrassed by Sukiman's pro-Western foreign policy. On questions of economic development he made no secret of his suspicion of foreign capital and his desire to see the Indonesianization of the economy – a view which brought him into conflict even with the second Ali

Sastroamidjojo government. But though, on occasion, he might have embarrassed his governments he kept himself, for the most part, from overt intervention. The significance of his public posture during this whole period was not that he interfered in important ways with the working of the parliamentary system but that he managed, through speeches and travel and through his patent concern with the trend of events, to preserve his independence and authority in the public eye. He was a political force in himself, matching the parties and the army. As such he could influence in some degree the play of events as they occurred, and he did so by working upon existing divisions. More important, however, than his actual influence was his potential influence: like the army he was standing on the edge of the political arena and was clearly visible as a potent source of action in the future should circumstances require it.

Within these limits it is true that Sukarno during these years was a divisive rather than a unifying force. It is instructive to compare his actions in the early fifties with the part he had played in the revolution. Then he had indeed been a national symbol and the sustainer of unity. True, during the revolution also he had taken sides in political struggles, but he had been aspiring to a leadership above faction fighting, and in taking sides he had always supported those groups which could claim to be the legitimate government. Now, though still claiming to stand above party rivalry, he was much more partisan. His opposition to Natsir and to Wilopo was as marked as his preference for Ali Sastroamidjojo. His Javanese outlook made it difficult for him to appreciate the problems of the Outer Islands and this, together with his casual adherence to Islam, went hand in hand with the growth of his opposition to Masjumi, which he later rationalized in terms of the latter's obstruction to the completion of the revolution. Certainly Sukarno was careful never to identify himself with the PNI. He might have taken the party and made it the basis of his own political action. He was almost certainly wise not to do so, for though this would have given him an organization to support his initiatives, it would have focused and localized his partisanship.

The absence of a party basis of strength was never a handicap to Sukarno so long as the forces about him were divided, and it enabled him to preserve more than a pretence of an 'above the battle' neutrality. But it was clear enough by 1956 that he had aligned himself with certain elements and was opposed to others; and when, later, he really was seeking a new consensus, he failed to achieve it. To bridge the divisions of Indonesia was, no doubt, an impossible task. The important point is that Sukarno, in the early fifties, was manipulating these divisions in order to advance his political preferences rather than make a genuine attempt to conciliate opponents.

How does one judge his political skill in pursuing his goals through these early years of independence? His flexibility and resourcefulness were particularly striking. Sukarno had no clear plan of action which enabled him to move purposefully from the position of circumscribed president in 1950 to that of man of the hour in 1956. Once again it was a case of a tentative and pragmatic handling of events as they occurred, and only gradually did he come to define his goal. For the most part he waited upon developments, fitting in with events sometimes, and sometimes pushing them along just a little in a desired direction. His intuitive sense of the possibilities of a political situation rarely failed him; he could judge just how far he could go – when to press on and when to concede. He pressed on when demanding action to recover West Irian but yielded when faced by Wilopo's list of ministers. His actions were prompted in some measure by the relations he could develop with individuals – he was prepared to fit in with Sukiman's policies even when he disliked them, but he had not been so accommodating with Natsir; he was able, in 1955, to achieve a reconciliation with Nasution, who had formerly been an opponent.

In skilfully adapting to situations as they unfolded Sukarno was showing his Javanese temper, concerned not to look too far ahead but to allow the forces of historical development to reveal themselves gradually. Nevertheless by 1956 there was a marked change in his method of action. In the past his hesitation at moments of crisis might be ascribed in part to uncertainty and indecisiveness. Now, though his ideas remained essentially unchanged, there was a new assurance to his approach and a sign of a more confident style of leadership, less rhetorical than before and more shrewdly resourceful. The reason was, at least in part, to be found in his personal life. In 1955 he had taken another wife.

Sukarno's affair with Mrs Hartini Suwondo, the wife of an oil company official, had developed over the course of 1953. It was conducted at first through the intermediary offices of Major-General Suhardjo who managed the meetings of the two. Hartini lived in Salatiga but she would fly frequently from Semarang airport to meet Sukarno in Djakarta. By 1954 the liaison was becoming a matter of widespread gossip and was the subject of comment in the Djakarta Press.

Hartini was an intelligent and sophisticated woman, more worldly than Fatmawati, and Sukarno's attraction to her was not just a matter of passing fancy. It became clear to those in close contact with him that he was in fact determined to marry her, as he was entitled to do under Muslim law, as soon as her own divorce had been arranged. Since Sukarno's sexual proclivities were to become a byword his handling of his relations with Hartini has been too easily assumed to fit into that pattern. The assumption is open to the gravest doubt. On this occasion Sukarno, in fact, was in love – in quite an ordinary and old-fashioned sense.

The Hartini affair necessarily became a concern of government, and Ali Sastroamidjojo, as Prime Minister at the time, was concerned to avoid scandal. For this reason he urged upon Sukarno what seemed to be a straightforward solution. If he was attracted so fatally to Hartini why shouldn't he simply keep her as a mistress without plunging into the mass of problems which marriage would pose. Sukarno's reply was that he loved Hartini and that it would be immoral, in those circumstances, to keep her as a mistress. The honest thing to do – the only thing for him to do – was to marry her openly.

The marriage took place in 1955. Fatmawati, though still accepted as Indonesia's First Lady, was no more prepared to share her house with her rival than Inggit had been fifteen years before and she moved out of the palace to a house in Kebajoran. Unlike Inggit she did not seek a divorce from Sukarno, who in his turn promised his son Guntur that he would never advance

Hartini formally to the position of First Lady (*Ibu Negara*) – a promise which he kept, though perhaps with some difficulty.

Sukarno's marriage to Hartini, coming at a critical time, seems to have provided him with a new source of strength. At least Sukarno himself later attributed his courage and determination in intervening in the political scene in 1957 to the emotional support she gave him. Certainly he showed a confidence which, as we have seen, had sometimes been lacking before.

## 11
## The Making of Guided Democracy

When Sukarno made his 'Bury the Parties' speech on 28 October 1956 he was still not clear where he was heading. He was merely testing the political temperature. Beyond his conviction that parliament and the party system had failed the country and that, in his desire for change, he was responding to the real wishes of the Indonesian people, he had not yet determined his precise goals or evolved a precise plan for attaining them. The way in which he gradually did so showed his resourcefulness and his mastery of political manoeuvre as he cajoled doubters, took the initiative from opponents, adapted himself to circumstances when he could not get his way and waited for his next opportunity.

The immediate reactions to the speech were mixed. Party spokesmen were, naturally, opposed to the idea of self-immolation, but they were also confused and hesitant in defining their opposition. Masjumi, as was to be expected, was clearer than most in rejecting the implications of Sukarno's suggestion. Its chairman, Natsir, remarked that there were many unsatisfactory features in Indonesian political life, but he asked whether they should all be attributed simply to the party system and claimed that 'If the parties should be buried, democracy would also disappear'.[42] Others saw the speech as a bid by Sukarno for absolute power for himself.[43] Even from those who usually supported Sukarno there was anxiety and doubt. PNI leaders were extraordinarily hesitant.[44] Aidit, Secretary-General of the PKI, agreed with the idea of the rationalization of parties but not, of course, with their abolition.[45]

Encouraged by the confused nature of these reactions, Sukarno, in an address to the Indonesian Teachers' Association, two days

42. *PIA News Bulletin*, 30 October 1956.
43. *Abadi*, quoted in *PIA*, 30 October 1956.
44. See, e.g., Suwirjo, PNI Chairman as quoted in *Merdeka*, 30 October 1956.
45. *Harian Rakjat*, 30 October 1956.

later, returned to his theme in slightly stronger terms. 'I no longer simply dream,' he said. 'Rather, the burying of the parties is now something I positively recommend.' At the same time he insisted that he had no desire for dictatorial powers for himself. 'I am not a managing director of the Indonesian republic and I don't want to become a dictator because it is contrary to my conscience. I am a democrat. But I don't desire democratic liberalism. On the contrary I want a guided democracy . . .'[46]

Here once again was the idea to which he had referred from time to time ever since 1950. He spoke of it further in his opening speech to the newly elected Constituent Assembly on 10 November. 'Indonesia's problems can only be solved by means of an intrinsically Indonesian formula. . . . I implore you to see that the constitution you are to draw up shall not be a copy of, or an adaptation from, constitutions existing in other countries. . . . Always bear in mind that the constitution to be drawn up is intended for the Indonesian people, and that therefore the soul of the Indonesian people, the character, the identity of the Indonesian people, should be reflected in this constitution.'[47]

In all of this Sukarno was feeling his way, sounding out reactions and not looking too far ahead, creating suspense and then delaying a resolution of it. A hint on 28 October became a recommendation on 30 October and the subject of an appeal to the body drafting the constitution on 10 November. But so far he had spoken only in the broadest of terms. What was meant, precisely, by 'guided democracy'? What kind of institutional changes did he envisage? If the parties did not agree to bury themselves were they to be coerced? If so, by what power? According to one view, Sukarno could only achieve his aims if he resigned his office and entered directly into the political arena himself in order to lead the struggle against the parties – presumably forming his own political organization and finding his own power base.[48] None of these things was made clear for Sukarno had no planned campaign. The very openness of his proposals gave him a certain initiative and left potential opponents uncertain of his intentions.

46. *PIA*, 31 October 1956.
47. *PIA*, 12 November 1956.
48. *Merdeka*, 30 October 1956.

Such opponents existed and they were not inconsiderable. Military voices in Djakarta and in the provinces had condemned the self-seeking civilian politicians and their failure to come to grips with urgent problems; there were civilian leaders who expressed the same criticisms. To many of these however it seemed that a possible solution to Indonesia's ills lay in the foundation of an emergency presidential cabinet under the premiership of Hatta and they were therefore suspicious of the President's initiatives. A Hatta government was, of course, the last thing Sukarno wanted, but for the moment, given the large public support for such a solution, he had to move gingerly, probing the situation bit by bit and waiting for it to show its potentialities.

By early 1957 certain tendencies had revealed themselves. First of all the series of regional coups had changed the whole political situation in Indonesia. Colonel Husein's successful seizure of power in West Sumatra and Colonel Simbolon's unsuccessful attempt to do the same in North Sumatra gave force to Sukarno's anxiety about national unity. In South Sumatra, too, the regional commander, Colonel Barlian, was able to act with a considerable degree of independence of Djakarta, and northern Sulawesi – a centre of army-protected smuggling – was also a region of doubtful loyalty. Now that they had become overt these movements of regional resistance confirmed the bankruptcy of the Ali government and made plain its inability to deal with the deteriorating situation.

By January the main initiative seemed to lie with the colonels and with their political supporters. Masjumi, with its strong Outer Island ties and its now well established opposition to the President, was to a considerable extent in sympathy with the regional movements, and in January, against this apparently favourable background, Masjumi and Parkindo initiated discussions among the government parties with a view to getting Hatta back into a team with Sukarno and heading a new presidential cabinet.[49] The other partners to the coalition were not prepared to yield, and when this move failed Masjumi, on 9 January, withdrew its ministers from the government. Sukarno was alarmed at

49. *PIA*, 3 and 5 January 1957.

the possible consequences of Masjumi's withdrawal. He was not yet ready for the government to fall and he brought his personal influence to bear on the Parkindo leader, Johannes Leimena, to dissuade him from following the Masjumi example.[50]

There was in fact no need for him to worry, though the fact may not have been plain to him at the time. Regional dissidence and the impotence of the government to deal with it had created a sense of crisis and expectancy – and it had also produced a fluidity about possible alternatives. In these circumstances a growing number of people looked to the President to find a way out. At the very least they were reluctant to oppose him; but also, more positively, there was a growing acceptance of the need for radical change and the belief that it could be introduced only by the President. Partly through the drift of circumstances and partly through his own boldness a considerable degree of initiative had passed into Sukarno's hands. There was opposition to him in Djakarta and in the regions, but he sensed also a strong tide of feeling flowing with him.

Even so he moved cautiously. During January he engaged in discussions with a wide range of political leaders. He had by this time recognized the strength of party opposition to his idea of a dissolution of the parties and he quietly put that aspect of his thinking on one side. No further references were made to it. Having thus shifted his ground he was able to reassure possible opponents and to exploit the sense of crisis which they shared with him. Finally in February he judged that the time was ready for a further step. Giving full play to his sense of theatre Sukarno summoned a gathering of some 900 political and other leaders to the palace on 21 February and outlined to them his *Konsepsi*.

His opening remarks indicated the role in which he had cast himself: simultaneously the servant of his people – as one among others, offering his views in all humility for their consideration – and their leader, able to speak with special authority, to give voice to their inner aspirations and to lead them to a solution.

His Concept was an attempt to put in more specific terms the ideas he had hinted at from time to time over the years. He took as his starting point, once again, the assertion that Indonesia

50. *PIA*, 16 January 1957.

should not imitate the political forms of other countries but should look for institutions which were in accordance with her own inner nature. He rejected the idea of liberal democracy on the grounds that it was a Western import and that it allowed the coercion of minorities by mere majorities. That was not the Indonesian way. Sukarno claimed to find an alternative mode of reaching decisions at the heart of Indonesian society – within the village assembly. There decisions were made only after prolonged and careful consideration. As long as a substantial minority remained unconvinced by a proposal deliberation would continue until, at length, under the guidance of a leader, a consensus was reached. These distinctively Indonesian procedures of deliberation and consensus – *musjawarah* and *mufakat* – together with leadership, allowed all views to be considered and were tolerant of minority feeling; they should thus be the model for the nation. Liberal democracy was based on conflict – the procedures of deliberation and consensus would promote harmony.

Translating these principles into terms of actual political machinery Sukarno made two proposals. First of all he suggested the formation of what he called a *gotong-royong* (mutual help) cabinet, representing all the major parties. The PKI was now too important an element to be excluded from power, he argued. It was an authentic part of the revolution and it should be allowed to play its part in forming a national consensus. Thus a four-legged government, consisting of PNI, Masjumi, NU and the PKI, aided possibly by representatives of the more substantial of the smaller parties, would be better able to shape an acceptable national policy and to promote national harmony than would a coalition government faced by a significant opposition party. The term *gotong-royong*, said Sukarno, was 'an authentic Indonesian term' a term 'which gave the truest reflection of the Indonesian soul'. He went on to argue that this was not a leftward step. 'It has been said that Bung Karno proposes this concept to turn the cabinet to the left. No, my brethren, as for me there is neither left nor right. I merely wish that the Indonesian nation may become whole again.'

Secondly, he proposed the formation of a National Council, under his own leadership, which could deliberate upon the broad lines of national policy. The Council was not to be a party body but was to be representative of functional groups – workers, peasants, intelligentsia, national entrepreneurs, religious organizations – Muslim, Protestant, Catholic – the armed services, youth organizations, women's organizations and also the regions of the country. The National Council, he argued, would reflect the composition of the nation as a whole in the same way that the proposed four-legged government would reflect the composition of parliament. By including the main elements of the nation both government and Council would be able to reach decisions based not on the overriding of minority by majority but on general consent, and they would thus command support in the country at large.

Sukarno's ideas of decision by consensus and of functional representation were not new. The former was merely another aspect of his insistence on the possibility of harmonizing competing streams of Indonesian thought. The latter was a return of the character of the KNIP of the revolution, after the expansion of its membership in 1946. Whether deliberation by representatives of this kind would be more effective than the party system in resolving genuine differences was, however, very much open to question. In his concern for unity Sukarno, as always, was apt to underestimate the depth of the gulfs separating opposing points of view. Certainly it was true that in practice the parliamentary system in Indonesia had tended markedly to play down elements of open conflict and to emphasize procedures making for harmony. In parliament, as in regional and local councils, attempts were made as a matter of general practice to resolve contentious questions outside the formal sessions of the assembly by prolonged discussion, subtle bargaining and compromise, and to avoid the taking of an open vote.

Such procedures made for flexibility in individual attitudes. So long as a person was not committed by public vote he might still be persuaded to give ground a little without loss of face, in the interests of an acceptable compromise. On the debit side was the fact that important and controversial issues were often shelved because of the difficulty of securing general agreement about them. Even if Sukarno was accurate in his ideal picture of decision making at the village level it did not follow that village procedures were capable of effective application at the national level, and the idea of constructing political machinery specifically to give effect to the Indonesian desire for harmony was at best a dubious enterprise.

At the practical level Sukarno's account of his plans still left a great many questions unanswered. Who was to choose the members of the National Council? What would be its exact powers? Was it intended to usurp some of the functions of parliament? He had no intention, he said, of dissolving parliament, but he did not say where it was to stand in relation to the Council, or how the Council was to be brought into being. The broad outline was as far as he was prepared to go for the moment. How much further he might try to go subsequently would be determined by circumstances as they revealed themselves.

Sukarno concluded his remarks by giving the parties a week to consider his plans. He would call on them, he said, to give him their views on 28 February. The intervening week saw a good deal of organized public support for the Concept. Across the country dozens of meetings of trade unionists, students, political and other groups gave it their endorsement. In Djakarta slogans appeared in paint and tar on the walls of office buildings, on shop windows and on telegraph poles. *Laksanakan Konsepsi Presiden Soekarno* ('Implement President Sukarno's Concept') was painted on the walls of the parliament building. The headquarters of the large Dutch firms, KPM and Royal Dutch Shell received their share of attention. A good deal of this 'spontaneous' support represented the application of the communist party's mobilization techniques, but when the delegations of party leaders came to give their reports to the President on 28 February it was apparent that there was a much lower degree of enthusiasm among the other parties. Of the major parties only the PNI and the PKI were in favour.[51] Masjumi, equally wholeheartedly, was

51. Aidit, when asked whether the idea of *gotong royong* was not in conflict with the idea of class struggle, replied that the PKI was not dogmatic but creative, and was prepared to take account of Indonesian circumstances (*PIA*, 28 February 1957).

opposed. Even NU, traditionally an opportunistic party and tending to ally itself with the Java-based PNI rather than with its former Islamic partner Masjumi, was on this occasion firm in its opposition to the idea of bringing the PKI into the government.

In the face of these reactions Sukarno hesitated. On 2 March, after promising to make a further statement on his Concept on 4 March, he left for Surabaya where he was to open the Indonesian Youth Week. Before 4 March arrived, however, others had made their own pre-emptive moves.

On 2 March Colonel Sumual, territorial commander of East Indonesia, declared a 'State of War and Siege' in the region under his command. The intention of his move was to place civil administration under military control and it was therefore in effect not unlike Colonel Husein's coup in Central Sumatra three months earlier. Three days later Colonel Barlian took control of civil administration in South Sumatra and thus made formal and public what had already been the *de facto* situation in the province. By these two actions the political initiative was seized, if only temporarily, from Sukarno's hands.

The action of Sumual and Barlian was intended in part to strengthen demands for Hatta's return to office. In Sulawesi Sumual's seizure of power was accompanied by the announcement of a so-called 'Charter of Common Struggle' (*Piagam Perdjuangan Semesta* – abbreviated to 'Permesta') which, together with the presentation of a series of regional economic and political demands, called for a restoration of the Sukarno–Hatta partnership. Nasution, who had been attempting ever since December to mediate between Djakarta and the regional commands, discussed this possible solution at a meeting with the President on 5 March[52] and efforts were made to arrange a meeting between the President and the former Vice-President. When it came to the point, however, Sukarno dug in his heels. Hatta waited at home for a telephone call from the palace but it never came. Sukarno did agree, nonetheless, to a second proposal of Nasution's – that a State of War and Siege should be declared over all Indonesia. Such a proposal would legalize the coups which had occurred in East Indonesia and in Central and South

52. *PIA*, 3 March 1957.

Sumatra, and it would anticipate similar actions in other regions. It would also have the effect of placing civil government in the regions under the general authority of the army. It would thus give the army at last a formal role in government, although theoretically its powers would be exercised under Sukarno's authority as Commander-in-Chief.

This was not the solution that Sukarno would have chosen. It meant a check to his own plans. Though he kept his ability to initiate new moves and to return (as he did persistently over the next two years) to the goals embodied in his Concept, he was faced by the army as clearly the major political force with which he had to contend; but given the regional movements of resistance he had very little alternative and he agreed to Nasution's proposal.

On 14 March the second Ali cabinet resigned and the President proclaimed a State of War and Siege immediately afterwards.

By early March 1957 Sukarno and the army had established themselves as the major forces in Indonesia's political scene. The few days following the fall of the Ali government were a period of re-grouping of forces and a preparation for the next stage of what was coming to be seen as a tussle between them. The declaration of a State of War and Siege served the political purposes of the army, but Sukarno still had room to manoeuvre.[53] Indeed the fall of the government placed the immediate initiative in his hands since it was his constitutional function to prepare the way for the next government. In exercising that function he still had no intention of submitting to army and regional demands by calling on Hatta to form a cabinet.

He moved first in an orthodox fashion by appointing PNI chairman Suwirjo as *formateur* and then withdrawing to his Bogor palace leaving Suwirjo to his task. When Suwirjo failed to form a coalition government Sukarno instructed him to try again, aiming this time at a 'business cabinet' not dependent on parties. By the

53. Cf. Daniel S. Lev, *The Transition to Guided Democracy; Indonesian Politics, 1957–1959*, Ithaca, 1966, which is the best account of the changing balance of forces between 1957 and 1959. On this point, Lev tends to consider that Sukarno as Commander-in-Chief held the real political authority under the State of War and Siege. He does, however, stress 'the immense legal authority given to army leaders under martial law' (p. 16).

beginning of April Suwirjo had reported his second failure, and Sukarno then decided to make this failure his own opportunity. He called a meeting for the evening of 4 April of about seventy party leaders and senior officials, together with military leaders. Some of those summoned had been recalled dramatically by radio from other islands and had hurried back to Djakarta, while the capital busily studied the list of those invited, raised its collective eyebrows at the omissions and wondered what the President had in mind now. When the meeting assembled behind closed doors at the palace he announced that he proposed to appoint a new cabinet *formateur* – himself. President Sukarno, he said, had called on Citizen Sukarno to accept responsibility for creating a government – an extra-parliamentary emergency business-cabinet. He then passed round slips of paper on which those present were asked to indicate whether or not they would be willing to serve in such a cabinet. Some refused, but the majority indicated their willingness even though they were necessarily in ignorance of who their colleagues would be.

Predictably there was angry criticism from Masjumi about the President's action but otherwise the sense of crisis ensured its general acceptance and four days later Sukarno was able to report success in his efforts. A team had agreed to serve under the leadership of Dr Djuanda, a non-party figure, formerly Minister of Planning in the second Ali government.

It was a limited success, certainly. Though the majority of ministers were members of parties, they were chosen and had accepted office as individuals. Government policy therefore did not depend on party consent. But as a government the *Karya* (Work) Cabinet, as it was called, did not even approximate to Sukarno's original plan for a four-legged government. The cabinet's main strength was drawn from the PNI and the NU, who supplied four members each. Masjumi refused to allow any of its members to serve and in fact expelled those who accepted office. Two members were close to the PKI in sympathy, but the government certainly did not reflect all the main streams of Indonesian political thinking and its formation was a clear indication of Sukarno's retreat from the position he had taken up in announcing his Concept.

Further compromises were ahead. In May the new government took steps to create a National Council along the lines, it seemed, of the council suggested by Sukarno; but again the reality was very different from Sukarno's ideal. In elaborating his *Konsepsi*, as we have seen, though Sukarno was vague about the constitutional standing of his proposed Council he did appear to suggest the formation of a body which would rival parliament and become an alternative source of authority. In fact the new National Council turned out to be much less than that. It was established by law and was therefore in effect a creation of parliament, and, legally speaking, dependent upon it. Its powers were defined as merely advisory and Djuanda made it clear that the cabinet was still responsible to parliament according to the provisions of the 1950 constitution.

Djuanda, in effect, was concerned to play down the elements of change in the situation and the formation of his government did restore a degree of normality to the Indonesian scene after the uncertainty of the preceding months. For a time it had seemed as though anything could happen – regional revolt, military coup, a presidential seizure of power or other radical changes in the workings of constitutional government. With the new government in office catastrophe was at least postponed.

It was a precarious equilibrium certainly. Over the next few months efforts were made by Sukarno and by military and political leaders to assess the possibilities of the new situation. For all groups they were months of caution and limited manoeuvre. Power was not focused at any one point and the strength of the various parties in the political balance could only be determined in practice. For Sukarno, however, there was a new exhilaration. He might not have got what he wanted in February, April or May, but at least he had dropped the pretence of presidential remoteness from political conflict and had stepped openly into the thick of day-to-day affairs. From the beginning of 1957 the palace had been the scene of comings and goings as he had consulted with ministers, with party leaders and with Nasution and his colleagues. It had become a political forum in its own right and Sukarno was at the centre of its activity, keeping it in motion. It was politics by bargaining and the trading of favours. The palace style of politics had begun to establish itself, though Sukarno was, for the moment, content to leave the details of government to Djuanda.

A primary concern of the Djuanda government was, inevitably, the regional problem. Efforts at conciliation were made at several levels. Steps were taken to implement the local government law which had passed through parliament at the end of 1956 and which went far to meet regional demands for greater autonomy. Regional elections were held in Java and South Sumatra between June and August and revealed a considerable advance in the position of the PKI since the general elections (an advance made essentially at the expense of the PNI).[54] More important on the surface was a national deliberative conference (*Musjawarah Nasional*) held in Djakarta in September. The conference brought together civilian and military leaders from throughout Indonesia, including the dissident regions of West Sumatra, South Sumatra and Sulawesi. The presence of such figures as Husein and Barlian was a sign of the Indonesian ability to sink differences temporarily in the interests of discussion.

Though the original idea of the conference came from the National Council it was taken up by the government and it became very much a Djuanda rather than a Sukarno production. It was opened by Djuanda on 10 September and was conducted under government rather than Presidential auspices. Sukarno could not, of course, afford to stay away from a conciliation attempt of this kind and he took part in its deliberations. In the end little was achieved. Much goodwill was displayed on all sides and discussions ranged over the political and economic grievances of the regions. Attention was also given to the problem of military dissension including the relations between the Army Chief of Staff and regional commanders. But on other questions of substance the conference resolutions were cast in such general terms that they provided no real basis for future agreement.

At the heart of much of the discussion was the Sukarno–Hatta question and it seemed on the surface that progress was made. The conference provided the opportunity for the first meeting between the pair for many months (except for a meeting on a

54. The PKI was now the strongest party in Java, in terms of electoral support, its main stronghold being Central Java.

formal occasion in early July) and it was a matter for Press comment that they did not shake hands as they came together on the first day. The omission was rectified later in the day. Thereafter the two met at the palace and they were photographed day by day at the conference, standing together, walking together, smiling together and seeming to be reconciled. They made a joint statement asserting their 'absolute obligation' to co-operate in defending the State. But the accord which this seemed to represent did not carry beyond the conference. If a Sukarno–Hatta partnership was really the goal of the regions, Sukarno was not prepared to give it substance. Pressure continued to be brought to bear on him to this end in the succeeding months; even as late as December 1957 a parliamentary committee was going to and fro between Hatta and the President, seeking ways and means to re-unite them. Sukarno professed himself anxious to see Hatta back as Vice-President and possibly as chairman of a proposed national planning board. To Hatta this seemed, with some reason, to be an attempt to shunt him aside. He was not willing to accept such terms and Sukarno certainly would not have him as premier.

While participating in the national deliberative conference Sukarno also kept his own initiative fresh. One of the issues he used for this purpose was that of West Irian. In February 1957 the UN General Assembly had turned down a proposal for a Good Offices Committee to facilitate negotiations between Indonesia and the Netherlands. Now the Assembly was scheduled to consider in November a further motion calling on the two parties to negotiate a solution. Against this general background Sukarno spoke frequently of the need to carry on the national struggle and to perfect the revolution by recovering the territory. He visited the eastern end of Indonesia at the beginning of September as a symbolic gesture to focus attention on West Irian. As November approached, with the scheduled date of the UN debate, he lent his support to mass meetings to express Indonesian determination. As a climax to his efforts he dropped a number of significant remarks in speeches towards the end of a visit to Nusa Tenggara in early November. If the motion before the General Assembly was lost, he said, it would be necessary to take a new course of action in the struggle – a course which would 'startle the world'. In Lombok on 8 November he outlined more clearly what he had in mind. Indonesia should have the courage to switch the direction of her trade – away from Holland and West Germany to the countries of Eastern Europe – to China, Japan and India.[55]

Sukarno's capacity to ignore considerations of economic advantage or political stability in the interests of prestige, or to assuage wounded pride, was to be an increasingly familiar characteristic in the future. 'To hell with your aid,' he cried a few years later, when the US seemed reluctant to continue its support to an Indonesia engaged in an adventurous foreign policy. His unexpected and petulant withdrawal from the United Nations at the end of 1964 was another example. His threats to Holland in November 1957 were in the same category and were to prove in due course a particularly drastic and expensive piece of policy dictated by pride. The public campaign mounted in intensity throughout November. There were critics, of course. Natsir was heard to condemn the violence of its slogans. Such phrases as 'Dutch pigs' or 'Kill the Dutch' were against the manners of an Eastern people, he felt.[56] Hatta, while supporting the object of the campaign, criticized its methods by implication. A way should be found, he said, which would show 'the sincerity and dignified fighting spirit of a high-minded people'.[57] But Sukarno continued to speak in more threatening terms. At a rally in Lapangan Banteng, after his return from Nusa Tenggara, he spoke of the need to build up power and to press the Dutch 'in such a way that they would have to yield'.[58]

An agitational strategy of this kind suited Sukarno's temperament but it had its risks for him – both personal and political. The personal risks revealed themselves dramatically on 30 November, the day after the UN vote had eventually been taken and the motion had failed to secure the necessary two-thirds majority. On the evening of 30 November, as Sukarno was leaving an anniversary celebration at his son Guntur's primary school in Tjikini,

55. *Merdeka*, 12 November 1957.
56. *PIA*, 9 November 1957.
57. *PIA*, 19 November 1957.
58. ibid.

homemade grenades were thrown by a group of young men (later alleged to be supporters of Zulkifli Lubis) into the crowd surrounding him. He escaped unhurt, but eleven people were killed and dozens of others wounded. The Tjikini incident was the first of five assassination attempts spread over the next few years (including a spectacular strafing of the palace from the air in 1960). On this and other occasions his escape fed a public belief (and perhaps even an inner and private belief) in Sukarno's invulnerability.

The political risks could be seen soon afterwards. With the defeat of the West Irian motion an angry campaign was launched, first of all in the capital, and then elsewhere in the archipelago, against Dutch property. It began with a decision to withdraw KLM's landing rights and was followed by a government-supported twenty-four hour strike; it then moved to mass demonstrations in the streets, the painting of more slogans, the overturning of Dutch-owned cars and finally the seizure of KPM, the big Dutch shipping line, of Dutch banks, and of other Dutch concerns. The movement swept across the country and in a matter of days Dutch estates in Sumatra had been taken. Shortly afterwards thousands of Dutch nationals began a massive return to Holland.

The campaign, though violent in one sense, was not accompanied by violence against persons and it was a remarkable testimony to its disciplined character that no lives were lost. The spontaneous seizure of property though had important consequences. To some it represented the development of the struggle for independence; political independence had been achieved in 1949 but economic dependence had remained until now – this was the true completion of the revolution. But it was at a cost to Indonesia. It dealt a tremendous blow to the Indonesian economy, disrupting communications and affecting the production of the exports on which the nation's finance depended. The government, after its first alarm at the seizures and its attempts to check them, found itself compelled to accept the *fait accompli* and announced that it would assume control for the time being of the seized enterprises. In practice 'the government' meant, in many cases, the army, which for a time became heavily involved in estate administration under the reconstituted Government Plantations Enterprise. This was a temporary arrangement, but for the time being it was to mean an increase in power for the army. Though Sukarno had intended to use the West Irian campaign as a means of keeping the political initiative in his own hands it had served, by the end of December, to endanger his control of the situation and to enhance the position of the political force which was soon to become his main rival.

The attempted assassination of Sukarno and the subsequent mass seizure of Dutch property injected a new sense of crisis into the Indonesian situation, similar to that which had marked the early months of the year. The formation of the Djuanda government had seemed to resolve the earlier crisis or at least to have moderated the urgency of it. A government was once more in existence within the framework of the constitution and it seemed to be tackling urgent problems. National disintegration had been avoided. But by December 1957 the Republic was again experiencing a situation with wide open, and perhaps catastrophic, possibilities.

The feeling of crisis was heightened when, in January 1958, the Press reported that a number of leading critics of Sukarno's actions and of the government's policies had begun to gather in West Sumatra, the home of the original separatism of over a year before. Sjafruddin Prawiranegara, Governor of the Bank of Indonesia and one-time premier of the emergency government of the Republic after the Dutch seizure of Jogja in 1948, Natsir, chairman of Masjumi and former Prime Minister, and Burhanuddin Harahap, former premier, were the main figures in the new Padang group. They were in touch also with Sumitro, a leading PSI member, Professor of Economics in the University of Indonesia, Minister of Trade and Industry in Natsir's cabinet, and of Finance in the Wilopo cabinet, who had fled from Djakarta in the course of 1956. During January this group of leaders conferred at length with Husein, Barlian and Simbolon, the military architects of Sumatran dissidence, and with Sumual of Minahasa.

The crisis came to a head during Sukarno's absence from Indonesia. Resorting to his common tactic of withdrawing from the scene and allowing a confused situation to sort itself out, he had left on 6 January for an overseas tour. The journey was planned ostensibly for health reasons but it was the kind of royal progress that he enjoyed, taking him to India, Egypt, Yugoslavia, Pakistan, Ceylon, Burma and Thailand, and finishing up in Japan, where his playboy tendencies could be generously indulged. On 10 February Colonel Husein broadcast an ultimatum to the President and the government, calling for the government's resignation and demanding its replacement by a new cabinet to be formed by Hatta and the Sultan of Jogjakarta. If these terms were not met, he said, a new government of Indonesia would be formed in Padang.

It was an oddly impractical ultimatum. Even had the government been so lacking in grip as to be prepared to resign, the prospect of conducting the negotiations which could test the delicate possibilities of agreement and co-operation and come up with something as specific as a Hatta government – all in a matter of five days – was remote indeed. The real motive was perhaps to force army leaders to support the regional initiative and in this way to bring about a change of government. With the advantage of hindsight that might seem an unlikely consequence, but to observers at the time it was a genuine possibility. The government however was not disposed to bow to the threat. The ultimatum was rejected and on the evening of 15 February Husein announced the formation of the 'Revolutionary Government of the Republic of Indonesia' (Pemerintah Revolusioner Republik Indonesia – PRRI) under the premiership of Sjafruddin. It still professed loyalty to the Republic and offered itself as an alternative government claiming the support of all Indonesians.

The regional challenge had thus come to a head at last and brought into question the very survival of Indonesia as a single country. Sukarno returned to face the crisis on 16 February, and had two meetings with Hatta over the next couple of weeks. A Hatta government, formed at this point, would meet the central rebel demand, but Sukarno's willingness to go as far as that after so long a resistance to this solution depended finally on the military prospects of defeating the rebellion. In fact it quickly became clear that the revolutionary government lacked the military power to force that sort of concession from him.

It is not necessary here to trace the details of the military campaign launched by Djakarta against the rebel areas. In early March landings on Sumatra's east coast were quickly followed by a parachute attack on the oil town of Pakan Baru and by its capture. From there the campaign to crush the rebellion moved rapidly. Padang fell to central government troops in mid April followed by Bukit Tinggi, the capital of the province of West Sumatra. In June the main force of the central government attack shifted to Sulawesi where resistance was more effective, but where the outcome was the same – a speedy defeat of rebel forces leaving only pockets of guerrilla opposition behind. Extravagant hopes of foreign intervention sustained the rebels for a while. They had proclaimed their anti-communism and had condemned what they saw as the communist leanings of the Djakarta government. In return they hoped for Western support. There was little: American military advisers had been present in Padang before the rebellion broke out and planes flew into North Sulawesi from bases in Taiwan and the Philippines. In May 1958 an American pilot, Allan Pope, was shot down over Ambon. The public statements of John Foster Dulles had certainly left no doubt about where American sympathies lay.[59] But what were regarded as firm promises of American support (given possibly by irresponsible CIA officers) were never fulfilled and the rebels obtained no international recognition as a government. As the rebellion ebbed away Sumitro continued to live a life of shadowy intrigue in Singapore, still hoping for outside support, while in North Borneo and the Philippines smuggling operations continued to support the hopeless cause of the remaining guerrillas. By late 1958 the rebellion was effectively over.

59. American encouragement of the rebels helped to confirm Sukarno in the view of the world which had been shaping itself in his mind ever since the Tjikini incident. The assassination attempt had shaken him and predisposed him to see enemies about him, foreign as well as domestic. In early 1958 he had good reason to believe that America would like to see him toppled. It speaks volumes for his flexibility that he was nevertheless able to respond when the new ambassador, Howard Jones, emerged in mid 1958 as the agent of a more conciliatory American initiative.

The defeat of this open challenge to Djakarta did not leave things as they were before. It transformed the Indonesian political situation, or at least completed its transformation.

At the beginning of 1957 the regions and their military leaders, with considerable sympathy from Masjumi, had faced a party-based government and a hesitant army High Command, with the President about to intervene in his own way. By the end of 1958 the army and Sukarno between them dominated the scene. The regional separatism of the last two years was crushed. Masjumi, compromised by its association with the rebellion, was no longer an effective political force and, together with the PSI, it was to be banned two years later. The other parties were still there and with some influence still, but they were no longer accepted in the nation at large as the principal agents of political action. Nor did the constitutional system which had conferred power on them in the first place any longer command respect.[60] The army, its rebellious elements defeated in the field, was now a much more unified and coherent force under Nasution's leadership, its prestige having been enormously increased by its effective handling of the rebellion. Under the state of emergency it was acquiring considerable responsibility in routine administration. It was the concern of Nasution to make this participation, or something like it, permanent. He did not want a military dictatorship but an established place for the army in the country's institutions – a place which would not depend upon the temporary arrangements of martial law.

Finally the President, for his part, had preserved his own independence and his capacity for effective action. Unlike the parties, the army and the factions within it, Sukarno had no organized power base of his own. He had to fit into this constellation of forces and use it as best he could for his own purposes. His political strength came from his personal standing as well as from his skill both in persuasion and in balancing his opponents against each other. His one advantage was his capacity, as a single individual, to move quickly and in unexpected directions and to keep the world guessing. He used this advantage to the full.

60. Lev, op. cit., chapters 3 and 4, gives a thorough account of the parties' moves of this period.

The P K I was, of course, an exception to the general picture of party decline. Because it had been excluded from power in the past it had escaped the tarnishing effects of responsibility. Unlike the other parties it had devised programmes with specific appeal to the rural and urban masses and its membership continued to grow. It did not depend upon a parliamentary constitution for its powers. Indeed it was preparing to play a direct role in politics, sustained by its coherence of organization, its numerical strength and its control over its subsidiary organizations of workers, peasants and others. For the moment, however, it was still feeling its way. The President and the army were therefore the chief partners in power, and together they formed an irresistible combination.

It was in many ways an uneasy partnership. On some vitally important matters the two partners were in firm agreement with each other. They were at one, for example, in their criticism of the party-based conflicts of the past, and in their desire for a less open, more authoritarian political structure for the future. But they were wary of each other and on some issues of policy they disagreed sharply. Despite Nasution's deep loyalty to Sukarno (not to mention his unwillingness – due possibly to a lack of political nerve – to oppose the President on matters at issue between them) the Chief of Staff distrusted the unpredictability and volatility of Sukarno's political temperament. In particular Nasution was concerned at Sukarno's leanings towards the P K I. Sukarno, for his part, thought the army was insufficiently radical and he also saw it as a possible threat. It was too independent a force for his liking and he recognized the danger that it might indeed destroy his own independence unless he could find some way to contain it. Yet each needed the other. The army needed the legitimacy which the President could confer on its political role, and Sukarno needed the backing of the army in the last resort. It was therefore a love-hate relationship which bound the two together. In the context of Indonesia's balanced politics the accommodation between them – the maintenance of a Sukarno-army axis – was the only guarantee of stability for the moment. The respective roles which each was to play in the new structure were still to be determined, however.

The army's authority was exercised directly through its powers under martial law and through its control of a large sector of the economy, but it also attempted to extend its political influence indirectly through a national front organization. A national front was one of Sukarno's ideas – ever since the failure of the state party proposed in 1945 he had wanted an organization embracing all parties and functional groups and able, under his own leadership, to mobilize the population in support of national policy. In early 1958 the army took over the proposal by forming its own 'National Front for the Liberation of West Irian'. Against this direct and indirect influence Sukarno could pit his personal standing, his persuasiveness and his greater speed of manoeuvre. (The army had its own internal divisions and uncertainties which gave the President an edge.) He also began to develop his alliance with the communist party to offset the dangers inherent in his alliance with the army.

Against the background of these new patterns of power Sukarno returned once more to his guided democracy plans, which had at last begun to define themselves more clearly. When he had first outlined his Concept in February 1957 it was not certain whether he intended it to be realized within the framework of the provisional constitution or not. He probably had not explored this side of the question very thoroughly. Certainly the Djuanda government and the National Council fell far short of his goal. By mid 1958 he had a better picture of the kind of constitutional changes he wanted. The fundamental issue as he saw it now was the principle of functional representation. The extension of this principle, not only into a proposed new national planning council but also into parliament, would meet much of his demand for a specifically Indonesian political system to replace liberal democracy. It would have the effect of cutting down party power, though without necessarily eliminating parties altogether. It would give the army the sort of permanent and legitimate voice that Nasution wanted for it, but without giving it an unchallenged position of dominance. And it would call for his own guidance of the consequent deliberation and consensus seeking.

But how was this change in parliamentary representation to be achieved? Through elections or by appointment? How many functional representatives were to be added? Would the new arrangements require constitutional change or could they be introduced simply by means of a new electoral law? In either case the support of party leaders would be required to implement them. This was Sukarno's dilemma. His plan to cut down party power required action by the Constituent Assembly or parliament, or by both together, and they were party-based bodies. Though the parties had come, reluctantly, to accept the principle of functional representation they differed widely from Sukarno on the details of its introduction. The National Council under his chairmanship had recommended that fifty per cent of parliamentary members should be functional representatives. The parties wished to limit the proportion to one third of the total. They also wanted such representatives to be chosen by elections, though in the eyes of the National Council this would merely enable the parties to advance functional group candidates, with the result that the functional group representatives would merely be party representatives in disguise. The cabinet, comprised largely of party members, was itself divided on these questions. On the sidelines of this discussion the army, under Nasution's leadership, was firm in its support of the President and the National Council. Indeed Nasution, by this time, was in effect a co-sponsor with Sukarno of the whole guided democracy idea.

Sukarno had to move slowly in resolving these differences. With army support he might get his own way but at the possible cost of becoming the army's prisoner. He preferred to rely on persuasion, brought to bear through extended discussions with interested parties. On 5 December he held the first of a series of 'Open Talks' with the cabinet and the National Council in his palace at Bogor. By this stage the cabinet had come to accept his demand that functional groups must in some way be introduced into parliament.[61] On 11 January leaders of the main political parties were called to the Merdeka Palace for a series of private meetings with the President. On 15 January a second 'Open Talk' with ministers was held in Djakarta. Finally, on 26 January, the third of the 'Open Talks' was held at Bogor, beginning at 10.30 in the morning and running on till the early hours of the following day.

61. Lev, op. cit., p. 235.

Despite a soothing communiqué after this meeting stating that a 'formula' had been reached, it quickly became apparent that party agreement was still some distance away. The details of the Bogor 'formula' were withheld from the public while party meetings were called hastily to consider its terms. In fact it provided that fifty per cent of the seats in parliament would be filled by functional group representatives, that of these the army would have thirty-five seats (out of a total of 260), that a new national front would be formed and that functional group candidates would be chosen through the national front. Of the major parties only the PKI was willing to accept the formula. A series of meetings failed to resolve the PNI's internal arguments and a week after the Bogor meeting the party was reported to be 'still talking'.[62] NU committed itself to the view that guided democracy should be implemented only through the 1950 constitution and that functional representatives should be party-based.

Sukarno once again left the capital to its discussions and went to fulfil speaking engagements in Central Java, and during a good part of February he was preoccupied with the state visits of Prince Norodom Sihanouk and Ho Chi Minh. Finally at a two-day cabinet session on 18 and 19 February it was decided that the time had come to cut through the morass of deliberation and to take more decisive action. The cabinet now proposed that guided democracy be introduced by a return to the constitution of 1945. This constitution, with its provision for a strong executive president and for a hierarchy of deliberative bodies, would provide a suitable framework for the functional representation that Sukarno desired. An important feature of this solution was that, if the adoption of the '45 Constitution could be achieved through the Constituent Assembly, it would preserve proper constitutional procedures and would avoid the danger that the constitution might be introduced by direct action.

The idea of a return to the 1945 Constitution was not a new one. It had been advanced by Nasution during the previous year in a National Council committee and it had been canvassed from time to time since then. But only in February was it given government endorsement as a single key to the whole guided democracy plan.

62. *Antara*, 4 February 1959.

All that was needed, said Djuanda, was for the Constituent Assembly to adopt the constitution and for parliament to legislate to simplify the party system. Guided Democracy would then be in existence.

All that was needed? In fact – given party attitudes – it was still a tall order, though there seemed a possibility of NU support which, with that of the PNI and the PKI, could ensure the necessary two-thirds majority in the Constituent Assembly. On 6 March cabinet leaders conferred with the Assembly's consultative committee to discuss ways of realizing the cabinet plan. From their discussions there emerged a proposal that Sukarno should speak to a plenary session of the Assembly which would then – so it was hoped – meekly accede to his wishes and adopt the 1945 Constitution. At the same time a public campaign for guided democracy was initiated.

On 8 March Sukarno addressed a large and sympathetic crowd in front of the palace and, in succeeding weeks, a series of public meetings produced floods of resolutions in support. At last on 22 April the plenary session of the Constituent Assembly was held and Sukarno delivered his plea. In a two-and-a-half hour speech he criticized the lack of progress made by the Assembly in the two years, five months and twelve days since he had opened its proceedings and he called now for speedy acceptance of the government's proposal.[63] The 1945 Constitution would not resolve the nation's difficulties, he said. There was never a revolution whose problems had disappeared overnight, but the '45 Constitution would enable the nation to face its difficulties more directly. Then, once again, he resorted to his withdrawal-and-return technique. On 23 April he left on an extraordinary overseas tour which embraced Turkey, Poland, Hungary, Russia, Scandinavia, Brazil, Argentina, Mexico, the USA (Los Angeles only), Japan, Cambodia and North Vietnam. While he was being fêted in foreign capitals the Assembly settled down to its debates – but in no uniformly submissive state of mind. Two of the major parties – PKI and PNI – accepted the government plan and one of them – Masjumi – was in opposition. Among the opponents there was some anxiety about the consequences of Guided

63. Published as *Res Publica! Once More Res Publica!*

Democracy for the party system, but in the end the ideological issue, the place of Islam under the constitution, became the decisive one. On this question, NU, despite its earlier pliability, lined up with Masjumi and with the lesser Muslim parties, Perti and PSII.

Discussions of this issue focused on the apparently trivial matter of the old Djakarta Charter which had been drafted in 1945 for the purpose of serving as a preamble to the constitution. As we have seen, the wording of the Djakarta Charter represented a compromise between secular nationalist and Islamic opinion. It had sought to place upon Muslims the obligation to observe Islamic law, but the meaning of the obligation was not precisely defined. In 1945 Muslim opinion had been against the Charter on the grounds that it was too permissive and Sukarno's powers of persuasion had to be called into play to secure its acceptance.[64] The controversial passage had then been omitted from the preamble before the constitution was finally adopted in August 1945. In 1959 Muslims pinned their hopes to the Charter and NU demanded that it be adopted as the constitution's preamble, thus, it was argued, giving constitutional effect to the obligations of Islam. Paradoxically what had been a compromise document in 1945 became the central plank of the Muslim position in 1959.

The government refused to accept the NU proposal. It would accept the Djakarta Charter, said Djuanda, not as an integral part of the constitution but only as 'an historic document', giving the 'essential spirit to the formulation of the Preamble'. As a compromise proposal Djuanda suggested that the full text of the Djakarta Charter be included in a document – to be known as the Bandung Charter – by which, it was hoped, the Constituent Assembly would ultimately adopt the 1945 Constitution. And so in these somewhat rarefied terms the Assembly debates continued.

Towards the end of May it was becoming clear that for all the confident expectations of 22 April the President's appeal to the Assembly was in grave danger of being rejected.[65] On 29 May the

64. See above, pp. 188–9.

65. Given 114 Masjumi members, 90 NU members, 17 PSII members and 7 Perti members as against 117 PNI and 59 PKI members (not counting the representatives of other minor parties), it was obvious that the possibility

Assembly rejected the NU proposal to write the Djakarta Charter into the constitution as its preamble. Then came the votes on the constitution itself. Three ballots were taken. On 30 May, though there was a clear majority for the proposal to adopt the 1945 Constitution (269–199), it fell short of the required two-thirds majority. At the second vote on 1 June the proposal fared even less well (264–204), and the final vote on 2 June made no appreciable difference (263–203). Muslim opinion had held solid and Sukarno's appeal had been decisively rejected. On the following day Nasution, as Chairman of the Supreme War Authority under the state of emergency, imposed a ban on all political activities. He then called on the absent President to by-pass the Constituent Assembly decision and implement the constitution by Presidential Decree.

This was the situation to which Sukarno returned at the end of the month. For the third time in three years the political public of Indonesia felt that the situation had almost unlimited possibilities.

Official receptions at Kemajoran airport were not at all unusual, given Sukarno's taste for overseas travel and his requirement that he be seen off and welcomed back with appropriate protocol; but the distinguished assembly of ministers, senior officials, service leaders, members of parliament and foreign diplomats that waited for him on the evening of 29 June was in a more than usually heightened state of anticipation. Having left the country two months before, after his charge to the Constituent Assembly to adopt the 1945 Constitution, Sukarno had created the drama of his own return. He had received official news of the progress of the debates and ultimately of the Assembly's rejection of his proposal. Roeslan Abdulgani had flown to Japan to bring him up to date on developments. He did not cut his journey short as he had been asked to do however, but he now returned, free of the in-fighting of the last two months, and appearing as the man

---

of the Assembly recording the required two-thirds majority in favour of adopting the 1945 Constitution depended on whether the solidarity of the Muslim parties could be broken. The government had counted on NU's traditional opportunism to achieve this, but that hope gradually faded. By mid May it seemed that Muslim solidarity would be maintained.

above the crisis and the only person who could resolve it. Acting-President Sartono had broadcast to the nation two days before, calling upon it to be ready for Sukarno's return and to await the instructions he would give. The army had played its part by prescribing the slogans which the organized crowd of welcome would be permitted to use. Variations of 'Long Live Bung Karno' were supplemented by the more pointed appeal: 'The people who have suffered hardship for so long urge the President to take firm measures'.

Sukarno waited for a few days after his return to assess the possibilities of the hour for himself. On 2 July Sartono returned his powers to the President at a palace ceremony. On the following day at Bogor the President conferred with Sartono, Djuanda and other ministers, with army leaders and with his National Council aides, Roeslan and Yamin. Then he acted. At a fifteen-minute ceremony at the palace on 5 July he dissolved the Constituent Assembly and adopted by decree the Constitution of 1945.

In retrospect this clear-cut decision has an air of inevitability about it, but in fact it was not taken lightly. Over the past two years Sukarno had placed a fairly broad interpretation on his constitutional powers but he had been anxious not to overstep them in an obvious way. In July 1959 there were other possibilities open to him. He could have allowed things to drift under the old constitution, resorting perhaps to a cabinet reshuffle, but without any other major change. To follow that course might have involved the risk of an army coup. He could have called the Constituent Assembly together again and thrown his personal influence more directly into its discussions in the hope of leading it to revise its decision. He probably weighed these alternatives but he judged that a decisive presidential intervention was expected of him, and this gave him, for once, an unusual degree of freedom. By removing himself from Indonesia and leaving the Constituent Assembly to its debates, he had allowed the parties finally to discredit themselves; he could now act on his own initiative and amend the provisional constitution single-handed.

There can be little doubt that the decree was unconstitutional. Sukarno claimed to be acting on the basis of *staatsnoodrecht* – the right of compelling national emergency – but the powers of the president under the 1950 Constitution did not appear to extend to constitutional amendment on that basis. Earlier in the year Sukarno had on several occasions sought advice on his powers from the Dean of the Faculty of Law in the University of Indonesia, Professor Djokosutono, and no doubt this particular question was explored. But when it came to the point there were few who were concerned to challenge the 5 July decree on constitutional grounds. Sukarno had promised in his airport speech on 29 June that within a short time he would act in accordance with the wishes of the people and in his decree of 5 July he did just that. Even his critics, wearied by the uncertainty and disagreements of the past two months, were disposed to feel a sense of relief that, for good or ill, the constitutional question was now disposed of, and the framework for Guided Democracy was now in being.

With the July decree the goals defined by Sukarno in broad outline over two years earlier were at last achieved. How much was it his own personal achievement? Circumstances, certainly, had been favourable. In 1956 he had been able to use the widespread mood of disappointment with parliamentary democracy and in 1958 the rebellion and its repression had transformed the balance of forces and tilted the situation in his favour. Even so, he had played his own skilful part in shaping his environment. The one power which could claim to share the achievement with him was the army, which under Nasution's leadership had made Guided Democracy its own to the extent that some observers have considered that it provided the main driving force.[66] The view that the 1945 Constitution would provide a suitable framework for it was espoused by Nasution in the National Council in the course of 1958, and during the 'Open Talks' and the Constituent Assembly debates the army was an open supporter of the Sukarno plan. When the Assembly rejected the proposal it was Nasution who banned political activity and called on Sukarno to resort to action by Presidential Decree.

Even so, against that background, Sukarno's own initiative was

66. See, e.g., Lev, op. cit., pp. 59 and 175. Lev sees the army as 'the main driving force', 'the prime mover behind Guided Democracy'. Sukarno 'was as much a follower as a leader in his alliance with the army.'

crucial. He had used the army's support for his own purposes while keeping intact his freedom of action in dealing with party and government leaders. It was he who had set things moving and whose manipulative skills had kept them moving in the direction he desired. It was true that he defined his precise objectives only little by little, as the situation about him unfolded – this was part of his characteristic tendency not to look too far beyond the next step. It was true, also, that he was cautious in his probing of the possibilities open to him at any one time, seeking to convert opponents by persuasion and avoiding an open breach with them where he could. But there was a new decisiveness and persistence about him through these two years. He kept his general goal always in view, circling it when balked, approaching it from new angles, modifying inessential points to conciliate opposition, redefining his position and attacking again when the time seemed opportune. In 1956 he had called for the disappearance of parties. He dropped that point in early 1957 as he tested the resistance to it. In his *Konsepsi* he had spoken of a four-legged government including the PKI, but when, as Citizen Sukarno, he came to form the next cabinet he did not risk trying to implement the original plan. He used the West Irian question to rally support for himself and he consolidated his own position in the aftermath of the rebellion. His unpredictability and his capacity always to be one step ahead of potential rivals gave him an enormous advantage.

Sukarno had to depend, as we have seen, on his capacity to preserve a balance among the forces about him. He could find some supporters in the PNI as well as among the younger and more radical Murba party members, and as parties in general were being discredited his protection of the PKI provided, in some measure, a counterweight against army power. (His liking for the communists was not solely due to that, of course. The party also spoke the right language, and it fitted his own radical image.) However, it would be a mistake to see Sukarno's success between 1956 and 1959 as simply a balancing act or as a masterpiece of manipulation, managed simply by force of personality. In part it was that, but in part his success depended upon his tremendous stature in the eyes of his public – on his charisma, for want of a better term, which enabled him to exert an authority of his own and to establish a right to arbitrate between other forces. His charismatic authority owed something to his past role as a revolutionary leader and to his present handling of the symbols of revolution, but it also owed much to his ability to project himself to the Javanese in traditional terms. To the appeal of his Jacobin radicalism was added something of the aura which had surrounded the old Javanese rulers. Thus while the party system was facing its crisis of legitimacy, as Feith puts it, Sukarno remained a source of legitimacy in himself – a fact which the army well realized. And if Sukarno acted at times against convention or set aside the constitution unilaterally it did not hurt him. He was expected to act in that sort of way. In his secret mind Sukarno possibly shared these popular attitudes – at least to the extent of feeling that hidden forces were with him.

If the creation of Guided Democracy was in a large measure his own achievement it was one for which a price had been paid. The old consensus which had established itself during the revolution and had held together during the first years of independence had disappeared. That it had done so was partly due to the logic of circumstances, but it was also due in part to Sukarno's deliberate choice in isolating those who were not in tune with him. We have already seen his partisanship in the early years of constitutional democracy and his success in counterbalancing Masjumi. By 1958 the victory was his. Masjumi was discredited. In the negotiations with party leaders in late 1958 and early 1959 he was able to ignore it completely and in 1960 the party was banned. Despite the continuing existence of NU, Masjumi's fall represented a decisive reverse for Islam as a political force. In the Constituent Assembly the combined forces of the Muslim parties had been insufficient to carry the idea of an Islamic state and Sukarno no longer had to fear an Islamic challenge. The NU never dared to stand up against him thereafter.

There was also a more personal element in his defeat of his political opponents. In some measure the July decree constituted Sukarno's final victory over his old rivals, the dull, emotional Hatta and the 'vicious' and critical Sjahrir. He had never forgotten their ability to puncture his self-esteem as they had done in the early thirties, and his own political ideas, he felt, were always vulnerable so long as they could bring their criticism to bear on him. He remembered the way in which they had elbowed him aside during the first three months of the revolution, when, by a few decisive moves, the presidential constitution had been adapted to the use of parliamentary conventions. As we have seen Sukarno accepted these changes under the pressure of political realities, but he felt the humiliation nonetheless and a good part of his later attack on liberal democracy was an attack on the political conventions enforced on him in 1945. He remembered also how he had played second fiddle during Hatta's premiership in 1948 and even more he recalled the insults he had suffered at the hands of Sjahrir in Brastagi and Prapat.

Sukarno usually preferred to conciliate his enemies and win them over to his side, but he could be a good hater if he chose. In fact his battle with Hatta and Sjahrir had been won long before 1959. Sjahrir had not been a public figure since 1949 and Hatta had removed himself from office in 1956, since when Sukarno had managed with comparative ease to resist the popular demands for the restoration of the partnership between them. Yet his feelings still smouldered and could burst into flame at the touch of a breeze as when, on one occasion, he threw an ashtray at a minister who had proposed conferring a public honour on Sjahrir. July 1959 was thus, for Sukarno, a kind of public vindication – a sign that he had read the forces of history more accurately than they and that his view of the world was at least as valid as theirs. He had still to put his views to the test of policy formation, but the times seemed clearly to be with him.

July 1959 was his hour of victory, then. He had recovered his central position in the nation's affairs; it remained to be seen how he would use it. So far his concern had been with the machinery for ordering of the affairs of the nation and with the politics of creating it. It had not been with the substance of policy. His arguments for guided democracy were that the country needed a political system which would reflect distinctively Indonesian values and which would enable a national consensus to emerge – under guidance. But in what direction would that guidance operate? Did Sukarno know? Or did his vision stop short with the machinery which might give effect to the consensus? Some observers saw the July decree as part of a deliberately conceived leftward trend – a step on the way to Sukarno's elevation of the PKI and the fashioning of the Djakarta–Peking axis. Others saw it simply as Sukarno creating a dictatorship.

Any such judgements must wait, pending an examination of Sukarno's record as the guide in Guided Democracy.

# 12

# Great Leader of the Revolution

The July decree confirmed the change in political realities which had taken place since 1956. The parties had declined in importance over the intervening three years, together with the parliamentary system which had given them their *raison d'être*. By the end of 1958 they had lost all hope of recovering their initiative.[67] The army, strengthened by the defeat of the outer regions revolt, was determined to maintain a permanent position of influence in national affairs, and to change Indonesia's institutions to enable it to do so. Sukarno, using army power but seeking simultaneously to contain it, was working in his own way to achieve a constitutional change. Faced by this powerful combination the parties could do no more than delay the course of events and ultimately accept the new dispensation. In proclaiming the decree Sukarno was representing a new order of power. That new order was, and continued to be, based on a balance of forces, but with Sukarno as the fulcrum on which others turned. He set the tone. He gave Guided Democracy the impress of his own personality. He was the dominating figure, the source of authority and of ideological leadership and the centre of a glittering court.

As his own Prime Minister under the new constitutional dispensation Sukarno's first task was to form a new government. On 6 July the Djuanda government returned its mandate and the President quickly brought together a new team of ministers. Though formally this was Sukarno's cabinet, responsible to him as chief executive under the constitution, Djuanda, now with the title of 'First Minister', in fact continued to perform essentially the same role as he had done hitherto as Prime Minister. The

67. In 1958 they could have lent their support to Djuanda's efforts to secure reform through parliament and the Constituent Assembly without destroying the parliamentary system entirely. In fact, as Lev points out (*The Transition to Guided Democracy; Indonesian Politics, 1957–1959*, Ithaca, 1966, p. 288), 'each party was not so much defending the political system which sustained it as trying to protect its own position in whatever system happened to emerge'.

*Kerdja* cabinet (Work Cabinet) as it was called was arranged in two tiers. There were, in addition to Sukarno and Djuanda, nine senior ministers and twenty-four junior ministers. The former held the major portfolios – Security and Defence, Finance, Foreign Affairs, Home Affairs, etc., and they also co-ordinated the work of the junior ministers who operated in a wide variety of lesser fields such as Information, Veteran Affairs, Agriculture, Public Works, Transmigration, Communications and Health. Finally the three Chiefs of Staff, the Chief of Police and the Chief Prosecutor were appointed *ex officio* ministers.

Members of the cabinet were expected to renounce party affiliation on their appointment. In fact, though a number of ministers had belonged to one or other of the parties, none of the major party leaders was included and the cabinet was able to regard itself as non-party with some justice. Its composition was yet one more indication of the loss of ground which the parties had suffered.

The '45 Constitution provided for two principal deliberative bodies in addition to parliament, a People's Deliberative Assembly (Madjelis Permusjawaratan Rakjat – MPR) and a Supreme Advisory Council (Dewan Pertimbangan Agung – DPA). The former was intended to be the repository of popular sovereignty and was to be a large body. (The provisional People's Deliberative Assembly – MPRS – formed in 1960, comprised 616 members.) Its functions were to choose the president and the vice-president and to determine the main lines of state policy. The latter function, however, was to be conducted at a somewhat rarefied level, for the constitution required only one meeting of the MPR every five years. It might in fact meet more frequently but it was obviously not intended under the terms of the constitution to exercise any very close supervision over the nation's affairs. The more compact Supreme Advisory Council was likely to be more important for practical purposes. Meeting frequently it was intended to provide for the president an alternative source of advice to that available from his cabinet. To these two bodies, provided for in the constitution, Sukarno added others for *ad hoc* purposes. The most important was the National Planning Council whose task was to prepare the blueprint for Indonesia's economic development under Guided Democracy.

This complex cluster of councils was intended to provide an appropriate framework for the deliberation which, under Guided Democracy's rationale, was intended to secure a national consensus. At the centre of the system was Sukarno. Pending the adoption of electoral laws to provide for the election of members to the MPR and to parliament, those bodies were filled by presidential appointment, as was the DPA. Though he was constitutionally responsible to the MPRS, its control over him would obviously be of the slenderest, at least until elections were held.

Having formed the *Kerdja* cabinet Sukarno moved gradually to the completion of this institutional structure. The DPA was quickly formed. It contained forty-three members who, apart from Sukarno as chairman and Roeslan Abdulgani as vice-chairman, were selected on the basis of three criteria. Leaders of the ten major parties, having been left out of the cabinet, were given twelve of the seats in the DPA. Representatives of the regions (a total of eight) formed the second group. The remaining twenty-three members were representative of functional groups. The members of the National Planning Council, to serve under the chairmanship of Yamin, were also chosen within a month. Over a year was to elapse, however, before the 616 representatives (of whom half were the members of the provisional parliament) were appointed to a provisional MPR. For the time being the elected parliament was allowed to remain in being – though very much on a bond of good behaviour. Early in 1960, in an unexpected show of independence, it rejected the government's budget. Sukarno immediately dissolved it and enacted the budget by decree. (Presidential action of that kind, once carried off with success, was habit-forming, and Sukarno resorted with increasing frequency to the use of decrees to deal with matters which formerly would have required legislation.) He replaced the old parliament by a nominated body – a *gotong royong* parliament, as he called it – which was to sit until new elections were held on the basis of a new electoral law. (In fact elections were not held in Sukarno's lifetime.) There had already been broad agreement about the distribution of party and functional group representatives in a future parliament, and in nominating the members of his *gotong royong* parliament Sukarno followed the outlines of that agreement. He appointed 130 party representatives (the principal parties being PNI: 44, NU: 36, and PKI: 30). The remaining 153 members were functional group representatives, with 15 seats going to the army, 7 each to the navy and the air force, 5 to the police and the rest to workers, peasants, Islamic authorities, youth, women and the intelligentsia.

Here was functional representation with a vengeance. Though the deliberative bodies were as yet appointed rather than elected Sukarno seemed, with the establishment of the DPA, the *gotong royong* parliament and the MPRS, to have constructed the kind of machinery he had desired. Bodies composed in this way, he had argued, could deliberate in an Indonesian fashion and reach a consensus which, because of the manner of its formation, would command enormous authority.

Finally, in addition to the deliberative bodies, constitutional and *ad hoc*, a new National Front was created to replace the existing army-dominated 'National Front for the Liberation of West Irian'. The National Front revived Sukarno's long-standing idea of a mass organization which could mobilize and canalize the will of the nation. Though parties were not abolished it was his hope that the National Front organization would give him a direct line of access to the population at large and enable him to bypass the political parties.

In this way, in a little over a year, Sukarno had transformed Indonesia's political institutions. Did the transformation make possible the new political life that he had promised?

In examining the performance of Guided Democracy as distinct from its institutions one feature becomes quickly apparent. Though Sukarno's had been the initiating hand in building the machinery of deliberation and control, he was still reluctant to accept detailed responsibility for government. That attitude was to be expected. Even during his attack on the party system and his call for a distinctively Indonesian solution to Indonesian problems he had not envisaged taking executive responsibility upon himself. What he would really have liked, if he could have had it, would have been a position in which he could exert his leadership without having to bother himself with day-to-day administration

– a position, in effect, of power without responsibility. In 1958 he had been slow to endorse Nasution's idea of a return to the '45 Constitution, and only when it seemed that alternative methods of extending functional representation into parliament and other bodies were likely to fail did he come to accept this solution as the best way of ending the evils of party government. Having decreed the constitution into being he still wanted to avoid being the sort of executive president which the constitution appeared to prescribe. His appointment of Djuanda as First Minister was a sign of his approach, for Djuanda was left to supervise the operations of ministers while Sukarno continued to act as the formal head of state – though now with the important difference that he had the right to interfere when he chose.

This division of labour was partly the result of the structure of Guided Democracy itself which quite specifically attempted to play up leadership and deliberation and to play down the hard, responsible, and often unpopular task of governing. It was partly the result of Indonesia's diffusion of power which made it, in any case, very difficult for anybody to be an effective chief executive. But it was also partly the result of Sukarno's own style which leant towards show and the handling of national symbols rather than towards dealing with the concrete details of administration. He evoked a sense of movement and euphoria in the nation, if not a clear conception of practical purpose. He called for the perfection of Indonesian independence through the recovery of West Irian; he pointed to the necessity for continuing revolution, to the ultimate goal of a just and prosperous society and to the need to stand firm against the besetting dangers of neo-colonialism. He conveyed the feeling that Indonesia was an important nation, great in international stature and recovering a sense of identity in the glory of its past civilizations.

This approach to government was embodied in the titles which he took for himself or allowed the MPRS to shower on him: 'President for Life', 'Mandatory of the MPRS', 'Great Leader of the Revolution', 'Bearer of the Message of the People's Suffering'. As his own Prime Minister Sukarno saw his task as that of defining broad goals while others were responsible for achieving them, and indeed there was some acceptance of that role within the political élite. 'Now that he has given us a sense of our general direction it is up to us to work out what he means,' was a common attitude which almost assumed that Sukarno's utterances were inspired – and perhaps not even understood by him – so that an understanding of them had to be patiently searched for. Sukarno was certainly not unwilling to portray himself as merely a vehicle by which messages from a higher source were conveyed. *Pantja Sila* was not his own creation, he once said. 'I only *dug it up* from the soil of our Motherland, Ibu Pratiwi. The Political Manifesto was born from the womb of Mother History.'[68] He was not in the least modest in speaking of his role as the source of national inspiration. What other leader could get away with such an easy assumption of authority as Sukarno when he solemnly said to his audience on 17 August 1962:

'I know that on this present 17 August you are all looking to me. And because I know that, I feel somewhat troubled because I am conscious of the size of the responsibility I hold. I know that on this present day, this out-of-the-ordinary day, in your hearts it is as though you were taxing me with questions: "What does Bung Karno want to say?" "What is the President going to enjoin upon us?" "What will the Great Leader counsel?"'

But though Sukarno tried not to be a chief executive he was at the centre of political life and he could not, in the end, avoid responsibility for what happened. With the increase in deliberative bodies the cabinet was reduced in importance, and gradual changes in the structure of the cabinet itself had the effect of weakening its corporate character and making individual ministers much more dependent upon their separate relationships with the President. The first cabinet under Guided Democracy, with its two-tiered structure, was the forerunner of a more elaborate organization whereby portfolios were grouped under eight 'Deputy First Ministers' (Wakil Menteri Pertama – WAMPA). The extension of this principle and the proliferation of portfolios until the cabinet ultimately came to consist of seventy-seven members in 1964 was a further indication of its growing ineffectiveness as a deliberative and decision-making body, responsible for the conduct of the nation's affairs. Parliament no longer constituted a

68. 'A Year of Living Dangerously', 17 August Speech, 1964.

check on executive action, the DPA was merely an advisory body and the handpicked MPRS was completely submissive. The application of the functional representation principle to these bodies, of course, enabled Sukarno in any case to select his own supporters. Under Guided Democracy in fact there were no effective formal limits to restrict the arbitrary exercise of power by the President.

It was this kind of central position, acquired after Sukarno's three-year-long attack on political parties, on the selfishness of politicians and on the parliamentary system as a whole, which led many observers to see in Guided Democracy an example of personal dictatorship. The dubious legality of the July decree showed a lack of concern with constitutional procedures and now within the framework of the political machinery carefully established by himself, and with a hand-picked parliament and MPRS, Sukarno seemed to have acquired almost absolute power. As time passed there were many signs of the increasingly authoritarian character of his régime: the sense of orthodoxy which accompanied his elaboration of the ideological props of Guided Democracy, the banning of the main opposition parties Masjumi and PSI, the 'simplification' of the remainder bringing the total of parties down to ten, the 're-tooling' of the civil service ('retooling' was the process by which civil servants of doubtful loyalty were replaced by others who were sympathetic to the régime), the placing of some critics under house arrest, the adoption of indoctrination courses at universities, the removal of university staff who were regarded as opponents of the régime[69] and the control of the Press. At the airport on his return from Tokyo in July 1959 Sukarno had insisted that he did not want to become a dictator. He had said the same thing on 17 October 1952, and again in his speech to teachers on 30 October 1956, when he had urged the dissolution of the parties. But by the early sixties some observers insisted that had become one.

Such judgements were misplaced. Sukarno was not a dictator in any accepted sense. First of all, one must take seriously the rationale of his drive to guided democracy. In seeking to replace

69. Professor Mochtar Kusumaatmadja of Padjadjaran University and H. B. Jassin of the University of Indonesia were among such casualties.

Western liberal democracy, based on majority rule, by what he regarded as the distinctively Indonesian method of deliberation and consensus, Sukarno meant what he said. The idea of government through wide consultation rather than through coercion was an integral part of his thinking, and the array of deliberative bodies that he erected was intended to be much more than a mere facade. Secondly, it must be noticed that, in spite of the ideological controls, the Press censorship, the 're-tooling' of the civil service and the many other measures designed to suppress opposition and to induce conformity, Sukarno's régime was not a harshly coercive one. House arrest was not uncommon but the imprisonment of political opponents was the exception rather than the rule, and there was no attempt to secure conformity by the brutal elimination of opposition. Sukarno's Indonesia had no concentration camps. Finally, a hard practical barrier stood between Sukarno and absolute authority. A dictatorship implies a tremendous concentration of power. In Indonesia power was widely diffused, even to the point of frustrating proper authority.

Indonesia's problem was not that an authoritarian régime had emerged but rather that the new régime, like the old one, was unable to mobilize the power that was needed if government was to be effective and if the gigantic problems of the economy were to be tackled seriously. The regions, the parties (even in their weakened condition), Islam organized in various ways, the army and the other services, the bureaucracy – each had its own effective weight to use in the political arena. Not only did Sukarno's political thinking stress the importance of conciliation – even had he wanted to be a dictator the facts required him to share power. He could not eliminate rival forces and was compelled to operate within and through them. The balance of forces surrounding Sukarno did not remain stable; but the fact of a balance of some kind was permanent. Paradoxically his own freedom of action was, at one and the same time, dependent upon that fact and limited by it.

The main elements in the balance were the army and the P K I. In 1959, as we have seen, the President and the army were the dominating partners in the political scene. In succeeding years the communist party – the one party to have emerged with increased strength from the events of 1957, 1958 and 1959 – became the army's most important single competitor. Under the effective nine-year-old leadership of Aidit, Lukman and Njoto, the party had achieved a remarkable growth and, by 1963, its membership was in the region of two and a half million. Beyond its actual member-ship it asserted its influence through a network of subsidiary orga-nizations and the fronts which it controlled. Through its peasant union (Barisan Tani Indonesia – BTI), its women's organization (Gerwani), SOBSI, the trade union federation under its control, its 'League of People's Culture' (LEKRA) and other groups it had an extensive and efficient network of organizational links with different sections of the population. In 1955 and 1957 the party had demonstrated its electoral appeal in rural Java, to the alarm of the other parties. Now that electoral contests had been set aside for the time being, the PKI had adapted itself to the new situation. While other parties floundered and retreated in the face of Sukarno's action to curb their powers the PKI had developed alternative means of preserving its influence. It did so to a great extent under his personal protection.

The President, the army and the PKI were thus, by 1960, the dominant forces in the political constellation and the history of Guided Democracy is in great measure the history of a shifting balance between the three.

The story of Sukarno's relations with the army and the PKI is central to an understanding not only of Guided Democracy but of the whole purpose and character of Sukarno's leadership during the closing years of his political career.

Earlier in the present study it was suggested, as a preliminary judgement, that there were three principal periods of political creativity in Sukarno's career. The first of these fell in the late twenties when, as the maker and the leader of the PNI, Sukarno gave a new direction to Indonesian nationalism. Again, during the Japanese occupation, whatever one's judgement upon the morality of his collaboration may be, he established himself as *the* national leader of Indonesia. Finally, between 1956 and 1959 he was the maker of Guided Democracy. He was not the unaided maker, it is true, but the skill with which he worked within the existing political environment justifies the view of him as the prime-mover in changing the nature of Indonesian government and politics.

These three periods stand out from other parts of his career. The years before 1926 were years of preparation – we have seen that he was a late starter as a nationalist leader. The thirties saw him in exile. During the revolution others took the control of events from his hands. His stature remained great and his support was vital at periods of crisis during those years, but he did not 'make' the revolution. The early years of independence saw him restive, but confined within the bounds of the parliamentary system. Only in 1957 did he break through them.

But what of the years after 1959? Though he was not a dictator they were the years of his greatest formal power. Were they not also creative years? What criteria would be relevant to a judgement on this question? The nature of his policy, certainly; if he contributed to the maintenance of political stability and to economic recovery he would certainly appear to have been a creative leader. To anticipate a conclusion on these points, it will be argued that he did preserve a remarkable degree of stability in what might be judged an inherently unstable situation. For this he gets high marks. But against that must be set his catastrophic failure to come to grips with economic problems. It is proposed, however, to suggest a different framework for the consideration of this question than would be contained in a balance sheet of his administrative achievements and failures. The real question to be asked is: What were his ultimate intentions during those years? What, if anything, was he working towards? Was he simply using the PKI as a factor in the immediate political situation, an ally in his relations with the army? Or did his plans go further than that and include a long-term goal? Was he, in brief, pushing Indonesia on a new leftward course? If so one could attempt to assess the skill with which he pursued such a policy.

From the beginning of Guided Democracy there was no doubt of the warmth of Sukarno's feelings for the PKI, and the expansion of its power and prestige thereafter was to a considerable extent promoted by him. In the face of army hostility to the party he readily assumed the role of its protector. In September 1959 the army attempted to prevent the PKI from holding its annual congress. Sukarno reversed the decision and gave a public demonstration of his attitude by attending the congress and giving an address. In March 1960, when selecting the new *gotong royong* parliament, he safeguarded the PKI's position, giving it thirty seats as against the PNI's forty-four and NU's thirty-six; he also gave it additional representation in the lists of functional representatives.[70] And, as will be seen, he was able in more concrete ways to contain the anti-communist proclivities of the army leaders. How are these actions to be interpreted?

During the period of Guided Democracy there were several schools of thought concerning the nature of Sukarno's protection of the PKI. In 1963 Arnold Brackman surveyed the advance of communist power with misgiving, and noted the party's own conviction that it was riding the crest of the future.[71] However, in Brackman's view Sukarno had 'no intention of putting the PKI into power', and he felt that, if Sukarno were to pass from the scene the odds on the whole were that the power of the army rather than that of the PKI was 'likely to flow into the void'.[72] Two years later, writing also with very great caution, van der Kroef was a little more pessimistic. He examined the way in which the PKI had skilfully adapted itself to its environment and considered that, more than any other force, it could capitalize on 'the popular Indonesian mystique that the present era is one of tribulation, but that a glorious future lies ahead'. Despite the party's occasional setbacks he considered that 'the long, but generally steadily ascending curve' gave a more accurate picture of the party's development, and he concluded that its 'charismatic and volitional omnipotence' might well lift it into a position of dominance in the future.[73]

By a somewhat different route Herbert Feith reached much the same conclusion. He depicted the Sukarno–army–PKI balance as a triangle of forces, gradually changing in shape. At first Sukarno

70. J. M. van der Kroef, *The Communist Party of Indonesia*, Vancouver, 1965, p. 115.

71. Brackman, *Indonesian Communism*, New York, 1963.

72. ibid., p. 303.

73. Van der Kroef, op. cit., p. 304.

and the army were the main elements, more or less equal to each other. Then Sukarno, by his manipulative skill, using on the one hand the PKI's need for protection and on the other the army's hesitancy and its uncertainty of purpose, was able to secure a central and pre-eminent position, holding the other two forces in balance, as it were, beneath him. Then the triangle again changed shape with the army corner slipping down and the PKI's rising closer to the level of the Sukarno apex.[74] While pointing out that after Sukarno had left the scene the army would treat the PKI as an enemy, Feith did not rule out the possibility of the PKI coming to power, and it was a question in his mind whether this did not represent the President's actual intention. Feith thought it possible that Sukarno at least might be attempting deliberately to move Indonesia to a position analogous to that of Cuba, with the PKI dominating the scene and with Indonesia heavily dependent on the support of the communist powers. Seeing the PKI as the one truly revolutionary and also efficiently mobilized force, was Sukarno intending to make it his heir?

Against these views was that of Donald Hindley who believed that the rise of the PKI was apparent rather than real. It had grown in prestige, admittedly, but its price for that improvement in its position was that it should bind itself to Sukarno and to his revolutionary ideology. Its own ideological purity and its moral fibre suffered in consequence. Its apparent rise in national status had not in fact brought it any nearer to the threshold of power – it had, like the army, been contained. Sukarno's policy towards the PKI had been an exercise in the 'politics of domestication'.[75]

Even with the advantage of hindsight it is not easy to resolve this conflict of observers' judgements. In the outcome Brackman was right. A break in the continuity of events did allow the army ultimately to fill the void. But was his judgement based on a

74. Herbert Feith, 'President Sukarno, the Army and the Communists: The Triangle Changes Shape', *Asian Survey*, IV, 8, August 1964. See also Ewa T. Pauker, 'Has the Sukarno Regime Weakened the PKI?', *Asian Survey*, IV, 9, September 1964. Mrs Pauker gave a decided negative to her own question.

75. Donald Hindley, 'President Sukarno and the Communists: the Politics of Domestication', *American Political Science Review*, LVI, 4, December 1962.

correct reading of the situation in 1963? And what did Sukarno really intend during those years?

The evidence is not conclusive, but a survey of it will help to clarify the possibilities. Certainly an impressive list of Presidential actions can be advanced in support of the view that Sukarno was deliberately concerned to improve the position of the PKI in the political constellation of Indonesia. Shortly after he had given a sign of his favour by cancelling the ban on the 1959 congress, and by lending his own presence to the occasion, he found it necessary to protect the party from a much more serious threat. After the dissolution of parliament in 1960 an anti-communist reaction began to assert itself. A group of people drawn from the ranks of Masjumi, PSI, NU, IPKI ('League for the Upholding of Indonesian Independence' – a small party with strong military connections) and other anti-communist parties, set up the 'Democratic League' (Liga Demokrasi) ostensibly to protest against the dissolution of parliament and to demand the preservation of the parliamentary system. The League secured the unofficial support of some of the army's regional commanders and, though Nasution was not prepared to go along with them, neither did he, for the time being, act against the new movement. Sukarno at the time was absent on an overseas journey. (From now on these were to be annual events. They enabled Sukarno, through his contacts with other national leaders, to build up his position as an international figure. They also enabled him to indulge his taste for uninhibited relaxation.) On his return he indicated his firm opposition to the League and in due course he banned it.

In July and August of the same year a further series of manoeuvres revealed very clearly the complexity of the political situation with which Sukarno had to deal, the nature of the limits placed on him, and the way in which he worked within those limits to protect the communist party's position. On 8 July, the PKI paper, *Harian Rakjat* ('People's Daily') carried an extensive criticism of the government's record over the past year. The article praised Sukarno, but Djuanda, other ministers and the army were the subjects of hostile comment. The army reacted sharply. The Djakarta Military Commander suspended the paper and summoned the members of the politburo, including Aidit himself, for questioning. Shortly afterwards the Military Commanders of South Sumatra, South Kalimantan and South Sulawesi banned all PKI activity in their respective commands.

Sukarno sought to reverse these moves but his success was limited. The ban on *Harian Rakjat* was lifted in early August, but the President was not able to secure a complete reversal of the anti-communist moves in Sumatra, Kalimantan and Sulawesi. He summoned the three commanders to Djakarta for consultation and, as a compromise solution, they imposed a temporary ban on all political acitivities and not simply on those of the PKI. At the end of the year the ban was lifted, but the three commanders continued to keep a close check on PKI moves. During this tussle Sukarno, though he could not bring the recalcitrant Military Commanders completely to heel, continued to extend marks of his own favour to the communists. On 25 July, in an address to the annual congress of the PNI, he launched an attack on political leaders who suffered from 'communist phobia'.[76] In August he appointed Aidit and Njoto to the executive of the National Front and in September he named Aidit as a member of the delegation which was to accompany him to the United Nations.[77] At the end of the year he began to canvass the possibility of bringing the communists into a NASAKOM cabinet – a cabinet which, he claimed, would represent the main streams of the Indonesian revolution: *Nasionalisme*, *Agama* (religion), *Komunisme*.

These incidents gave an illuminating illustration of the way Indonesia's political balance was maintained. Sukarno and the army each had their distinct areas of initiative within which they were not easily coerced. But even within those areas their powers were not unlimited; each side had to move warily, and might feel it prudent to give way a little in the face of pressure. But of course for Sukarno the mere existence of the PKI was an important element in his maintaining his independence in the face of army pressure.

During the course of the next two or three years the balance continued to oscillate, though with signs that the army's leverage against the PKI was weakening and that the PKI was, in consequence, gradually improving its position. In March 1962 Sukarno

76. Van der Kroef, op. cit., p. 237.      77. ibid., p. 239.

included Aidit and Lukman in the State Leadership Consultative Body – which carried something equivalent to cabinet status, but without executive responsibility. The party was successful in its campaigns to remove anti-communist regional officials as part of the 're-tooling' process. Sukarno's pro-PKI moves were accompanied by other actions designed to weaken the position of preponderant anti-communist elements within the army leadership – in July 1962 Nasution was 'promoted' from the position of Army Chief of Staff to the new position of Chief of Staff of the Armed Forces, and was replaced as army leader by General Yani whom Sukarno considered more pliable. Nasution retained the defence portfolio in the government, but Sukarno's intention was clearly to remove him from his main base of strength as army commander. Yani, of course, was no pro-communist; his attitude to the party was little different from that of Nasution, and army agreement on this central question was far more important than the divisions and rivalries within military ranks. Nonetheless the divisions were important enough to give Sukarno an opportunity to play upon them as he did in July 1962.

As well as fostering intra-army divisions, the President also attempted to promote inter-service rivalry. He found elements of support in the air force in particular, and was able to play on the vanity of Air Vice-Marshal Omar Dhani, whose support gave him an additional element of leverage against the army. Sukarno also used the re-structuring of command arrangements to strengthen his own influence. In 1959 a Supreme War Authority (Penguasa Perang Tertinggi – PEPERTI) had been set up under the President, and regional Military Commanders, hitherto directly responsible to the army Chief of Staff, were now formally responsible to him. In 1962 a Supreme Command for the Liberation of West Irian (KOTI) was again headed by Sukarno. It contained representatives of the three services and the police, and it thus represented a weakening of the army's special position. In the same year Sukarno successfully frustrated service plans for the formation of an integrated command of the armed services as a whole – an achievement which he was able to bring about once again by playing on inter-service rivalry. The decision that martial law would be lifted in May 1963 was also designed to cut back the routine administrative responsibilities which the army had acquired.

Throughout these years Sukarno's alliance with the army remained a fundamental fact of political life, but clearly its place in the balance of forces had been altered in important respects by 1963. How was it that Sukarno was able to act so consistently against the army's wishes? A number of factors help to explain his remarkable success in preserving his independence. First of all there was his own quickness and his ability to take his main rival by surprise. If Sukarno had once seemed indecisive in the face of great events he was no longer so – or at least he was decisive in the use of the day-to-day devices of political manoeuvre. His promotion of Nasution, for example, or his use of the proposals for a NASAKOM cabinet, were examples of his capacity to be a step ahead.

Secondly the army's own lack of certainty about its purposes was important. It had acquired considerable power after 1958 but with no clear idea of how to use it. It was therefore easily outmanoeuvred by the President when he knew exactly what he wanted. It was not so cohesive a force as it had been. Rivalries and differences of interest had developed within it and Sukarno could use them to his own advantage. Moreover in becoming involved in the tasks of routine administration the army had lost a good deal of its reforming thrust and its reputation for incorruptibility. Like the civilian politicians whom they had condemned, many army officers had laid themselves open to charges of corruption. As an additional factor there was the essential weakness of Nasution – or was it his essential loyalty to Sukarno? Again and again he seemed reluctant to confront the President, until at last he had lost the power to do so. He held himself aloof from the Liga Demokrasi movement, though some of his regional commanders supported it; he accepted his promotion meekly in 1962; he accepted the creation of KOTI and his subsequent removal from it. Whether his submissiveness was due to loyalty or to weakness, he was certainly not the man to lead the army into an anti-communist crusade once it was clear that to oppose the PKI was to challenge Sukarno himself.[78]

78. In view of his subsequent comparative eclipse it is worth stressing the

The evidence for the view that Sukarno had set a leftward course under Guided Democracy would thus seem to be impressive. But what was the general outcome of this seemingly pro-PKI, anti-army policy of the President? And what was his motive? Was Sukarno really advancing the PKI or was he simply protecting it and, from time to time, acting to redress a balance which had become tilted against the party? The army, after all, possessed armed strength, and in that sense it was always more powerful than its political rival, whatever Sukarno might do to contain it. It was notable, too, that though Sukarno continued from 1960 onwards to talk of the desirability of a NASAKOM government and was frequently believed to be on the point of re-shuffling the cabinet to bring it about, he never did. Was it that he wanted to do so but felt insufficiently confident of getting away with it? Or was it that he wanted to keep open the possibility of a NASAKOM cabinet – but no more than the possibility?

It is at least arguable that Sukarno's aim was to bring the PKI to a position of greater prestige, but not to bring it very much nearer to actual power. For the party that last step was always to remain so great that its other gradual advances over the years of Guided Democracy were unimportant by comparison; instead of reaching power it was being incorporated in the régime, ideologically caged-in, made to support Sukarno in return for his protection and being tamed in the process. The party itself by 1963 was becoming afraid that its increasing numbers and its

---

importance of Nasution and of the personal relationship which had existed between him and Sukarno since 1957. A professional soldier, KNIL trained, restrained in political action, a devout Muslim, a Batak, Nasution perhaps played down any chance of seizing power that he might have possessed. He was politically skilled within certain limits – witness his restoration of army unity, his part in formulating a political role for the army in Indonesian government and his share in the campaign for Guided Democracy. Outside observers continued for years to regard him as an inevitable candidate for the presidency if an open struggle for power should ever develop in Indonesia. But either his personal ambition was limited, or he lacked the will and the ruthlessness to play the part for which many had cast him. He was a secretive man, careful to conceal his emotions and hard for his colleagues to judge. He was given many opportunities of advancing himself personally but by the middle of 1966 it was clear that history had passed him by.

increasing respectability were being accompanied by a loss of discipline, moral fibre and revolutionary *élan*.

It is difficult to be positive about these trends. By 1963 the PKI appeared stronger than before, certainly, and the army less strong or at least less unambiguously under the control of a cohesive anti-communist leadership. By this time the whole question of the domestic political balance had become entangled with issues of foreign policy. The West Irian question, resolved at last in 1962, had been followed by the confrontation with Malaysia. It will be convenient to suspend our judgement on the intentions of Sukarno's policy towards the PKI until these aspects have been examined – and also until attention has been given to the character of Sukarno's ideology during this period.

Against this background of domestic rivalry the content of Sukarno's economic and social policy after 1959 must be examined. Here there is no need for suspended judgement: Sukarno may have been the supreme artist in balancing opposing forces and in maintaining his own central position, but the record shows that he had little grasp of the hard economic problems facing the nation and little capacity for seeking the kind of advice that might have enabled his government to come to grips with them. The point needs to be made, of course, with a full appreciation of his purposes. It would be vain to condemn Sukarno for failing to follow what Western economists, operating within a given economic structure, would regard as 'sound' economic policies, for he had political objects to pursue.[79] The seizure of Dutch property in December 1957, for example, was for him, and for many other Indonesians, a necessary piece of surgery to end Indonesia's dependence on Holland. His careless attitude to foreign aid in 1964 was associated with his insistence that Indonesia's self-respect required her to stand on her own feet. His subordination

79. Cf. Samuel P. Huntington, *Political Order in Changing Societies*, New Haven, 1968, p. 309, which criticizes the conservative assumption that economic collapse produced by revolution is a sign of the failure of the revolution. He cites Trotsky that these are 'the overhead expenses of historic progress', and adds that economic deprivation may often be essential to the success of the revolution.

of economic development to the dictates of recovering West Irian was a matter of national pride, as was his public expenditure. ‘I consider money for material symbols well spent,’ he said to Cindy Adams. ‘I must make Indonesians proud of themselves. They have cringed too long.’[80]

In brief, Sukarno dealt all kinds of blows at the economy by doing just those things which a revolutionary might be expected to do. His fault was not that he had these priorities but that, in pursuing them, he did not take sufficient precautions to minimize their effect on the economy, nor did he recognize the way in which the economic situation as a whole might get out of hand. The expropriation of Dutch estates, for example, might have been an economically viable policy had Indonesia possessed adequate bureaucratic and management skills to handle the task of running them. (The case of Nasser's seizure of the Suez Canal makes an instructive contrast.) In fact, however, Sukarno ignored or failed to understand the dangers of some of his actions, and the economic story of Guided Democracy is one of increasing government helplessness in the face of declining exports and accelerating inflation. For this Sukarno must bear a full share of responsibility.

In August 1959, a month after the July Decree, Sukarno dramatically introduced a drastic confiscatory reform of the currency. Rp 500 and Rp 1,000 notes were reduced to one-tenth of their face value. Bank deposits of over Rp 25,000 were ‘frozen’ at ten per cent of their value, and the exchange rate of the Rupiah was simultaneously cut to almost a quarter of the earlier official rate. This action merely purchased time, and it was not long before deficit budgeting and falling exports had once more produced runaway inflation. Between the end of 1960 and the end of 1962 the increase in money in circulation from Rp 47·8 billion to Rp 135·3 billion was reflected in steeply rising prices.[81]

In August 1960 the National Planning Council had announced Indonesia's Eight-Year Plan for economic development. It called for a huge investment programme, but beyond indicating that much of the funds for investment were expected to come from

80. *Autobiography*, p. 293.
81. See J. A. C. Mackie, *Problems of the Indonesian Inflation*, Ithaca, 1967, for a discussion of the inflation problem.

external sources it contained no clear indication of how the plan was to be financed.

In a number of ways the government's policy was calculated to weaken the private sector of the economy and to contribute to the growth of a new bureaucratic capitalism. The seizure of Dutch property in December 1957 had started this process with disastrous results, both immediate and long term. Subsequent foreign exchange controls, the encouragement of state trading firms and the monetary 'reform' of 1959 contributed to the trend. So did the attempts to curtail Chinese dominance of retail trade in rural areas, though the notorious Government Regulation 10 of 1959 which was designed to achieve the curtailment, was not adopted at the instance of Sukarno. On the contrary, it reflected the wishes of the army and of certain sectors of Indonesian business which were, in general, opposed to the whole Sukarno régime.

Sukarno never lent his authority to that kind of discrimination. It should, indeed, be emphasized very strongly that, in a society in which anti-Chinese feeling ran so high, he consistently maintained that Chinese who had committed themselves to Indonesia must be accepted as a part of that Indonesian unity to the creation of which so much of his exhortation was directed. 'It is of primary importance to wipe out all traces of racialism,' he said in his 17 August speech of 1964, with obvious reference to the problem of anti-Chinese feeling. He sought to put the Chinese problem into the more general context of national unity: 'You all know that what I am always dreaming of is a harmony of *Pantja Sila*-ist Manipolists among all the *suku*, the peoples of the nation. . . .'[82] Harmony among all the *suku*, including the peoples of mixed descent or of foreign descent, whether Arab, European, Chinese, Indian, Pakistani or Jewish. . . . It is, for example, impossible for us . . . to eliminate the "jaw of the Batak" or "the Chinese slanting eye" or "the large nose of the Arab" and so on. Indeed this is not the problem! The problem is: how to cultivate harmony, to cultivate unity, to build the Indonesian *Nation* amongst all and of all.' But on this aspect of economic regulation others were too strong for him.

82. Manipol – the Political Manifesto – was the name given to the 17 August speech of 1959.

As government attempts to regulate the economy increased so did corruption. The bureaucracy was ill-equipped to operate control mechanisms and this, together with rising living costs and absurdly low civil service salaries, helped to make bribery, the illegal disposal of government goods and other rackets a part of Indonesia's economic way of life.

Sukarno's lack of understanding of economic questions was monumental. 'They tell me there is a problem of inflation in Indonesia,' he once remarked to an astonished foreign diplomat. 'Do you think that is true?' In his 17 August speech of 1962, Sukarno referred to 'some people who say: "Bung Karno is clever at making political speeches, but he completely ignores economic questions"'. He went on: 'I know about such criticisms. But I say to you: "The strategy of my leadership has already taken into account the implications of such criticisms!"' Comforting, perhaps, to his listeners, but not very informative about his economic plans. His strategy, he said, was to give priority to the restoration of internal security, the consolidation of that security and the recovery of West Irian, rather than to economic questions. A year later he defended his policies in terms of his revolutionary goals. 'I am not an economist. . . . I am a revolutionary. . . . My feelings and ideas about the economic question are simple, very simple indeed. They can be formulated as follows: If nations who live in a dry and barren desert can solve the problems of their economy, why can't we?'

At only one point – in 1963 – did the government seem prepared to take realistic economic advice. In March a speech by Sukarno, to be known as the Economic Declaration (DEKON), seemed to indicate a concern for the economic situation, though unfortunately in no very clear terms. He reiterated well-worn themes and gave little by way of specific recommendation. The task at the present first stage of the revolution, said Sukarno, was to complete the eradication of imperialist and feudal remnants in the economy and to mobilize the national potential in order to create a national economy leading to a socialist Indonesian economy. Leadership, he said, must continue to be in government hands, though foreign interests would be welcome in production-sharing agreements. (He showed no recognition of the fact that production-sharing, in which foreign credit would be used but with ownership remaining in Indonesian hands, might not be popular with foreign investors.) The provision of food and clothing would remain the highest priority for the moment.

But how was all this to be achieved? Sukarno's recommendations were so vague as to be meaningless: improvement in the organization and management of State enterprises, the making of changes 'where necessary' in regulations, the improvement of financial institutions, the perfecting of the labour force by improvement of skills. However, DEKON was followed on 26 May by a set of regulations which in some measure reflected the influence on government thinking of the International Monetary Fund and an associated consortium of Development Aid Committee countries. The 26 May regulations represented an 'economist's' approach to Indonesia's economic problems. They envisaged devaluation, the raising of prices, the search for price stability and the freeing of the economy from some of its bureaucratic controls. Perhaps they were seriously intended to effect a reversal of past policy, but the death of Djuanda shortly afterwards removed their main sponsor, and with the adoption of the policy of confrontation with Malaysia this particular attempt at reform was doomed.

Economic decline was accompanied by an increase in the flamboyancy of the régime, and the two were not unconnected. Economic hardship made the development of political controls to preserve stability more urgent, and Sukarno paradoxically attempted to maintain political stability in part through his expressive and agitational style of politics. He insisted on the importance of continuing ferment, of carrying the revolution forward, of shaking established institutions and of preparing resistance to abstract enemies. Slogans tended to replace considered programmes of action. The ideological basis of the régime was expressed in Manipol/USDEK. 'USDEK' was an acronym made from the initials of the 1945 Constitution (Undang-Undang Dasar '45), Sosialisme à la Indonesia, Guided Democracy (*Demokrasi Terpimpin*), 'Guided Economy' (*Ekonomi Terpimpin*) and the 'Indonesian Identity' (*Kepribadian Indonesia*). Round this were strung many other acronyms and abbreviations - AMPERA ('the Message of the People's Suffering' – *Amanat Penderitaan Rakjat*), *Resopim* ('Revolution, Socialism, Leadership'), Nekolim ('Neo-colonialism, colonialism and imperialism'), NASAKOM, the need to avoid 'textbook thinking', the 'return to the rails of the revolution' and many others. Terms such as these became the language of political discussion, and the ability to use them a sign of acceptance of the régime and its basic ideology. (The character of the ideological system elaborated by Sukarno during the years of Guided Democracy will be examined more closely in the next chapter.)

Through his integrative slogans Sukarno sought to urge his people on to the task of nation-building. He was obsessed by the concept of national greatness. Though hating the West he admired its technological achievements. He failed to see, however, that technology required economic development as a basis, and that this would involve a change in society too. To him, greatness for Indonesia simply meant the grafting of an advanced technology on to an Indonesian identity drawn essentially from a distant past. He therefore went ahead with arms purchases (especially from the Soviet Union) to develop Indonesia's military strength, and also concentrated on monumental building schemes for Djakarta, the capital. The multi-storeyed department store, Sarinah, was a symbol that Indonesia too could aspire to the perquisites of an affluent society. He sprinkled Djakarta with strident statues in the worst of socialist-realist taste – muscled men with arms uplifted, throwing off chains, leaping to the sky – and began to build his giant tower in the centre of Medan Merdeka, to be taller, he boasted, than the Eiffel Tower and bigger than the Borobodur.

In international affairs he was anxious to assert the claim to leadership which Indonesia had staked for herself at Bandung. He wanted the voice of the Indonesian revolution to 'reverberate throughout the world'.[83] In his speeches to the United Nations in 1960, and to the conference of non-aligned nations at Belgrade in 1961, Sukarno made his own claim to the leadership of the 'new emerging forces'. The Fourth Asian Games, to which Indonesia played host in 1962, were a demonstration to the Djakarta populace

83. 17 August speech, 1962, 'A Year of Triumph'.

of Indonesia's standing in the eyes of her neighbours. (They secured, for the nation a fine sports complex at Senajan, though the Indonesian exclusion of competitors from Israel and Taiwan, in contravention of previously given assurances, subsequently led to her suspension by the International Olympic Committee. In defiant response Sukarno organized Ganefo – the Games of the New Emerging Forces, which were held in 1963 – another sign of the nation's greatness and of her independence from established power.)

Sukarno's concern with symbolism, says Feith, reflected an effort to focus attention on what the government *was* rather than on what it was *doing*.[84] Much the same idea is conveyed by Geertz's characterization of it as a 'Theatre State', acting out before the people the inner meaning of the kingdom, making the ruler's court, and his capital, the mystical centre of the realm from which power radiated outwards and downwards, and serving as a model of the cosmos. After 1960 says Geertz, Sukarno was expressing 'the doctrine that the welfare of a country proceeds from the excellence of its capital, the excellence of its capital proceeds from the brilliance of its élite, and the brilliance of its élite from the spirituality of its ruler'.[85]

In the Theatre State the life of the palace was an integral part. To a large extent Guided Democracy was government by access to the ruler and his court, with all the palace intrigue which that entailed. An important figure at the centre of it all was Hartini, although Sukarno kept his promise to his son Guntur that she would never be made First Lady. On one occasion in 1963 Hartini allowed a women's congress at which she was present to consider a resolution that she be accepted as *Ibu Negara*. Hearing of it, Sukarno broke off his morning's business, descended on the hall where the meeting was taking place, brought Hartini out of the meeting and ordered that she be taken back to Bogor forthwith.[86]

84. Feith, 'Dynamics of Guided Democracy', in R. T. McVey (ed.), *Indonesia*, p. 385.

85. See Clifford Geertz, *Islam Observed*, New Haven, 1968, p. 86.

86. Rosihan Anwar, 'Djakarta Diary', extracts from which were published in *Pedoman* during 1969. For this story see 'Djakarta Diary', 16 May 1963, *Pedoman*, 12 June 1969.

Her position posed problems of protocol at public functions. She could not accompany Sukarno to the podium or sit with the ministers and their wives – even Sukarno could not insist on that sort of place for her. Nor was she allowed to enter the palace in Djakarta. But in Bogor Hartini ruled, and from there she could control much of the access to Sukarno.

Hartini had developed politically since 1955. At first she had kept herself in the background but, by the early sixties, perhaps because of her own growing feeling of insecurity, she made great efforts to keep up with Sukarno, to be both mistress and political helpmeet to him, an effort that Fatmawati had never made. With coaching, she trained herself to make 'impromptu' speeches and to play a part on formal occasions. More significantly she developed her own web of independent contacts – with party leaders, with other interest groups, and even with the army. She stood between the President and his suitors. People who wanted to get to Sukarno frequently found it convenient to go through her. Only a few high leaders could afford to ignore her. (It was rumoured that Mrs Suryadarma, wife of Air-Marshal Suryadarma, could do without Hartini, but even Yani's wife and Subandrio's wife had had to establish good relations with her in order to preserve relations with the palace itself.) At Bogor, Hartini had a court of her own from which she was not to be displaced when Sukarno took other wives – Dewi the highly talented Japanese bar-girl whom he had met in Tokyo on the eve of his return to Djakarta in 1959 and later Hariati and then Yurike Sanger, though the latter, as a fifth wife, was not recognized in Muslim eyes as formally married to him.

His role as Javanese ruler, the central actor of the Theatre State, had its corrupting effect on Sukarno. One may be tempted to see signs of his coarsening character even in his physical appearance. The trim figure which he managed to keep even until the mid fifties was lost by the early sixties. Though he remained vain and concerned about his appearance, his waistline had expanded and the folds of flesh about his jaw and neck came to give him the heavily jowled look so loved by hostile cartoonists. These changes were, no doubt, simply the natural thickening of the body in later middle age. But there was undoubtedly a moral coarsening which was not so inevitable. It was not just his sexual appetites which support that judgement, though these seemed to have acquired elements of a new brutality by this time. His playboy leanings of the fifties had become a massive preoccupation with sex in the sixties. (This was a matter of admiration rather than of disapproval in Indonesia – a demonstration, perhaps, of Sukarno's continuing virility and thus of his political potency as well.) But beyond these characteristics was a growing insensitivity to his own deficiencies of leadership, a hardening of his attitude to opponents and the quickening of a potentate's temper.

Despite all this Sukarno did manage, in an environment of economic decline and growing leadership, to maintain stability in an inherently unstable situation. He continued to appeal to the mass of the population as the Great Leader of the Revolution and his *rapport* with them was important to him. On one occasion, as he was saying goodbye to a foreign ambassador who had visited him at Bogor, his eye lighted upon his helicopter. 'Have you ever ridden in a helicopter?' asked Sukarno. 'No,' said the ambassador, whereupon Sukarno carried him off for a short flight. Sukarno, seeing the town of Sukabumi below, decided to make an unexpected descent. He gathered the amazed local population about him, talked to them, joked with them and finally led them in community singing. No security officers were about. It had been a spur of the moment departure from routine. After renewing his contact with the source of his strength for an hour, Sukarno and his companion climbed back into the helicopter and returned to the day's business.

Sukarno did not succeed in bridging the major divisions in Indonesia, but during the early years of Guided Democracy he managed to preserve a degree of balance between the major forces in his political environment. The question of his ultimate purpose, however, remains to be answered.

# 13

# Ideological Reformulations

Sukarno's claim to be a fashioner of ideology marked him off from most other Asian leaders. Gandhi was concerned with the quality of life rather than with the construction of a political orthodoxy. Nehru's urbanity, drawn from his Cambridge education, had no need of an ideology to sustain it. Sun Yat-sen's Three Principles had been little more than a very general programme of action for the Kuomintang. Communist leaders whether, like Mao, they could acquire prophetic status and could claim to contribute to the evolution of party theory, or whether like Ho Chi Minh they were content to accept a given doctrinal framework, at least worked within an established intellectual tradition. Only Sukarno saw himself as prophetically called upon to provide a distinctive body of ideas for his followers. After 1959 they took on the flavour of an orthodoxy. Supporters and opponents alike of Sukarno's régime found it convenient to speak in the language of Guided Democracy, using its slogans, its abbreviations and its acronyms. Against these, the earlier formulations of Sukarno's thinking – in particular the *Pantja Sila* speech of 1945 – were superseded and tended to reappear mainly in the views of those who were critical of his later radicalism.

While Sukarno's claim to ideological leadership must be taken seriously there is no point in looking for system or logical coherence in his ideas. Sukarno was not a disciplined thinker; indeed he was contemptuous of those who were concerned with argument and discipline – they were guilty of 'textbook thinking'.[87] He scoffed at those 'led astray by science *à la* Rotterdam [Hatta obviously] or *à la* Harvard'.[88] He complained of 'the Indonesian hyper-intellectuals – people here and there whose brains are so rusty with the teachings of Western constitutional law, of liberalism and liberal parliamentary democracy' that they were quite

87. This phrase was used in the address to the Constituent Assembly or 22 April 1959 and was a recurring theme thereafter.
88. 17 August speech, 1964.

incapable of grasping the essence of the Political Manifesto.[89] Though the world of thought was important to Sukarno he was by nature not analytical. Ideas in the round moved him: he was gripped by them and he used them for their evocative power, but his speeches and writings showed little analysis, little reflection, no expressions of hesitation or doubt. His characteristic method of handling opponents was to brush their views aside. He re-defined terms to suit his purpose and accused his critics of misunderstanding the issues at stake.[90] He was not, in brief, an intellectual's intellectual. He never wrestled at midnight with traditional philosophical questions; he was not concerned, as was Sjahrir, with the validity of an argument (and he was not torn, as was Sjahrir, by a sense of conflict between the sophistication of his Western learning and the cultural heritage of his homeland). It is important that his experience of the world outside the Indies was limited. Not until 1945 did he make his first journey abroad and thereafter, on his many overseas visits, he saw the world only with the limited vision of a head of state.

Sukarno was widely read, but in the fields of political and social theory he was essentially self-taught. He was not particularly original. His originality lay in the use he made of his ideas rather than in their content. He picked from many sources those ideas with which he felt an affinity and attempted to construct his own synthesis. If his eclecticism was not in the least systematic, the resulting flavour was distinctively his.

Though Sukarno's political thinking was accumulative rather than systematic his ideas obviously had great potency. He could sense intuitively what would appeal to his audiences. He could express the frustrations and disappointments of those in rural villages, disturbed by new forces of change which they could not understand, and of the rootless in the urban kampongs. To the élite he could convey a sense of national stature and hold out hopes for a significant role for Indonesia in the world at large. His view of the world helped to give meaning to the existence of

89. 17 August speech, 1962.

90. Dahm examines effectively Sukarno's tendency to ascribe differences as arising from 'misunderstandings'. See *Sukarno and the Struggle for Indonesian Independence*, Ithaca, 1969, especially pp. 70–77, and 95–8.

his people at all levels as traditional values were becoming less rigid. As Benda suggests, there were also elements of verbal magic in his ideology-making, which performed a function not so very different from that performed by Sanskrit as a sacred language in the Hindu kingdoms of the past.[91] By blending Western and traditional concepts Sukarno was able to legitimize the authority of a new élite.

Most of the component parts of Sukarno's view of the world have already been mentioned in tracing his political career, but a brief recapitulation will make it easier to consider his ideas as a whole, to assess their relevance for Guided Democracy, and to judge the extent to which they changed in character in the later years of his career.

In the 1920s nationalism was the all-absorbing idea. It involved, as we have seen, the creation of a united movement of resistance, based on non-cooperation with the Dutch and aiming at the mobilization of the moral power of the awakened masses against the authority of the colonial régime. So far as Sukarno was concerned the nationalist idea, supported by a Leninist analysis of imperialism, marched closely alongside an anti-Western outlook. Not all of his colleagues shared that hostility to the West. Nationalist leaders who had studied in Europe had managed to distinguish their hatred of imperialism from their attitudes to Western culture; they could respect the latter while fighting against the former. Indonesian intellectuals, said Sjahrir, should reject the idea of a central opposition between East and West 'because for our spiritual needs we are in general dependent on the West'.[92]

Sukarno saw no need for any such dependence. He stressed not the stimulus to modernization and the other possibly beneficial side-products of Western domination, but rather the economic exploitation, the discrimination and the distortion of social patterns which accompanied it. This was one feature of his outlook which remained constant. His desire in 1927 to draw the line clearly between *sini* and *sana* – between our side and theirs – had

91. H. J. Benda in the prefatory note to Donald E. Weatherbee, *Ideology in Indonesia: Sukarno's Indonesian Revolution*, New Haven, 1966.

92. Sjahrir, *Out of Exile*, New York, 1949, p. 67.

its echoes thirty years later when he warned that 'the tricks of the imperialists are many and various', and called on his audience to be united in resisting the imperialist enemy.[93] Such had been the theme of his address to the Afro–Asian Conference in 1955 and it was reflected in his rejection of Western liberalism, in his insistence on the importance of the Indonesian identity and in his continuing memory of the fact that the atomic bomb was dropped by a Western country upon 'us of Asia'.[94] It showed itself even in his opposition to what he saw as the cultural decadence of the West as exemplified in rock and roll. Recognition of this continuing hostility to the West helps to make sense of his insistence on non-cooperation with the Dutch and his readiness to co-operate with the Japanese.

The positive side of his outlook was his concern with the unity of the Indonesian side in the confrontation. In his determined efforts to bring together all sections of the Indonesian community and to build an Indonesian nation, Sukarno was making his most distinctive contribution. When he said that a nation was based on the desire to be together, or that political democracy without economic democracy was no democracy at all, or that imperialism was the last stage of capitalism in decline, he was expressing views which were a part of him, but they were not his own ideas. When he spoke of the unity of the nation he was expressing his own distinctive vision.

'The problem is: how to cultivate harmony, to cultivate unity, to build the Indonesian nation amongst all and of all. To achieve this every *suku* has . . . to accept positive contributions from the other *suku*. In short all *sukus* have to integrate themselves and become one big family of the Indonesian nation.'[95]

This was the authentic and distinctive Sukarno voice.

To bring this nation into being required the common effort of Muslim and communist, democratic socialist and straightforward nationalist, whatever their long term differences might be. The possibility of such co-operation was the subject of his first

93. 17 August speech, 1964

94. 'To Build the World Anew', address to the UN General Assembly, September 1960.

95. 'A Year of Living Dangerously', 17 August, 1964.

major statement 'Nationalism, Islam and Marxism'. To some extent he was able to persuade others to share his vision as when, in 1927, he brought together within the PPPKI groups which were fiercely opposed to each other on many questions.

Sukarno's search for unity was followed by his attempt at ideological synthesis. There were distinct stages of development here. When he wrote 'Nationalism, Islam and Marxism' he was concerned essentially with strategy. Given the power of the Dutch it seemed a matter of simple common sense that communists and Muslims should close their ranks and work together under the banner of nationalism. From that idea of a co-operative effort he was enticed by the further hope that it might be possible actually to blend differing currents of thought so as to create, by selective borrowing, a single acceptable synthesis. He had no difficulty, himself, in adhering simultaneously to a variety of world-views. 'What is Sukarno? A nationalist? An Islamist? A Marxist?' he had asked in 1941 in his article, 'Soekarno by Soekarno Himself'. 'Readers, Sukarno is a mixture of all these isms.' He made the same claim often thereafter. 'I have made myself a meeting place of all trends and ideologies. I have blended, blended, and blended them until finally they became the present Sukarno.'[96] The *Pantja Sila* speech of 1945, in its attempt to bring together nationalism, humanitarianism, democracy, social justice and belief in God, represented his most coherent statement of such a view, and the platonic nature of his quest was revealed in his ultimate claim that the five principles could be compressed into three (socio-nationalism, socio-democracy and belief in God) and the three into one – the basic and distinctively Indonesian principle of *gotong royong*.

It was significant that, in speaking of unity, Sukarno thought in terms of the barriers to unity posed not by class differences but by ethnic loyalties and by opposing cultural and ideological streams. Given that perspective it was easier for him to think of himself as the great unifier. Had his appeal been in class terms – to farmer, proletarian or businessman – it would have been of necessity a sectional appeal, seeking support from one group

96. Quoted in Louis Fischer, *The Story of Indonesia*, New York, 1959, p. 154.

against others. But since he saw Indonesia as composed of *Marhaens*, he could appeal to all simultaneously on the basis of his own synthesis, uniting all ethnic groups, all religions, all social philosophies. The *Marhaen* concept was an important insight which, despite its simplistic character, did grasp an important feature of Indonesian society – namely that class distinctions were not significant bases of cleavage. But quite apart from its intrinsic validity it was an added support to his vision of Indonesia as a diversity of cultural streams brought together into the one great unity under his own leadership.

Nationalism with an anti-Western flavour, pursued through an awakening of the masses, the drive for unity and for synthesis – these ideas were established in Sukarno's thinking by the end of the thirties, and the later evolution of his thought seemed largely a matter of adapting them to changing circumstances. Indeed, the striking thing about Sukarno's political thought is the apparent permanence of its leading themes. There were changes of emphasis from time to time and reformulations of particular points – as when the idea of the mass party in the twenties became the idea of a combined mass-plus-vanguard party in the early thirties. But, in appearance at least, there was a remarkable continuity over the years. In charging liberal democracy with being divisive and in stating that the truly Indonesian way of reaching decisions was through deliberation, consensus and leadership, he was concerned once again with the problem of unity. 'Our democracy is not a battlefield of opponents,' he said in his 17 August speech in 1960. 'Our democracy is nothing else than a search for synthesis, a search for an accumulation of ideas and energies.'

In the early sixties, when he coined the new acronym NASAKOM to symbolize the unity of nationalism, religion and communism, he seemed to be reviving in almost exactly parallel terms his 1926 assertion that the interests of nationalism, Islam and Marxism were complementary. Similarly with the idea of an Indonesian identity, which became part of his stock-in-trade after 1957, though the exact nature of that identity was never made clear. At first glance the concept of Indonesian identity may appear to be a new element in this thinking. In fact it merely reflected a new sense of anxiety. In the 1920s he *knew* that an Indonesian nation existed and he felt no need to stress the importance of a special Indonesian identity. By the mid-fifties he had reason to doubt whether it did exist after all. He feared the influence of foreign mass culture. He also had a clearer perception of the precarious nature of unity and of the practical difficulty of preserving it. But in both the twenties and the fifties, though the language may have been different, the idea of nationhood lay at the centre of his concern.

. His view of the outside world, too, did not appear to change greatly. His anti-imperialism clothed itself in new terms but its flavour seemed the same. Nekolim (neo-colonialism, colonialism, and imperialism) was the sixties version of the anti-imperialism of the twenties, designed to fit a situation where direct colonial rule had been thrown off, but where imperialism in the form of economic domination or of Western spheres of influence still existed. Another version of the same feeling was the concept of a struggle between the new emerging forces and the old established forces, soon to be compressed, in Sukarno fashion, into the concepts of NEFO and OLDEFO. The essence of these concepts was given a preliminary exposition in Sukarno's address 'To Build the World Anew', delivered to the United Nations in September 1960, in which a distinction was made, not yet in capital letters, between 'the emergent nations and the old established'. Sukarno had been quick to grasp the implications of the Peking–Moscow split and to see its long-term impact on existing international alignments. To his UN audience he argued that the real conflict in the world was not the cold war (with the possibility of a neutral third force) but that between imperialism in its new forms on the one hand and justice, equality and freedom for the long exploited peoples of the world on the other. To the 'older established nations' he pointed out that 'Imperialism is not yet dead.' ... 'Many of you in this chamber have never known imperialism.' 'However my brothers of Asia and Africa have known the scourges of imperialism. ... They know its dangers, and its cunning and its tenacity.' Phrases like 'the revolution of mankind' were employed to indicate the boundaries of the struggle, and the Indonesian revolution was seen to run together with this revolution of mankind. In Belgrade a year later, at the

344 Sukarno: A Political Biography

conference of non-aligned nations which Indonesia had helped to sponsor, Sukarno developed the idea further, this time specifically in terms of the New Emerging Forces (NEFO), the forces 'of freedom and justice' and the Old Established Forces (OLDEFO), 'the old forces of domination'. 'The safety of the world is always threatened by the Old Established Order.'

The concepts reflected Sukarno's real and, of course, justified, suspicion of the West and of Western power. He never forgot that a good deal of Western sympathy had lain with the rebels in 1958. From his point of view, and from that of Indonesia, the West did not cease to be a threat once Indonesia had attained independence – or even after the economic ties with Holland had been broken. There were other forms of domination, and Sukarno's ear was closely attuned to the resentment of the whole third world at its economic backwardness and inferiority of status in an international situation dominated still by the great powers. He gave passionate expression to his feelings in 1963 when he said:

'Colonialism and imperialism are living realities in our world. Their sentiment of superiority, of arrogance towards us who were once their colonial subjects is thrust down our throats by their press, by their politicians, by their very tourists who only reflect attitudes inculcated in them by the forces in their own societies. Their political, economic or military interference is always with us, sometimes subtly, often insultingly. At every move we make for economic reconstruction and up-building, we find that they exploit their technological superiority to manipulate conditions in order that our nations can be kept eternally subservient to their selfish interests.'[97]

Even so his distinction between NEFO and OLDEFO was hardly precise. It was not clear how the new emerging forces were to be distinguished from the old established forces, and the classification might appear little more than a set of emotional terms to attack those of whom Sukarno disapproved. (Indeed the same comment might be made upon the concept of non-alignment – the very *raison d'être* of the Belgrade conference. Non-alignment, said Sukarno, 'is not directed against any one country or against any one bloc or against any one particular type of social system'. It did not even mean being 'a buffer state between giant blocs'.

97. Address to the Conference of the Peoples of Indochina, 1965.

What did it mean then? The assertion that it was a dynamic force 'startling in its freshness' did not help very much to indicate precisely which nations fell into the non-aligned group.)

The NEFO–OLDEFO antithesis was defined in some measure in terms of former colonies and their former masters who 'want to preserve as much as possible of their economic – and sometimes also of their political and military – interests', but this did not sum it up completely. There were elements of the antithesis between wealth and poverty – the new emerging forces, said Sukarno, were warning the affluent societies that they could not go on exploiting the poverty-stricken nations. There was also a hint that the conflict was between socialist and capitalist countries. In his 17 August speech in 1963 Sukarno announced that the new emerging forces were composed of 'the Asian nations, the African nations, the Latin American nations, the nations of the socialist countries, the progressive groups in the capitalist countries'. But there were many marginal cases. China, North Vietnam and North Korea, 'the nations which have been ignored and attacked', were newly emerging.[98] But what about Russia – communist and yet locked in ideological conflict with China? What about France – old established undoubtedly, but making conciliatory approaches to emerging forces? Perhaps, after all, one can get no further than such terms as Afro–Asia or Third World. Yet the emotional thrust of the concept was clear. The idea of the new emerging and the old established forces was not a scientific theory to explain the international order, but a broad classifying device to be used in distinguishing friends from foes in the struggles within that order. At the very least, however, it did indicate that Sukarno still, as he had always done, saw the West as Indonesia's prime enemy.[99]

The new formulations of the sixties then appear, at first glance, to be continuations of ideas Sukarno had already developed or adaptations of them to new circumstances. Yet, largely true though this is, there were some important changes in temper, and

98. Statement on Indonesia's withdrawal from the UN, 7 January 1965.
99. For discussions of the concept of the NEFO and OLDEFO see Donald E. Weatherbee, op. cit., and G. Moldelski (ed.), *The New Emerging Forces*, Canberra, 1963.

even in substance. At the very least there was a marked change – and no doubt an entirely natural change – in style between the ideas of Sukarno in power, President for Life and Great Leader of the Revolution, and those of the attractive young activist of the twenties and the revered exile of the thirties. The ideological concern of the young Sukarno had been to analyse reality in popular terms and to point to possibilities of changing it. He had been romantic and idealistic, and these qualities were reflected in considerable measure in his great defence speech of 1930. He spoke then as a man fighting against odds, but believing that the world could indeed be changed if one fought hard enough.

By 1960 a good deal of his romanticism remained but the idealism had been eroded. Ideas were no longer attempts at a description of reality, or even weapons of revolution, but were a means of manipulating the immediate political environment. In the twenties his anti-imperialism was specific and precise. It meant fighting to overthrow Dutch rule. Now it was a struggle against vaguely perceived and abstract forces. His demand for unity had once been linked to skilful action to conciliate specific opponents. Now there was a strident condemnation of those who did not see the world in his terms. Slogans, and the abbreviations to which they were reduced, now replaced the comparatively straight-forward, if unsophisticated, presentation of his ideas.[1] Manipol, USDEK, AMPERA, NEFO and OLDEFO, Nekolim and NASAKOM, BERDIKARI ('standing on one's own feet' – *Berdiri di atas kaki sendiri*), TAVIP ('the year of living dangerously' – *Tahun Vivere Pericoloso*), RESOPIM ('revolution, Indonesian socialism, national leadership' – *revolusi, sosialisme à la Indonesia, Pimpinan Nasional*) and others. There was an incantatory flavour about the repetition of such terms. If ideology has an element of verbal magic it had become a rather crude magic under Guided Democracy. Sukarno's speeches continued to play

1. Cf. Weatherbee's argument that, since ideology has the political function of supporting authority, and since it is self-validating, there is no point in considering its truth or falsity. 'The proper question is, did it serve its political purpose?' (p. 17). That is *a* proper question, certainly, and the view of ideology as having a legitimizing function is part of our argument here, but there is still a very important difference between Sukarno's earlier and his later thinking with regard to its relation to reality.

with words, piling up adjectives and nouns often without any clear meaning. 'Revolution is a dynamically dialectical process or a dialectically dynamic process.'[2]

'Our duty is to stay united . . . while firmly adhering to the Political Manifesto and Resopim and to expand and intensify the execution of the Political Manifesto and Resopim . . . . The negative characteristic, the destructive characteristic and the characteristic of breaking down of our revolution has now begun to decrease.'[3]

Or again:

'The Romanticism of Struggle – the primeval source of strength (oerkracht) of Struggle, the oerkracht of the stamina of Struggle, the oerkracht of mental strength, the oerkracht of spiritual strength . . . the oerkracht which gives understanding that the dynamic and dialectic of Revolution are needed . . .'[4]

And so on.

One aspect of this change in style was that ideology was fast turning to an orthodoxy of which Sukarno was the inspired interpreter. Ability to use this extraordinary language of political discourse was tending to become a test of loyalty. Even so Sukarno was always on the alert for those who could use his terminology and yet were opposed to him – 'the double-faced manipolist, the hypocrite manipolist, the false manipolist'.[5] It was significant that Sukarno, the great unifier, was increasingly conscious of whether people were for him or against him. To some extent this had always been so; the desire for reassurance and agreement had always made him vulnerable to criticism, as we have seen, and anxious to overcome it. He had made no bones about opposing those whom he regarded as enemies, as was apparent in his gradual isolation of Masjumi in the fifties and his banning of the party together with the PSI in 1960. But now, in the early sixties, there was a compulsion on his entourage to make a continuing show of support for him. Sukarno's rule was not harshly coercive but it contained strong pressures towards conformity. For the

2. 17 August 1957.
3. 'A Year of Triumph', 17 August 1962.
4. 'A Year of Living Dangerously', 17 August 1964.
5. ibid.

doubters there was the threat of political isolation or house arrest if not of actual imprisonment. A passage of his 17 August speech of 1964 warned dissenters of the risks they were running:

'Sometimes when I sit by myself, or when too I sit face to face with people whom indeed I know to be actually hypocrites (I rather often come across such people) I ask in my heart: What is it actually that makes them so obstinate and pig-headed? What makes them so bold as to make arbitrary interpretations of my speeches? Do they think that what they say publicly does not reach my ears? Do they think that I do not read the papers, that I do not follow the radio and television? Do they think when they whisper and mumble words in conspiratorial meetings, that there is no one among those urged to conspire who is faithful to the great leader of the revolution and who reports everything to him . . .?'

The change in Sukarno's ideology-building, from attempting to describe – and thereby change – the world to manipulating it, was illustrated in the idea of NASAKOM. It has been pointed out that, to all superficial appearances, NASAKOM was a revival of his old 'Nationalism, Islam and Marxism' article.[6] But on closer inspection its functions are seen to be very different. The 1926 essay was a statement designed for the years of struggle and it really was intended to bridge divisions and to secure a common effort. NASAKOM was a device of Sukarno in power. In the early sixties, certainly, Sukarno was still concerned about conflicts and divisions, but in a slightly different way. He no longer believed that he could unite the opposing forces in Indonesian politics and he saw the problem shrewdly, not in idealistic terms, but in terms of the practical exigencies and pressures of day-to-day political action. He saw the necessity of conciliating the main streams of opinion, but his desire was to contain them and hold them in balance rather than to unite them. The union between them was to be achieved only within himself. NASAKOM must be seen in these terms: it was a tactic calculated not to unite contending forces but to preserve his own position as their balancer and arbiter. Its meaning was never made very clear. The PKI, for a time, argued that NASAKOM involved the creation of a balance between nationalism, religion and communism in all

6. Cf. Dahm, op. cit., p. xii and chapter 11.

executive as well as deliberative bodies, so that even in the military high command these three elements should be represented. In this sense the party demanded the NASAKOM-ization of the army. The army argued in reply that the term referred only to the general spirit of co-operation which should inform the conduct of the nation's affairs. It suited Sukarno to leave the doubt unresolved as long as he could, for in advancing the idea of NASAKOM his purpose was to control opposing forces, not to unite them except through himself. 'I am NASAKOM,' he is reported to have said in 1963 when rejecting the PKI's demand for the inclusion of communists in the cabinet.[7]

The most important single theme in Sukarno's speeches in the sixties was that of revolution. Though he had spoken and written of Indonesia's revolution in the past, it was another concept which took on a different aspect in the environment of Guided Democracy. As a young man he had been concerned with the revolution which would overthrow Dutch power. In the thirties, in *Achieving Indonesian Independence*, he had recognized that, beyond the 'golden bridge' leading to independence, there were other problems to be solved before a just and prosperous society could be achieved. His distinction between national and social revolution was further elaborated in *Sarinah*, where he developed, in terms analogous to those of Marxism, a theory of stages of revolution. It contained little sign of the Marxist idea of class maturity which would be a part of the preparation of each stage of revolution, but there was at least a sense of successive phases, with social revolution having to wait upon the completion of the national revolution. Sukarno spoke of the 'national phase in which we build the National State, and social phase in which we build Socialism'.

In this present phase [the national phase] the political chains, economic shackles and subjugating laws of colonialism are being struck, attacked, shattered. . . . But within this present phase the task will also be commenced of gradually preparing . . . the coming social phase. . . . But the social phase cannot come before the national phase is finished . . .

During the fifties, however, the programmatic element of this

7. K. Krishna Moorthy, 'Indonesian Tug-of-War', *Far Eastern Economic Review*, 18 April 1963.

thinking began to disappear and, in talking of revolution, Sukarno seemed to be referring merely to the turmoil and flux of events – not to any goal to which revolution should be directed. It was now a concept of undifferentiated revolution, and, in the sixties, of 'continuing revolution'. Here again one can use Hatta as a foil to Sukarno. Hatta had regarded the revolution as over with the achievement of independence and he saw the task facing Indonesia thereafter as that of coming to grips with the hard problems of economic development. Without solving those problems there could be no social betterment. 'A revolution shakes the floor and the foundations, it loosens all hinges and boards,' said Hatta. Unless it was 'dammed up at the appropriate time' it would cause chaos.[8] Sukarno, by contrast, welcomed the turbulence and confusion of change. 'Revolution is revolution because it is a flood in spate that is not still.'[9] And though he continued to speak of achieving a just and prosperous society there seemed no longer to be any connection between that goal and the programme of revolution which was supposed to bring it about. The important thing was the struggle itself, not the goal:

'Revolution is only truly Revolution if it is a continuous struggle. Not just an external struggle against an enemy, but an inner struggle, fighting and subduing all negative aspects which hinder or do damage to the course of the Revolution. In this light Revolution is . . . a mighty symphony of victory over the enemy and over oneself.'[10]

Revolution was important for its spiritual rather than its practical consequences. Sukarno called for 'a spirit that dares to think and re-think, dares to shape and re-shape, dares to make and re-make. A spirit that dares to plunge into the seething ocean and to seek the pearl.'[11]

The exaggeratedly emotional flavour of Sukarno's concept of revolution received one of its most typical expressions in his 17 August speech of 1960.

'Well, frankly I tell you: I belong to the group of people who are bound in spiritual longing by the Romanticism of Revolution. I am

8. Mohammad Hatta, *Past and Future*, Ithaca, 1960.
9. 17 August speech, 1962.
10. 17 August speech, 1957.
11. ibid.

inspired by it, I am fascinated by it, I am completely absorbed by it, I am crazed, I am obsessed by the Romanticism of Revolution . . .

'There are people who do not understand Revolutionary logic. Those are the people who say in the midst of a journey: the Revolution is over – while in fact the Revolution is not yet concluded and still goes on, on, and again on. This is Revolutionary logic: once we start off a Revolution we must continue that Revolution until all its ideals have been implemented. This constitutes an absolute Law of Revolution, which can be denied no longer, this can be debated no further! Therefore, do not say 'The Revolution is already over', whilst Revolution is on the march . . .

'There are also people who . . . ask: "Do we need to be always inflaming the spirit of Revolution?. . . . Could it not be done more patiently . . . slow but sure?"

'Good heavens! Slow but sure! That is not possible! That is not possible, unless we want to be crushed by the People! . . .

'This world today is a revolutionary ammunition dump. . . . This world today is loaded with revolution. . . . It has never before happened that the history of man has gone through such a revolution as this at present . . . a Revolution of Humanity which simultaneously surges, flashes, thunders, in almost every corner of the earth.

'And we want to creep like snails, to crawl like tortoises! . . .

'Wake up, you people who suffer from revolution-phobia. We are now in the midst of a revolution . . . greater than the past American Revolution, or the past French Revolution, or the present Soviet Revolution. One year ago I explained that this Revolution of ours is at the same time a National Revolution, a political Revolution, a social Revolution, a cultural Revolution and a Revolution in Man. Our Revolution, I said, is a five-facetted Revolution, a multi-complex Revolution, a revolution which is 'a summing up of many revolutions in one generation.' One year ago I said that therefore we must move fast, we must run like the obsessed, we must be dynamically revolutionary, we must, incessantly and relentlessly, extract every idea, all fighting energies, every creative power, every atom of sweat in our bodies, in order that the outcome of our Revolution can balance the dynamic of social consciousness which surges in the breast of society as a whole.'[12]

What did all this hyperbole amount to? Was it mere rhetoric? Certainly statements like these – and many others could be given – contain no hint of any view of the precise changes he wished to

12. 'Like an angel that strikes from the skies: the march of our Revolution', 17 August 1960.

bring about in society or of how they might be brought about. There were plenty of references to abstract evils that needed to be overcome – to poverty, oppression and the '*exploitation de l'homme par l'homme*' (one of his favourite phrases), but no specific analysis of them or plans for remedying them. Attention has already been drawn to Sukarno's subordination of economic policy to political ends and to his lack of interest in problems of economic organization in general. He desired that Indonesia should be great and that she should possess the external signs of greatness in the form of advanced technology and its products. But even at this level there was no grasp of the nature of the industrial development and social change which would be required to produce that advanced technology. Similarly with issues of social welfare. In his desire 'always to be in rhythm with the waves of the Revolution'[13] there was certainly a feeling for movement, but not for direction. In conversation with a visitor he once used a revealing analogy. Guiding a Revolution, he said, was like riding a bolting horse. You could not properly control it, and you were not sure where it was taking you. The important thing was simply to stay on as best you could, and be carried with it.[14] Movement was therefore the thing. But the tempest and the flux which excited him so much were within a stable balance, without purpose beyond themselves.

This throws some light on Sukarno's alliance with the PKI – the one party which did have a concept of changing society. Sukarno said that he supported the PKI as a revolutionary party:

'There are still people who accuse Sukarno of 'taking sides' who accuse Sukarno of 'favouritism'. Sukarno taking sides? Taking sides with whom? If it is against imperialism, feudalism, and the enemies of the revolution in general, yes! Certainly Sukarno is taking sides, certainly Sukarno has favourites, that is he sides with the *people* and he sides with the revolution itself . . .

'I have been accused of bringing advantage to one group only among our big national family. My answer is also, yes. Yes, I am giving advan-

13. ibid.
14. Author's interview with Soedjatmoko, to whom Sukarno made these remarks in the early fifties.

tage to one group only, namely – the revolutionary group! I am a friend of the nationalists, but only the *revolutionary* nationalists! I am a friend of the religious group, but only the *revolutionary* religious group! I am a friend of the communists, because the communists are *revolutionary* people.'[15]

But, beyond this recognition of the importance of the PKI in the political balance which surrounded him, his approval of it was an approval of its general *temper* of thought. It was not an approval of its social programme. Unlike the PKI, Sukarno did not see the possibility of social change – he would not have wanted it in any case. Like a good Javanese he probably felt that, in basic structure, Indonesian society was all right as it was. At the very most the nationalism he had led for so long had represented a levelling challenge to an aristocratic social order (as well as a struggle against the Dutch), but it was made on behalf of a political élite which was concerned thereafter to maintain its own position. Even the programme of land reform which he supported did not represent an attempt to introduce a basic change in the structure of Indonesian society. Whether he was conscious of it or not, a good deal of Sukarno's radicalism, together with his abstract talk of revolution, was designed to serve the goal of preserving a social *status quo*.

If this interpretation is correct it helps to explain the absence of a social programme for Guided Democracy. Ideology was a manipulative device rather than the presentation of a plan of action; it had meaning in the sense that the slogans marshalled by Sukarno evoked a deep response from his hearers and it also, in a very general way, embodied a view of the world and a set of values about it. But there were other functions. Ideology provided a test of orthodoxy and served as a means of securing conformity. In its emphasis on nation-building, national identity, dynamism, it suggested quite different criteria of success than the more prosaic tests of practical achievement. Its 'verbal magic' thus helped in legitimizing Sukarno's own position and the authority of his régime against those who might challenge it on the grounds of its failure to curb inflation or to stamp out corruption. And despite its revolutionary language it was conservatively directed

15. 17 August speech, 1964.

in the sense that the régime it supported was essentially representative of an existing élite.

Attention has already been drawn to elements of a traditional outlook in Sukarno's ideas and in the manner in which he elaborated them, but this question needs to be faced again briefly. The game of detecting the traditional elements may, perhaps, be overdone. The self-conscious and atavistic character of his search for an Indonesian identity may indeed lead one to ask whether Sukarno's Javanism was not, after all, an artificial construction. In examining the elements of his ideology, certainly, the classification of them as 'modern' or 'traditional' can often be played both ways. We have seen that as a political activist in the company of his PNI colleagues in the 1920s he thought very much in the categories of Western political analysis. Marxism, in particular, supplied him with the weapons to use against imperialism and he attempted to apply dialectical thinking to Indonesian circumstances, seeing Indonesian nationalism specifically as a dialectical opposite of Dutch nationalism.[16] Similarly with his insistence on the direct confrontation of 'us' and 'them'. It can be argued that Marxism appealed to Sukarno because it echoed the polarities of Javanese thought, with its pairs of opposites – right and left, light and dark, mountain and sea, refined and coarse. But why should one speak in either-or terms when assessing the importance in Sukarno's make up of Marx and Java? In both there are polarities and struggle, and in both there is a concept of stability.

Again Sukarno's drive to unite opposing streams of Indonesian thinking is often seen as reflecting the proverbial syncretism of Java. This point has been argued in the preceding pages. But it could equally be seen simply as good tactics in the political situations of colonial rule and independent Indonesia alike. There may be little point in identifying a particular element in his thought as reflecting his traditional cast of mind. Tradition and modernity are, in any case, crude categories. They are certainly not precise enough to catch the enormously subtle and complex inter-weaving of characteristics within the one person or the one society, and any general judgement must inevitably be crude.

16. See above, p. 97.

Nevertheless, with this warning it is worth emphasizing the peculiarities of certain aspects of Sukarno's world-view which do seem to make him a product of the Javanese tradition. His attempt at unity and the accompanying attempts at ideological synthesis were indeed more than the tactics chosen by a master political strategist. They were genuinely Javanese in a more profound way, in that they reflected a body of views about the structure of reality itself. In a crude way Sukarno's compression of five points of the *Pantja Sila* into one principle reflected his conception of a totality and wholeness of the universe, of which the terrestrial order was but a reflection. The totality reconciled differences, for it involved the concept of the 'fitting together of things' in perfect equilibrium, with everything in its place in the whole.

The ideas of cosmological equilibrium and the fitting together of things, with conflicts reconciled in one-ness, were very much in the tradition of the *priyayi-abangan* spectrum of Java. Perhaps the failure of those ideas in practical application was also the failure of the *priyayi-abangan* tradition. The *abangan* element in Javanese society had no difficulty in absorbing a variety of diverse elements – animinism, Hinduism, Buddhism and, in due course, Islam – but the amalgam, existing in whatever different forms, was not equivalent to 'the' tradition of Java. There were less syncretistic streams as well. What Sukarno seemed not to understand was that it was precisely this syncretism which the Javanese *santri* and the non-Javanese Muslim condemned as compromise. Muslims, for their part, failed to understand the dangers of their own intransigence. Perhaps Sukarno was right in the end. *Abangan* tolerance might be the only thing which could enable Indonesian unity to survive. The fact was, however, that, in his approach both to Muslims and communists, Sukarno saw them through *abangan* spectacles, not as they were – committed each in their own way to an uncompromising goal – but as he thought that they ought to be – as parts of a possible Indonesian consensus. He believed in his capacity to make them so.

While attempting to accommodate them within that totality he was, as we have seen, more alert to the dangers of Islamic intransigence than to those of communism. There was a background to that tendency. In the 1917–23 period, when Sukarno was experiencing infant nationalism at its source, the radicals were the ones who talked of unity and the moderates were those who were intent upon forcing a division. The crushing of the PKI three years later prevented it from disturbing that image and, in the sixties, once again it was the PKI which Sukarno saw as endeavouring to fit into the consensus, its conservative opponents who were divisive.

Unity – or rather its central position in Sukarno's thought – can be regarded then as belonging to a world-view which stressed the harmony and the wholeness of the universe. Secondly, his political thought and action reproduced a certain ambiguity of Javanese cosmology. We have referred to his belief in the presence of supernatural forces within which man must operate. At the same time he believed that an exceptional person, possessed of spiritual power, could shape events. There were elements here of the Javanese view of reality as portrayed in the *wayang*. Though the forces governing the unfolding of events were broadly determined, the *dalang* could play his part in manipulating the puppets and shaping the story.

This brings us back to unity. A part of his special power (*kesaktian*) was his ability to project himself as the blender of opposing views. Leadership in Javanese terms involves the capacity of an exceptional person to hold opposites in balance. This capacity was particularly important in view of the times with which he was dealing. Sukarno's era was genuinely a period of turmoil and his ideology of revolution was born of that sense of instability and uncertainty. He did not create the confusion but in that setting he could appear to Indonesia's 'little people' as the focal point of stability, as the man who could interpret the confusion and lead them to safety.

Finally, in so far as Sukarno was consciously or unconsciously reviving something of the Javanese *kraton* in his presidency, he was not only fulfilling the messianic expectations of his Javanese peasant subjects, but was also expressing the Javanese aristocratic idea of the parallelism of the cosmic and the terrestrial orders – the view that the job of the state was to mirror the cosmos in its hierarchy and its harmony, the spiritual superiority of the ruler in his capital serving as the analogue of the superiority of God in the universe. In Geertz's terms this was the function of the Theatre State. The Indonesian identity which Sukarno was concerned to establish was, it would seem, a Javanese aristocratic identity; Sukarno's ideology, for all its apparent radicalism, was a means of securing that end, even though the aristocracy was no longer an aristocracy of blood but an élite forged in the struggle against the Dutch.

# 14
## Foreign Adventure and Domestic Balance

Sukarno's leadership during the last years of his unchallenged dominance of Indonesia was increasingly frenetic – a characteristic particularly apparent in the field of foreign policy. From the neutralism of the early fifties – a 'free and active' neutralism, but with a marked westward inclination – Indonesia moved by a series of stages to adopt a totally different posture barely even retaining the pretence of neutralism. By 1965 she had become, instead, one pole of the Djakarta–Peking axis (or the Djakarta–Phnom Penh–Peking–Pyongyang axis as Sukarno called it). The acquisition of West Irian was followed by the confrontation with Malaysia on an increasing level of violence, by Sukarno's withdrawal from the United Nations in January 1965 and by his plans for calling a Conference of the New Emerging Forces (CONEFO). At first glance these trends would seem to emerge naturally from the domestic politics of the period and from its ideology. The apparent leftward leanings of Sukarno, as expressed in his protection of the PKI, could be regarded as having their natural counterpart in the increasingly close ties with Peking; and in ideological terms it seemed that the concept of continuing revolution in domestic affairs had overflowed, through the concepts of NEKOLIM and NEFO and OLDEFO, into the sphere of international relations. But was the revolutionary flavour of Sukarno's foreign policy, like that of his domestic policy, perhaps less revolutionary than it seemed at first glance?

Explanations of Sukarno's approach to the outside world have been sought at various levels. Apart from the view that it represented a planned and reasonable response to Indonesia's national interests there have been three main schools of thought: that it was ideologically motivated, reflecting his view of the world about him, that it was the product of a deep psychological need – both personal and national – for self-assertion and national prestige, and again that it was a response to domestic political pressures.[17] These views are not necessarily mutually exclusive. An adventurous foreign policy reflecting, it would seem, the concept of the world divided into progressive and reactionary forces certainly fitted neatly into Sukarno's stock of ideas. The impulsive assertiveness of such a policy also contributed to Indonesia's need – and to Sukarno's – for self-respect and international stature, as well as having a function to perform in domestic politics. These judgements do not necessarily mean that it was an artificial policy having no relation to a reasonable perception of the interests of the nation.

The West Irian issue, which had preoccupied Sukarno from the very beginning of Indonesia's experience as an independent nation, was finally brought to a settlement in 1962 – Indonesia's 'Year of Triumph' as Sukarno called it in his Proclamation Day speech of that year. It had been a long struggle. As long ago as 1954 Indonesia, in a minor way, had begun its infiltrations into West Irian territory. With the failure of the United Nations vote in 1957 Sukarno foreshadowed a more forceful Indonesian approach to the problem. The seizure of Dutch estates and business houses and the repatriation of Dutch nationals was followed by the shattering of other commercial ties as Indonesia reduced the volume of her trade with Rotterdam. In what was to become a recognized technique she began to harass Dutch diplomatic representatives in Djakarta, making their position more and more untenable, until, in August 1960, Indonesia broke off diplomatic relations with the Netherlands.

The break was followed by the stepping up of Indonesia's military pressure on West Irian. (At the end of 1959 she had negotiated a major purchase of arms from the Soviet Union, and her dependence on Russian military support became more and more pronounced in subsequent years.) During 1961 Indonesian forces continued to operate on the fringes of the territory while at the same time the Dutch were taking their own steps to promote the

17. For one discussion of these questions see Frederick P. Bunnell, 'Guided Democracy Foreign Policy: 1960–1965', *Indonesia*, (Ithaca), No. 2, October 1966.

political development of West Irian, with a view to transforming the territory into an independent state. In February 1961 elections were held for a newly-created council in which the indigenous population was given its first taste of political representation. At the beginning of 1962 Indonesia created an area command for West New Guinea under Major-General Suharto. In the following months infiltration of the territory – the dropping of paratroops and the landing of guerrillas – was used in support of Subandrio's diplomatic pressure on the Netherlands. At length, after strong American persuasion, and after several abortive attempts earlier in the year to negotiate a solution, Holland was brought to accept a face-saving formula, reached under United Nations auspices, which could relieve her from what was becoming an increasingly unprofitable and distasteful commitment to the last remnant of her former Indian empire. Sukarno's skill and boldness in applying a calculated mixture of agitation and threats, fluctuating military action and diplomacy, had paid off.

The agreement of August 1962, reached through the mediation of the senior American diplomat, Ellsworth Bunker, provided for a cease fire to be followed by the handing over of the territory on 1 October to a temporary United Nations administration. On 1 January 1963 the Indonesian flag would be flown side by side with the UN flag – a symbol of great moment to Sukarno. Then, on 1 May, the United Nations would hand West Irian over to Indonesia, to be administered by the latter until a final determination was made through an act of free choice on the part of the people of West Irian, to be held before the end of 1969. At best this agreement was seen as a means of saving face on all sides. There was considerable doubt in the world at large as to whether the West Irianese would ever be allowed their act of free choice, but even were Indonesia ever to honour that part of the agreement it was assumed that it would be handled in such a way as to confirm Indonesian control.[18]

On 1 October the United Nations Temporary Administration

18. The act of free choice was finally held by process of *musjawarah* ('deliberation') through representative councils in July 1969 and resulted in the West Irian decision on the part of about 1,000 representatives to remain a part of Indonesia.

(UNTEA) took control. Not content with the favourable terms of the Bunker agreement Indonesian spokesmen almost immediately began to raise the possibility of the shortening of the term of United Nations administration and the earlier transfer of West Irian to Indonesia. This was an unrealistic demand. The time, in any case, was so short that no such alteration of the original agreement could possibly have been negotiated. It served merely as an additional sign of Indonesian assertiveness even at the moment of victory and lent support to the view that, with the settlement of the dispute, Indonesia still needed a functional equivalent of West Irian. On 1 May the final transfer of the territory took place, and three days later Sukarno arrived to assume, as it were, his personal control of West Irian. As though to confirm the change there was a good deal of renaming of places. Hollandia, the capital, became Kota Baru and then Sukarnopura, and the territory's highest peak, Mount Wilhelmina, became Mount Sukarno.

If the rest of the world hoped that the settlement of the West Irian question in Indonesia's favour would make her once more a peaceful member of the community of nations it was soon to be disappointed. That issue was hardly out of the way when a new bone of contention appeared in circumstances which, to some, suggested either that Sukarno had grander expansionist goals or that an external issue was necessary to him.

When the Tengku Abdul Rahman, Prime Minister of Malaya, in May 1961 proposed the idea of a federation of some kind to embrace Malaya, Singapore and the British Borneo territories, Indonesia offered no objection (though in due course the Philippines did, by lodging a claim to a substantial part of North Borneo).[19] The Tengku's suggestion was preceded and followed by close discussions between himself and the Prime Minister of Singapore, Mr Lee Kuan Yew, and it represented an extraordinarily close (if only temporary) *rapport* between the two. Lee Kuan Yew had argued that merger with Malaya formed the only possible basis for the development of a stable Singapore. The

19. For a thorough discussion of the Malaysia plan, the circumstances surrounding its adoption, the problems facing it and the opposition of Indonesia, see J. A. C. Mackie, *Confrontation: The Indonesia–Malaysia Dispute 1963–66* (forthcoming).

addition of the Borneo territories was part of a package deal. The predominantly Chinese character of the city of Singapore posed serious obstacles to the idea of merger, since Malaysia was already concerned at the strength of the economically powerful Chinese community in the Peninsula as against that of the Malay community. It seemed, however, as though Singapore could be absorbed if, at the same time, the populations of Brunei, Sarawak and North Borneo could be brought into the new federation. In spite of the apparently statesmanlike dimensions of the proposal this was at best a doubtful argument – the Borneo territories were not predominantly Malay in population; they had their own Chinese minorities along with a variety of other ethnic groups which could complicate rather than ease Malaya's plural society problems. But the scheme had other advantages, among them the fact that the proposed federation would enable Britain to withdraw easily from this corner of her former empire.

In November 1961 at the United Nations Subandrio insisted that Indonesia had no claim to the Borneo territories and stated that, when informed by Malaya of the merger proposal, she had raised no objection. Thereafter continuing negotiations between Malaya, Singapore and London led to the agreement in 1962 that Singapore and the Borneo territories of Britain would be given independence on the formation of the Malaysian Federation in August 1963. Brunei subsequently decided not to be a party to the agreement but Sarawak and Sabah were willing to enter the new federation. However, despite Indonesia's original acquiescence, she was ready, very late in the day, to take advantage of an unforeseen event to crystallize her opposition to the whole Malaysia concept.

The unforeseen event was the outbreak in December 1962 of a revolt in Brunei under the leadership of A. M. Azahari, leader of Brunei's largest party, the Party Rakjat ('Peoples' Party'), aiming at the creation of an independent state of Kalimantan Utara, embracing the three territories. The revolt was short-lived but it raised considerable doubts as to the willingness of the populations of the Borneo territories to enter the new federation, and it gave Sukarno, until recently preoccupied by the West Irian dispute, the opportunity to formulate his latent suspicions of the

Malaysia plan. On 8 January 1963, he rejected the idea of Malaysia and shortly afterwards Subandrio announced Indonesia's 'confrontation' with the new federation. The meaning of the term was not entirely clear, but Subandrio was not proposing a declaration of war upon Malaysia. In due course confrontation did go beyond the maintenance of continuing diplomatic and economic pressure to the application of military force, but it was force maintained at a comparatively low level. The successful West Irian campaign, and the mode of conducting it in the first half of 1962, had provided the model.

There were many reasons why Indonesia under Sukarno's leadership might have been expected to react adversely to the Malaysia idea. Despite Subandrio's disclaimer in November 1961, Indonesia, as the major power in the region, could well feel that she had a right to intimate consultation on all questions relating to the disposition of territories near her borders – in this case actually adjoining those borders. Sukarno, as the embodiment of the nation's pride, was always quick to detect anything which might seem a slight and on this occasion, since it was a matter of an imperial power disposing of her imperial possessions in ways calculated to maintain its own influence, he was particularly sensitive. The formation of Malaysia, indeed, seemed in his eyes to represent an act of the forces of neo-colonialism and to be part of an encircling movement directed against Indonesia. In the terms of his world-view, Indonesia, with Malaysia composed of former British territories and protectorates to the north, and with Australia and New Zealand to the south, could well feel herself to be an isolated NEFO in a hostile OLDEFO environment.

Sukarno had not forgotten his suspicions that Malaya had sympathized with the rebels of 1958. His feelings were buttressed by an awareness of other vital differences between Indonesia and Malaya. The latter, it seemed, had obtained her independence the easy way; she had not had to struggle for it and it was therefore an inferior commodity when compared with Indonesia's hard-won freedom. Moreover, this independence was, almost certainly, a cover for continued British economic, political and military influence. The Singapore base was a particular concern for Sukarno, and so were Britain's financial interests in the peninsula and in Borneo. 'Malaysia is to be set up to save *tin* for the imperialists. Malaysia is to be established to save *rubber* for the imperialists. Malaysia is founded to save *oil* for the imperialists,' said the President to a meeting of central and regional officials of the National Front in February 1963.[20] In social terms Malaya, with no revolution to launch her into the modern world, appeared a conservative, aristocratic country as compared with Indonesia's radical nationalism. Symbolizing this difference of temperament was the personal contrast between the Tengku and Sukarno – the English-trained, racehorse-owning, Malay prince and the Jacobin leader drawn from the lower aristocracy of Java and trained through the long struggle against Dutch rule.

Other arguments, too, were forthcoming. Nasution contested that the real danger of Malaysia to Indonesia was that it offered the Chinese of the region an opportunity to establish their dominance and it therefore represented an opportunity for Peking to increase its influence. (This, oddly enough, was completely the reverse of the Sukarno–Subandrio view that the danger of Malaysia lay in its possible subordination to British influence and in the possibly reactionary character of the new state.) Finally there were a number of domestic pressures on Sukarno. The army was a supporter of confrontation, for it offered the prospect of increased military budgets and a reinforcement of army prestige at a time when it was endangered by the forthcoming end of martial law. For the PKI, confrontation provided an atmosphere in which the party's brand of radicalism could flourish and in which it could side-step internal criticisms that its leaders had become too dependent on the Sukarno régime.[21]

In assessing the ostensible reasons for Sukarno's sudden declaration of opposition to the Malaysia plan, these arguments must be taken seriously. Indonesia's general ideological perspectives were particularly important. Under Sukarno's leadership the country had built up a coherent view of the outside world which, however extreme and far-fetched it might seem to outside

20. 'Implement the five-point program, overcome all challenges.' 13 February 1963.

21. See Donald Hindley, 'Indonesia's Confrontation with Malaysia: A Search for Motives', *Asian Survey*, IV, 6, June 1964.

observers, did have meaning within Indonesia. The NEFO – OLDEFO dichotomy was not patently absurd and the national sense of insecurity was not an artificial creation. The Indonesian ideological framework may have distorted reality, but it was held with profound conviction. Nevertheless the circumstances in which Sukarno announced his opposition appeared suspicious, to say the least, to the sceptical. Was it that, having disposed of the West Irian question, he felt the need of another external issue – perhaps to buttress his claim to leadership in the region as a whole, perhaps to divert attention from economic hardship at home, or to contain opposition to the régime which might otherwise have resulted in violence? More positively, was Sukarno following his own dictum of a dozen years before: 'A nation always needs an enemy'?

These are easy charges to make. A brief examination of the way in which Sukarno handled the Malaysia issue up to the actual formation of the new federation may make the degree of their relevance a little clearer.

Sukarno's initial attack on the Malaysia idea in January 1963 was very quickly followed by overt action, indicating that Indonesia meant business. In February General Nasution, after announcing in no uncertain terms his own agreement with Sukarno and Subandrio, sent the first Indonesian infiltrators across the Sarawak border. From April there were reports of clashes with British security forces. An ECAFE meeting in Manila in March gave representatives of other Southeast Asian countries an opportunity to take informal notice of the growing threat which Indonesia's attitudes posed to the stability of the region as a whole, and the Philippines' President Macapagal proposed that talks be held on the question. The suggestion bore fruit in a meeting in Manila of the Deputy Foreign Ministers of the Philippines, Indonesia and Malaya, early in April. The object of this sub-ministerial gathering was to prepare an agenda for a Foreign Ministers' conference and the omens, briefly, seemed favourable.

The optimism did not last for long. While the Manila discussions were still in progress Sukarno chose the occasion of the appointment of a new ambassador to Malaya to launch another attack on Malaysia, speaking of it again as a neo-colonial creation.[22] From this point on, though confrontation was not the invention of Sukarno alone, the distinctive character of the President's personal diplomacy became a major factor in the gradual crystallization of Indonesia's attitudes. From April to September the story is one of erratic fluctuations of mood as Sukarno, with apparent deliberation, adopted a strategy of alternating aggression and conciliation which seemed calculated to reduce the Tengku to a state of nervous confusion with regard to Indonesia's ultimate intentions. After the April conference angry verbal exchanges continued between Djakarta and Kuala Lumpur, with Sukarno and the Tengku apparently vying with each other in their search for the most offensive epithets to hurl across the Java sea. The slanging match continued during mounting Indonesian action across the Sarawak border. In these circumstances the proposed Foreign Ministers' meeting was not held.

At the end of May came an unexpected change of tone. In the course of a journey to Europe Sukarno paused for a few days in Tokyo to conduct negotiations with representatives of American oil companies seeking mining rights in Indonesia. He invited the Tengku to meet him there. The latter accepted and the two men, in the course of their discussions, appeared able at least to re-establish cordial personal relations. Their new accord was followed, on 7 June, by the postponed Foreign Ministers' meeting. In the wake of the Sukarno–Tengku summit the Foreign Ministers' discussion went well and an unexpectedly broad consensus seemed to emerge. Not only was there an agreement that action should be taken to ascertain the willingness of the inhabitants of the Borneo territories to enter Malaysia, but President Macapagal also managed to secure the assent of Indonesia and Malaya to the idea that some permanent machinery – a confederation of sorts – should be set up to enable the three countries to deal on a regular basis with matters affecting them. This concept of 'Maphilindo' (*Ma*laysia, the *Phil*ippines and *Indo*nesia), to be based on 'the historic community and common heritage of the Malay peoples', was not spelt out in detail, but it appeared to reflect a bold vision and it would have seemed quite out of the question a fortnight earlier.

22. *Suluh Indonesia*, 12 April 1963.

The euphoria of Manila, however, was broken by a new exchange of charges and counter-charges between Sukarno and the Tengku. Abdul Rahman was not prepared to take a vote in Borneo, said Sukarno, and was therefore guilty of breaking his promises. '*Ganjang Malaysia*' ('Crush Malaysia'), he cried in a speech at a palace reception on 10 July.[23] It was Malaysia, not Indonesia, which was doing the confronting, said Sukarno in a speech to staff college officers on the following day; Malaysia's formation was a 'confrontation against the Indonesian Revolution'.[24] Then, yet again, harmony was unexpectedly restored in time to allow a summit meeting between Sukarno, the Tengku and Macapagal at the end of July. It seemed that, at last, it might be possible to devise a solution which would allow Malaysia to be formed, but under conditions which, through the acceptance of some of his terms, would permit Sukarno to retreat from confrontation without loss of face.

The essence of the Manila agreement was that before Malaysia was formed a further attempt would be made to discover the willingness of the populations of the Borneo territories to enter the federation. This would be done not by a time-consuming and expensive referendum but more expeditiously by a representative of the UN Secretary-General. U Thant was consulted by cable and agreed to send such an envoy. An inquiry conducted in this way represented a retreat from Indonesia's earlier extreme position that only a full plebiscite would be satisfactory. At the same time, from Malaysia's point of view, merely to allow such an inquiry to be made at all constituted a quite extraordinary concession for a sovereign state to make, particularly as it would involve the postponement by a week or two of the formation of Malaysia, originally scheduled for 31 August. These mutual concessions seemed to reflect a willingness on both sides to find a way out of the impasse. If U Thant was satisfied that Sarawak and Sabah were willing partners to the Malaysia plan the Philippines and Indonesia agreed to 'welcome' the new federation. On 26 August U Thant's representative began his survey of Borneo opinion.

Once again, however, the accord was no sooner reached than

23. *Suluh Indonesia*, 11 July 1963.
24. *Suluh Indonesia*, 12 July 1963.

it began to disintegrate. Two new issues emerged and on these the breach between Indonesia and Malaysia became final. The two issues were, first of all, the question of sending observers to be present during the UN inquiry and, secondly, the determination of the date of Malaysia's formation. The Manila agreement did not specify the number of observers to be allowed in Sarawak and Sabah, but Indonesia subsequently demanded the right to send ten and Britain would give visas for only four. Indonesia interpreted this as an attempt to prevent an honest scrutiny of the procedure. On the second issue the Tengku, who had gone a great distance towards meeting Indonesia's demands already, announced on 29 August – i.e. before the United Nations mission had completed its work – that Malaysia would be formed on 16 September. Sukarno branded this decision as a breach of the Manila agreement in that it showed a determination to go ahead with the formation of the federation without waiting for U Thant's verdict.

Though U Thant, in due course, announced that he was satisfied that the Borneo territories were willing to enter Malaysia the President, after his on-again-off-again diplomacy of the past six months, committed Indonesia to continuing confrontation. The decision was accompanied by attacks on British diplomatic buildings and personnel of a kind unprecedented even in Djakarta, where inspired demonstrations had been a well-tried means of showing official displeasure at the policies of other countries. Mobs attacked the Malayan and British Embassies and subsequently the British Embassy was seized and sacked. The somewhat provocative posture adopted by Ambassador Gilchrist and his staff did not help matters. (The bravado of one kilted member of the Embassy, who marched up and down playing the bagpipes in order to show his contempt for the mob, might have been intended to figure nobly in the pages of future school textbooks, but it was hardly appropriate in the circumstances of Djakarta in September 1963.) The houses of British diplomats were attacked, their cars were burnt in the streets and the sacred cricket club was taken over. British estates in Java and Sumatra were seized and subsequently the government announced the sequestration of all British-owned properties. As on former occasions Sukarno was prepared to disregard completely Indonesia's economic interests. The seizure of British plantations on the pattern of the nationalization of Dutch properties six years earlier and, more importantly, the severing of trade connections with Singapore and other Malaysian ports were hardly calculated to aid the Indonesian economy.

Thereafter confrontation became Indonesia's settled policy and 'Gangjang Malaysia' her war-cry. Infiltration into Sarawak continued, though never on a massive scale, and was countered by British, Malaysian and Australian action. In 1964 attempts at mediation by Robert Kennedy led to a cease fire and a Foreign Ministers' conference in Bangkok, but no agreement was reached. In June Sukarno was persuaded to meet the Tengku and Macapagal in Tokyo, where the latter proposed an Afro–Asian conciliation commission. The Tengku however made the withdrawal of Indonesian guerrillas from Borneo a precondition of any negotiations and the conference broke down. In August confrontation entered a new phase when a party of Indonesians landed on the Malay Peninsula. They were quickly seized but other seaborne landings and small incursions of paratroops followed.

Confrontation went far to undermine Indonesia's leadership of Afro–Asian opinion. In the United Nations her Afro–Asian colleagues failed to stand by her. At the non-aligned conference in Cairo in September 1964 – a meeting composed of the very powers Indonesia might have expected to support her – she was criticized by implication and, in the preparations for the second Afro–Asian Conference in Algeria (ultimately to be postponed and then cancelled because of the fall of the Ben Bella régime) it seemed likely that, despite Indonesian opposition, Malaysia would be admitted as a member. Finally on 7 January 1965, in response to the seating of Malaysia as a non-permanent member of the United Nations Security Council, Sukarno confirmed his threat, made a week earlier, to take Indonesia out of the United Nations. A few days later he was to propose a further UN testing of Borneo opinion, announcing that this time he would abide by the result, but it was no longer remotely possible.

As the year wore on, further signs of Indonesia's isolation were discernible. The leadership of the Afro–Asian world which he had claimed for himself in 1955 was slipping from him and there was desperation in his attempts to pretend that the struggle for the new emerging forces was still being conducted with vigour. In April the tenth anniversary of the first Afro–Asian Conference was held in Djakarta, but only thirty-six nations of the sixty invited sent representatives. Peking and Hanoi were among them. At the same time Sukarno confirmed his country's new alignment by bringing the same kind of pressure to bear on American property and aid programmes – USIS and the Peace Corps – and against United States representatives as had marked the earlier attacks on the Dutch and the British. Individual diplomats were subjected to petty harassment – mail was interfered with, telephones and other services refused to work – and to many people an open breach of diplomatic relations seemed only a matter of time. Simultaneously Sukarno was planning his conference of the New Emerging Forces (CONEFO) which, he hoped, would provide a grouping of powers to rival the United Nations itself. The policy of confrontation was in fact to end only after Sukarno's dominance of Indonesia had begun to fade.

Was this new course in Indonesian policy to be ascribed to perceptions of national interest, to ideology, or to whim?

To some, the whole story of Sukarno's confrontation of Malaysia suggested that the 'Greater Indonesia' ideas which he had advanced in 1945 were an essential part of his outlook,[25] though in fact none of the demands made in the course of the Malaysia dispute was couched in terms of claims to territory, or of the building of *Indonesia Raya*. Others have taken the view that Sukarno had not meant to push his opposition to Malaysia to the point of continuing confrontation, but that, having raised his opposition in principle to some features of the Malaysia proposal – its formation by agreement between Britain and Malaya alone, its apparent disregard of the wishes of the Borneo population (though on this point Indonesian authorities seem to have been genuinely, but nonetheless seriously, misinformed) – he had then not been allowed the possibility of retreat from this position, even

25. B. K. Gordon, *The Dimensions of Conflict in Southeast Asia*, Englewood Cliffs, 1966, chapter 3.

when it became apparent that it was against Indonesian interests to proceed. Rather the unco-operative and even provocative behaviour of Britian and Malaya had forced him in the end to the final conflict. This view was advanced by Kahin, who argued that Indonesia's suspicions of Malaya and Britain were genuine and not unreasonable, but who held that there were nonetheless limits to Sukarno's desire to maintain his opposition to Malaysia.[26] At Manila in July 1963 there had been prospects of a genuine and lasting accommodation which were destroyed by the Tengku's disregard of the proprieties when he announced in advance of U Thant's findings that Malaysia would be formed on 16 September. By that announcement, said Kahin, Sukarno was manoeuvred into a 'corner of humiliation'. If the dispute was to be resolved it was therefore necessary to provide Sukarno with 'a dignified way of disengaging from the strategy of military confrontation'.[27] Such a view tended to forget that the Tengku, too, had his domestic problems and that there were limits to the extent to which he could be seen to be bowing to Sukarno's demands. He had gone as far as could reasonably be expected in allowing the United Nations investigation and he had accepted his own share of humiliation. At the end of August 1963 his freedom of manoeuvre was, perhaps, more limited than Sukarno's.[28] Indeed it is incredible that Sukarno could not have abided by the Manila decision if he had really wanted to do so, despite what certain elements within Indonesia may have wished.

The same argument also presupposed that Sukarno's handling of the Malaysia problem was rational in the sense that it was prompted by the reasons which we have already noted – by the pressure of Indonesian interests, or at least by the way in which Indonesia's interests were ideologically perceived in terms of the

26. G. McT. Kahin, 'Malaysia and Indonesia', *Pacific Affairs*, XXXVII, 3, Fall 1964. A somewhat similar interpretation is given by Gordon, op. cit.

27. It should be noted that Kahin's judgement of Sukarno's intentions in July, August and September 1963 was based on conversations with him and on close observation of him before and after the Manila conference. Kahin, op. cit., footnote 18.

28. It should also be noticed that before the announcement was made of the new formation date a Malayan mission had gone to Djakarta to warn Subandrio and to explain the reasons to him. Bunnell, op. cit., note 41.

new emerging forces, neo-colonial encirclement and so forth. Indonesia was concerned with her self-respect and she did desire leadership in the region; she was angered that Borneo's affairs were disposed of in such a cavalier fashion by Britain and Malaya. She believed in the dangers of neo-colonial encirclement and resented the continuing presence of British influence. But could considerations of this kind, concerned though they were with Indonesian interests, be regarded as the real *causes* of Indonesian policy? Did her Malaysia policy reflect a carefully conceived design to achieve defined goals?

There are some grounds for doubting it. In particular, such a hypothesis would not account for the erratic character of Sukarno's approach to Malaysia over the whole course of 1963. The puzzling switches of mood suggest that the ostensible objects of diplomacy were not the real objects. What was important, it seemed, was not simply the goal to be achieved by negotiation, threats or ultimately by confrontation itself, but something lying beyond the Malaysia question altogether. The erratic application and withdrawal of pressure seem to have been of the essence of Sukarno's handling of the Malaysia issue, and part of the explanation is the function which the issue fulfilled in Indonesia's domestic affairs. In brief, confrontation was finally adopted not only because the Tengku was tactless, or because Sukarno could not otherwise achieve sufficient diplomatic gains to satisfy his psychological need to assert his own and his country's claims to regional leadership, but also because foreign policy was an extension of domestic policy.

To interpret confrontation in this way, as in large measure a product of domestic policy, needs further definition, however. There have been several variants of this interpretation – that it was a means of diverting attention from problems of poverty and economic decline; that it was a means of arousing the national spirit and preserving unity ('every nation needs an enemy'); that different pressure groups, in particular the army and the PKI, had their own distinct reasons for supporting confrontation and that Sukarno, in effect, was responding to those pressures. No doubt all these factors were present in some measure. Certainly the army and the PKI each had its own interest in a radical foreign policy, and foreign policy did have its part to play in the preservation of domestic unity. If the army and the PKI could be persuaded to confront Malaysia jointly it might be possible to prevent them from confronting each other. Our contention here, however, goes a little beyond these aspects of explanation and involves a distinction between the substance and the methods of policy. It is that an assertive foreign policy was related not just to the content of Sukarno's domestic policy – to his goal of preserving a balance between opposing forces – but to the 'mechanics' of policy – to the modes and procedures by which he pursued that goal. Essential to his domestic political style was the element of constant movement – the sudden, unpredictable manoeuvres, catching opponents or doubters off their guard and the resourceful responses to potential challenges. The maintenance of a mood of crisis and agitation helped him to keep the initiative always in his own hands. This style had its foreign-policy counterpart – boldness of posture, readiness to take risks, swiftness of adaptation to setbacks or challenges and, once again, unpredictability. Such a style of revolutionary diplomacy could indeed achieve occasional successes, but it was also related to Sukarno's constant need to hold the initiative at home. Sudden switches of policy thus had a systematic function to fulfil, and the whole apparatus of negotiation, *détente*, *démarche*, confrontation, the sudden advances and retreats, was an integral part of his political method.

Given motives such as these the Malaysia affair did nonetheless evoke a deep response within the country. There was a genuine suspicion of the new federation and of the way it was created even among Indonesians critical of the Sukarno régime, and the Brunei revolt released their feelings. It appeared as a classic NEFO–OLDEFO clash. As far as conservative Indonesian opinion was concerned, there was certainly a growing anxiety about Indonesia's gradual isolation from the West and her alignment with Peking, and about the military dangers of confrontation; but these elements of disillusionment with confrontation as a policy did not amount to a disagreement with the view that Malaysia was one of the old-established forces.

This interaction of foreign and domestic policy returns us to the question we have left in suspension: that of Sukarno's ultimate aims in the management of his two partners in power. Was he pushing Indonesia in a leftward direction and preparing the way for the PKI to succeed him?

So far we have surveyed the evidence relating to this question as it appeared during Guided Democracy's first four years. The events of the following two years appear, at first glance, to represent an acceleration of the earlier slow trend towards growing PKI power. Sukarno continued to show favour to the party and to resist army moves against it. The PKI, for its part, had responded to his favour and to all intents and purposes was riding high, aided enormously by the atmosphere generated by the Malaysia dispute.

One sign of the PKI's confidence was its ability to silence ideological dissent. In 1963 a group of writers adopted a 'Cultural Manifesto' (*Manifesto Kebudajaan* – '*Manikebu*'), stressing the importance of freedom of expression for artists and writers, and arguing that art should not be made to serve political ends. The PKI attacked the movement and Sukarno banned it in April 1964. Shortly afterwards the PKI organized a partially successful boycott of American films. At another level there was its ability to resort to direct action in certain areas of policy: it played a leading part in the seizure of British enterprises after the formation of Malaysia and its direct action in the field of land reform was a particularly important new departure. Delays in the distribution of land under the Land Reform Programme led the party to organize what were called 'unilateral actions', by which peasants were encouraged to seize land which they considered to be theirs under the government's land legislation. In his 17 August speech of 1964 Sukarno seemed to lend his active encouragement to the peasants to take the law into their own hands in this way: 'I am getting impatient, I can no longer wait,' he said in criticism of the Land Reform Programme. 'Perhaps the farmers will also box the ears of those officials who are moving too slowly.' On 23 May 1965 Sukarno addressed a mass rally on the occasion of the PKI's forty-fifth anniversary celebrations. 'Onward PKI,' he cried, 'onward, onward and never retreat.'[29] There was a personal

29. *Indonesian Herald*, 24 May 1965.

warmth in this speech which seemed to suggest that Sukarno felt himself to be in a special relationship with his audience. Was he really giving it a promise of his aid to bring the party ultimately to power?

As on former occasions the growing prestige and power of the PKI evoked moves against it. In late 1964 a new organization was formed with the object of mobilizing anti-PKI feeling but seeking to achieve its aims by an appeal to Sukarno's own ideas. By this stage close observers of Indonesian affairs could detect a subtle development in the handling of ideology. Those opposed to Sukarno and his policy tended to appeal to the *Pantja Sila* rather than to MANIPOL–USDEK as the source of inspiration. Since the *Pantja Sila* speech was also Sukarno's creation it seemed an unimpeachable basis of correct thinking and the tactic gave the PKI's opponents some room for manoeuvre. The formation of the 'Body for the Upholding of Sukarnoism' (Badan Pendukung Sukarno – BPS) was one of the moves in the laying of an ideological smokescreen behind which an anti-PKI campaign might be launched. Trade Minister Adam Malik and the Murba party to which he belonged were among the architects of the campaign. So was B. M. Diah, the proprietor of the newspaper *Merdeka* and now a diplomat of the Republic. Some sections of the army, too, were behind the BPS.

In many respects the formation of the new body resembled strongly the earlier anti-PKI campaign which had been mounted through the Liga Demokrasi in 1960, and its fate was the same. The ingenious idea of a movement designed to oppose the President's purposes while claiming to support him was not likely to deceive Sukarno, though he moved as cautiously as ever in deciding what line he would take towards it. At last in December he called a marathon meeting of party leaders and ministers at Bogor.[30] He stressed the importance of all of his revolutionary formulations, MANIPOL–USDEK and NASAKOM as well as the *Pantja Sila*. On this kind of occasion Sukarno was irresistible. Even doubters and opponents found it difficult to resist the pressure of his personality in a face-to-face encounter. Having assured himself that the BPS had not yet acquired extensive

30. *Suluh Indonesia*, 14 December 1964.

support he acted a few days later to ban the movement on the ground that it was divisive. This was followed in January by a temporary suspension of the Murba party. This was indeed a replay of the Liga Demokrasi story – an anti-communist movement was quickly brought to a halt.

There were other signs too of Sukarno's desire to protect the PKI and to contain its enemies. Nasution, the figure on whom most anti-communist elements had pinned their hopes, suffered further reverses after his removal from the position of Army Chief of Staff in 1962. In June 1963 he was dropped from the operational body of KOTI, the supreme command organization which had been created for the purpose of the West Irian campaign, and was relegated to its advisory council. In May 1964 he lost his chairmanship of PARAN (the 'Committee for the Re-Tooling of the State Apparatus') and PARAN itself was then replaced by a new body under Subandrio with Yani as deputy chairman.

In cutting down the position of Nasution, Sukarno was not, however, necessarily succeeding in dividing the army on the crucial question of its attitude to communism. There were divisions and rivalries within the army, as we have seen, and, among other groupings, it was possible to speak of a Yani faction and a Nasution faction. After Yani's appointment as Chief of Staff, for example, he advanced his own men to the commands of South Sumatra, South Kalimantan and South Sulawesi to replace those who had resisted Sukarno on the matter of the PKI in 1960; he also replaced the military chief in East Java, where the previous commander had sponsored a clandestine conference of the more strongly anti-communist territorial commanders. These two factions, the Yani and the Nasution, overlapped considerably with other alignments – between Javanese and Sumatran officers, between PETA-trained and KNIL-trained officers. But too much must not be made of such factional divisions. On essential questions Yani and Nasution saw eye to eye, and though Sukarno was no doubt correct in regarding the Javanese Yani as somewhat more pliable than the Sumatran Nasution, at least to the point of accepting Javanese rules of doing business and Javanese restraints on methods of expressing opposition, his attempts to play on factional rivalry did not erode to any great extent the army's opposition to the PKI. The army had learned much from the ease with which Sukarno had outmanoeuvred it in the past and was determined not to allow it to happen again. When, in 1964, Air-Vice-Marshal Omar Dhani was appointed to the command of the inter-service command body KOGA (Komando Siaga) formed to control the confrontation with Malaysia, the army acted to limit the functions of the new body and to keep effective command of the Malaysia campaign in its own hands.[31]

The army was alarmed in January 1965 when Subandrio, in a speech on the occasion of the 11th anniversary of the NU newspaper *Duta Masjarakat*, spoke of the coming year as the most critical yet to be faced by Indonesia, and went on to say that, as the forces of the Indonesian revolution crystallized it might be necessary to discard some former comrades-in-arms because they had become counter-revolutionary.[32] Was this a veiled threat to army leaders? A little later, on 27 May, Sukarno warned the army of the need to be alert and to guard against the possibility that the British and American imperialists would use the Malaysia issue to interfere in Indonesian affairs.[33] Two days later he announced that he had documentary evidence of a plot against the lives of himself, Subandrio and Yani, to be carried out by 'henchmen' of the imperialists.[34] These statements were made in the context of the 'Gilchrist letter', produced by Subandrio and purporting to be a telegram of the preceding March from the British Ambassador, Mr (later Sir Andrew) Gilchrist, to the British Foreign Office. It referred to 'our local army friends', and thereby could be held to imply the existence of close connections between the British Embassy and members of the Indonesian army. Whether or not the telegram was genuine it was undoubtedly the kind of telegram an ambassador might have sent to his government, but it was not evidence of any particularly sinister plotting either on the part of Britain or on that of the Embassy's local military contacts. Sukarno, nonetheless, put that construction on it in order to sow dismay in army ranks.

31. P. Polomka, *The Indonesian Army and Confrontation*, unpublished thesis, University of Melbourne, 1970.

32. *Duta Masjarakat*, 5 January 1965.

33. *Suluh Indonesia*, 27 May 1965.

34. *Antara*, 28 May 1965; *Suluh Indonesia*, 29 May 1965.

A further piece of evidence was his role, in August, in bringing pressure to bear on the PNI to expel a group of its leaders in Central Java who had emerged as an anti-communist faction in opposition to the docile central executive of the party under Ali Sastroamidjojo.

There would thus appear to be many pointers to indicate where Sukarno's preferences lay in his handling of the forces about him and to suggest that his long-term strategy was indeed to divide the army and make it more submissive, while at the same time working to bring the PKI gradually to power. But it might still be argued, even in the face of this evidence, that his purpose was in fact no more than to maintain the balance between the two. The army was, in fact, inherently more powerful than the PKI, and it would be possible to interpret all Sukarno's actions in the light of that fact. In reversing policies which the army supported – banning the Liga Demokrasi and the BPS – in encouraging intra-army factional rivalries and inter-service rivalry, in establishing KOTI and, later, KOGA, in 'promoting' Nasution and in favouring Dhani, in threatening the army for its counter-revolutionary tendencies, it is arguable that he was redressing a balance which constantly tended to weigh against the PKI. What seemed like a series of actions to advance the PKI might be no more than a holding of the PKI position – and a maintenance, therefore, of Sukarno's own independence from both army *and* PKI. He would no doubt have liked a more submissive army, but, had he got it, it did not follow that he would then make the PKI his effective partner in power. As far as the other side of the balance was concerned Sukarno was not worried – he was not afraid of the PKI. He saw it as dependent upon himself and he believed, perhaps with some justice, that he could destroy it by a single speech if he felt that it was getting out of line.

There can be no firm and final conclusion on this question but there are some actions which are difficult to fit into the hypothesis of a simple pro-PKI, anti-army strategy. The willingness of Sukarno to allow the army its own newspapers, for example, is hard to reconcile with the theory that he was consistently opposed to army interests. In March 1965 his personal support enabled the army to found the daily paper *Angkatan Bersendjata* ('Armed

Forces'). His decision to ban public demonstrations unless they had received prior approval was a measure adopted at the army's instance and was designed to curb the PKI's skill in the techniques of mass mobilization. A further test of the President's thinking was provided by his skilful handling of two key issues: the idea of NASAKOM (including the idea of a NASAKOM government), and the very crucial idea of a 'Fifth Force' armed in defence of the revolution.

The idea of a unity of nationalism, religion and communism in government had been a part of Sukarno's thinking since 1957, as we have seen. His criticism of communist-phobia had been linked with his emphasis on the desirability of welding the three forces together. But, as we have also noticed, the oft-predicted cabinet reshuffle which was to bring communist representatives into the government never materialized. It was as though Sukarno wanted to keep the possibility alive for manipulative purposes without ever actually doing anything about it. In August 1964 when Njoto was added to the national leadership with cabinet status he was immediately balanced by the addition of extra military and religious representatives, and this cabinet status (which was also enjoyed by Aidit and Lukman) stopped a good way short of actual control of a portfolio. Very significant was Sukarno's attitude in 1965 when he supported the army against the PKI on the question of the meaning of NASAKOM. The PKI had insisted that the term involved the idea of restructuring all government agencies (including the armed forces) so that the three streams would be represented at each level. Sukarno supported the army's view that NASAKOM merely referred to a general spirit of co-operation and not to a mechanically achieved balance, with a commander being a nationalist, one of his deputies representing the religious group and another representing the PKI. 'What I mean,' said Sukarno, 'is that all members of the Armed Forces [should] uphold firmly the spirit and unity of NASAKOM. Let there be no phobias amongst the Armed Forces.'[35]

The question of a Fifth Force was more fundamental. Such a force would inevitably have been open to communist techniques of infiltration, and for Sukarno to give in to this demand might

35. *Antara*, 28 May 1965.

well have been to give the PKI what it had hitherto lacked – the effective control of armed power. It would be difficult to argue that such a concession would not have been part of a long-term strategy designed eventually to bring the PKI power. The party's demands for a Fifth Force were presented with gathering vigour from towards the end of 1964. In the context of the confrontation campaign and the landings of Indonesian troops on the Malay Peninsula the idea of an 'Armed People' could be presented as a desirable part of Indonesian defence. In a speech to the National Front, party leaders and the leaders of mass organizations on 17 January 1965, Aidit called for the arming of five million workers and ten million peasants to carry on the war against Malaysia.[36]

Politically, of course, the purpose of the Fifth Force was otherwise, and Sukarno maintained an ambiguous position, appearing to favour it but never deciding to introduce it. His clearest reference to the idea was made in a speech to a rally of SOBSI unions in February when he referred to the existence of twenty-one million volunteers ready to fight side by side with Indonesia's regular forces if the country were ever subjected to aggression. 'And we will arm the workers and peasants as well if need be,' he added.[37] The qualification 'if need be' took the force from his remark and this was, no doubt, the way he wanted it. He discussed the whole idea with Chou En-lai, who came to Indonesia in April for the tenth anniversary of the Bandung Conference and who was reported to have offered arms for the purpose of creating a Fifth Force.[38] In May, when opening the National Defence Institute, Sukarno praised the defence systems of China and North Vietnam and the importance of guerrillas in national defence.[39] A few days later he urged army commanders to give the Fifth Force proposal their serious consideration and to report their views to him at a later date.[40] He seemed thus to want to retain the possibility as a means of disciplining the army, but not to want it

36. *Indonesian Herald*, 19 January 1965.

37. *Indonesian Herald*, 12 February 1965.

38. Sukarno to members of the National Defence Institute. *Suluh Indonesia*, 2 June 1965.

39. *Indonesian Herald*, 21 May 1965.

40. *Suluh Indonesia*, 2 June 1965.

as an actuality. The alternative view was that he did want the Fifth Force, but was unable to accede to the PKI's demand in view of the army's opposition. (It was later alleged that Dhani, in August, had flown to Peking to negotiate a secret small-arms deal.) The evidence is not sufficient for a clear-cut answer either way, but the method of playing with the possibility, keeping it alive but not making a decision, would be in keeping with Sukarno's style.

The absence of hard evidence makes it impossible to reach a final resolution of this question of Sukarno's ultimate intentions towards the PKI and the argument is one of those in which each side has no great difficulty in accommodating the evidence used by the other. It must also be remembered that the PKI had its own purposes and its own views of how it could best handle the situation in which it was placed. It was no doubt trying to take its own initiatives and to secure Sukarno's support for them in order to outmanoeuvre its opponents. Subject to these qualifications the view advanced here is that Sukarno's domestic balancing act, and his foreign adventures, combined to serve the same purpose. Together they constituted elements in a system of conciliation in internal politics by which powerful rivals to Sukarno's power were neutralized or contained, and his own independence assured. The PKI's radicalism supported his foreign policy and gave a bite to his slogans, so that it became dangerous to challenge the ideas of Guided Democracy, OLDEFO versus NEFO, continuing revolution and the rest. Even the army had to work within that framework, developing its own double-talk to make its actions consistent with its words, and in that manner it was contained by Sukarno's skill and counterbalanced by the PKI. But the PKI, too, was contained – Sukarno was not intending to make the party his heir. It was curbed in considerable degree by the fact that the Sukarno–army partnership was still in existence to balance the Sukarno–PKI partnership, but also by its own adherence to the régime's orthodoxy. In securing Presidential protection it had lost much of its doctrinal purity and its revolutionary will, and by 1965 it was aware of the corrupting influence of respectability. It had acquired much prestige; it was praised by the President and assisted by him, but it was really not very much nearer to the exercise of genuine power.

Foreign policy had its own place in this conciliation system. Between 1959 and 1965 the whole balance of Indonesian policy had shifted, a westward looking neutralism giving way to the alignment with Peking. Sukarno's speeches in 1964 and 1965 were pervaded by condemnations of imperialism – by references to its continuing strength and its sinister purpose – and by praise of those attacked by the West – China, North Korea and North Vietnam in particular. This shift of position had few of the signs of a cautiously planned realignment, conceived either in terms of interest or of ideological requirements. Rather it appears as though foreign policies were shaped, and indeed pulled out of shape, by quite arbitrary considerations. There was no *plan* to align Indonesia with Peking but a series of *ad hoc* adjustments to the pressures of the moment. Even confrontation appears to have been not a response to Indonesia's encirclement or a means of resisting the pressure of neo-colonialism, but part of the machinery by which Sukarno controlled his rivals for power at home.

By 1965, as the economic crisis grew, the tempo of Sukarno's efforts to preserve political stability through confrontation abroad and through continuing display at home became increasingly frantic – hence the state visit of Kim Il Sung, the essentially unsuccessful tenth anniversary of the First Afro–Asian Conference in April and the plans for a conference of the New Emerging Forces to replace Indonesia's membership of the United Nations. The displays of the Theatre State could not, however, permanently reconcile the opposing forces within Indonesia's political élite. The Sukarno system offered no real prospect of permanent stability and it seemed that resolution could only come, in the end, through cataclysm.

In the midst of the political whirl was Sukarno, the *dalang*, but in danger at last of losing control of his play as it caught him up in its own momentum. In his system of conciliation Sukarno was compelled to be always on the move, to be unpredictable and to be ahead of his rivals. He gave a brilliant and sparkling performance, hinting at plots against him from within the army while allowing the army its own Press. He spoke of NASAKOM while rendering it meaningless; he countenanced the Fifth Force while stopping short of allowing it. Through it all he kept himself on top of a constantly shifting base.

There are two comments to be made on his performance. First of all is the fact that it was indeed a performance. Sukarno, as his political career drew to its close, appeared more and more as the manipulator, rather than as the ideologue or the visionary leader. As such he stood in marked contrast to the Sukarno of the independence struggle, fighting imaginatively, though in very different ways, first against the Dutch and then against the Japanese. He stands in contrast also to the Sukarno of the mid fifties, distressed by the shortcomings of parliamentary democracy and anxious to renew national unity in a distinctively Indonesian way. In so far as he was caught up and carried along by the momentum of his own performance this period of his career was less creative than that which preceded it.

Secondly, as we have already suggested, his manipulative skills served an essentially conservative end. The manoeuvres and the game of politics had become more important than the substance of political programmes. Even had he wanted to restructure Indonesian society he would have recognized instinctively the danger to Indonesian unity of so doing. Sukarno was well aware of the fragile character of the nation and of the imperative need to conciliate its component parts. He was thus given to inspirational tasks rather than to even mild measures of practical reform. Had he, for example, attempted to implement the 26 May Regulations of 1963 he would inevitably have alienated certain sections of his support and made himself increasingly dependent upon army support. In lending himself to the pursuit of vague and abstract goals rather than of specific and practical ones he was serving the interests, as he saw it, of the highest goal of all – the preservation of the nation.

In fact it is doubtful whether he really wanted a radical restructuring of the social order. For all his talk of continuing revolution he had no real conception of class conflict or of fundamental change. Sukarno had been a revolutionary in the sense of urging the nation in the twenties, thirties and forties to the struggle against the Dutch. The making of the nation was a revolutionary

act, as were its accompaniments. The national language in itself represented an element of social change. But by the sixties
Sukarno's sense of creative change had evaporated. The *idea* of
revolution could now be served by the struggle for West Irian, by
confrontation with Malaysia, by the idea of a struggle between
NEFOs and OLDEFOs in the world at large while domestic
upheaval was carefully contained. Whether he knew it or not his
political style was protective of the *status quo* – of the position,
that is to say, of the existing (and corrupt) élite.

Sukarno was not aware of his motives. His protection of the
élite was not practised in a conscious way by a deliberate alliance
with the army against the PKI. His affection for the PKI was
genuine.[41] He valued it as part of the Indonesian Revolution –
but only as a part. He saw it as he saw Islam, not as making a
total claim but as fitting into its own niche in a broader totality,
and he was in no way anxious for it to be anything more. In his
view of society and political order the people were to be led by
benevolent rulers (pre-eminently himself) and their needs were to
be attended to, but without a fundamental alteration in the
structure of society.

Once again this was a change from the earlier Sukarno. When
he had been opposing colonial rule he had a clear and identifiable
enemy and a concept of what victory would be. When he was
attacking constitutional democracy he could see its very real
faults though the remedies were less clear. But once in power,
constricted by the constellation of forces of which he was a part,
his clarity of vision faded.

41. Cf. J. M. Pluvier, who, in *Confrontations*, Kuala Lumpur, 1965, saw
the whole operation – the alliance with the army, the confrontation with
Malaysia, etc. – as part of a long-term and *conscious* plot to curb the PKI.

# 15

The Fall of Sukarno

In retrospect it is tempting to see a mounting sense of crisis over the course of 1965. The year opened with another opposition movement – the BPS – in ruins and with Sukarno's sudden action to withdraw Indonesia from the United Nations. Confrontation continued to delay any prospect of economic reform and the state of the economy was reflected in the inflationary spiral which was touching new levels of acceleration. As a result of falling exports and huge borrowings for military purposes Indonesia's foreign debt had reached US$2,400 million. A series of state visits, the celebrations to mark the tenth anniversary of the Bandung Conference and the initial preparations for the proposed Conference of the New Emerging Forces continued to indicate the propensity of the régime for display. PKI confidence revealed itself in the party's forty-fifth anniversary celebrations, but there were also signs of new movements of opposition. In particular members of the 'Islamic Students' Society, Himpunan Mahasiswa Islam (HMI), were involved in clashes with communists in Central and East Java.

Sukarno's health, long a matter of political moment, continued to be the subject of anxious speculation. He had refused the advice of his Viennese doctors that his kidney ailment required an operation. His reluctance was said to be due to his having been advised by a *dukun* (traditional soothsayer) that he would die by the knife. More recently he had taken to consulting Chinese doctors and had resorted to acupuncture. In January 1965, in a ceremony at Bogor, he decorated his Chinese physicians and scoffed at 'Nekolim rumours' that he was about to die.[42] In the same month, at a meeting of ministers at the palace, Sukarno expressed concern at the circulation of rumours about his health.[43] He took every opportunity to deny them and to boast of his good

42. *Merdeka*, 5 January 1965.
43. Author's interview with Frans Seda, formerly Minister of State Enterprises, 4 March 1969.

health to foreign diplomats. Certainly his stamina was sufficient to allow him to keep his sparkle throughout late-night entertainments, while distinguished guests wilted and waited for the President to retire. Nevertheless there was evidence that his powers were increasingly being eroded. He was protected by his senior advisers but signs of deterioration could not be entirely concealed. Tantrums became more frequent and journalists began to notice his incoherence in his meetings with them. On 5 August, he became ill at a public meeting, which gave rise to rumours that he was seriously ill and accentuated fears of a coming struggle for power. Again on 30 September he interrupted a speech, apparently because of an indisposition, though he resumed his discourse a few minutes later.

The growing sense of crisis and rumour may tempt observers to see a history of events working their way to an inevitable and dramatic climax. Yet despite the fact that a coup was always regarded as a possibility in Sukarno's Djakarta, neither Indonesia nor the outside world was really prepared for the events of the night of 30 September and the day which followed.

The main facts are familiar enough, but the details and their inner meaning may perhaps never be the subject of agreement. In the early hours of 1 October, seven trucks containing armed soldiers left Halim airbase, six for Djakarta, and one for the satellite town of Kebajoran. Their task was to kidnap seven generals, using the pretext that they had been summoned urgently to the palace by the President, or to kill them if they could not be taken alive. The plan was carried out with almost complete success. The seven parties had no difficulty in taking by surprise the guards at the homes of their intended victims, and in making their way inside. Three of the generals on the list, Major-General Parman, Major-General Suprapto and Brigadier-General Sujoto were captured before they could resist and were taken alive to Halim. Two others offered resistance and were shot down, Brigadier-General Pandjaitan in the front garden of his home, and Major-General Harjono as he struggled with one of his assailants in his bedroom. Yani, the Army Chief of Staff, when summoned to accompany his visitors, insisted on dressing first and was shot as he stood. The bodies of these three were dumped in the waiting trucks and taken to Halim. But the seventh general, Nasution, managed to escape by climbing over the back wall of his garden and dropping into the grounds of the Iraqi Embassy. He broke his ankle as he fell and lay there for some hours until the coast was clear. One of his aides, Lieutenant Tendean, who resembled him, was seized. Nasution's daughter, who had been caught in a burst of shooting in the house, was to die several days later.

While these actions were being carried out, other troops were seizing the radio station and telephone exchange, and by morning the authors of the coup, with the airfield as their base, appeared to be in a commanding position. When the trucks returned to Halim the most hideous of the night's events took place. The three living generals were killed in a particularly brutal fashion. In the presence of members of Gerwani (the PKI women's movement) and of Pemuda Rakjat (the PKI youth movement) they were beaten, stabbed and shot in what seemed to have been a ritual killing. Their bodies and those of the other three generals were allegedly mutilated through the gouging out of eyes and the cutting off of genital organs.[44] They were then dropped into what was known as the Crocodile Hole (Lubang Buaja), where they were discovered three days later.

Just after seven, Djakarta radio, under the control of the conspirators, came on the air to give the capital its first official news of the coup. It was announced that the '30 September Movement' under the leadership of Lieutenant-Colonel Untung, one of the officers of the Tjakrabirawa Regiment (the palace guard), had acted to forestall an army coup against the President. This army coup, it was said, was planned by a 'Council of Generals' and was scheduled to take place before Armed Forces Day on 5 October. According to the broadcast the 30 September Movement would set up a Revolutionary Council in Djakarta and would create Regional Revolutionary Councils too. In the meantime, it was announced, Sukarno was under the protection of the Movement. (In fact at that stage he was nothing of the kind.) In the broadcast Untung did not claim to be acting in Sukarno's name, and he himself accepted responsibility for the actions which had been performed.

44. John Hughes, *The End of Sukarno*, London, 1968, p. 44, gives some reason to doubt the reports of the extent of the mutilation.

While the night's events were in progress, Sukarno, after delivering a speech to a meeting at Senajan and collecting his wife Dewi from a reception at the Hotel Indonesia, had spent the night at Dewi's house at Slipi. In the early hours of the morning he was awakened and told of the shooting and disturbances in Djakarta during the night. He first set out for the palace but on hearing of troops in Medan Merdeka he changed his destination, first to the house of his fourth wife, Hariati, and then to Halim. On his arrival there at 9 a.m. or soon after he found other figures including Aidit, Secretary-General of the P K I, Air-Vice-Marshal Omar Dhani, Colonel Latief and General Supardjo. Supardjo, in charge of the 4th Combat Command of the Strategic Reserve in Kalimantan, had left his post without leave some days earlier but had failed to report to his superior, General Suharto, commander of the Army Strategic Reserve (KOSTRAD), on his arrival in Djakarta. Early on the morning of 1 October he looked for Sukarno at the palace, but not finding him there had himself flown by air force helicopter to Halim. At their first meeting at Halim Supardjo reported to Sukarno the events of the night and the President was later alleged to have clapped him on the back on receipt of the news.

In the meantime Untung's coup was evoking its responses elsewhere. Early in the morning General Suharto, the KOSTRAD commander, was awakened at his home to learn the news of unusual happenings near the house of one of the generals, and of shots fired in the night. Suharto had not been on the conspirator's list of victims, an omission they were later to regret. He dressed and made his way to the KOSTRAD office in Medan Merdeka where he began, in a quietly decisive manner, to piece information together, to pick up the threads of the coup and to take his own measures to counter it. He confirmed the disappearance of the six generals and learned later of the survival of the seventh. He heard the seven o'clock broadcast and identified the troops gathered at key points in Djakarta as the 454th Battalion from Central Java and the 530th Battalion from East Java, brought to the capital to take part in the Armed Forces Day celebrations. He learned of the presence of Sukarno at Halim and later of Dhani's action in committing the air force to the support of the coup.

Gradually Suharto moved to neutralize the opposition, making contact with other officers through the army's own communications system and securing their support, making contact with the two rebel battalions and negotiating with their commanders, and preparing to act against Halim itself. At 2 p.m. Untung made his second broadcast, in which he announced the 'arrest' of the generals and gave the names of members of the Revolutionary Council. The forty-five members listed did not fall into any recognizable pattern. The names of the coup leaders Untung and Supardjo were there, service leaders were included and so were some of the political leaders of the country, First Deputy-Premier Subandrio and Leimena. No reference was made to Sukarno. It did not take Suharto long to discover that many members of the Council had not been consulted in advance and that the list of names did not represent a list of supporters of the coup. He continued his negotiations with the two rebellious battalions and by evening had secured their surrender and taken over control of the points they had held. He was then ready for an assault on Halim if it were to prove necessary.

By evening the initiative was thus completely in Suharto's hands. Early in the day the coup leaders had appeared to be in a strong position: they had secured critical points of the city, they had Sukarno with them at Halim and the air force was on their side. Sukarno was the key to the consolidation of their position. If he could be persuaded to throw his weight behind the coup, accepting the idea that Untung had moved to forestall action by a 'Council of Generals', it might be possible for them to make their authority good. But Sukarno cautiously held his hand, with the result that his name could not be invoked in the two o'clock broadcast. During the day he conferred with Supardjo, Leimena and the navy and the police commanders whom he had summoned to Halim – but not, it would seem, with Aidit. It was characteristic of him that he avoided participating in any general round-table discussion with the coup leaders and his other advisers, but dealt with them as individuals. From Supardjo's reports he tried to assess the trend of the day's events; from Leimena he attempted to gauge possible reactions to his own presence at Halim and to decide his next move. He even found time to retire for a sleep. His only overt action during the course of the afternoon was to issue an Order of the Day announcing that he had taken the leadership of the army into his own hands and had appointed Major-General Pranoto to be responsible for day-to-day administration of army affairs. There were other more senior contenders for that position (including Suharto), but Sukarno saw Pranoto as likely to be more amenable to his own wishes. But this appointment did not arrest Suharto's gradual assumption of the real control of the situation and by evening the Halim headquarters was crumbling from within. Sukarno took steps to detach himself from the rest and at about 10 p.m. drove to Bogor. Aidit flew to Jogjakarta where he successfully attempted to prevent any large scale PKI uprising. (At the end of November it was to be reported that he had been captured and shot there.) Supardjo flew to Madiun.

Early on the morning of the next day Suharto's forces took possession of Halim and the coup was over.

It is not intended here to attempt a definitive resolution of the intricacies of the attempted coup. Much has been written about it, and more will follow.[45] In view of the controversial character

45. An official Indonesian view of the coup is given by Nugroho Noto-susanto and Ismail Saleh, *The Coup Attempt of the '30 September Movement' in Indonesia*, Djakarta, 1968. Perhaps the best piece of reportage covering the coup and its aftermath is that of John Hughes, *The End of Sukarno*, London, 1968, also published as *Indonesian Upheaval*, New York, 1967. More sensational and less accurate is Tarzie Vittachi, *The Fall of Sukarno*, New York, 1967. Arnold C. Brackman, *The Communist Collapse in Indonesia*, New York, 1969, in a treatment which sometimes goes a good way beyond the hard evidence, interpreted the coup as a communist plot in which Sukarno was involved. So does Victor M. Fic, 'The September 30 Movement in Indonesia: The 1965 Gamble that Failed', an unpublished paper presented to the Conference on Asian History, University of Malaya, August 1968. This account is based upon the evidence accumulated at the proceedings of the Special Military Tribunal which tried the conspirators. J. M. van der Kroef, 'Gestapu in Indonesia', *Orbis*, X, 2, Summer 1966, also accepts the view of a pre-emptive strike by the PKI. These accounts however differ from each other in emphasis and on detailed points of inter-pretation. Brackman's book discusses the so-called 'Cornell paper', now published as B. R. Anderson and R. T. McVey (with the assistance of F. P. Bunnell), *A Preliminary Analysis of the October 1, 1965, Coup in Indonesia*, Ithaca, 1971, which gave the view (also to be found in Lucien

of the events, any interpretation of the coup and of Sukarno's role in it must necessarily be speculative and tentative.

Several main categories of interpretation have established themselves. At one extreme was Untung's own explanation of his actions – that he had acted to protect the President from a generals' coup. The PKI, in disarray after 1 October, attempted to brush aside the coup as an internal affair of the army. The army saw it as a simple and straightforward PKI bid for power and this interpretation, buttressed by the confessions and the trials of those involved, became the received view and the justification for the appalling massacres of communists which swept across Java and Bali in the months that followed.

All interpretations have their inconsistencies to be explained away. If the PKI was as innocent as it claimed how did Aidit happen to be at Halim on the morning of 1 October? On the other hand, if the coup was a PKI plot how was the absence of key PKI leaders – Njoto who was in Medan with Subandrio's party, Lukman and Sakirman who were in Semarang – to be explained? Why were they not standing by to assist in the direction of events? Why were not plans made for a mass insurrection to support the coup if necessary? Why was there no prior deployment of communist forces to seize power outside the capital? How does one explain the extraordinary clumsiness by which *Harian Rakjat*, the PKI daily, came out in support of the coup on

Rey, 'Dossier of the Indonesian Drama', *New Left Review*, March–April 1966) that the PKI had become entangled in an internal army conflict. A similar view was advanced by W. F. Wertheim, 'Indonesia Before and After the Untung Coup', *Pacific Affairs*, XXXIX, 1–2, Spring–Summer 1966, Daniel S. Lev, 'Indonesia in 1965: the Year of the Coup', *Asian Survey*, VI, 1, February 1966, gives a more suspended judgement. A judicious exploration of some of the issues in the debate is given by Jerome R. Bass, 'The PKI and the Attempted Coup', *Journal of Southeast Asian Studies*, I, 1, March 1970, and van der Kroef gives another general survey of the discussion in 'Interpretations of the 1965 Indonesian Coup: A Review of the Literature', *Pacific Affairs*, XLIII, No. 4, Winter 1970–71. Some transcripts of the proceedings of the *Mahmillub* (*Mahkamah Militer Luar Biasa* – 'Special Military Tribunal') are now available and can provide a quarry for future studies of the coup, but since the Tribunal was concerned to establish a particular case it cannot, in itself, yield a complete answer. Neither, however, can its massive accumulation of evidence be entirely brushed aside as representing an attempt to frame the PKI.

2 October, after it had been effectively crushed? Why did the PKI subsequently take no steps in its own defence, but passively await its fate? Had it, perhaps, as some observers argued, become implicated in a plot which was not of its own making?

There were other questions too of fact and motive about which hard information was lacking. Was there in fact a 'Council of Generals' in the Untung sense? The coup leaders, under investigation, produced little evidence of it. The army admitted to the existence of a body by that name which confined its attention to questions of promotion, but in any case informal contacts within the army high command certainly would have allowed plenty of opportunity for the preparation of contingency plans, with or without a formal council.

How ill was Sukarno? Or how ill was he believed to be? It was later said that his Chinese doctors had informed the PKI that the President was very ill indeed and that this had prompted the party's leaders to make their own pre-emptive strike before Sukarno's death allowed the army to move against them.

Finally how far was Sukarno himself implicated in the coup attempt? Did he know about the plans in advance? If so, how much did he know? Did he in fact have a meeting with Supardjo on 29 September after the latter's arrival from Borneo as was later to be alleged? Did he agree to the seizure of the generals, even if not to their murder? Did he know that something was afoot but decide to remain ignorant of the details, giving his assent by a hint or a nod? Or was he caught entirely by surprise by a coup engineered by people who counted on securing his assent after the event?

Any examination of the events of 30 September and 1 October would seem to produce more questions than answers. In attempting to assess the evidence it is perhaps a mistake to look for a single interpretation in terms of a plot, rationally conceived, masterminded by a group of efficient conspirators and taking account of all contingencies. Human affairs are complex and proverbially unpredictable and in any political situation, whether it is a coup situation or not, conflicting motives are likely to interweave with each other and miscalculations are likely to be as important as careful planning. Untung's purposes and his view of his role were no doubt different from those of Supardjo or of Aidit.[46] In the absence of conclusive evidence the opposing judgements which observers have made of the attempted coup have really been based to a great extent on their opposing assessments of what the inherent probabilities of the situation were. If the PKI was heading for power under Sukarno would that make it more probable – or less – that it should plan a pre-emptive strike against the army? Alternatively, if it had been domesticated under Sukarno, would this make the party anxious to break free from its constraints by removing its most powerful military enemies and by making the President dependent upon itself? If Sukarno had been working to contain the PKI rather than to bring it to power, would that make his own involvement more or less likely? There can be no sure answers and the following judgements are subject to that *caveat*.

The coup was not, as the army would have it, a communist bid for power in the orthodox sense. Rather it seemed to have been designed, with or without Sukarno's connivance, to bring about a more limited shift of power within the existing régime. (Whether this would have ultimately meant the consolidation of communist party control, or whether it might have meant, on the contrary, that Sukarno, with a more submissive army leadership behind him, might then have used the army to control the PKI, are other questions.) But, following from this, it seems no longer possible to contend that the PKI was not a prime-mover in the coup. Certainly there were internal rivalries within the army and there were elements of an attack by a closely-knit group of puritanical young officers of the Diponegoro division of Central Java upon an army leadership which they saw as corrupted by power, diverted by luxury and as no longer guarding the revolution. The story of the coup cannot, however, be told primarily in these terms.

46. An important question here is whether Supardjo, as was claimed by Sjam in his trial, was under the tutelage of the PKI's Special Bureau (Biro Chusus) from 1968. If he were, it would lend more substance to the idea of an over-arching, long-term, coherent PKI plot. (See Mahkamah Militer Luar Biasa, *Perkara Kamarusuman bin Ahmad Mubaidah Dalam Peristiwa Gerakan 30 September* ['Extraordinary Military Tribunal, Case of Kamarusuman bin Ahmad Mubaidah in the 30 September Affair'], p. 45).

To see a major PKI involvement is not to argue that the coup was planned by the politburo and approved by the central committee of the party. There seems an inherent probability in the account of Sudisman at his trial that knowledge of the plans for the coup was confined to a few members of the party's leadership. Preparations were in the hands of the party's 'Special Bureau' (*Biro Chusus*) under the direction of the mysterious Sjam (later identified as Kamarusuman bin Achmad Mubaidah) and his deputy, Pono. This organization of the planning, it was believed, would protect the party from attack if the coup went astray; it would be, in any case, consistent with the view that the coup was not designed to be a full-scale communist revolution but a much more limited action to shift the balance of power within the Sukarno régime. It would also help to explain the party's failure to prepare for a general insurrection in support of the coup. To have planned a general uprising would have been foolhardy in view of the erosion of the PKI discipline over the years of Guided Democracy. The PKI was now a large and sprawling party and it has been part of our argument that its accommodation to Guided Democracy, while boosting its numbers and prestige, had also weakened in some respects its sense of revolutionary purpose, its doctrinal purity and even the moral fibre of its leadership. Its enormous membership was not composed of people who understood the precepts of Marxism or who could be trained to effective revolutionary action. To plot a general insurrection far ahead of the event would have been for the party to risk a gradual leakage of its plans and to invite retaliation in advance. And, once again, the coup was clearly not intended to be that kind of PKI bid for power.

The PKI, in this view, was thus a leading partner in a limited plot designed to shift the domestic power balance in its favour and to improve its position without endangering its existence. It interacted with a group within the army – a group which had its own purposes and which is not to be regarded as composed of secret communists or of puppets under PKI control. Even if the official version of the coup in its most simplistic form is rejected, even if the confessions of PKI leaders are brushed aside as false and if the tribunal evidence is regarded as suspect, an interpretation in terms of a major PKI involvement in a plot which also had elements of intra-army rivalry would seem to fit the main facts and be very credible.

Given this tentative assessment, what was the degree of Sukarno's involvement? If he had no advance knowledge of the plot how did he come to go so naturally to Halim when he turned back, on his way to the palace, on the morning of 1 October? He went, he said, of his own free will and in order to be near a plane if something unexpected happened. Was that really the reason? What of the story that he patted Supardjo on the back when the latter reported to him the arrest (and killing?) of the generals? Was this a gesture of congratulation or a warning that in murdering the generals the plotters had gone too far? His remark: 'Such things happen in a revolution' – if in fact he made it – would seem to indicate a casual acceptance of the news. Certainly, whether he made that remark or not, there was no question that, during the following days, he was determined to minimize the significance of the assassinations and to treat the whole coup as a comparatively minor incident. On the other hand, if he was a party to the plan why did he not lend his support to the conspirators without delay? This would have given them their only chance of success, whereas his hesitation over the course of 1 October, as he waited for the situation to define itself, was a factor which contributed directly to the loss of their earlier initiative. Sukarno's Order of the Day by which he announced his assumption of control of the army was careful to preserve his independence from Untung and his colleagues. Later in the afternoon, when pressed by Dhani to take flight to Madiun (a suggestion which must have had an ominous ring in his ears), he seems again to have hesitated until he was persuaded by Leimena to dissociate himself completely from the Halim group and to go to his palace at Bogor.

Whatever the actual facts about Sukarno's behaviour during that morning and afternoon, he seemed at the cabinet meeting which he called at Bogor five days later to be comparatively undisturbed – in sharp contrast to the cold anger of the military representatives who were present. He was beginning to try to adjust himself to the situation and to salvage what he could of his own prestige and authority. But he was not to succeed. The following months were to see the gradual reversal of his policies and the beginning of the massive wave of killings which eliminated the PKI as a force in Indonesian politics for years to come. These months were to be a test of Sukarno's talent for political manoeuvring and he played his cards, once again, with skill. But the game was lost from the beginning; the failure of the coup shattered the triangle of forces on which Guided Democracy had been based; the army, under Suharto's leadership, acted gradually, with Javanese indirection and enormous patience, but at the same time with immovable determination, to bring the Sukarno régime, at least in its old form, to an end.

Sukarno was faced almost immediately with a test of his strength as he stood amid the ruins of the coup, attempting to assess the political possibilities of the situation and to re-establish his authority. The issue at stake was the control of the army. On 1 October, Suharto, with the consent of the Djakarta garrison commander, Umar Wirhadikusuma, and of other senior officers, had taken over the army leadership. When he re-established contact with Nasution that afternoon Suharto offered him the leadership but Nasution refused. In the meantime, as we have seen, Sukarno had announced his own assumption of the army leadership and had appointed Pranoto to be responsible for day-to-day administration of army affairs. Suharto noted the fact, but went ahead, unperturbed, and assumed control. Two days later Sukarno was forced to accept the situation as it was. On 3 October he 'appointed' Suharto to be responsible for the restoration of security and order – though still without dismissing Pranoto. Again Suharto made no demur but carried on as though Pranoto did not exist. Finally, on 14 October Sukarno retreated further. Suharto was appointed Commander-in-Chief; he was installed two days later and Pranoto vanished from the scene.

These events revealed to Sukarno the weakness of his position and reflected the style of the two men – Sukarno determined to act as though authority was still effectively in his hands and Suharto prepared to leave unchallenged whatever formal dispositions the President might make, but ignoring them in practice and acting quietly according to his own decisions.

While Sukarno and Suharto manoeuvred for control of the army, the President was, in other ways, developing his long-term line of action to cope with the new situation in which he found himself. His concern was to act as though his position was unaffected and to minimize the significance of the events of 1 October. In two broadcast statements on the Sunday following the coup he had announced that he was safe and well, that he had gone to Halim of his own free will in order to be near a plane if necessary, and he claimed to be in full command of the government. In the second broadcast he was at pains to defend the air force from the charge of complicity in the attempted coup. He summoned a cabinet meeting at Bogor for 6 October and sought to treat it as a normal occasion. The meeting was notable for the presence of Njoto, who had returned from Sumatra with Subandrio (also present at Bogor), and of Lukman, who had come back from Central Java. The two communist leaders were trying, no doubt, to contribute to the appearance of normality and to seek, in this way, the President's protection of the party as a whole. Sukarno was in bantering mood as he talked, before the meeting, with ministers and journalists, but to some his manner appeared a shocking contrast to the mood of the preceding day when the murdered generals had been buried.[47] Sukarno had not attended the funeral and his conduct at Bogor seemed further evidence of his lack of concern about the crisis as a whole. At the cabinet meeting he announced that the situation called for a 'political solution' and he appealed for 'a calm and tranquil atmosphere' in which he could seek such a solution. According to a statement made by Subandrio at the close of the meeting he did condemn the 'atrocious' murder of the generals but he also stressed that 'we should not lose our heads and forget what we should do to continue and safeguard our revolution'. To be driven by emotion into the making of accusations against one another would play into the hands of Nekolim, he said.[48]

To appeal for calm while the situation was sorting itself out was one thing, to brush aside the happenings of 1 October was another. Ten days after the cabinet meeting Sukarno spoke of the

47. See John Hughes's account, op. cit., pp. 126–7.
48. *Indonesian Herald*, 8 October 1965.

coup as a 'ripple in the ocean of the Revolution'. Nevertheless, new forces had been released in Indonesia and these appeals for calm were insufficient to curb the momentum of events as the army acted to crush its communist enemies. In Central Java the abortive moves made in support of the 30 September Movement were quickly suppressed, but actions against the PKI and its supporters soon spread far beyond the steps necessary to crush an incipient rebellion. On 8 October the PKI headquarters in Djakarta was attacked and burned. Other attacks on PKI property – on SOBSI headquarters and that of the party's Youth Organization – followed. On 18 October the army banned PKI activities in Djakarta. Gradually throughout Java mass arrests were followed by mass killings of communists and of people who had had communist affiliations.

The slaughter was carried out sometimes by soldiers, sometimes by civilians, Muslim or other. In some cases the massacres were organized in a group manner with all present taking a direct part in the killing so that all would be equally involved. No doubt many of the dead were not communist in any sense. There were opportunities in plenty for the wiping out of old scores, whether purely personal or the product of deeper cultural enmities. There were also undoubted elements of class conflict following from the tensions produced by the land reform programme. The effect was to destroy at the village level the precarious consensus which Sukarno had attempted to create in the nation as a whole. The massacre rolled on through Java and Bali leaving villages decimated and in some cases obliterated. Estimates of the number killed varied between the 78,000 announced by Sukarno, and others which have gone as high as a million. There is no way of reaching exact figures. The same deaths may have been counted many times, as observers tried to estimate the toll in sample areas. It is widely agreed that somewhere between 200,000 and 250,000 people were killed.[49] In the face of this national rage the PKI awaited its fate with extraordinary passivity. (Was this once again a Javanese trait emerging? Did the party see itself as having lost the struggle before it began? The communists were on the left in the struggle of the sixties – politically left but symbolically left

49. See Hughes's discussion of this question, op. cit., chapter 16.

also. In *wayang* terms the party was on the side to the left of the *dalang* (Sukarno) – the wrong side, the losing side, the doomed side.[50])

Perhaps because it was communists who were being killed, the conscience of the outside world seemed comparatively undisturbed by what must rank, in any assessment, as one of the bloodiest massacres in modern history. And if Sudisman was speaking the truth when he said that the plans of the coup were known only to a small handful of leaders the massacres were eliminating the innocent. Many Indonesians, shocked by the killings, nonetheless tended to justify them on the basis of 'It was them or us,' and in those quarters there was little sympathy for Sukarno's patent horror at the course of events. There was nothing that the President could do to halt the massacre and his angry frustration made itself plain as he called again and again for an end to the killing.

Sukarno was, of course, concerned politically at the elimination of the party which had supported him, but it would be unfair to suppose that his anger could be adequately described in those terms. At a more fundamental level he was appalled to watch the destruction of a national unity that he had been concerned to create and preserve during a lifetime of political action. Some observers scoffed at his bitterness and saw his protests as a wilful and arrogant defiance of the wishes of the nation, which, to a certain extent, was undeniably true. He continued to mouth the old slogans; he insisted to KOTI in October that Nekolim was still the real enemy of the revolution[51] and a few days later he was urging the regional leaders to preserve the NASAKOM spirit.[52] But mixed with the repetition of the old ideological formulae was a simple, more straightforward and humane condemnation of 'racialism, arson and hooliganism' and an appeal not to overstep the proper bounds in dealing with a possible communist threat. At a meeting of students on 22 December 1965 he called once again for the preservation of NASAKOM. He admitted that the coup was 'an extremism of KOM', but said

50. I am indebted to Professor G. J. Resink for the suggestion that the PKI itself may have seen its fate in *Bharata Yudha* terms.

51. *Indonesian Herald*, 22 October 1965.

52. *Indonesian Herald*, 25 October 1965.

that this should not lead to a condemnation of communist ideology as such.[53] On the following day he made what was to become a famous statement of the same point when he said that the PKI had had 'one of the biggest shares' in the Indonesian national struggle. This did not mean that the elements involved in the coup attempt should not be punished, but the ideology should not be punished any more than Islam for the errors of Darul Islam or nationalism for the errors of Permesta.[54] A little later he repeated his view in more unqualified terms, saying that the PKI was 'the only party' which had made considerable sacrifices in the struggle for independence.

He could not stop the tide. With the PKI out of action and the army determined to have its own way, Sukarno found that his words on this and other matters were now simply ignored. He could maintain the appearance of leadership but its reality had slipped from him. He could no longer impose his personality on others. One of the defects of charismatic leadership is that once the magic has gone it cannot be brought back, and there was great bitterness in Sukarno's discovery that he was obviously alienated from large sections of his people. By December it was becoming clear to him that his policy of attempting to make light of the coup had failed. There was a growing sense of desperation as this was borne in on him. At the same time the game was not necessarily over: the army might have been determined to have its own way on all kinds of policy matters but it seemed strangely hesitant to move against him personally. Was this because Suharto and other leaders still retained their old feeling of loyalty to Sukarno?[55] Or because the army, too, was feeling its way,

53. *Indonesian Herald*, 22 December 1965.

54. *Indonesian Herald*, 23 December 1965.

55. This question has implications also for the pre-coup era. The army's material power was real enough right through the days of Guided Democracy. Did it hold its hand against the communists then because it did not want to challenge the President – a combination of humility before his superior authority and of loyalty to him as *Bapak* ('father') as Guy Pauker argued? (G. J. Pauker, 'The Role of the Military in Indonesia', in John J. Johnson (ed.), *The Role of the Military in Underdeveloped Countries*, Princeton, 1962, p. 217.) Or was it because it feared the real consequences? One speaks of a balance of forces between the army, the President and the PKI. Had it been a real balance or had it existed merely because it was believed to exist?

fearful of the strength of Sukarno's support in Central and East
Java and of the possible consequences of taking direct action
against him? Or was it a matter of Suharto's desire to resolve the
Sukarno question slowly and with Javanese patience? Whatever
the reason Sukarno still felt that he had some room for manoeuvre.
He made some concessions to opinion, dropping Subandrio
from the Supreme Operational Command and replacing Dhani as
air force commander but, at the same time, he prepared for a
determined gamble – against all odds – to re-assert his authority.
By this time, however, a new element had entered the situation –
the student groups of Djakarta and Bandung.

The Indonesian Students' Action Group – Kesatuan Aksi
Mahasiswa Indonesia – better known as KAMI – had been
formed on 27 October 1965. Together with its sister bodies KASI
(graduates) and KAPPI (senior high school students) it had
launched street protests in early January against such matters as
rising prices and had called for the dissolution of the PKI. Seven
successive demonstrations from 7 to 17 January were followed by
a lull, but the student movement was thus prepared for action
when Sukarno in February 1966 made his next move. On 21 February he announced a new cabinet. A number of anti-communist
members of the old cabinet were dropped, but the most conspic-
uous change was the dismissal of Nasution as Minister of Defence
and Chief-of-Staff of the Armed Forces. Major-General Sarbini
was named to replace him as Defence Minister, and the position of
Chief-of-Staff of the Armed Forces was abolished. Nasution, because of his past standing, and also because of his personal
bereavement as a result of the coup, had appeared as the main
figure giving authority to the anti-communist cause; his dismissal
was therefore an unambiguous challenge by Sukarno to his opponents. It brought the students once more into the streets. Their new
wave of demonstrations reflected the presence of an extraordinarily
sophisticated organization, with an effective communications
system to co-ordinate action and with logistical arrangements for
feeding the participants. They were acting within the framework
of army permissiveness and indeed there were clear signs of army
support in the provision of transport for demonstrations. On 24
February a massive demonstration blocked the streets outside the

palace and almost prevented the swearing in of the new cabinet. In the course of it warning shots were fired at the demonstrators and a medical student was killed. His funeral on the following day was the occasion for an impressive display of student anger and of the efficiency of their organization. During the next few days much of the student anger was focused on Subandrio, who remained Sukarno's closest confidant. Successive demonstrations culminated in attacks on the Foreign Ministry on 8 March and an attack on the Chinese Embassy followed the next day.

The climax came two days later. In a desperate attempt to retain his control Sukarno called political leaders to the palace on 10 March for a six-hour session in which he persuaded them to condemn the student demonstrations. He also set down the following day for a cabinet meeting. However, now that the students had prepared the way, the army was ready to take its own steps to resolve the crisis. As Sukarno chaired the cabinet meeting on the morning of 11 March he was informed that unidentified troops (they were in fact General Sarwo Ehdie's paratroops) were surrounding the palace. He wasted no time. Followed by a shoe-less Subandrio (he had slipped off his shoes during the meeting and did not even pause to pick them up) and by Chaireul Saleh, he made for his helicopter and took off immediately for Bogor. He was confronted there, later in the day, by three generals, Basuki Rachmat, Mohammad Jusuf and Amir Machmud, who had followed him from Djakarta more slowly by car. They had been sent by Suharto with what was, in effect, an ultimatum demanding that he step aside and confer upon others a formal responsibility for government. After a lengthy and sometimes angry discussion Sukarno signed an order delegating to General Suharto the authority 'to take all necessary steps to guarantee security and calm and the stability of the running of the government and the course of the Revolution', and also to preserve the personal safety of the President.

On the following day, Suharto, acting under this Presidential order, issued a Presidential Decree dissolving the PKI. On 18 March, fifteen members of cabinet including Subandrio and Chaireul Saleh and also Jusuf Muda Dalam, Governor of the Bank Negara, Indonesia, were arrested. (Subandrio at the time was still under Sukarno's protection in the palace and one reporter has conveyed a sense of the President's humiliation in the story that, as he was forced to leave the palace to enable the arrest of Subandrio to be made, Sukarno was reduced to pleading with Amir Machmud, commander of the Djakarta garrison, 'Amir, do not kill him.'[56]) On 27 March a new cabinet was announced which included, as three of the six deputy premiers, Suharto, Adam Malik and Sultan Hamengku Buwono of Jogjakarta. Over the following months close co-operation between these three made them, in effect, a triumvirate setting Indonesia's affairs on a new course.

For Sukarno the order of 11 March, was effectively, though not formally, the end of the road. On 16 March in a further gesture of defiance, he issued an 'Announcement' to explain the 11 March order and to state that he still had full authority as Chief Executive and as Mandatory of the MPRS. He was accountable, he said, only to the MPRS and to God, and he stressed that he, and he only, could appoint his ministers. This announcement was not a withdrawal of the delegation of his authority to Suharto. The fiction was still preserved that the 11 March order had been an act of free will on Sukarno's part. On 16 March he was concerned, rather, to reject the demands of those who were wanting a cabinet change. It was a futile gesture and it no doubt played its part in prompting Suharto to show who was really master by ordering the arrest of the fifteen ministers two days later. When the new cabinet was formed Sukarno was faced with the humiliating task of announcing its composition. It was too much for him – he read the first few names on the list, then handed the sheet to Dr Leimena to finish and left the room.

Though Sukarno remained as President and Prime Minister the way was now prepared, if he was not willing to accommodate himself gracefully to the new situation, for his eclipse by gradual stages. He was certainly not prepared to accept a diminished authority on those terms and the following twelve months were, accordingly, months of growing bitterness and frustration as his powers were reduced by appropriate constitutional steps, his

56. John Hughes, op. cit., p. 245.

orders ignored and his policy overturned. As if taking its cue from Sukarno's announcement of 18 March, the MPRS convened on 20 June to give its own sanction to the new political realities of the Republic. It began its proceedings by electing Nasution as its chairman. Sukarno addressed the congress, but without giving any sign of a willingness to accept a reduced role for himself. The congress, however, simply proceeded to give its own authority to what had been done. It confirmed the order of 11 March, thus giving it a new status beyond the power of Sukarno to recall. And, though it left Sukarno with the presidency and the title of Great Leader of the Revolution, it revoked its 1963 decision making him President for Life. Sukarno noted these decisions sourly; but when he heard that the Congress had called for elections within two years he remarked that he would indeed be interested to know what the results of an election would be. His faith that if 'the People' could only speak they would support him was, perhaps, not misplaced, but the question was not to be put to the test.

In the meantime Suharto continued to implement his own policies. In July he formed a new cabinet under the authority of the 11 March order and in accordance with the instructions of the MPRS; it excluded the well-known Sukarno men. On 11 August, after quick and cordial negotiations with Malaysia's leaders, the policy of confrontation was formally ended. Steps were taken to rejoin the United Nations. With the aid of his brains trust of University of Indonesia economists Suharto began to tackle economic problems, seeking to negotiate a rescheduling of debt repayments, and finding new instalments of foreign aid, applying 'Western' remedies to stimulate trade, encourage investment, control inflation and improve production. A more ominous feature of his rule was the growing penetration of soldiers into government and administration, but the question of how far a military régime was in process of formation is not for consideration here. It is enough to say that where Sukarno preserved political stability – an extremely fragile stability – by balance the new régime had its independent power base.

There were still occasions when Sukarno was allowed to speak as President. 'I am silent in a thousand tongues,' he said as he watched his powers gradually being taken from him, but in fact he was very vocal. On 17 August and 5 October (Armed Forces Day) he faced large audiences again. But instead of accepting the realities of power as they were, he repeated the old themes and continued to insist that he was still the man in authority. As if to rebuke him for the latter speech the MPRS Standing Committee called on him, in October, to make a supplementary statement to his MPRS address of the preceding June. It asked him to give an account of his own relation to the 30 September Movement (which he had persistently called *Gestok* – the 1 October Movement – rather than *Gestapu*, the army's acronym[57]) and also to give an explanation of the economic and moral deterioration of the nation under his administration. Sukarno ignored the request. In December, he began to feel further pressures upon him. The trial of Omar Dhani brought to the surface the story of Sukarno's meeting with Supardjo on the morning of 1 October 1965 and of the President's action in patting the General on the back. Other evidence also pointed to Sukarno's prior knowledge that some sort of coup was in the making. (These indications of Sukarno's involvement appeared to receive further corroboration when Supardjo was finally arrested and brought to trial in February 1967.)

As the case was built up against him Sukarno at last agreed to answer the MPRS request for an account of his stewardship. Unfortunately when it came to the point his explanation was not such as to satisfy his critics. In a written statement of 12 January he said that Gestapu had come as a 'complete surprise' to him. He blamed it on three causes: the blunders of the PKI leadership, the cunning of the forces of Nekolim and 'the fact that indeed there were persons who were "nuts"'.[58] On questions of Indonesia's economic and moral decline he asked: 'Is it fair to make me alone responsible?'

57. In using the term *Gestok*, Sukarno may have been attempting to indicate his view that the real offenders were those who led the counter-revolutionary movement against the PKI. His overt explanation of his term, however, was simply that the events referred to as the 30 September Movement in fact took place on 1 October and that the Movement should therefore be called *Gestok* rather than *Gestapu*.

58. *Antara*, 11 January 1967.

Against the background of student demands that Sukarno be tried and punished for his part in the coup, Suharto decided that the time had at last come for the final move against the President. On 17 February the MPRS Standing Committee under Nasution's chairmanship rejected Sukarno's account of his handling of affairs and called on the forthcoming plenary session of the MPRS Congress to seek a resolution of the problem. On 20 February, Suharto, accompanied by the armed forces commanders, presented himself at the palace at Bogor and spent three hours with Sukarno. Rumours that this confrontation had persuaded Sukarno to sign a surrender of his administrative powers to Suharto were confirmed two days later.[59]

What was the purpose of such a surrender? Since Suharto had already received the 11 March delegation of power from Sukarno, and had secured its confirmation by the MPRS, the new surrender would seem to have added little to his position. It was in fact merely a preparation for the next constitutional step. The MPRS convened on 7 March and addressed itself to the task of withdrawing its mandate from Sukarno and transferring it to Suharto. It did so, however, in characteristically ambiguous terms. It took from Sukarno the functions of President, but not the title. Suharto was made Acting-President, and foreign observers were left to wonder what exactly Sukarno now was, and who was President of Indonesia.

The full title came to Suharto surely enough a year later by a decision of the MPRS of 27 March 1968. It had been a slow process. Suharto had chosen, three years earlier, to stick to constitutional processes rather than to evict Sukarno by main force. He thus avoided the immediate risk that such an action would carry and also the unfortunate precedent which it would set. Only when it was clear that Sukarno's *de facto* deposition had been accepted by the nation did Suharto allow the MPRS to enact his formal deposition.

Confined at first to his house at Batu Tulis in Bogor, and then to Dewi's house in the Djakarta suburb of Slipi, Sukarno was now condemned to the loneliest of isolations. Dewi had left him before his deposition and was to secure her divorce from him early in

59. *Antara*, 23 February 1967.

1970. Hariati was also divorced from him and Yurike Sanger had never been formally married to him. Cut off not only from power but from life-giving contacts with people as well he declined physically and mentally. He was to appear – old, unable to walk without support and uncertain in speech – at his daughter's wedding and on other rare family occasions at Fatmawati's house. (Surprisingly, Fatmawati, too, was to secure her divorce from him in the end, leaving Hartini as his only legal wife.)

Could he have avoided the misery of those last three years? Could he have saved his position if he had played his cards differently in 1965 and 1966? He could probably have kept the presidency, but it would certainly not have been the presidency that he knew. Without the balanced situation which had given him power he would have had to accept policies of which he disapproved and obey orders from those he disliked. He would not have been any more the supreme and essential figure, but he might have saved for himself some of the outward signs of leadership had he settled for returning to the role of national figurehead which he had held in the early fifties.

It is not easy, of course, to be sure of Suharto's original motives and it must be recognized that his choices, too, were limited. On the one hand he had to cope with Sukarno's struggle to preserve his authority intact, and on the other with the pressures of students and others demanding more decisive action to remove, and perhaps to try, the President. Suharto used the student demonstrations in his campaign against Sukarno but he was also limited in his choices by them, as he was in a different way by his fear of unrest in Central and East Java if he were to act too swiftly and bluntly against Sukarno. His problem was illustrated in the tussle which occurred over such a simple matter as the setting of a date for the 1966 meeting of the MPRS. The meeting was originally scheduled for 12 May. Sukarno objected and Suharto agreed to a three months' postponement. This brought him into conflict with student opinion and a compromise date of 20 June was eventually agreed to. Up till the end of 1966, however, the record does suggest that wrapped up in Suharto's politeness and caution was a willingness to compromise with

Sukarno, allowing him status in return for reduced power, had Sukarno been willing to make the bargain.

In the event, whether for reasons of courage, pride, principle, or because he desperately hoped that he might still recover power on his own terms, Sukarno did not choose that path. 'Don't push me,' said Sukarno to his critics early in 1966. 'I am not a man to be pushed.' Whatever his motives there was a certain grandeur in his prolonged resistance to forces which were too strong for him. There is a temptation to view Sukarno's career in classically tragic terms – the idealistic leader who was corrupted by power or betrayed by the fatal flaw of his own pride. But it might be said that Sukarno's closing years in the presidency were years when he was most clearly standing by principle. He could have condemned the PKI in order to save himself, looking back to Madiun or even to his 1926 charge that communists who followed out-of-date tactics were 'the poison of the people'. He would not take this way out, however, and refused to deny the place of communism in the consensus he had always sought. Even if his stand was less a matter of principle than of mistaken pride it must still evoke some admiration though it led, in the end, to the picture of a pathetic, sick old man, shut away from the world he loved, kept under constant threat of trial for his involvement in the coup, but for the most part ignored.

On the evening of 16 June 1970, after a sudden deterioration in his condition, Sukarno was taken to the Djakarta Military Hospital and died there on the morning of Sunday 21 June.

With his death it was possible for President Suharto's government to soften towards him and a decision was quickly made that he would be given a state funeral. Official spokesmen remembered his achievements as well as his failures and he was viewed once again as the father of his country.

Before his death Sukarno expressed the wish to see his former wife Dewi once again. She flew into Djakarta on the day before his death, bringing with her the daughter she had borne him and whom Sukarno had never seen. On the Sunday of his death, Hartini and Dewi together begged Suharto to allow Sukarno to be buried in the garden of his Batu Tulis home. Sukarno had chosen this spot for his house because he believed that the nearby stone, with its fifteenth-century inscription, was a source of mystical power. Suharto, perhaps, did not wish to establish a place of pilgrimage so near to Djakarta and refused the request. On Monday 22 June Sukarno was buried next to his mother at Blitar.

# Bibliographical Note

The preceding pages are based on a variety of kinds of source material: on press sources – the nationalist Press of the twenties and thirties, the Indonesian-language paper *Asia Raya* of the Japanese occupation, the Press of the Republic – on Sukarno's own writings and speeches, on interviews with those who knew him at various stages of his career, as well as on the body of monographic material which, over recent years, has focused on many aspects of Sukarno's Indonesia. As indicated in the Preface, the author makes no claim to having combed all available material in an exhaustive fashion. Though he has tried to go behind the received story to the original sources at many points, and though he may have added in some places to the known 'facts' of Sukarno's life, for the most part he has seen his task as that of attempting to assess Sukarno's career on the basis of a fairly well-known record. Footnote references have been kept to a minimum but will indicate more specifically what sort of material has been drawn on and how it has been used.

For the general reader who wishes to explore further the political history of the Republic, George McT. Kahin's *Nationalism and Revolution in Indonesia* (Ithaca 1962) is the standard account of the revolution, Herbert Feith's *The Decline of Constitutional Democracy in Indonesia* (Ithaca 1962) examines the early years of independence, Daniel S. Lev's *The Transition to Guided Democracy: Indonesian Politics, 1957–1959* (Ithaca 1966) carries the story up to the adoption of the 1945 Constitution, and Herbert Feith in 'The Dynamics of Guided Democracy' in Ruth T. McVey (ed.), *Indonesia* (New Haven 1963), explores the character of the political system which emerged thereafter.

The bulk of Sukarno's own writings are available only in Indonesian, in the major two-volume collection of articles, pamphlets and speeches, *Dibawah Bendera Revolusi*, (vol. I, 1959; vol. II, 1965), in the collection of Independence Day Speeches, *Dari Proklamasi Sampai Resopim* (Djakarta 1961), in individual works such as his defence speech *Indonesia Menggugat* ('Indonesia Accuses' – Djakarta 1961), his pamphlets, *Mentjapai Indonesia*

*Merdeka* (1933) and *Sarinah* (1947), but some are available in translation. His important 1926 essay, *Nationalism, Islam and Marxism*, and his 1957 speech *Marhaen and Proletarian* have been published in the Cornell Modern Indonesia Project Translation Series. The Republic's Departments of Foreign Affairs and Information put out translations of many of Sukarno's individual speeches made on National Days and other occasions, e.g. *The Birth of Pantja Sila* (Djakarta 1950), *The Year of Living Dangerously* (Djakarta 1964), *To Build the World Anew* (Djakarta 1960), and these are likely to be found in libraries collecting Indonesian material. His speech to the Afro–Asian Conference can be found in George McT. Kahin, *The Asian–African Conference, Bandung, Indonesia, April 1955* (Ithaca 1956). *Towards Freedom and the Dignity of Man* (Djakarta 1961) is a collection of five Sukarno speeches.

For Sukarno himself his *Autobiography as Told to Cindy Adams* (Indianapolis 1965) is a revealing and eminently readable book. Bernhard Dahm's *Sukarno and the Struggle for Indonesian Independence* (translated by Mary F. Somers Heidhues, Ithaca 1969) is a scholarly examination of Sukarno's career and the evolution of his thought up to 1945. Donald E. Weatherbee examines the ideas of the Guided Democracy period in *Ideology in Indonesia: Sukarno's Indonesian Revolution* (New Haven 1966). Willard A. Hanna gives a brief biography in his *Eight Nation Makers: Southeast Asia's Charismatic Statesmen* (New York 1964), and the same author's *Bung Karno's Indonesia* (New York 1961) provides vivid, disenchanted impressions of Sukarno and the Indonesia of the late fifties. Louis Fischer, one of the journalists to whom Sukarno gave privileged access, gives perceptive impressions gained from interviews and from travelling with Sukarno within Indonesia in *The Story of Indonesia* (New York 1959). Cindy Adams's *My Friend the Dictator* (Indianapolis 1967) describes her collaboration with Sukarno in the preparation of the *Autobiography*. Herbert Feith and Lance Castles (eds.), *Indonesian Political Thinking 1945–1965* (Ithaca and London 1970) contains a number of extracts from Sukarno's writings and sets them in the context of other representative currents of Indonesian political thought from 1945 onwards.

# Index

## Penguinews *and* Penguins in Print

Every month we issue an illustrated magazine, *Penguinews*. It's a lively guide to all the latest Penguins, Pelicans and Puffins, and always contains an article on a major Penguin author, plus other features of contemporary interest.

*Penguinews* is supplemented by *Penguins in Print*, a complete list of all the available Penguin titles – there are now over four thousand!

The cost is no more than the postage; so why not write for a free copy of this month's *Penguinews*? And if you'd like both publications sent for a year, just send us a cheque or a postal order for 30p (if you live in the United Kingdom) or 60p (if you live elsewhere), and we'll put you on our mailing list.

Dept EP, Penguin Books Ltd,
Harmondsworth, Middlesex

Note: *Penguinews* and *Penguins in Print* are not available in the U.S.A. or Canada

## Political Leaders of the Twentieth Century

Each of these political biographies examines one great
contemporary statesman – the formation of his political
outlook and his route to power and subsequent methods
of exercising it.
*Some titles in this series:*

## Lenin\*  *David Shub*

David Shub was born and educated in Russia and exiled
to Siberia for his part in the 1905 revolution. He escaped
to the U.S.A. but kept up his contact with the leaders of
the revolution, many of whom he knew personally. His
biography of Lenin is both readable and scholarly.

## Stalin\*  *Isaac Deutscher*

An appraisal of a revolutionary despot which aroused a
storm of controversy on publication in 1949. This edition
contains a chapter on Stalin's last years but none of the
information released since his death has caused the author
to revise his views on Stalin.

## Ho Chi Minh\*  *Jean Lacouture*

Almost single-handed Ho Chi Minh revived a nation,
built a state and directed two wars against oppression.
'As a political biography it is a remarkable achievement' –
*The Times Literary Supplement*

\* *Not for sale in the U.S.A.*

## Political Leaders of the Twentieth Century

### Mao Tse-tung  *Stuart Schram*

By any reckoning Mao Tse-tung must be regarded as one of the greatest and most remarkable statesmen of modern times. This biography tells the long story of Mao's struggle to free the greatness of China and to give a new meaning to Marxism.

### Political Leaders of Latin America
### *Richard Bourne*

This volume contains portraits of six leaders: Che Guevara, Eduardo Frei, Alfredo Stroessner, Juscelino Kubitschek, Carlos Lacerda and Evita Perón.

### Macmillan*  *Anthony Sampson*

The political career of this intellectual, sensitive, and aristocratic Prime Minister culminated strangely in a riot of profligacy and scandal. Anthony Sampson's careful analysis probes the enigmatic character behind the mythological figure.

### Castro*  *Herbert L. Matthews*

Matthews has for many years been in personal contact with Castro – intimate knowledge, not second-hand research, inform this study of one of the most charismatic of modern political leaders.

*Also available*

Verwoerd  *Alexander Hepple*

Hitler  *Alan Bullock*

*\* Not for sale in the U.S.A.*

# Japanese Imperialism Today

'Co-prosperity in Greater East Asia'

*Jon Halliday and Gavan McCormack*

One Japanese design for 'co-prosperity with its Asian neighbours' ended in disaster in the 1940s. Since then, with solid backing from its old enemy, the United States, Japan has achieved a remarkable recovery.

Jon Halliday and Gavan McCormack have written a lively and convincing Marxist study of Japan's new economic empire in Asia, detailing the new forms of dependency and control built into its relations with the region. They argue that Japan, having established during the 1960s a powerful grip on South-East Asia's markets, is now tightening its fist on the supply of raw materials: by 1980 it plans to monopolize 30 per cent of the entire world's raw-material exports

While concentrating on East and South-East Asia, the authors set their analysis firmly in the context of Japan's changing relations with the United States and China, adding appendices on the Soviet Union and Australasia. To complete the picture, they describe the internal restructuring of Japan's society and economy that has accompanied overseas expansion, and in particular they pinpoint the speed and extent of Japan's rearmament.

# The Dutch Seaborne Empire
## 1600–1800

*C. R. Boxer*

For Holland the 'Golden Century' was the seventeenth. Astonishing indeed was the Dutch nation's sudden rise to prosperity and power, in view of the country's smallness, its religious and political divisions and its recent oppression by Spain.

In this 'fascinating and vividly written book' (as Christopher Hill called it in the *New Statesman*) Professor Boxer makes their large, even fabulous trading empire the key to the Dutch explosion – an empire in which the Dutch East India and West India Companies played an important part. He shows the Dutch brushing aside political, religious and even racial differences in their pursuit of profit and devoting all their energies and resources to the construction of a 'burgher' nation, inspired by trade and commerce. But there were flaws in the story of success, and Professor Boxer records how too often sober merchants succumbed, in the hot climates, to the temptations of gin and dissipation.

*The Dutch Seaborne Empire* admirably portrays the early Dutch incursion into the modern world, to which Holland added its full quota in scientific and artistic achievement.

*Not for sale in the U.S.A.*